Drugs, Crime and the Criminal Justice System

Edited by Ralph Weisheit
Illinois State University

ACJS Series Editor, Anna Kuhl

Academy of Criminal Justice Sciences
Northern Kentucky University
402 Nunn Hall
Highland Heights, KY 41076

Anderson Publishing Co.
Criminal Justice Division
P.O. Box 1576
Cincinnati, OH 45201-1576

Drugs, Crime and the Criminal Justice System

ISBN 0-87084-225-0
Library of Congress Catalog Number 90-80231

Kelly Humble *Managing Editor*   *Project Editor* Gail Eccleston

Cover Design by John H. Walker

Preface

As Series Editor for the conjoint Monograph Series between the Academy of Criminal Justice Sciences and Anderson Publishing Co., it is both exciting and humbling to introduce as the first volume in this series Ralph Weisheit's *Drugs, Crime and the Criminal Justice System*, a book that reviewers have deemed to be on the cutting edge of research in the field of drugs and criminal justice. Ralph has put together a group of authors who examine the dimensions of the drug problem specific to crime and criminal justice by "cutting through the smokescreen" raised by the government and other persons involved in key policy decision-making capacities. Indeed, what makes this book so stimulating is the depth and breadth of the analysis of the drug problem specific to crime and criminal justice through the diverse political and philosophical positions of the various chapter authors.

While this is the first book in the Monograph Series, let me whet your appetite for the future. Forthcoming in the early fall of 1990 will be Robert Bohm's volume on the "Death Penalty," followed by Gerald Robin's volume concerning "Gun Control." These two volumes will be followed closely by Gary Cordner and Donna Hale's book on "Police Administration" and Michael Steinman's book, which examines the latest research on "Domestic Violence." Please keep these volumes in mind either as reference books or as you plan your future classes.

Anna F. Kuhl
Eastern Kentucky University

Acknowledgments

Contrary to the warnings I received in advance, this book was a genuine pleasure to compile and edit. The authors were prompt and thorough in submitting their materials and to a person were easy to work with. The series editor, Dr. Anna Kuhl, was supportive throughout and gave me considerable freedom to shape the book into its present form. I would also like to thank Patricia Mott, who provided assistance at various stages of editing and mailing. The task would have taken much longer and been far more difficult without her help.

—Ralph Weisheit

Contents

1

Declaring a "Civil" War on Drugs

Ralph A. Weisheit
Illinois State University

The language of war is commonly invoked to describe current anti-drug efforts. The term "war" expresses the sincerity and zeal with which anti-drug efforts are undertaken, but thinking in terms of the language of war may also be a useful tool for examining current drug policies. The discussion that follows is designed to raise issues which haunt current anti-drug efforts; it is not intended to provide easy solutions. America has acknowledged the existence of a drug problem for more than three-quarters of a century, and during that time has employed a variety of countermeasures. Despite this, prohibited drugs abound. Anyone who argues that the solution is simple, obvious, or could quickly be determined with more resources has not seriously studied the problem. The purpose of this introductory chapter is to raise broad issues which transcend any single problem related to drugs and crime, setting the stage for what follows. The remaining chapters in this book explore specific aspects of the drug problem. The writers focus not only on different issues, but approach these issues from different philosophical and political positions. Combined, these authors provide a good sense of the breadth and complexity of the drugs-crime problem.

In 1971, President Richard Nixon declared a "war" on drugs. The phrase stuck and it has become almost obligatory for politicians to repeat it and to vow a new commitment to it. Nearly every current aspect of the drug issue is framed in the language of war or conflict. Using the language of war when discussing the drug problem is so common that its significance is sometimes lost as the phrase risks becoming a hackneyed cliche. Giving careful thought to all that the term "war" implies raises important issues. The language of war begs such questions as Who is the *enemy*?, Where is the major *front*?, What type of *warfare* is acceptable? and What constitutes *victory*?

WHO IS THE ENEMY?

To declare a war on drugs implies that chemical substances are the enemy, but these substances are themselves inert, at least prior to their ingestion. The war is not against drugs, but against people who hold particular values and consequently take particular actions regarding drugs. The significance of this point cannot be overstated, for it means that any war on drugs is really a civil war in which the forces of society are marshalled against some of its own citizens.

It is difficult to win a war in which the enemy is hard to identify, but this is precisely the problem with current anti-drug efforts. Except in extreme cases, drug users do not stand out from other citizens in either their appearance or behavior. If they did, employers would not find it necessary to conduct drug tests to identify users, and it would be unnecessary to test arrestees or probationers to determine whether they are drug-free. In fact, the current emphasis on drug testing seems at least partly related to the need to distinguish between "good" and "bad" people (i.e., drug-free vs. drug-using) in much the same way that mental testing was once used to distinguish salvageable from hopeless offenders. For many it seems important to identify these "bad" people and treat them differently from other "good" criminals. Viewed in this way, it is easy to see why some argue that we should have little concern for the rights of drug users or drug dealers, but such arguments are based on two presumptions. First, it is presumed that drug users can be easily identified and that everyone is either a drug user or is drug-free. But, it is precisely the risk that innocent people will be wrongfully labeled that makes a recognition of basic legal rights essential. Drug tests can be in error, informants can present misinformation, and prosecutors have been known to lie or to conceal evidence which would prove an arrestee innocent.

Second, such arguments presume that drug offenders really are unlike other citizens or other offenders, and that the differences merit considering them as something "less than human." According to these presumptions, legal rights are for "good" drug offenders, and "bad" drug offenders are not deserving of their legal rights.

WHERE IS THE FRONT?

Characterizing the regulation of drugs as a civil war implies that the *front* in the drug war is within the United States itself. Some might argue that the real front should be the drug-producing countries, that if production were to stop in these countries, consumption would stop in the United States. While it is wise to be concerned with these producer nations, no successful policy to end drug use in this country can or should depend on regulating foreign production. There are several reasons for this.

First, with all its wealth, the United States cannot afford the prisons and police required to end drug consumption in this country. Most producer nations are far less equipped to afford the resources required to end drug production and trafficking within their borders. Economic forces have a way of defining and shaping moral imperatives. As the United States demonstrates in its subsidies to tobacco farmers, it is easy to rationalize the production of harmful addictive substances if enough citizens are economically dependent on them.

Second, as Peter Reuter (The RAND Corporation, 1988) argues, increased interdiction at the borders is likely to have little impact on the street price or availability of drugs in the United States. Most producer nations are only generating a fraction of their production capacity, and consequently, drugs from these countries are readily available at a low cost. Further, most of the value added to street drugs is added after they enter this country, which means that much of the wealth generated by the drug business (and the problems which arise from that wealth) is created after drugs enter the United States.

Third, there is almost no evidence that curtailing foreign sources of drugs would end the drug problem in the United States. Foreign sources have been heavily used because their drugs are cheap and readily available. It is foolish to presume, however, that if foreign sources were cut off, there would be no increase in domestic production. This is precisely what has happened in the marijuana trade. The domestic production of methamphetamines also demonstrates our ability to become a producer nation, and the development of "designer drugs" assures that heroin and cocaine substitutes will be available long after foreign sources of these drugs are shut down. It is even possible that, within the next 20 years, the United States will become an *exporter* of some drugs. Curtailing foreign drug supplies may lead to a temporary shortage of drugs and may lead to a change in the types of drugs used, but it is not a long-term solution to the drug problem.

Finally, while stopping drugs at the source has been supported by the rhetoric of the U.S. government, official actions have been ambiguous. Pressuring producer nations occurs only when it does not conflict with other foreign policy objectives. In reality, other considerations often place the United States in a position of tolerating or even facilitating international drug trafficking. There is evidence, for example, that the United States arranged the safe transport of drugs during the Vietnam War and, more recently in Central America. In some cases this included providing planes, pilots and instructions for avoiding radar detection. As long as such practices continue (and it seems likely they will), attacking the drug problem by ending production in source countries is unlikely to have much impact.

These conditions suggest that, for both practical and political reasons, the primary front in the war on drugs will continue to be the domestic front. The idea that the problem can be blamed on someone else has considerable public appeal, however, and the *rhetoric* of a foreign front is likely to continue for some time.

WHAT TYPE OF WARFARE IS ACCEPTABLE?

Although it is sometimes said that "All is fair in love and war," even war is supposed to be conducted following basic rules of human decency. Engaging in a war against ourselves demands a different set of rules than that used against foreign enemies fighting on foreign soil. Waging a domestic war against an internal enemy places restrictions on the intensity of the war and limits the tactics which will be defined as acceptable. It would be a small consolation, for example, for the United States to win the war against drugs at the price of abandoning democracy itself. Thus, the domestic drug war must be conducted within a social and political environment which supports extensive civil liberties for all citizens, a notion which contradicts the rules of conduct on a true battlefield.

In the past, the United States has adopted two strategies for fighting the war on drugs: the use of force through law, and the use of education and treatment programs. The language of war is the language of force, and force has been the primary strategy for fighting the war on drugs. In recent years the proportion of anti-drug expenditures which have gone to criminal justice agencies has steadily been growing, but in a war against ourselves, force proves to be of mixed utility. Police actions and strict legal sanctions clearly deter some from using drugs, and encourage some users to stop. But, force alone is unlikely to end the drug problem. Even in totalitarian states with extreme legal penalties, drug use continues. Following the Iranian revolution, for example, the death penalty was liberally used for drug dealers, but drug dealing and drug use continued and may have actually increased. In this country, marijuana use by young people is declining, but this reduction is apparently unrelated to the threat of arrest or formal legal action. While there are thousands of drug arrests each year, there are so many more drug transactions that the objective likelihood of arrest is remote. Further, proponents of get-tough strategies should be reminded that relaxing penalties for marijuana during the 1970s was partly a response to the dramatic increase in marijuana use, an increase which *followed* a long period of harsh penalties for possession and sale.

Harsh penalties may also have unintended consequences. For example, as the number of drug offenders in prison continues to grow (the Federal prison population will soon be more than one-half drug offenders), this will provide an opportunity for the social networks of drug offenders to expand and may provide these offenders with a common sense of identity. Further, the simple fact that so many offenders are placed together will not only allow them to share skills and perfect techniques of drug trafficking, but sets the stage for the development of even stronger national networks of drug traffickers when these inmates are released.

As an alternative to force, some suggest that education and treatment are the most effective ways to deal with the drug problem. Like the use of force, a reliance on education and treatment will likely have some impact, but is of mixed utility. Education which focuses only on the "facts" about drugs is of questionable value. Doctors and nurses are very well-educated regarding the facts about drugs, but as a group they remain highly susceptible to drug abuse. Further, to focus on the "facts" is to deny that this is a war of values. Unfortunately for drug education programs, our educational system is much better suited to teaching facts than to changing values, and despite loud vocal expressions of concern by the public, our society holds considerable ambiguity about drugs. There is no doubt that people's values and beliefs change, but we simply do not know how to *make* them change in the desired direction, particularly on a national scale.

Like education, the idea of treatment is appealing but the process of effectively carrying it out is more elusive. People do stop using drugs, often without any formal treatment program, but current treatment approaches are not very effective at forcing people to stop. For even the best of programs, success rates of 25 percent are probably optimistic. Further, for many drug users, treatment may not be necessary. Using current estimates of users and of addicts, for example, suggests that about 10 percent of heroin and cocaine users can be classified as addicts, about the same percent of alcohol users who can be considered alcoholics.[1] For the other 90 percent, moderate or occasional use is the rule. Treatment also implies that the user has some form of physiological or psychological dependence on, or addiction to, the drug. To date, however, the very notion of addiction is controversial, with some suggesting that such intangible things as love may be considered addictive. It is easy to understand why treatment programs have such low success rates when the very thing they are treating is poorly understood.

In recent years, two new strategies have begun to take form, strategies which raise particularly troublesome issues and which may force many citizens to confront the conflicting values they hold regarding drugs and drug users. The first strategy, a peculiar mix of force and community education, encourages citizens to tell the police about drug use by friends and family members. Thus, the government is encouraging a civil war in the truest sense. Like any action which directly pits brother against brother, only time will tell if communities and families are eventually made stronger or are destroyed in the process.

A second evolving strategy is to shift the burden of proof to the citizen to demonstrate that they do not use drugs. Refusing to take a drug test, however noble the principle, easily leads one to be categorized as a drug user or as one who condones the behavior of drug users. Extending this reasoning sets the stage for intrusive programs which make every citizen a suspected "enemy." As an example, businesses in a Texas community are even giving 10 to 50 percent discounts to high school students who submit to drug tests and agree to periodic unannounced spot testing to assure that they are drug free. Students are not only joining the program in large numbers, but report that those unwilling to take part are ostracized and generally presumed to be drug users. Willingness to take part in such programs may quickly become modern-day versions of loyalty oaths given during the McCarthy era.

Sorting out proper strategies and deciding the appropriate blend of punishment, treatment, and prevention requires an understanding of what these strategies should ultimately accomplish. In other words, whether a particular set of strategies makes sense depends almost entirely upon the goals these strategies are intended to achieve. In the war on drugs, goals are often vague, making for better rhetoric than public policy.

Before turning to the problem of establishing goals, it is worth noting that arguments about strategy are among the most heated in this area. Three great myths underlie many arguments regarding appropriate strategies for responding to the drug problem, and the use of these myths transcends any particular philosophical approach to the drug problem. Not everyone premises their argument on these myths and few rely on all three. Nevertheless, these myths are common and have had a strong influence on the shape of current arguments.

Myth #1: *It is better to do something than to do nothing.*

Americans are people of action. It is unthinkable to stand by and do nothing when faced with a pressing social problem. While few would suggest that the current drug problem simply be ignored, this is not to say that any well-intentioned action must do some good, or at the least will do no harm. In fact, policies may have detrimental (though inadvertent) effects. For example, the crackdown on marijuana use by soldiers in Vietnam did lead some to stop using marijuana, but also led others to begin using heroin, which was easier to conceal. Few would argue that soldiers with a heroin problem are better off than those with a marijuana problem. Whatever policies are adopted, there is always the risk that the policies may exacerbate the problem. In such cases, inaction may well be better than action. A corollary to this myth is the belief that if some action is not solving the problem (or is making it even worse) then even more of the same is needed. If harsh penalties do not reduce the drug problem, then the penalties are simply not harsh enough. Conversely, if reducing penalties leads to no increase in use, then eliminating penalties will also have no impact on use.

Myth #2:   *Current drug problems prove the failure of current drug policies.*

It is tempting to cite current drug problems as evidence that past policies have failed. The truth is the level of drug problems under alternative policies is unknown. Some societies, such as that of the Netherlands, have taken a more tolerant stance toward drugs, and have a smaller drug problem. But the culture of the Netherlands differs from that of the United States in a number of ways. Their homicide rate, for example, is nearly one-eighth that of the United States. It is not obvious that successful drug policies in that country would have the same result in the United States. In fact, it is not even clear whether different policies *create* different patterns of drug use in the Netherlands and the United States. It is just as likely that different patterns of drug use give rise to different policies. The truth is that we have only a vague idea about the extent to which current policies reduce or exacerbate the drug problem.

Myth #3:   *When policies fail, their opposites will succeed.*

This is perhaps the most disturbing myth which pervades current thinking about drugs. If drug use escalates in the face of increasingly repressive laws, then the problem is best dealt with by abandoning repressive laws altogether. Similarly, some would argue that if treatment is not effective, then the idea of treatment should be abandoned in favor of harsh punishment. This myth is a natural outgrowth of our compulsion to take some action to deal with the problem. Rather than systematically testing and modifying policies, this myth leads to a frenzied thrashing about and sends mixed messages to the public as policies dramatically shift from one direction to another (as occurred during the Carter years with marijuana).

WHAT CONSTITUTES VICTORY?

Most drugs, at least those which occur in nature, have in one society or another been integrated into the culture in such a way that use is regulated. Put differently, most cultures have found ways to encourage moderate use and to discourage excess. Much of the current problem with drugs derives not only from its illegal status, but also from patterns of excessive consumption. The debate over strategies for dealing with the drug problem must also be a debate over the objectives of the war on drugs. The issue is whether the problem is in the drug's effects, or in the way they are used. That is, whether the goal should be to eliminate drugs (through legal restrictions and punishments) or to change cultural definitions which shape individual patterns of use (through education and treatment). Although the mix of punishment and prevention varies from one country to the next, most countries have policies which include elements of each.

Most would agree that ending the drug problem requires some degree of consensus among citizens, a set of shared values about drugs, drug users, and a sense of obligation by drug-free citizens to both the user and to society. But in the United States, a land known for conspicuous consumption in which success and excess are almost synonymous, the conflicting values which provide the context for national drug policies are particularly striking. This country's historical experience with alcohol is a testimonial to its long-standing resistance to adopting culturally benign patterns of drug use.

The issue of drugs calls forth very deeply held and conflicting basic values in our society, including individualism and free choice, which suggests that people should be able to choose their own poison. These same values elicit strong opposition to mandatory helmet laws for motorcycle riders and explain the hesitation to ban tobacco use despite its known harm and addictive quality. Viewed at this level, drug use is an individual act of free will; if it were not, then legal penalties for use would make no sense.

On the other hand, drug users (particularly addicts) are seen as helpless pawns, who no longer have a will of their own and whose actions affect all of society. They are sick, not bad. Thus drug use, particularly drug addiction, undercuts the principles of individualism and free choice. The particular abhorrence felt in the United States for addiction explains why there is more concern with abstinence by offenders on parole than with the general condition of their life and health. It similarly explains why many addiction treatment programs (such as Narcotics Anonymous) see addiction as the primary problem and other life problems as secondary to or derived from addiction itself. In this country successful drug treatment is synonymous with abstinence, but this view is not universal. Successful drug treatment in the Netherlands makes no presumption that the addict will stop using drugs, only that his or her life will get in order.

A third basic value is the belief in hard work and the uneasy tolerance of hedonism. Pleasure for its own sake is simply incompatible with the Protestant ethic that shapes American society. One of the most commonly cited justifications for drug testing employees is that drug use undercuts productivity. Thus, while treatment for addicts is justified because they are dependent and lack free choice, treatment for recreational users is justified because they are not fully productive.

Merging these competing values into a single coherent policy is difficult, and accounts for such inherently inconsistent policies as: (1) legally mandating drug treatment but underfunding treatment programs; (2) utilizing mandatory treatment by giving drug offenders the option of jail or treatment. The idea of legally forcing someone to help themselves is a contradictory concept in a democracy. Mandatory treatment is not possible in the Netherlands, but is a mainstay of American drug policy.

The point of noting these conflicting values is not to argue that the debate over drugs is a debate over whether drugs are good or bad. Most proponents of legalization acknowledge the harm resulting from drugs and many are themselves avowed abstainers. Neither are these conflicting values noted because the problems are merely technical oversights, such as insufficient funding for treatment programs. The problem lies not in these internally inconsistent policies, but in the conflicts in fundamental values which give rise to these policies. Victory in the drug war can never come about because one value "wins" and another "loses." In a war against ourselves even the victor emerges with battle scars. Rather than victory, the term "negotiated settlement" is probably more accurate.

CONCLUSION

This book is about one particular dimension of the drug problem, that aspect related to crime and criminal justice. That the twelve chapters of this book can only deal with a few of the issues raised in the study of drugs and crime attests to the complexity of the subject. This introductory chapter has taken a broader perspective because the study of drugs and crime cannot be fully separated from the broader problem of drugs and drug policy. The criminal justice system has been chosen as the primary force in the war on drugs, and it is likely that it will continue to play the primary role in drug control in the United States. The language of war in drug policy has taken a more literal meaning in recent years, with efforts to include the National

Guard and the armed forces in the domestic battle. In addition, a growing number of police departments are preparing for drug-related violence with training in military-type exercises. Separating the threats to the security of citizens posed by the drug lords from the threats posed by minimally regulated police and military anti-drug activities will be one of the major challenges in the coming decade. The authors in this book do an excellent job of detailing the issues which will need to be addressed as these distinctions are drawn.

NOTES

[1] Undoubtedly some will quibble with this figure of 10 percent, particularly given the inexact numbers upon which any such estimates must be based. This figure is consistent with materials I have seen estimating, for example, the number of heroin addicts and (as a separate estimate) the number of heroin users. From my perspective, the actual percent is only of secondary interest and should not obscure the larger point that, even for such addictive drugs as heroin, there are more controlled users than addicts.

Section I

DRUGS AND THE
CRIMINAL JUSTICE SYSTEM

As the first line of defense in the war on drugs, the criminal justice system not only shapes the nature of the drug problem, but is shaped by it. The chapters in this section address issues raised by this relationship.

In the opening article, of this section, Peter Reuter takes aim at a cornerstone of U.S. drug policy: interdiction at the border. Few policies are so uncritically accepted by the public. Reuter argues, however, that increased resources for border interdiction are likely to have little impact on the supply or the price of drugs. He assesses the utility of using the military and strategies of conventional warfare to respond to the problem, noting that, in key respects, the problems of border interdiction are distinct from those on a more conventional battlefield.

In "The Impact of Drug Offenders on the Criminal Justice System," Steven Belenko documents the far-reaching ways in which the drug problem affects the criminal justice system. There has been growing public pressure to use the law to respond to the drug problem, and the system has responded with more arrests, more convictions, and a greater likelihood of confinement for drug offenders than was true a few years ago. Unfortunately, the demand to get tough with drug offenders has occurred at the same time that a punitive attitude has already filled our system with other offenders and at a time when each level of the system is severely underfunded. Belenko points out that drug offenders place greater demands on the system than other offenders in regards to screening, treatment, and behavior problems. Finally, the chapter describes the types of programs and the problems encountered in utilizing the criminal justice system to provide treatment for drug-using offenders.

One of the more disturbing aspects of using the criminal justice system to deal with the drug problem is the problem of corruption and drug use by criminal justice employees. David Carter presents his research on drug-related misconduct by police, presenting a model of how police organizations

11

discover, come to terms with, and resolve drug problems among police officers. He distinguishes between drug corruption driven by officer drug use and drug corruption driven by greed. Drug corruption by police is particularly disturbing, not only because the behavior itself is illegal, but also because it is an abrogation of trust and requires associating with others in the drug business. Carter carefully outlines the factors which contribute to police drug corruption and notes the policy issues which must be addressed by departments seeking to prevent or respond to the problem.

In the final chapter in this section, Peter Kraska presents the arguments for the "unmentionable alternative" of decriminalizing drugs. Like the "get-tough" stance they oppose, proponents of decriminalization are drawn from across the political spectrum. Kraska presents the history of drug use and drug controls in this country to argue that a precedent for decriminalization exists. He also outlines the problems generated by drugs, arguing that many of these problems are more the result of drug laws and of the effects of drugs themselves. The issue is not whether decriminalization would incur costs, but whether these costs would exceed those arising from our current policies.

2

Can the Borders Be Sealed?*

Peter Reuter
RAND Corporation

Notwithstanding the new rhetorical emphasis on demand-side measures, the United States, in 1989, is still heavily committed to enforcement of drug prohibitions as the primary method of controlling drug problems. Federal efforts get most of the attention in this respect, though it is estimated[1] that local expenditures on drug enforcement in 1986 greatly exceeded those of federal agencies. For police alone, Godshaw, Koppell and Pancoast estimate a total expenditure of $4.4 billion by state and local governments, to which must be added another $1 billion or $2 billion for prosecutors, courts and prisons. That compares with federal enforcement expenditures of about $2.5 billion in the same year. Expenditures for treatment, counting all levels of government, came to less than $2.5 billion in 1987.[2]

A great deal of the federal enforcement budget has gone to interdiction, the effort to seize drugs and smugglers on their way from the source countries (principally Colombia and Mexico). In Fiscal Year 1988 interdiction expenditures totaled $1.04 billion. Congress has been particularly eager to have the military assume more of the growing interdiction burden; it reasons that the military's $300 billion annual budget and its enormous arsenal of apparently relevant equipment -- from helicopters, to sophisticated radar devices, to fast ships -- should enable it to dramatically reduce the capacity of smug-

---

*   Reprinted with the permission of The RAND Corporation. This chapter was drawn from Peter Reuter, Gordon Crawford, and Jonathan Cave, *Sealing the Borders* (Santa Monica, CA: The RAND Corporation, 1988).

glers to bring drugs across U.S. borders. In late 1986 the House of Representatives passed an amendment that would have required the military services to become the primary interdiction agencies, and to "seal the borders" within 45 days of passage of the act. The Senate, after a scathing attack on the proposal by Senator Sam Nunn (who argued that it was "the equivalent of passing a law saying the President shall, by Thanksgiving, devise a cure for the common cold") rejected the amendment, but the 1986 Omnibus Drug Control Act did require the military to become much more active in the interdiction effort. Some members still support the view that the military should take on this task. Senator DeConcini, one of the leading drug warriors, has even broached the prospect of using Strategic Defense Initiative (SDI) if all else fails in this struggle.

In May 1988 the House passed another bill putting more of the burden on the military; ironically, the House proposed shifting $475 million from SDI development to anti-drug efforts. Under this bill the military services would also have acquired the authority to make high seas arrests of drug smugglers, ending a century-long prohibition of use of military personnel for law enforcement purposes (the "Posse Comitatus" statute). The Senate passed a similar bill but then had second thoughts. In a hearing, unusual because it was held prior to the conference between the two chambers to reconcile the bills, the Senate Armed Services Committee heard an array of witnesses who argued that the expansion of the military role was unwise and unlikely to have much impact on U.S. drug problems. The final result was a bill (The Defense Authorization Act of 1988) which gave the military a rather narrow new role, namely "lead agency" in the detection and monitoring (but not the apprehension) of drug smugglers, and the responsibility for integrating command, control, communication and intelligence (C3I) for drug smuggling. Congress also appropriated an additional $300 million for the military to increase its assistance to the interdictors.

The Omnibus Anti-Drug Abuse Act of 1988 added another $500 million in supplemental appropriations for more interdiction equipment. This accounted for about 50 percent of the additional appropriations contained in the bill. Thus, even at a time when Congress was registering its enthusiasm for shifting more resources to domestic demand-side programs, it was investing heavily in expanding the interdiction effort.

Yet the recent results of cocaine-interdiction efforts are certainly not encouraging. It is true that as interdiction expenditures have grown (since 1981), the amount of cocaine seized also has grown dramatically: whereas in 1981 interdictors seized 1.7 tons of cocaine, the total may have been as high as 40 tons in 1987. Furthermore, even though total cocaine imports increased rapidly over that same period, a much larger share of shipments to the U.S. was seized in 1987 than in 1981; the interdiction seizure rate in 1987 may have been as high as one quarter.[3]   Nonetheless, not only did total imports apparently increase, but the price of cocaine, at both the import and retail levels, also fell rapidly. By late 1987 it was asserted that some large shipments of cocaine were selling for only $15,000 a kilogram in Miami (compared to about $55,000 a kilogram in 1981). At the retail level, where the kilogram is broken down into one-gram units, the price per kilo fell from about $600,000 to $250,000.

The recent past suggests that interdiction, even if it produces a high rate of seizures, will do little to decrease cocaine imports. The Congress, backed by numerous General Accounting Office reports, seems to believe that the problem lies in the execution of the interdiction program -- in particular, lack of coordination. There have been public squabbles among the agencies over who has primacy, as well as complaints about a lack of trained personnel and underfunding of operation and maintenance budgets. All this has fed Congress's suspicion that more could be accomplished with the resources currently allocated.

What in fact could an improved and expanded interdiction program do to reduce cocaine consumption in the United States? This is a question that Congress rarely asks. It has occasionally asked the interdiction agencies (notably the Coast Guard and the Customs Service) what they believe is required to "cut off" the flow of drugs. Since both agencies are too sensible to have any faith that they could actually accomplish that, they have answered in appropriately vague ways. Customs Commissioner Von Raab has described a program that would require a 25-mile cordon around the United States, with every entering vessel, plane, or vehicle having to submit to inspection before crossing the cordon. Commissioner Von Raab correctly assumed that this was not a realistic prospect, and little time was spent substantiating the proposal.

The more serious question is what might be achieved through large increases in the interdiction program, whether invested in large military or non-military resources. A recently published RAND study, carried out on behalf of the Department of Defense, argues that it is extremely difficult to reduce cocaine consumption in this country by even as little as five percent through a more stringent interdiction program. The problem lies in the adaptability of smugglers, the variety of methods by which cocaine can be brought into the United States, and the low price of both drugs and labor for smugglers.

ADAPTING TO CHANGING STRATEGIES

We know relatively little about the organization of the smuggling business. Those who get caught by interdictors are generally lower-level agents, pilots (who may be highly paid), crewmen on ships, and unloaders. Those who run the smuggling organizations remain fairly shadowy figures, probably residents of the source countries themselves. We cannot say whether they are, as press accounts often suggest, particularly astute businessmen. However, they have shown at least a modicum of shrewdness in their adaption to changes in the strategies of interdictors. When, in the early 1980s, the Customs Service improved its radar surveillance of the South Florida Coast -- then the primary entry point for both cocaine and marijuana -- smugglers changed their methods.

In the case of marijuana, as the Coast Guard increased its efforts against seaborne traffic into southern Florida, the smugglers shifted to smaller loads. Whereas the average seizure in 1978 was 9 tons, by 1986 it had fallen to 4.6 tons. "Mother ships," carrying 50 to 100 tons and off-loading to smaller, faster boats for the final run to the Florida coast, almost disappeared during this period. The result was an enormous dilution of the efficacy of maritime interdiction. It takes the same resources to interdict a 5-ton shipment as to interdict a 20-ton shipment, particularly since the Coast Guard vessels must generally tow the smuggler back to shore very soon after apprehension to begin legal proceedings; an arrested person cannot be held for long without the beginnings of formal prosecution. Thus by halving the size of the average shipment, the smugglers practically doubled the task confronting interdiction agencies. Indeed, since smugglers were then able to use smaller boats, the interdictors had to sort through a larger number of potential smuggling vessels.

Similarly, cocaine smugglers shifted much of their traffic to other routes. In particular, there seems to have been a substantial increase in the amount of cocaine brought in through Mexico. Once in Mexico -- and there are few barriers to entry from the south of that country (with or without General Noriega's assistance) -- the drugs may be brought across by small plane, private vehicle, or even by boat.

The peculiar problem presented by Mexico is that planes taking off from there may be at risk for only short periods of time. There are numerous landing strips less than 30 miles south of the U.S. border. A small plane can make the trip over the border and drop its load (if need be, without landing) in less than one hour. During this period, the U.S. interdictors must not only "see" the plane, but also identify it as a vessel used by smugglers and launch interceptors to catch it. This is not technically impossible, but it is exceedingly difficult. It is particularly difficult when there is no continuous radar coverage along the Mexican border, which has been the case until quite recently.

The number of methods that have been used for bringing in large shipments of cocaine is impressive. Air-cargo bays have been found stuffed with cocaine. The U.S. Rose-Growers' Association once tried to bring an action against its Colombian competitors for illegal subsidies in violation of the General Agreement of Tariffs and Trade (GATT), arguing that the cocaine smugglers were subsidizing the shipment of roses for purposes of concealment. The International Trade Commission correctly pointed out that any such subsidy was a private one, hence beyond the reach of the GATT rules.

Other large seizures have involved furniture or other objects stuffed with cocaine, cocaine carried in cargo ships, or cocaine concealed in trucks, coming over the Mexican border. One ton of cocaine was recently found hidden in a cargo of frozen fruit pulp arriving from Ecuador. Four tons were found in a cargo of Brazilian lumber, following a tip from a Colombian source. Though there are still occasional seizures of comparatively modest quantities of cocaine hidden on the persons of airline passengers, the declining cost of the drug is causing smugglers to move toward less labor-intensive smuggling methods. There have been no reports of smuggling over the border in model planes or remote pilotless vehicles, but these are clearly possibilities if the risks associated with other methods increase.

Smugglers have continued to change their methods for bringing cocaine into this country. In 1985, for example, the Coast Guard began seizing significant amounts of cocaine in private boats. Whereas in 1981 the first 100-kilogram seizure attracted considerable attention, the average seizure by the Customs Air Branch in 1986 was 250 kilograms. Even thousand-kilogram seizures barely rate a front-page reference now. Mere expansion of the total size of the cocaine market could not account for this order of magnitude increase in the size of shipments. That change reflects some important developments in the cocaine market.

THE COSTS OF SMUGGLING

Interdiction affects the consumption of cocaine in the United States by affecting its price. No one seriously claims now that interdiction can control the amount of drugs physically able to reach this nation. There are simply too many experienced smugglers, and too many producers and refiners for that to be feasible. Interdiction might be able to make smuggling costs so high that U.S. consumers would want less (so that less would be delivered); but interdiction could not be so effective that, say, only 100 tons of cocaine would reach our shores. Thus we need to look at how interdiction raises smugglers' costs and, eventually, the price of cocaine for users.

Smuggling entails four primary costs: *drugs, personnel, transportation,* and *corruption.* Not only is each cost currently modest (compared to the retail price of cocaine), but it is hard to see how any of them could be made significantly higher.

Producing drugs is inexpensive. The leaf that goes into making a kilogram of cocaine costs about $1,000; not much more goes into the refining process. Fully 99 percent of the price of the drug, when sold on the streets in the United States, is accounted for by payments to people who distribute it.

Seizing drugs close to the source thus imposes little penalty on the drug-distribution system. Drugs are cheaply replaced. One kilogram of cocaine seized on the beaches of Colombia in 1987 probably cost less than $5,000 to replace, including the cost of getting it from the refinery to the point of export. Even by the time it made it out of Colombia into Mexico or the Bahamas, it probably cost less than $15,000. These figures are substantially lower than those of 1981.

As a result, it seems likely that smugglers will now spend less to protect their drugs. Precautions are expensive. A smuggler whose cocaine costs $10,000 per kilo will spend more to protect it (for example, by bribing the local sheriff) than a smuggler whose replacement cost is only $5,000 per kilo. With lower replacement costs, the smuggler may also find it sensible to send larger shipments in a single load. The transportation costs are the same for a 200-kilo shipment in a private plane as for a 100-kilo shipment. The pilot's risk of long-term imprisonment is also the same. A smuggler who wants to transport 200 kilograms a month will be more likely to do it in one rather than two shipments when the price of cocaine falls.

Simple arithmetic demonstrates how little the seizure of the drug itself can affect the retail price of cocaine. Assume for the moment that instead of seizing 20 percent of all cocaine shipped from Colombia, the interdiction agencies had been able to seize 50 percent in 1987. The 1987 retail price was (approximately) $250,000, which includes compensation for lost drugs. If an additional 30 percent of drugs were seized, the kilo sold in the street would incur an additional $6,000 in replacement costs (assuming that a kilo costs as much as $20,000 to replace). Thus, our successful drug-seizure program would have added less than 3 percent to the retail price of cocaine.

An analysis of labor costs is even more discouraging. The problem is simply that smugglers of cocaine need very little skilled labor per kilogram. Even if their workers demand high compensation for the risks of long prison terms, it will have little effect on the final price of the drug.

Consider the pilot who flies in 250-kilogram shipments over the Mexican border. A fair guess is that in 1987 he received about $250,000 for incurring the risks of the business -- attempting to land under difficult conditions, and possibly going to prison. Assume that we had much more effective interdiction -- that is, that the pilot was more likely to be caught, and that he faced a much longer prison term if caught. Assume further that, as a consequence, the pilot then tripled his demand, and would make the trip only if paid $750,000, surely a fair down payment on his daydreams of wealth. Unfortunately, this adds only $2,000 to the per-kilogram cost of bringing cocaine into the U.S., less than one percent of the retail price in 1987.

The tale is at least as depressing when we consider the other types of labor used by smugglers. Pilots presumably value their freedom rather highly; they have, after all, prospects of reasonable earnings in legitimate positions. The same cannot be said for crewmen on ships coming up from Colombia. Their earnings from other employment may be quite modest, and the rigors of a U.S. federal prison may not appear too daunting when compared with life on a Colombian fishing vessel. They already face at least a one-in-nine chance of being arrested on any marijuana smuggling trip, and the federal judiciary is not lenient in these matters; in South Florida, the average 1986 sentence was 46 months for those caught by the Coast Guard. Nonetheless, crew members are believed (a stronger statement is unfortunately not possible) to earn only about $15,000 each for taking the trip; the master may get as much as $25,000. Total crew costs are probably between $100,000 and $150,000. Even if better interdiction were to double this cost, it still would add little to the cost of bringing in a kilo of cocaine, assuming that smugglers are willing to put aboard a hundred kilograms at a time.

The reader need not be burdened with details concerning transportation. Adequate vessels and planes are available for $100,000; defrayed over a 250-kilogram shipment, that amounts to only $400 per kilogram. Seizing equipment has no more promise than seizing drugs or couriers.

THE RISKS OF SMUGGLING

Given these facts, it should come as no surprise that an effort to simulate the effect of increasingly effective interdiction (through a formal mathematical model) found that improved interdiction is likely to have little impact on U.S. cocaine consumption. In the model, interdictors seized increasing quantities of cocaine, even increasing shares of total shipments, but were able to reduce total consumption by more than five percent only when they could raise the risks for almost every mode of bringing in the drug. And there lies the rub; it is hard to see how all the many and disparate methods of bringing in this compact drug could be made very risky.

We built a model in which smugglers had to make a choice among different routes for bringing in cocaine. Each route was associated with a particular risk, and with particular transportation/personnel costs. As the interdictors raised risks along a particular route, the smugglers were induced to shift away from that route and to send more of their shipments along alternative routes. Increasing the probability of interdiction raises the smuggler's costs, since he must now face higher drug-replacement, transportation, and labor costs. With few hard data available, assumptions were made that favored the interdictors. For example, we assumed that labor costs were quite sensitive to risk, so that raising the risk of being caught from 0.25 percent to 0.50 percent led to a quadrupling of a pilot's payment.

Even with these favorable assumptions, it proved very difficult to raise smugglers' costs enough to greatly increase the retail price of cocaine, and thus reduce total consumption. In the model, smugglers had eleven routes available to them -- five by air, five by sea, and one by land. (The land route represents shipment across Mexico.) The interdictors were assumed to be able to raise risks on all of the routes except the land route, in which the drug is, in effect, walked across the border in small shipments. The probability of a shipment's being intercepted on the land route stayed fixed at 10 percent, but other costs (particularly personnel) were assumed to be high relative to other routes.

When we raised the risk of capture along one route from about 0.25 percent to 0.50 percent, smugglers negated this by shifting to other routes; their costs rose by less than two percent, or about $117 per kilo. It was only when five out of eleven routes were subject to the higher risk that imports fell by more than 10 percent. When the risk was raised on all ten of the non-land routes, smugglers' costs per kilo rose by $7,663, or about three percent of the retail price. Consumption now fell by more than 20 percent, reflecting model assumptions very favorable to interdictors. As smugglers incurred greater risks from more routes, an increasing share of total shipments was imported via the Mexican land border.

THE UNINTENDED CONSEQUENCES
OF DRUG POLICY

The astute reader will now have identified a puzzle. Disheartening though the above analysis may be, it still suggests that more interdiction, even when smugglers adapt, will raise prices. Yet more intense interdiction since 1981 has been accompanied by *declining* prices, contrary both to intuition and to the foregoing projections. The explanation may lie in the phenomenon of "learning by doing": most individuals and organizations get better at their job as they do it longer. This is the basis for the famous strategy suggested by the Boston Consulting Group in the early 1970s: "investing in the learning curve."

Our conjecture (and it is not more than that) is that the rapid growth of the cocaine market has increased the number of experienced smugglers, and that this has driven down the cost of bringing cocaine into the United States. Experienced smugglers can control their risks better than novices can; they know more about the risks of particular methods of importing, have better connections with corrupt officials, and can obtain better credit from their suppliers. Prior to 1980, there were relatively few experienced smugglers, and they could not, without raising their risks a great deal, provide enough cocaine for the entire market. Thus the price of cocaine smuggling was determined by the marginal smuggler, a novice trying to become an expert.

Novices, if they are not caught, eventually become experienced. Interdiction is obviously more successful with novices than with experienced smugglers, because the latter are better at avoiding interdictors. But enough novices make it through, at least when the market is expanding rapidly, that the stock of experience may grow relative to the size of the market. A sufficient number of experienced smugglers in the business can supply the entire market, and the price for smuggling services will fall. This seems to be a plausible account of why the cocaine import price has tumbled by as much as two-thirds since 1981.

If this account is correct, we must accept some possibly shameful consequences of intensified interdiction. Experienced smugglers can benefit from interdiction, since it catches the potential competition; their profits will rise without a corresponding increase in risk. If there is a cartel of experienced smugglers, with an interest in trying to set prices for cocaine smuggling, then its prospects may certainly be enhanced by intense interdiction, the disproportionate weight of which falls on the newcomers. The recent 4-ton seizure mentioned above was generated by a tip from Colombia, though the shipment came from Brazil; perhaps the cartel is attempting to gain control of the market by helping interdictors.

Another irony that emerges from systematic analysis of the interdiction program concerns the source countries. Interdiction can impose costs on smugglers in a variety of ways. But inasmuch as it involves the seizure of drugs, interdiction will increase the earnings of source-country producers, thus exacerbating the problems with which the U.S. Government is urging the source-country governments to deal.

The explanation for this conundrum lies in the fact that source-country earnings come from all drug shipments, not just from those drugs that are actually consumed. Some of these shipments reach users. Others are seized. Total demand for producers equals the sum of shipments that are seized and those that reach their destinations. As more is seized, total export demand goes up. Of course, higher rates of seizure will raise smuggler costs and thus reduce demand, but it is possible to show that only under highly improbable conditions will the price increase reduce demand by more than enough to compensate for the increase in replacement demand caused by the seizure it-self.

It is not inevitable that more successful interdiction leads to an increase in export demand. If interdiction can make smugglers take more precautions and raise their non-drug costs (personnel, transportation, or corruption pay-ments), then it will reduce total shipments. It is difficult to determine whether such a goal can be achieved in practice, however.

THE MEXICAN BORDER

Clearly the porousness of the Mexican border is an important part of the problem. It has become the principal gateway for all three of the major im-ported drugs: cocaine, heroin, and marijuana. Yet among the source coun-tries, Mexico is the only one that seems not to have developed its own signifi-cant drug problem (in that domestic drug consumption has not increased there); hence it is the one source-country in which pressure might actually have some impact.[4]

In trying to persuade the other major source countries (Bolivia, Colom-bia, and Peru) to make a serious effort to curtail drug exports, the U.S. gov-ernment is usually restricted by two factors. First, the earnings from drug production are an important source of income for large peasant populations, and generate a significant share of the nation's export earnings. Second, the source-country government either has weak political control of some of the growing areas (Bolivia and Peru) or is facing an opponent that has the ca-pacity to threaten the lives of government leaders (Colombia). The first con-dition creates ambivalence, the second incapacity.

Neither of these conditions applies to Mexico. Drug earnings are not a significant share of total export income or even of the regional income in the areas in which drugs are produced. The Mexican government does not incur any major political threats by cracking down on the drug trade. In fact, the government has been reasonably active, and the Mexican Attorney General has pointed, with considerable ire, to the large number (154) of Mexican po-licemen that have died in drug-enforcement efforts, undertaken largely for U.S. interests. Indeed, it is likely that more Mexican than U.S. police have died while attempting to enforce U.S. drug policies.

Clearly, it would be naive to expect that Mexico could eliminate either drug production or transshipment; after all, the United States domestically produces an increasing share of its own marijuana (perhaps as much as one-third), despite highly publicized and well-funded efforts at eradication. Transshipment is, of course, even harder to stop; the United States does not manage to capture a large share of the drugs that move within its domestic commerce, either. However, it is not unreasonable to expect Mexico to co-operate with the United States in cross-border control (to allow "hot pursuit" of smugglers, for example).

Mexico has chosen not to do so. U.S. planes must turn back at the border, and cannot receive coordinated support from Mexicans in pursuing those planes further. The explanation for this seems to lie less in corruption, which U.S. politicians often claim, than in the sensitivity of Mexico about its political autonomy. History provides some basis for that sensitivity, which has probably been heightened by recent finger-pointing. Getting cooperation from the Mexicans on border control is one way of making progress on the interdiction front (though it may be doubtful that it will make a major difference for the long-term availability of cocaine or heroin, given their compactness).

THE ROLE OF THE MILITARY

The temptation to reach for the military is understandable. The armed forces have vast quantities of equipment designed to ensure that we can see our enemy, rapidly close in on him once he has been seen, and attack him if he does not agree to follow our orders. Surely the armed services must be able to do this against drug smugglers, still not a very high-technology foe, if they are to be competent against the nation's better-armed strategic adversaries.

The problem is that smugglers have a different set of goals from those of America's other adversaries, and that drug-interdiction efforts require acceptance of certain constraints that do not apply in wartime. Smugglers do not seek to cross the border in large numbers in a short period of time; they seek instead to enter in a steady flow, disperse once they are over the border, and never reassemble. More importantly, this nation is not willing to impose the strict entry requirements that are almost automatic during wartime. We still wish to allow regular commerce and tourism. Long delays at the Mexican border for commercial traffic, such as those that resulted from Operations Intercept and Alliance, are regarded as intolerable for any length of time. Pleasure-craft owners, as formidable a middle-class lobby as the private-pilots' association, are not going to agree to increased restrictions on their activities for the sake of catching a few extra drug smugglers.

Thus the heart of the problem -- especially after adopting more stringent interdiction measures -- is distinguishing smugglers from innocent citizens. Data from the Coast Guard, which has sole jurisdiction outside U.S. territorial waters (sometimes using Navy equipment), point to the problem. Even when the Coast Guard has prior information that a vessel may be carrying drugs, only one out of eight of those boarded is found to have drugs. This figure is about five times higher than the agency's success rate when it has no prior information, but nevertheless it does point to the difficulty of recognizing smugglers.

The military can ensure that the Coast Guard will see more vessels and pursue more of them for the purpose of boarding, but it cannot do much to help the maritime services distinguish the indistinguishable. Smugglers do not need distinctive equipment, and can readily blend in with other traffic. As a result, the book of hull types issued to Coast Guard commanders is a thick one; the thicker the book, in this case, the less information it imparts.

Maritime interdiction has been oriented primarily toward catching marijuana smugglers, and has certainly made smuggling from the Atlantic coast of Colombia a fairly risky business. But an increasing amount of cocaine now seems to move by sea as well, and represents a much more difficult target than marijuana. A 100-kilogram shipment of cocaine is much harder to detect, once the boat is boarded, than a 5-ton cargo of marijuana. Thus even if the military does increase the number of ships seen, halted, and searched, it is likely that the cost of smuggling cocaine by sea will remain modest.

The military problem here, unfortunately, is similar to that faced by the United States when it attempted interdiction of North Vietnamese supplies heading into South Vietnam. It is the simplicity of the enemy's needs and technology that makes interdiction difficult; there are no large, fixed targets whose destruction makes a difference. Smuggling organizations are also capable of the decentralization, adaptability, and capacity to camouflage themselves in the civilian traffic and population that made the Vietcong such an elusive target.

THE POLITICS OF INTERDICTION

However original the foregoing analysis, its conclusions are familiar: greater efforts toward interdiction are not going to have much of an effect on the nation's cocaine problem. A similar argument can be made with regard to much of the federal enforcement effort.

Given the general lack of faith in the effectiveness of enforcement, why does it still attract so much support? Clearly no member of Congress wishes to be on record as being "soft" on drugs. A vote against a proposed increase in drug enforcement incurs the risk of such an accusation. Budgetary limits, in theory, force any increase in the drug budget to be weighed against some other (presumably desirable) program. In fact, as was shown in the 1988 contingency bill passed by the Senate referred to above, it is possible to get around these trade-offs by labeling the drug problem a crisis.

Those politicians who are more thoughtful about the problem, and see beyond the rhetoric of the drug warriors, face further obstacles if they wish to achieve visible results in the short run.   Maybe prevention is the principal long-run hope, but does that necessarily mean that the nation should immediately spend large sums on prevention efforts?   Precisely because prevention has been slighted in the past, we have no well-developed models of what works.   We know a good deal about what does not work -- programs that aim to scare adolescents, for example, or simply telling them about the pharmacology of drugs -- and we know, from smoking-prevention programs, something about the design of what does work.   But moving from principles of design to working programs, particularly for schools in inner cities, is a long step.   A lot of research is necessary before good prevention programs are readily available.

Given these facts, it is scarcely surprising that Congress continues to push enforcement programs on an administration that is visibly wearying of the fight it entered with so much enthusiasm.   Interdiction does produce visible results: drugs seized, assets confiscated, smugglers imprisoned.   Spending more will almost certainly produce more of each of these desirable outputs. What effect this has on the drug problem is almost secondary -- or at least Congress acts as if it were; for Congress never seems to raise the issue, either with the interdiction agencies or with its own watchdog, the General Accounting Office.

What is largely neglected by both branches of the federal government is the less glamorous set of programs that make up the drug-treatment sector. There is not much of a constituency of these programs, which are often staffed by ex-drug offenders, and which offer services primarily to underclass drug users.   Few of the programs' clients seem to be cured of their drug problem, and many have long histories of arrests and continued drug use while in the programs.

Public treatment programs have been systematically starved of funds since 1981; their share of the federal drug budget has shrunk from about 19 percent in 1981 to 14 percent in 1988.   Yet intensified enforcement and the more addictive nature of crack have greatly increased the demand for their services.   There are long waiting lists for treatment in most major cities.   Creating better treatment programs, which can handle the variegated populations now at their doors, should be an important goal.

This is not to say that the interdiction program should be abandoned. The standard estimate of the economic cost of drug abuse in this country is somewhere between $50 billion and $100 billion -- and that does not include a number of social costs, such as the fear of crime, that might add substantially to the figure.   If the billion-dollar interdiction program reduces that cost by a few percentage points, society might judge it as money reasonably spent.

The real issue is whether we would obtain a greater reduction in the social costs of drug abuse if some of that money were allocated to other programs. Although there may be no analysis that would provide a firm answer to that question, the nation may well be better off putting more money into treatment and less into interdiction. A few more resources put into research, so that we can base policy choices on something firmer than instinct and image, also sounds like a reasonable expenditure.

NOTES

[1]   Godshaw, Gerald; Ross Koppel and Russell Pancoast *Anti-Drug Law Enforcement Efforts and Their Impact.* Washington, DC: U.S. Government Printing Office.

[2]   National Institute on Drug Abuse *Main Findings for Drug Abuse Treatment Units: Data from the National Drug and Alcoholism Treatment Unit Survey.* Rockville, MD, 1989.

[3]   A stronger statement about interdiction rates is not possible because there are no systematic estimates of cocaine consumption.

[4]   For an analysis of the obstacles of effective control of source-country exports, see "Eternal Hope: American's Quest of Narcotics Control." *The Public Interest*, No. 79 (Spring, 1985).

3

The Impact of Drug Offenders on the Criminal Justice System

Steven Belenko
New York City Criminal Justice Agency

BACKGROUND

Over the past few years, an unprecedented surge in the number of drug arrests and in the percentage of drug-involved offenders has caused enormous management and policy problems for the criminal justice system. The focus on control of street drug dealing and emphasis on enforcement and punishment instead of treatment and rehabilitation have been fueled in part by a recent evolution in American society's attitudes toward illicit drug use, leading to widespread repudiation of those who use illegal drugs. Accompanying this widespread sentiment that drug use is a cause, or symptom, of many of society's ills is a readiness to blame much of America's crime and violence problem on the use, and sale, of illicit drugs, unprecedented media coverage of the issue, and increased clamoring for more effective measures to control drug offenders. In the midst of this latest wave of public concern about drug use, now focusing on cocaine and crack, the criminal justice system has struggled to react to these pressures while simultaneously confronted by severe courtroom congestion and jail overcrowding. This combination of strains on the system has resulted in frequent crisis management and a continuing search for more effective ways for the system to absorb the increase in drug arrests and to reduce the cycle of drug use and arrest for these defendants.

The criminal justice system's relationship to the drug-abusing offender, and the ways in which he or she should be treated by the system, have historically been uneasy and mutable. At different times in the past 50 years, the courts have taken a tolerant, rehabilitation-oriented view or a punitive, sanction-oriented one. The former approach still largely remains in the juvenile justice system, where drug charges tend to be handled more like status offenses than criminal cases (Schneider, 1988). To some extent, these shifts have reflected changes in the public's attitudes toward drugs and their perceived relationship to crime and public order. Further, the type of drug with which the public and the criminal justice system has been concerned has also shifted, and with it the level of concern and the type of system response. While there has long been a concern about the relationship between illicit drug use and criminal behavior, and a perception that by reducing drug use we can reduce crime, it is only relatively recently that the drug-using offender has commanded such an intense focus by the system.

Concomitant with a growing intolerance for drug abuse and demise of the rehabilitative ideal has come the emergence of crack and powdered cocaine as the drugs of choice in poor urban areas, and the fear that use of these drugs is criminogenic and particularly associated with violent behavior. The confluence of these trends has meant an emphasis on law enforcement control of drug use and sale at a time when available treatment facilities were severely limited, resulting in a flood of cases into the system, with few options but to respond with punitive sanctions.

Growing Impact of Drug-Using Offenders on the Criminal Justice System

The past decade has seen a dramatic change in the composition of the defendant population. Nationally, both the number of drug arrests and the percentage of all arrestees that are charged with drug offenses have increased substantially since 1980. In New York City the percentage of defendants arrested for drug charges has increased from 11 percent of the arrestee population in 1980 to 30 percent in 1988 (New York City Police Department, 1989). In Washington, D.C., a similar trend has occurred, with the number and proportion of drug arrests soaring in recent years as a result of intensified street enforcement efforts against crack and other drugs (*U.S. News & World Report*, 1989).

The National Institute of Justice's Drug Use Forecasting program, a 12-city effort to monitor drug use rates through urine testing among new arrestees, has found drug-positive rates ranging from 23 to 86 percent (excluding marijuana) for the period April - June 1988, with an average of about 58 percent. Positive tests for cocaine were found in 83 percent of

Manhattan arrestees, 65 percent in Los Angeles, and 55 percent in Washington, D.C. (National Institute of Justice, 1988). In the latter city, where all arrestees have routinely been subject to urine tests at arrest since May 1984, the percentage of defendants testing positive for cocaine rose steadily, from about 20 percent in 1984, to over 60 percent in the first half of 1988.

It is difficult to extricate the extent to which these trends reflect changes in law enforcement priorities, the offender population, prosecutorial strategy, legislative changes, actual increases in illicit drug use, or public/political/media pressures on the criminal justice system. Yet it is important to understand how these forces operate and interrelate in order to elucidate the system's response to serious social and public health issues, and to help develop more effective policies in the future. Clearly, the changes in law enforcement strategy in the early to mid-1980s, from long, elaborate investigations to target the major drug sellers, to a street-level strategy aimed at sweeping low-level dealers and steerers off the streets and into less visible locations, has had a major impact on the flood of cases into the system. The emphasis on street dealers and undercover buy-and-bust operations (Zimmer, 1987; Kleiman et al., 1984; Kleiman, 1986) inevitably results in a much larger number of defendants than enforcement efforts aimed at the high-level dealers.

This change in police strategy, in part, a response to intense community pressure to reduce open street drug markets (Belenko & Schiff, 1984), has had an enormous impact on the courts, pretrial agencies, defense, prosecution, probation, corrections, and parole. A major focus of the courts has become the processing of cases as quickly as possible to clear calendars, such as through increased use of felony waivers. Also, the pressure on defendants to accept plea bargains may increase as a result of caseload demands. Further, federal, state, and local jail and prison populations have soared during the 1980s, a result of substantial increases in the number of drug arrestees, higher conviction rates, increased probability of receiving a jail or prison sentence, and longer sentences. In New York City, drug offenders are now the largest single category of arrestee and jail inmate, and the most common type of New York State prison inmate. Legislative initiatives to increase penalties for drug offenders or drug-related crime, and the existence of mandatory sentencing laws for repeat offenders in most states, have placed additional pressures on the system at all phases of case processing.

Public Pressure to Use the Criminal Justice System to Alleviate the Drug Problem

Reduced tolerance for illicit drug use, and frustration with open street dealing led to law enforcement efforts like Operation Pressure Point and

Tactical Narcotics Teams in New York City, and similar efforts in Washington, D.C., Lynn, Massachusetts, and elsewhere. At the same time came a growing disenchantment with the inability of the criminal justice system to reduce crime ("soft judges", "revolving-door justice," etc.) and a lack of confidence in and reduced funding for treatment, non-incarcerative supervision and other rehabilitation-oriented efforts.   Interdiction efforts were also viewed as having limited utility, including efforts to eradicate growing areas in South America, increase border patrols, etc; increased seizures have not reduced the amount of drugs available on the streets (Nadelmann, 1988). The South Florida Task Force, a major interagency federal effort to reduce the incoming supplies of cocaine and other drugs and thereby drive up street prices, was widely viewed as a failure.

Finally, the emergence of crack and the fears generated by its use may have helped to alter the criminal justice system's views about drug-using offenders. The appearance of crack in urban areas in the mid-1980s and the apparent epidemic of use has caused enormous problems for an already overloaded criminal justice system. The drug's low cost, ease of manufacture and distribution, and high addiction potential may have contributed both to the spread of its use and to the development of new types of entrepreneurial marketing systems that have fostered increased violence among dealers (*Newsweek*, 1988; *U.S. News & World Report*, 1989). Also, no effective, readily available treatment modalities currently exist for crack or powdered cocaine, at least for the poor, uneducated urban population. Proliferating use of these drugs along with increased poverty and the opportunity to make large sums of money rather quickly, have attracted a large number of young, inexperienced dealers.

What Should the Criminal Justice System Do?

Faced with this flood of drug cases, the criminal justice system must consider policy responses within the framework of several sometimes-competing concerns:

* move cases through the system so as not to clog courts

* maintain legal/constitutional rights

* respond to legislative and public pressures to treat drug cases seriously

*   develop resources to increase understanding of the effects of crack and cocaine use and the appropriate treatment and other interventions for the different types of drug offenders processed through the system.

The emphasis in this chapter will be on adult arrests for drug law violations, since these types of crimes are the most readily quantifiable measures of the impact of drugs on the criminal justice system. While there is evidence that arrestees for non-drug offenses in urban jurisdictions also may have a high probability of using drugs (National Institute of Justice, 1988), precise data on drug-use patterns and long-term trends among arrestees are not readily available. Further, the low prevalence of illicit drug use among juveniles, and the relative lack of data on the processing of juvenile arrests, make analysis of the impact of drugs on the juvenile justice system difficult. The focus here is not necessarily to analyze drug-crime interactions, which have received much attention in the research literature for many years (e.g. Inciardi, 1986; Wish & Johnson, 1986; Anglin & Speckart, 1988; Nurco et al., 1988) but to examine how the criminal justice system has responded to the drug crisis, what the effects of the growing emphasis on enforcement and punishment have been, and what types of system responses might be both appropriate and effective.

EFFECTS ON COURT CASELOADS

Volume of Arrests

The impact of the drug-using offender on the criminal justice system has been driven primarily by the large increase in the number of drug arrests during the last few years. Nationally, the Federal Bureau of Investigation's Uniform Crime Reports data show that an estimated 937,400 arrests for drug-law violations were made in 1987, representing 7.5 percent of all arrests. Between 1980 and 1987 drug arrests in the United States rose by 52 percent, while the number of total arrests increased by only 11 percent (Table 3.1). Not only has the arrest volume increased, but so has the relative severity of the offenses: the proportions of drug arrests that are for drug sale and for heroin or cocaine have been increasing in recent years, while the percentage of marijuana arrests has declined (Table 3.2). For example, in 1986, 41 percent of drug arrests were for heroin or cocaine, compared to 12 percent in the beginning of the decade.

Table 3.1
**Number and Percentage of Total and Drug Arrests
in United States, 1980-1987**

Year	Total Number of Arrests	Number of Drug Arrests Actual	Number of Drug Arrests Estimated	% Drug Arrests (Actual)
1980	9,686,940	533,010	580,900	5.5
1981	10,278,107	586,646	559,900	5.7
1982	10,053,324	565,182	676,000	5.6
1983	10,275,047	616,936	661,400	6.0
1984	8,905,289	562,255	708,400	6.3
1985	10,278,380	702,882	811,400	6.8
1986	10,384,722	691,882	824,100	6.7
1987	10,784,199	811,078	937,400	7.5

SOURCE: U.S. Department of Justice, Federal Bureau of Investigation. *Crime in the United States.*

Table 3.2
United States Drug Arrests, 1980-1987:
Percentage of Drug Sale and Marijuana Arrests

Year	% Sale Arrests	% Marijuana Arrests	% Heroin or Cocaine Arrests
1980	22	69	12
1981	20	72	12
1982	20	67	13
1983	22	61	23
1984	22	59	26
1985	24	56	30
1986	25	44	41
1987	26	40	N.A.

SOURCE: U.S. Department of Justice, Federal Bureau of Investigation. *Crime in the United States.*

Table 3.3
New York State Drug Arrest Trends, 1983-1987

	% Change 1983-1987
ALL ARRESTS	+25
Drug	+98
Non-Drug	+13
FELONY ARRESTS	+26
Drug	+118
Non-Drug	+11
DRUG ARRESTS (EXCLUDING MARIJUANA)	
Sale	+152
Possession	+75
Felony Sale	+161
Felony Possession	+112

SOURCE: New York State Division of Criminal Justice Services. *New York State: Trends in Felony Drug Offense Processing 1983-1987*. October 1988.

The arrest statistics for New York State and New York City tell an even more dramatic story, and help illustrate the scope of the impact of illicit drugs on the criminal justice system in a large, urbanized state that has both a major drug problem and an active anti-drug enforcement effort. From 1983-87, the number of drug arrests in New York State increased by 98 percent, compared to a 13 percent increase for non-drug arrests (Table 3.3). More important in terms of its impact on local and state correctional institutions, as well as the court system, was an even larger growth in felony drug arrests of 118 percent in that five-year period, including a 161 percent increase in felony drug sale arrests. Moreover, the severity of these felony drug arrests has increased: 75 percent of the felony drug arrests in New York State in 1987 were Class B felonies (see page 41) compared with 52 percent in 1983. Among the felony drug arrestees in 1987, 72 percent had been arrested previously, and 25 percent had a prior felony conviction (Division of Criminal Justice Services, 1988a).

To a large extent these state trends have been driven by changes in the New York City arrest population over the past nine years, as street enforcement policy and the nature of the urban drug problem evolved. In 1980, the New York City Police Department made 18,521 felony or misdemeanor arrests for drug offenses, about 40 percent of them for heroin or other opiates; drug arrests in that year comprised 11 percent of all arrests in New York City. By 1988, the number of arrests had grown to 88,641 (44 percent of them for crack), representing 30 percent of all arrests (New York City Police Department, 1981-89). In contrast to the United States and New York State figures cited above, drug arrests in New York City increased by 379 percent from 1980-88 (127 percent since 1983), with a 427 percent increase in felony arrests.

Processing of Drug Arrests

The extraordinary number of drug arrests has placed tremendous burdens on already overloaded urban court systems, leading to severe overcrowding of detention facilities, increased prosecutor and public defender caseloads, case delay, and the need for substantial additional court resources. Although court and related resources have increased, they have not kept pace. Frequently, police enforcement decisions are made in a vacuum, without considering their impact on other parts of the criminal justice system. An ancillary effect of the burgeoning drug caseloads is the access to and quality of defense representation. With more cases to defend, and increasingly limited resources, caseloads for public defenders are higher and the quality of defense perhaps is compromised.

Table 3.4
Number of Convictions and Incarceration Rates for Drug Law Violations,
U.S. District Courts, 1980-1986

	1980	1981	1982	1983	1984	1985	1986	% Change 1980-86
Number of Convictions								
All Drug Cases	5244	6067	7152	7929	9175	10500	12285	+134
Heroin/Cocaine	2677	2714	2997	3624	4660	5910	7769	+190
Marijuana	1267	2204	2839	3070	3285	3261	3221	+154
Other	1300	1149	1316	1235	1230	1329	1295	0
% Sentenced To Incarceration								
All Drug Convictions	71	72	73	72	72	75	77	
Heroin/Cocaine	76	78	79	80	79	80	81	
Marijuana	63	65	66	62	62	66	66	
All Convictions	46	48	51	51	49	50	52	

SOURCE: U.S. Department of Justice, Bureau of Justice Statistics. *Drug Law Violators 1980-86*. Washington, DC: June 1988.

The tremendous media and political attention toward illicit drugs, and the increasing clamoring of public officials to "get tough" on drugs, together with the more general public hardening of attitudes toward drug use, has put substantial pressure on the judiciary to look at drug cases from a different perspective and to process these cases more quickly and perhaps more harshly. One response has been to create special "Narcotics Court" divisions, designed to handle only felony drug cases and to get quick felony pleas with perhaps more lenient sanctions. This, perhaps, has had a reciprocal effect on the police arrest policy since the special parts imply that the courts can handle more and more drug cases without affecting the processing of other cases. Changes in the way drug cases are processed, or other policy or legislative initiatives, have generally been implemented in a piecemeal fashion, in a crisis atmosphere, with little long-range planning and insufficient funding. To some extent, the lack of coordinated response and primary emphasis on simply building more jail and prison cells to house the large numbers of detained and sentenced drug offenders has been understandable, given the rapidly changing nature of the street drug problem, and the conspicuous public and political outcry against drug use and associated crime.

The trends in convictions and sentences, both in federal and large urban courts, show an increasingly punitive response to the incoming drug arrests. During Fiscal Year 1986, 20 percent of the criminal case filings in U.S. District Courts (19,646 cases) were for drug law violations (Bureau of Justice Statistics, 1988a), mostly for sale or manufacture. As Table 3.4 shows, the number of drug law convictions in 1986 (12,285), represents a 134 percent increase from 1980. In contrast, the number of non-drug case convictions in U.S. District Courts increased by only 27 percent during that period. This difference, in part, reflects that the federal prosecutors are much less likely to decline to prosecute or refer drug cases to the U.S. Magistrate (20%) than non-drug cases (42%).

Drug convictions in the U.S. District Courts have also had a higher probability than non-drug convictions to receive an incarcerative sentence, and this rate has been increasing during the 1980s (Table 3.4). The percentage of convicted drug offenders sentenced to incarceration rose to 77 percent in 1986, and was 81 percent for heroin or cocaine cases. In contrast, the incarceration rate for all U.S. District Court convictions was 52 percent in 1986. The impact of this pattern on federal prisons is exacerbated by the fact that the average sentence length has been increasing for drug offenders at a faster rate than for non-drug cases (Table 3.5). In 1986, the mean length of all federal drug sentences was 61 months, a 33 percent increase from 1980; drug possession cases showed a much greater 181 percent increase to a mean of 45 months. Overall, U.S. District Court sentences had a mean length of 51 months in 1986, a 24 percent increase from 1980.

Table 3.5
Mean (Median) Sentence Length for Sentences on Drug Law Violations, U.S. District Courts, 1980-1986

	1980	1981	1982	1983	1984	1985	1986	% Change 1980-86
All Drug Sentences	46 (24)	49 (36)	54 (36)	54 (36)	55 (36)	57 (36)	61 (42)	+33 (17)
Sale/Manuf.	47 (36)	50 (36)	57 (36)	56 (36)	57 (36)	56 (36)	60 (42)	+28 (17)
Possession	16 (6)	29 (18)	28 (24)	26 (24)	29 (30)	39 (32)	45 (36)	+181 (500)
All Sentences	41	44 (24)	45 (24)	44 (24)	45 (24)	49 (24)	51 (30)	+24 (25)

SOURCE: U.S. Department of Justice, Bureau of Justice Statistics. *Drug Law Violators 1980-86.* Washington, DC: June 1988.

The situation in the states has largely paralleled the federal data. A 1984 study of dispositions of felony arrests in 11 states found that 78 percent of drug arrests were prosecuted, 69 percent of the prosecuted cases resulted in a conviction, and 65 percent of the convictions received a jail or prison sentence, mostly more than one year (Bureau of Justice Statistics, 1988b). These conviction and incarceration rates were comparable to those of violent felonies (67% and 64%, respectively). In New York State, the percentage of felony drug arrests prosecuted as felonies was the highest of any offense type in 1987 except homicide (Division of Criminal Justice Services, 1988a). While overall conviction rates in New York State from 1983-87 remained stable for drug arrests at about 70 percent, the percentage of felony arrests that resulted in a felony conviction increased from 42 percent in 1983 to 63 percent in 1987. In contrast, felony conviction rates for non-drug felonies rose slightly from 35 to 38 percent. Of the convictions resulting from felony drug arrests, 70 percent were sentenced to jail or prison, a large increase from the 50 percent rate in 1983. Incarceration rates for non-drug felony arrest convictions actually decreased slightly from 49 to 45 percent between 1983 and 1987.

Bail Setting

The available data on bail setting and pretrial detention rates also suggest a tendency toward harsher treatment of drug offenders by the Courts. For example, among all U.S. District Court cases in Fiscal Year 1986, 31 percent were detained pretrial, compared with 38 percent of the drug cases. Among those not detained, 22 percent of all defendants, but only 13 percent of the drug defendants, were released on their own recognizance. A recent study in New York City on arraignment release rates showed a large increase in the percentage of drug defendants held in detention, beginning in early 1986, with a concomitant decrease in the held rates of non-drug defendants (Nickerson & Dynia, 1988). Figure 3.1 shows how this clear shift in the arraignment release patterns has remained through 1988. Most of the change occurred between 1985 and 1986, when New York City, as much of the nation, began to be buffeted by a rising wave of concern over drugs, especially crack and cocaine, and enforcement efforts began to shift toward these drugs.

Figure 3.1
Citywide Percentage Held at Criminal Court Arraignment:
Drug and Non-drug Cases

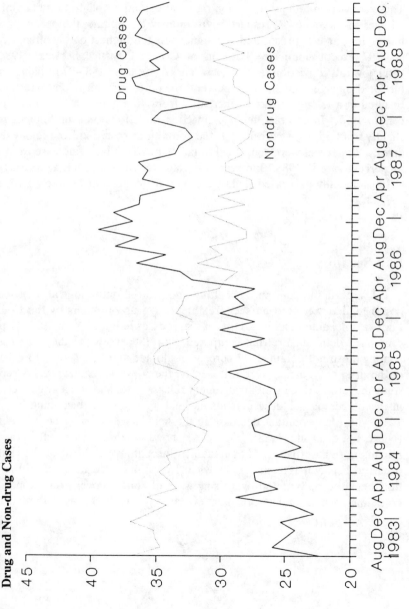

SOURCE: New York City Criminal Justice Agency, *Semi-Annual Reports.*

Other Effects

The response of the courts to cases is necessarily strongly influenced by the actions of police and prosecutors whose decisions and enforcement policies determine the stream of cases entering the system. A consensus among the participants in the judicial process (Church et al., 1978; Church, 1982) often guides responses to various offender types by establishing implicit or explicit "going rates" for various offender types. However, new problems such as crack, or a general shift in focus toward problems such as drugs, may change this consensus by altering perceptions of their relative importance within the general stream of cases. The altering of that stream by a huge influx of drug felonies may influence the actions of the court, whether in response to external events such as an emerging new drug problem, changes in public attitudes, or internal events such as a shift in prosecutorial polices and priorities. If court and prison resources remain relatively stable, then, shifts may occur within a "zero-sum" context, in that harsher treatment of and focus on drug crimes may ameliorate the responses to certain non-drug crimes, especially non-violent crimes. Whereas several years ago New York City prosecutors and criminal justice system officials were giving major attention to auto crimes and so-called quality-of-life offenses, concern about these types of crimes has virtually disappeared in the face of the new drug crisis.

Although the types of drug defendants being processed through the courts (at least at the state and local level) are primarily low-level street users and dealers, typically involving $10-20 transactions, the cases are usually labeled as serious both in terms of the operative Penal Law and public attitudes. For example, in New York State, sale of any amount of "narcotic" substance (including cocaine) is a Class B felony (the second most severe felony class and of the same severity as attempted murder, first degree rape, or armed robbery) punishable by up to 25 years in prison. Although 11 states decriminalized possession of small amounts of marijuana during the mid-1970s, marijuana use and sale is still a common arrest charge (about 375,000 such arrests were made in the United States in 1987), and sale of any amount of this drug is still subject to maximum prison terms of life in Missouri and 15 years in Alabama and Nevada (Department of Justice, 1988). Labeled as such serious crimes by the law, it becomes more difficult for judges to treat these cases other than punitively.

The Emergence of Crack

Beginning around 1985, a potent form of cocaine began appearing on urban streets, available in small quantities at relatively low-dosage costs.

Although lower-cost powdered cocaine had begun to emerge as the drug of choice among many users, replacing heroin to some extent, crack was a new way of producing and marketing free base cocaine for smoking. Reports from users suggest that it produces a brief but very intense high, followed by rapid onset of depression and a compelling drive to get high again. The appearance of crack on the streets of New York and other urban areas (earlier reports about the drug came from Los Angeles, where it was known as "rock" cocaine) and its widespread popularity as a drug of abuse have caused enormous problems for the already overburdened criminal justice system. Officials fear that crack's low cost, intense high, and high probability of addiction make this drug more available and attractive to poor populations, especially to those who could not previously afford cocaine. Since the surge in crack use, media coverage has proliferated, with almost daily coverage of the drug and crime crisis in urban newspapers (*New York Times*, 1989a).

In particular, early reports of crack's effects on user's behavior in New York City's newspapers fueled the public's fears about crack's criminogenic effects and increased demands for a strong enforcement response to the problem. The early stages of New York's crack crisis in the summer of 1986 coincided with a more general wave of anti-drug sentiment nationwide. This response to a real or perceived drug epidemic has been observed periodically in this century (Musto, 1981), driven by the fear that use of the drug caused violent behavior, that "pushers" were readily foisting the drug on innocent people, and that the rapid onset of compulsive and addictive use was accompanied by the commission of crimes to sustain the craving for the drug. The Harrison Act of 1914 was a response to widespread concern about opiate use, which had been legal previously; the marijuana scares of the 1930s and 1960s were exacerbated by discovery of the drug by youth and musicians; the heroin epidemic of the late 1960s and early 1970s, epitomized in part by the deaths of popular rock stars, as well as high addiction rates among returning Vietnam soldiers, led to the development of a large heroin treatment industry and the spread of methadone maintenance programs; in the late 1970s, the PCP scare raised concerns that young people were now prone to irrational drug-related violence; finally, in the early 1980s America was panicked over the use of powdered cocaine, primarily by middle-class users.

Together with growing intolerance for illicit drug use, the perception that crack use and violent behavior are inexorably linked (crystallized in the murder of a New York City police officer guarding the home of a witness in a drug case in late 1987, allegedly on orders from a major crack dealer) has increased the sense of urgency for effective sanctions against crack. This killing was a direct impetus for the New York City Police Department's Tactical Narcotics Team (TNT) undercover street enforcement strategy.

Further, the ease and cheapness of manufacture, and the enormous profits that could be made, attracted many makeshift distribution networks and drew young, inexperienced dealers into the trade (Johnson, Hamid & Morales, 1987). A large number of neighborhood-based cottage industries have emerged in recent years to process, package, and sell crack -- minimal equipment is needed and low-quality cocaine can be used. In addition, numerous "crack houses," where users can purchase and smoke the drug, have materialized in the inner cities, bringing large profits to landlords and considerable concern to neighborhood residents. The heated street competition for sales markets has generated a large amount of drug "warfare" and violent crime (Hunt, 1987). Homicide rates in major cities have increased, according to police officials, because of internecine drug-related violence. The attendant street violence attributed to crack dealers and their employees has heightened the sense of urgency and pressures to increase law enforcement efforts and toughen criminal justice sanctions against crack and, by extension, other drug dealers.

The impact of the wave of drug arrests, especially crack, has been viewed so seriously by criminal justice system officials and policymakers that the Association of the Bar of the City of New York devoted its annual criminal justice retreat in December 1987 entirely to the system's response to the crack crisis. The retreat ended with calls for better interagency coordination, more effective management and planning, expanded court resources, and more efficient and proactive use of case data to anticipate and monitor system crises and the impacts of the drug cases (Anderson, 1988; Press, 1988).

At the same time, the non-punitive options available for cocaine or crack abusers are severely limited. With the drug treatment industry focused mainly on heroin since the late 1960s, effective treatment for cocaine or crack is generally unavailable to the inner-city population. Also, there is no equivalent drug therapy, like methadone maintenance, with which to stabilize cocaine use by removing the urge to get high. Since we are in the relatively early stages of the crack epidemic, it is not clear whether or when any effective treatment modalities will be developed for this population. Some claims for treatment success, at least through detoxification, have been made by acupuncture clinics. Private, expensive, inpatient programs such as Fair Oaks, Stony Point, Hazelden, and the Betty Ford Clinic treat cocaine users, and may have achieved some success with wealthy or middle-class users and athletes, but these are rarely treatment options for inner-city offenders. Residential programs based on the therapeutic community model do treat cocaine and crack abusers in limited numbers, but high dropout rates and the length of the ideal treatment period may make them potentially problematic for court-ordered treatment.

Analyses of New York City's early response to the crack crisis has demonstrated that the policy to control crack use and sales by street-level law enforcement has flooded the courts with cases. With crack dealing becoming much more prevalent throughout New York City in 1986, the police created a special Anti-Crack Unit and began making unprecedented numbers of drug arrests. During the latter half of 1986, almost 1,500 crack arrests were being made per month; since the initiation of TNT in 1988, crack arrests have soared even higher to an average of 3,216 per month for 1988 (New York City Police Department, 1989), 58 percent of them for felonies. Comparing the processing of crack cases to powdered cocaine in 1983-84, Belenko & Fagan (1988) showed that crack sale and possession cases more often were charged and prosecuted as felonies (78%). Felony arrests, of course, are more likely to result in pretrial detention, take longer to process through the courts than misdemeanors, and more often lead to jail or prison sentences. The data also showed that the New York City courts are treating crack cases more severely, regardless of the severity of arrest charge or the defendant's prior criminal record. Compared with cocaine defendants, crack cases were more likely to be held in detention (64% vs. 44%), to be indicted on felony charges (75% of the felonies compared with 51% for powdered cocaine), and to be sentenced to jail if convicted of a misdemeanor (57% vs. 35%).

Multivariate analyses, using logit models to determine the relative contributions of case and offender characteristics to lower court disposition and pretrial release, found that crack charges had significant independent effect on lower court dispositions and the pretrial release decision, relative to offender characteristics and prior criminal record. This suggests that the emergence of crack may have altered existing decision models in drug cases.

External Pressures on the System

The influx of large numbers of drug and drug-related arrests into the criminal justice system can affect the system's response to these cases in a number of ways. What makes the current crisis unique is that this increase in case volume is coming at a time when the combination of severe strains on system resources and a more conservative, punitive ethos makes traditional methods of absorbing case volume more difficult to implement. That is, these external pressures make it more difficult for prosecutors and judges to dismiss drug cases, reduce charges, or establish quick plea bargaining agreements by offering lower plea charges with non-incarcerative sentences. Coupled with the lack of diversion or community supervision options for drug offenders, the case surge has seriously clogged the courts.

Although the impact of public pressure on the courts is difficult to quantify, it is reasonable to assume that judges and prosecutors respond at least in part to media and political influences. Some research has suggested a limited effect: Glick and Pruet (1985) suggest that public opinion may affect sentencing policy at least in the short term, but that public opinion is too far removed from the courtroom or too imprecisely measured locally for the impact to be clear. Nonetheless, legislators are influenced by real or perceived public attitudes in fashioning anti-crime legislation, so that the penal and criminal procedure laws under which the courts operate reflect these non-judicial attitudes, at least in part. In addition, a more conservative electorate means the appointment and election of more conservative judges and prosecutors.

Along with the general attitude that the courts do not deal harshly enough with criminals (in a 1987 survey, 79% agreed with this -- Department of Justice, 1988), there is some evidence that the public wants serious drug offenders to be treated particularly severely. The 1987 National Survey on Punishment of Offenders found that respondents ranked cocaine sale as a more serious crime than assault with a weapon, residential burglary, or a robbery with a weapon if the victim was not harmed (Department of Justice, 1988). In addition, 89.9 percent preferred prison or jail as the sentence of choice for cocaine sale, a similar percentage as for vehicular homicide and higher than burglary, arson, or assault. The desired average prison sentences for cocaine sale (126 months) and use (67 months) were also relatively high.

Other surveys taken in 1986 showed somewhat contradictory attitudes toward the handling of drug offenders. While 32 percent agreed convicted heroin dealers should receive the death penalty, 85 percent agreed that the best place for most drug users is in treatment programs and not jails (Department of Justice, 1988). Although 56 percent of respondents felt that arresting drug sellers was a very effective means of controlling drugs, 30 percent felt that arresting drug users was not a very effective policy.

Finally, some recent studies suggest that, while there is a common perception that treatment and rehabilitation have failed to reduce drug use and crime, public support still exists for expansion of drug treatment and the use of rehabilitation as a legitimate goal of sanctions for certain offenders (Cullen et al., 1988; Gendreau & Ross, 1987; Gottfredson & Taylor, 1983)

Jail Overcrowding Issues

The existence of a severe jail and prison overcrowding problem exacerbates the problem by further limiting the court's options. To the extent that judges and prosecutors are affected by jail overcrowding pressures, bail and sentencing decisions may be influenced explicitly or implicitly (Price et al., 1983). What is not clear, however, is the degree to which decisionmakers are affected by these types of external constraints (Glick & Pruet, 1985).

Prior to the current caseload and overcrowding crises, it was common practice to treat drug arrestees (even felony defendants) who had no prior arrests or convictions leniently. Even during Operation Pressure Point in New York City, when the beginnings of the current wave of public and law enforcement concerns about street drug dealing were surfacing, the typical practice was to dismiss or reduce to a misdemeanor first-time felony offenders, to release them on recognizance if the case continued past arraignment, and to impose non-incarcerative sentences if convicted (NYC Criminal Justice Agency, 1985).

Judges and prosecutors faced with first-time drug offenders (50 percent of the NYC drug arrestees) are in a bind: there are few jail or detention alternatives, limited treatment options, and a strong sense that probation departments are overloaded and traditional probation supervision largely ineffective and, therefore, not always a desirable sentencing alternative. In recent years, the development of Intensive Probation Supervision (IPS) programs has raised expectations that closer supervision of relatively high-risk offenders with frequent personal contact and mandatory drug treatment or urine test monitoring would lead to greater use of probation as an alternative to incarceration, without increasing the risk to the community.

Evaluations of IPS programs have shown mixed results, however. A study of the Georgia IPS program by Erwin and Bennett (1987) found a relatively low absconding rate of 16 percent among the 2,300 offenders in the program from 1982-1986. This program targeted serious nonviolent offenders who were jail- or prison-bound. Drug offenders responded better under IPS than under regular probation supervision, with a 90 percent success rate over an 18-month follow-up period. On the other hand, the rearrest rate among a sample of IPS defendants (40%) within 18 months of sentencing was slightly higher than those under regular probation (36%), although lower than for a sample of prison releasees (58%); presumably the IPS sample was a higher-risk group than the regular probationers. On the other hand, studies of the New York State intensive supervision program, which began in 1978, have found that the failure rate during the first 18 months was the same for IPS and regular probationers (about 40%), that judges were not using the program as an alternative to incarceration, and that community resources were inadequately developed to meet the needs of this population (Committee on Corrections, 1987). Evidence from the New Jersey IPS program, which has a large percentage of drug and property offenders, has shown a high success rate and use as an alternative to incarceration (New Jersey Administrative Office of the Courts, 1985).

IMPACT ON JAILS AND PRISONS

One of the most dramatic and costly effects of America's "war on drugs" has been the enormous increase in jail and prison populations over the past few years.   The United States now has one of the highest per capita incarceration rates among any Western or industrialized nation (Bureau of Justice Statistics, 1987); the number of inmates per 100,000 population was 224 at the end of 1987, up from 154 in 1981 (Camp & Camp, 1988).   The surge in jail/prison admissions, coupled with increasing sentence lengths and more mandatory sentencing laws has sparked an unprecedented wave of prison construction at all jurisdictional levels, with no resultant easing of the overcrowding problem.   The costs incurred include not only capital construction costs, but increased operating costs.   Additionally, 102 jurisdictions were under Federal Court order, at the end of 1987, to maintain population ceilings (Bureau of Justice Statistics, 1988c), 15 states had Special Masters or other court-appointed monitors overseeing their prison systems at the beginning of 1988, and 16 states had emergency release programs to reduce overcrowding (Camp & Camp, 1988).

Local Jails

Between 1982 and 1989, the average daily population in local jails rose from 209,582 to 290,300, a 39 percent increase; a little over half of these inmates were awaiting trial (Bureau of Justice Statistics, 1988d).   During 1987, there were 8,627,000 admissions to local jails, up about 7 percent from 1983. The situation in those large urban jurisdictions with serious drug problems, however, is substantially more acute, with New York City, Washington, D.C., and Los Angeles facing serious overcrowding (*Newsweek*, 1988).   The jail population in the District of Columbia is expected to grow by 24 percent in 1989 alone (Camp & Camp, 1988).

Overcrowding of the New York City jails, while a problem at various points during the last ten years, has reached unprecedented proportions.   The average daily jail population has nearly doubled from 9,500 in 1981 to 18,600 in April 1989; two-thirds of these are pretrial detainees.   City officials attribute the bulk of this growth to arrests for drug possession and sale, especially crack.   The percentage of New York City jail admissions on drug charges was 42 percent of felony admissions and 27 percent of misdemeanors in 1987, and was the most common charge category (Division of Criminal Justice Services, 1988b). Under federal court order to maintain a cap on the population, New York City has had to turn to temporary, prefabricated housing and refitted floating jail barges to handle the overflow. Although there have been some efforts to develop and expand alternatives to incarceration programs, their scope, at present, is limited and has little impact on the jail population.

State Prisons

State prison populations have surged during the 1980s, due, in large part, to the increased drug enforcement activity in the large states. Table 3.6 shows the number of inmates in custody from 1980 to 1987, as of December 31. The 533,309 offenders imprisoned at the end of 1987 represents a 75 percent increase over 1980. Much larger increases occurred in the Northeast (97%) and West (139%) regions. In particular, California's state prison population stood at 66,975 at the end of 1987, a 173 percent increase over 1980, when 24,569 were in custody. These populations are expected to grow by an additional 8 percent each year in 1989 and 1990 (Camp & Camp, 1988).

In 1986, a Bureau of Justice Statistics study indicated that 8.6 percent of state prison inmates had been imprisoned on drug offenses (12% for females) up from 6.4 percent (10.5%) from 1979 (Innes, 1988). Moreover, 17.2 percent of a sample of inmates reported being under the influence of drugs at the time they committed the offense for which they were imprisoned, 22 percent had used cocaine regularly, and 17 percent heroin.

New York State

Paralleling the New York City trends (from which the bulk of the state prison admissions arrive) the State's prison population at the end of 1987 stood at 40,842, an increase of 89 percent over 1980. A major reason for this growth is the increase in sentenced drug offenders: in early 1988, drug charges became the most common committing offense for the first time, comprising over one-fifth of all admissions (Division of Criminal Justice Services, 1988b). A recent analysis of New York State drug felony arrests (by the State) for the five-year period 1983-87 revealed the dramatic impact of the drug arrest explosion on the prison population (Division of Criminal Justice Services, 1988a). The percentage of convicted drug felons sentenced to incarceration rose from 50 percent to 70 percent, while the percentage of incarcerative sentences for non-drug felons decreased from 49 percent to 45 percent. Over time the situation is likely to worsen as more and repeat felony offenders are arrested and become subject to mandatory second felony offender prison sentences.

Table 3.6
Number of State and Federal Prison Inmates on December 31

	NUMBER OF INMATES	
Year	State	Federal
1980	304,844	24,363
1981	341,255	28,133
1982	384,689	29,673
1983	405,322	31,926
1984	430,304	34,263
1985	463,048	40,223
1986	500,725	44,408
1987	533,309	48,300

SOURCE: U.S. Department of Justice, Bureau of Justice Statistics. *Drug Law Violators 1980-86*. Washington, DC: June 1988.

Federal Prisons

The growth in the federal prison system has paralleled that of the states. At the end of 1987, there were 48,300 inmates in federal prisons, up 98 percent from 1980 (Table 3.6). Had the proportion of prison admissions on drug charges remained stable after 1980, the population growth would have been much smaller: 34 percent of Fiscal Year 1986 admissions were for drug law violations, compared to 22 percent in Fiscal Year 1980, and the number of admissions for drug offenses rose by 128 percent between Fiscal Years 1981 and 1986 (Bureau of Prisons, 1987). The federal sentencing guidelines which recently went into effect called for increased penalties for drug-related offenses. Together with the harsher penalties legislated in the 1986 federal Anti-Drug Abuse Act, new sanctioning practices in the U.S. District Courts are expected to lead to explosive growth in the federal prison population. The U.S. Sentencing Commission estimates that this population will range from 85-108,000 in 1997 if the 1986 act is fully implemented, and 61-78,000 if it is not (U.S. Sentencing Commission, 1987).

Pretrial Detention

Increased detention rates for drug offenders, as well as new sentencing practices and mandatory sentencing laws, have affected the jail population in recent years. Over the past three years, the rise in drug arrests in New York City has been accompanied by an increase in the proportion of drug defendants held on bail, with fewer released on recognizance, placing even more burdens on already-strained detention facilities (Nickerson & Dynia, 1988). Over the same period, arrests and detention rates for non-drug offenses remained stable. Pressure to make drug-free status a condition of pretrial release also puts a burden on pretrial programs and detention facilities, especially in the absence of treatment alternatives.

Further strains on the jail and prison systems are likely to accrue from the effects of mandatory or enhanced sentencing laws for repeat felony offenders. A high likelihood of arrest on felony charges in jurisdictions with active anti-drug enforcement efforts, coupled with a substantial probability of rearrest (Belenko & Schiff, 1984), will increase the number of crack and other drug offenders entering the system. Repeat offenders facing mandatory prison sentences are much more likely to be held in detention and to receive longer sentences, placing additional burdens on correctional facilities.

Additional pressure is being brought to bear on the system because of legislative concerns over crack use: in November 1988, changes in the New York State Penal Law made possession of 500 milligrams of crack (about 5 vials) a Class D felony offense with a potential prison sentence of 1 to 7 years. Before this change, possession of up to 30 vials of crack was a misdemeanor, carrying a maximum sentence of one year in jail. While the impact of this law has not yet been analyzed, it is likely to increase further the pressures on the jail/prison facilities because of the higher likelihood of detention and jail/prison sentences for felony offenders.

The Costs of Incarceration

With the large increases in local, state, and federal prison populations has come a substantial increase in the costs of new jail and prison construction, as well as operational costs. For example, federal system costs, which were $614 million in Fiscal Year 1986, are expected to grow to $998 million in Fiscal Year 1989, a 63 percent increase (Department of Justice, 1988). Between 1979 and 1985, total state corrections costs in the United States increased by 129 percent, compared to a 98 percent overall growth in criminal justice system expenditures; local jail costs increased by 97 percent during this same period, and local system costs by 66 percent overall. In all, expenditures for corrections were estimated at $11.7 billion for the states in 1987, and an additional $4.3 billion for local jails (Camp & Camp, 1988). Capital costs, including the federal system, were $2.4 billion in 1987. The current costs, of course, are even greater with the recent increases in jail and prison admissions.

In New York State and New York City, the tremendous growth in prison costs has primarily reflected renewed emphasis on drug law enforcement. The operating costs for the New York State prison system were over 1 billion dollars in Fiscal Year 1987 (a 50% increase from Fiscal Year 1983), an average of $26,500 per year per inmate. In addition, estimated capital construction costs for a new prison bed expansion program begun in Fiscal Year 1987 (10,200 new beds) were an additional $1.5 billion dollars, including debt service to retire construction bonds, a cost of $147,000 per bed.

New York City's corrections capital construction plan for the 1989-1992 period calls for $495 million in new jail construction (adding a total of almost 7,500 new beds). The costs of New York City's new jail barges, being used as stopgap solutions to the overcrowding crisis until more permanent facilities can be built, are estimated to cost about $130 million each, an astonishing $171,000 per bed.

In addition to the tremendous construction costs that have been necessitated by the huge increase in drug arrests, convictions, and incarcerative sentences, the nature of these offenses and offenders generate substantial additional costs.

First, drug offenders require additional medical screening at admission, and follow-up services, compared with other defendants. This includes examination for addiction status, closely-monitored detoxification, and methadone maintenance. In addition, drug users often have myriad other medical problems which require costly interventions; chief among these are the high HIV-infection rates among intravenous drug users, hepatitis, and general physical trauma and neglect. The increasing number of women being arrested in street enforcement actions has led to the opening of a separate nursery facility on Rikers Island to house female defendants with newborn children (*New York Times*, 1989b)

Second, the influx of drug offenders initiates a need for prison-based treatment programs, including methadone maintenance, TC-model (therapeutic community model) programs, and counseling programs. Prison treatment programs such as Stay N' Out and Saturn are costly, but have great potential cost-effectiveness (Wexler et al., 1988). To attempt to break the cycle of continued drug use and high recidivism rates, there will be increasing need for in-prison treatment, both in local jails and in state prisons. Recent legislation introduced in New York would expand prison treatment programs and allow early parole for nonviolent inmates who successfully participate; they would then be required to enroll in an aftercare program as a condition of release.

Third, the extent to which crack and other drug abusers have psychological and behavioral problems or exhibit aberrant behavior as a consequence of their drug use, jails and prisons must deal with classification and housing issues for these inmates. The costs include enhanced psychiatric screening and evaluation, special housing needs including isolation or placement in hospital wards, and more intensive supervision by correction officers.

Finally, there is a need to provide drug offenders with additional post-release planning and services, again to try to reduce the drug use-recidivism cycle. This includes evaluation for treatment placement or other post-release community services, and enhanced parole supervision.

OPTIONS FOR THE
CRIMINAL JUSTICE SYSTEM

Concern within the criminal justice system about drug offenders, and heated debate about the appropriate response to the problem (punition vs. rehabilitation) are not new phenomena. The heroin epidemic of the late 1960s and early 1970s, though not generating the numbers of arrests and level of public concern that we are seeing today, nevertheless sparked considerable attention toward drug-related crime and legislative action to increase penalties for drug use or sale (e.g., Rockefeller Drug Laws in New York State).

However, research in New York has shown that increased penalties for drug possession and sale, including the provision of life sentences for selling two or more ounces of narcotics, had no effect on street drug use or drug-related crime (Japha, 1978). We have seen the same trend during the past few years, whereas increased sanctions and arrest activity have done little to reduce the demand for illicit drugs or the level of drug-related crime.

A second, less punitive approach, which became adopted more widely in the early 1960s, was the civil commitment process, whereby drug abusers could be committed to custody, often for a number of years, for simply being addicted to drugs and without having been convicted of a crime. In addition, civil commitment was used to divert arrestees from the criminal justice system into treatment, although the amount of time these offenders were required to remain in secure treatment facilities often greatly exceeded the amount of time they would have spent in jail or prison had they been convicted and sentenced to incarceration under the criminal law. Twenty-five states now operate various types of civil commitment programs.

The results of three early civil commitment programs (California Civil Addict Program [CAP], the New York State Narcotics Addiction Control Commission, and the 1966 Federal Narcotic Addict Rehabilitation Act [NARA]) were mixed. A follow-up study of California CAP admissions from the early 1960s showed somewhat reduced daily narcotic use, lower rearrest and self-reported crime rates, and higher rates of employment for those completing treatment compared to those admitted to CAP but discharged prior to outpatient treatment (McGlothlin et al., 1977). Successful participants used narcotics daily 31 percent of the time during follow-up compared to 48 percent for the comparison group of discharged clients. Researchers noted that the most effective aspects of the program appeared to be close community supervision coupled with regular testing for drugs, and a long parole-type follow-up of 5-10 years (Anglin, 1988).

The federal program had mixed success. Here, addicts convicted of a federal crime could be committed for treatment for an indeterminate period not to exceed ten years or the maximum term that could have been imposed on a prison sentence. Further, addicts not charged with any federal offense could choose civil commitment; those deemed to have a high likelihood of rehabilitation could be committed to treatment and aftercare for a 36-month period, and most of the NARA commitments fell into this category (Maddux, 1988). The two primary centers for treatment under NARA were the Lexington, Kentucky, and Fort Worth Public Health Service hospitals. Follow-up studies showed that one-third to one-half of those admitted to the program were found not suitable for treatment, and that attrition rates were high. When treatment was combined with compulsory aftercare, civil commitment patients did somewhat better than those in voluntary treatment;

however, only about one-third of those committed remained after the six-month treatment period and entered aftercare (Maddux, 1988).

The New York State Civil Commitment Program, established by the Narcotics Control Act of 1966, allowed commitment to treatment for three to five years for drug arrestees or non-defendants for whom a petition was filed with the court. For a number of reasons, including the low quality of treatment facilities and staff associated with the program, the intermingling of parole supervision with treatment aftercare, high absconding rates, and the prison-like atmosphere of the rehabilitation centers, the commitment program never achieved much success (Inciardi, 1988). In addition, poor record-keeping made it difficult for legislators or evaluators to adequately assess the program's operations. Further, the long commitment period, in rather unpleasant facilities, with limited treatment, meant that defendants tended to prefer the option of a short jail sentence to the civil commitment.

As attitudes toward illicit drug use began to shift in the late 1960s, and following the effects of a 1962 ruling by the U.S. Supreme Court (*Robinson v. California*) which overturned laws that made it a crime to be an addict, there was a tremendous expansion of treatment programs. The Comprehensive Drug Abuse Prevention and Control Act of 1970 reduced federal penalties for drug possession and provided increased funding for treatment, research, education, and prevention. Treatment availability and federal funding for treatment, especially methadone maintenance, expanded greatly during the early 1970s.

During this same period, the recognition that the drug-using criminal offender was an important subset of the arrestee population, and that a significant amount of crime was drug related, led to the creation of new types of interventions linking the criminal justice and treatment communities. The 1973 National Commission on Marihuana and Drug Abuse recognized this need:

> All states attempt to rationalize the operation of the criminal justice system as a process for identifying drug-dependent persons and for securing their entry into a treatment system. The states should establish, as part of their comprehensive prevention and treatment program, a separate treatment process which runs parallel to the criminal process, and which may be formally or informally substituted for the criminal process. (National Commission on Marihuana and Drug Abuse, 1973)

The widespread recognition that the criminal justice system provided a useful means of identifying drug-involved persons who might benefit from treatment led to a number of referral and diversion programs beginning in the early 1970s. Chief among these was the federally-funded Treatment Alternatives to Street Crime (TASC) program, initiated in 1972 and which continues today, albeit on a smaller scale. At its peak in 1981 (before federal funding was withdrawn with the dismantling of LEAA), there were 130 TASC programs in 39 states and Puerto Rico (Bureau of Justice Assistance, 1988). The basic goal of TASC is to identify offenders in need of drug treatment as early as possible in the criminal justice process, and under close supervision, provide community-based treatment as an alternative or supplement to more traditional criminal justice sanctions. The assumption is that, with the threat of criminal sanctions, if they violate conditions of the treatment program or TASC supervision requirements, the likelihood of successful completion of treatment is enhanced. The range of possible processing under TASC supervision now includes deferred prosecution, community sentencing, diversion, pretrial intervention, and probation or parole supervision.

In addition, the Federal Bureau of Prisons funded 13 Community Treatment Centers for drug offenders between 1961 and 1975; by the end of 1981, all had been closed (Bureau of Prisons, 1987).

Several evaluations of TASC programs over the past 15 years have concluded that these programs have generally been effective in reducing drug abuse and criminal activity, identifying previously untreated drug-dependent offenders, and establishing useful links between the criminal justice and treatment systems. The studies include a 1974 evaluation of five early TASC programs, a 1976 study of 22 projects, and a 1978 evaluation of 12 sites (Bureau of Justice Assistance, 1988). Studies from the National Institute on Drug Abuse's Treatment Outcome Prospective Study have found that TASC and other criminal justice referrals tend to remain in treatment longer and thus have higher rates of treatment success (Hubbard et al., 1988). In addition, criminal justice screening and diversion programs have tended to identify and refer defendants who had had limited treatment exposure and thus were at earlier stages of their addiction encounters. TASC clients also tended to have lower recidivism rates during treatment, although the independent effects of TASC on this finding were not determined.

Other research has found that court pressure on defendants and the threat of sanctions can increase the probability of treatment success for therapeutic community and other clients (Pompi & Resnick, 1987; De Leon et al., 1979; De Leon & Schwartz, 1984; Wexler et al., 1988; Ward, 1982), perhaps because court oversight helps keep the defendant in treatment during the first stages.

Despite some of these early success stories in the system's handling of drug-abusing offenders, the nature of today's drug problem and the context in which it has occurred are different in important ways:

(1) the drugs of chief concern are now cocaine and cocaine derivatives,

(2) there is a shortage of treatment slots and limited effective treatment modalities for cocaine and crack addiction,

(3) there is a more conservative political climate and less public tolerance for drug abuse and crime, and

(4) the sheer volume of cases entering the system often mandates that the first priority be to move offenders through the system as quickly as possible.

In the following sections, an overview of the options available to the criminal justice system is presented along with a discussion of the benefits and problems of each. While it is clear that the criminal justice system can play an important role in the identification and treatment of drug-using offenders, and obvious that some differential handling of these defendants is desirable, there are many difficulties and concerns associated with the implementation of new interventions and procedures.

Identification of Drug-Using Offenders: Costs and Consequences

Inherent in the criminal justice system's ability to establish and maintain innovative programs and procedures to handle the drug-using offender is the importance of adequate guidelines for screening defendants for the existence of drug problems, assessing the need for treatment, and targeting an appropriate intervention for a given defendant. Many issues relate to the effective identification of drug-abusing offenders for purposes of providing differential supervision, pretrial or post-conviction monitoring, or making sanctioning decisions. In order for the courts or other criminal justice agencies to deal with the drug-using offender, identification becomes a key problem. Not only must the use of illicit drugs be determined, but the type of drug and the degree of use (e.g., addiction level) are important determinants of the system's response to the defendant (Wexler et al., 1988). Data from the National Institute of Justice's Drug Use Forecasting program, begun in 1987, also suggest high rates of drug use among arrestees for non-drug offenses. To the extent that the courts would want or be able to identify drug-using offenders, many arrestees for non-drug crimes would also need to be screened.

There are a number of ways of identifying drug users, but each have their problems (Wish et al., 1988): these techniques include self-reports, urine or hair tests, medical examination, official criminal history records, and simple observation. Self-reports are the quickest and cheapest way to assess drug use status and need for drug treatment, but are subject to underreporting (Wish et al., 1986). Despite this, given the limited number of treatment or other program slots generally available, self-reports can easily identify sufficient numbers of defendants who abuse drugs and desire treatment. A recent New York City study projected that 42,000 defendants would self-report illicit drug use at arrest, and 62,000 would report current or past drug dependency, more than enough defendants to easily overwhelm the number of treatment slots that would ever reasonably be expected to be available (Belenko & Mara-Drita, 1987).

Urine tests have been promoted as a relatively quick screen for drug use in the criminal justice system, and several jurisdictions have implemented pretrial urine screening programs to identify drug users at arrest. Washington, D.C. has had an extensive urine testing program by the pretrial services agency for several years, including prearraignment mass screening of all arrestees, and urine monitoring for defendants released on recognizance (Carver, 1986). These tests, while generally accurate if newer technologies and careful controls are used, can be costly, especially if confirmatory tests are used. They also can impose delay on already strained processing time. In addition, there are legal and constitutional issues which arise and must be considered, especially when tests are administered pretrial (Rosen & Goldkamp, 1988).

Drug abusers might also be identified through official criminal justice records by searching for prior convictions on drug possession charges or other drug-use related charges such as possession of a hypodermic syringe. However, these records provide an incomplete picture of drug use history, since drug abusers are often arrested on non-drug charges, and drug sale convictions do not necessarily indicate that the defendant is a drug user himself. Other potential criminal justice record sources include prior court case files, probation department records, and jail or prison files, but these records are often difficult or very time-consuming to obtain.

Medical or psychiatric examinations can provide a reasonable assessment of addiction or drug use status, but are among the more costly and time-consuming options. These examinations are necessary at jail admission to determine medical needs, but would be very difficult to implement at any other stage of criminal justice system processing. However, medical examinations or in-depth interviews are necessary to determine abuse level or addiction status for defendants screened as drug users by simple screening techniques such as urine tests. Finally, observation of the defendant by trained personnel, especially within a short time of arrest, can reveal signs of drug intoxication or withdrawal symptoms.

There are also questions about who should be tested, and at what stages the testing should be conducted (Wish et al., 1988). The range of possibilities is large, including all arrestees prior to arraignment, defendants being considered for non-financial release after arraignment, as part of a presentence investigation, as part of a conditional discharge sentence or as condition of pretrial release, by probation or parole departments, or by non-criminal justice agencies supervising defendants pretrial or posttrial. At any stage of the criminal justice process, however, the costs of drug screening would be substantial and could increase case delay at a time when the courts are strained to their limits and trying to expedite the processing of cases. Legal and constitutional issues must also be resolved, and the purposes for which these tests would be used must be carefully described.

There are other problems with the identification of drug-abusing defendants. The pressure to move cases along restricts the points at which intervention might occur and limits alternative processing choices. Resources are limited in many jurisdictions and preclude the kind of close, effective monitoring of defendants that might induce more judges to release drug defendants pretrial or to consider alternatives to incarceration. Second, the types of identification and screening methods likely to be used in a court setting may not provide sufficient information to make an effective decision regarding the appropriate placement of a given defendant. Although some of the factors associated with treatment success are known (Sells & Simpson, 1976), matching a defendant with a treatment program to maximize the likelihood of success is a difficult art, and judges are likely to take a conservative stance when considering whether to release a defendant pretrial or sentence him to an alternative to jail. This is more likely in jurisdictions where drug offenders tend to have high recidivism rates or failure-to-appear rates, or where the judges perceive these rates to be relatively high. Further, judges and attorneys are usually not trained either to interpret the meaning of drug test results or other diagnostic tests, nor are they often very knowledgeable about the various kinds of drug treatment and the types of drug abusers for which they are appropriate. Previous research has pointed to the number of distinct types of illicit drug users (Chaiken & Johnson, 1988; Nurco et al., 1988), each requiring different types of responses from the criminal justice system. Chaiken and Johnson point out that most adult drug offenders are nonviolent and commit crimes at relatively low rates, but they represent the bulk of the drug-using criminal justice population. For these offenders, diversion to drug treatment or other community-based supervision may be an appropriate response and help to reduce the cycle of continued drug use and rearrest. On the other hand, the minority of drug users who are "violent predators," also committing large numbers of robberies and assaults, may demand more punitive sanctions.

A recent initiative funded by the Bureau of Justice Assistance, the Drug Testing Technology/Focused Offender Disposition Project, will attempt to address these problems by developing screening mechanisms to identify drug-using offenders, to assess the type of intervention needed for each defendant to reduce drug use and recidivism, and to formulate guidelines for matching defendants to treatment and monitoring programs. The range of recom-mended interventions would include urine monitoring only, outpatient treat-ment, short-term residential treatment, or long-term residential treatment, and could be used to supervise drug-involved offenders during the pretrial period, pre-sentence, or as a condition of probation. The pilot project is be-ing implemented in three test sites during 1989.

Once the system has identified the drug-using offender, potential inter-ventions can occur at a variety of points (from prior to arrest through post-conviction and parole), in a number of different ways, and involve a variety of criminal justice and non-criminal justice agencies (National Institute on Drug Abuse, 1978).

Points of Intervention

Effective handling of drug offenders should be aimed at achieving sev-eral objectives, depending on the type of offender. These include:

(1) accurate identification of the drug-using offender, the nature and degree of his drug problem, and his need for treatment;

(2) providing treatment of other community-based supervision to offenders whose primary problem is drug abuse and who do not pose an undue threat to the community;

(3) providing prison-based treatment and post-release follow-up to incarcerated drug abusers;

(4) using non-incarcerative monitoring or sanctions to control drug use where appropriate; and

(5) minimizing the use of program supervision for low-risk defen-dants in order to avoid net-widening.

As discussed above, the criminal justice system has historically had diffi-culty effectively identifying the drug-using offender and assessing the need for treatment. To accomplish this would require extensive training of judicial personnel, the provision of new resources, and possible establishment or ex-pansion of court-based referral and monitoring programs.

Pre-arrest Diversion

The initial entry of a drug user into the criminal justice system is primarily controlled by the police officer or other law enforcement officer. Using individual discretion or official guidelines, an officer could advise or order a suspect to enter a drug treatment program, perhaps even transporting the offender to a program. This type of intervention would be most suitable for minor drug offenses such as possession of small amounts of drugs, or for juveniles, and might include review by a superior or prosecutor of the decision not to arrest. An obvious drawback of this approach is the difficulty in making a snap judgment about a suspect's suitability for treatment, and the potential for discriminatory behavior or other abuse of authority stemming from the broad police discretion. Also, treatment facilities typically are not available to accept new admissions at night, when most arrests occur. The major advantage of pre-arrest diversion is that it offers the earliest intervention opportunity and thus the greatest potential for minimizing unnecessary costs to the criminal justice system, and helps the offender avoid the stigma associated with arrest and prosecution. Alternatively this type of diversion can be implemented upon bringing the offender to the precinct or prosecutor's office, where an assistant district attorney can review the case and decide whether to allow treatment in lieu of arrest. The lack of defense counsel to advise the offender at this stage is also potentially problematic.

Pre-arraignment Diversion

A second alternative is to arrest the suspect, have the prosecutor review the case, and then offer diversion to treatment before charges are formally filed with the court. If the offender does well in treatment, then no charges are filed and the case is dropped. This early intervention affords potential cost savings to the criminal justice system, benefits the defendant, and allows some time for further review of the arrest circumstances and the defendant's background.

Pretrial Intervention

At several pretrial stages there is an opportunity to provide special processing for drug offenders. This could include:

(1) *conditional release*, where a defendant is released from detention (at arraignment or following arraignment at a later bail
hearing) without financial conditions but subject to specific
monitoring or supervision conditions. These could include
participation in a drug treatment program, abstention from
drug use without treatment, periodic urine testing by a supervising authority such as a pretrial services program, or other
court-approved agency.

(2) *adjournment pending successful treatment participation or other
program supervision*, whereby the case may be dismissed, the
charges reduced, or a nonincarcerative sentence imposed if the
defendant completes the pretrial supervision period successfully. This procedure could be done with or without the prosecutor's approval under a court order.

(3) *"conditional plea" pending treatment participation*, where the
defendant pleads guilty to the charges but the plea is vacated
after successful treatment. Here, the court can retain the presumably deterrent effects of criminal sanctions.

One problem with the notion of referring defendants for treatment as a
condition of pretrial release is the briefness of the pretrial period relative to
the optimal length of treatment needed by most drug abusers. Once the
court's "hold" on the defendant is over, at the conclusion of the case, the incentive for the offender to remain in treatment is diminished. Further, individuals in drug treatment, especially when placed there involuntarily or under
threat, are likely to continue to use drugs, at least initially, increasing the
likelihood that they will violate release conditions, be held in contempt of
court, and be placed back in custody or otherwise receive harsher sanctions
than if they had not participated in a treatment program in the first place.
The net effect could be an increase in jail overcrowding and further clogging
of the court calendars, unless supervision conditions are structured to allow
some leeway for handling violations short of returning the defendant to custody. The use of urine tests as a way of monitoring abstention from drug use
under any type of supervision, of course, makes it even more likely that drug
abusers will at some point be found in violation of conditions of supervision.
Preliminary analyses of the District of Columbia's pretrial urine monitoring
program have suggested that for some defendants, this type of supervision
can reduce failure-to-appear and rearrest rates (Yezer et al., 1988). Other
research on supervised pretrial release has found that closer monitoring can
reduce pretrial misconduct but that the ability to statistically predict which
defendants are likely to fail is limited (Austin et al., 1985).

Post-Conviction Intervention

A number of potential options are available to the court for handling drug-involved offenders after conviction. These options include:

(1) *court-ordered referral to treatment after trial but before judgment is rendered*, whereby successful program participation might result in dismissal of the charges;

(2) *presentence intervention* to refer a defendant for treatment or supervision after conviction -- if successfully completing the program, the court can sentence the defendant to probation or conditional discharge;

(3) *suspension of sentence* pending treatment completion, where the court would re-sentence to a nonincarcerative sentence or not execute the sentence;

(4) *probation sentence with treatment requirement*, with a violation of probation imposed if the defendant drops out of treatment or otherwise violates treatment conditions -- this option includes Intensive Probation Supervision programs which often include urine monitoring but do not necessarily involve drug treatment, and which have shown mixed success (Erwin & Bennett, 1987; Committee on Corrections, 1987);

(5) *split sentence of jail and treatment*, with a short jail term followed by mandated treatment participation with a return to jail if treatment is not successful;

(6) *other sentence combined with treatment*, where the court imposes a combination of nontraditional sentences such as community service or restitution with treatment enrollment;

(7) *post-incarceration review*, either following successful participation in a prison treatment program or a defense motion for a reduction in jail or prison time to enroll in treatment under parole supervision. Examples of these kinds of interventions would be Intensive Probation Supervision, or a new experimental crack treatment program in New York City for jailbound adolescent defendants who will be referred from existing alternatives-to-incarceration programs.

In all of these potential interventions, the focus should be on decision points in the processing of the case where treatment referral is appropriate and can serve as an alternative to incarceration. An effective use of community-based treatment can reduce court caseload and jail overcrowding, maximize the use of scarce jail resources for more dangerous offenders, provide a source of clients for treatment programs (not currently a problem given the waiting list for most treatment programs -- see below), and benefit the defendant who might reduce illicit drug use during treatment. Potential problems include the loss of general or specific deterrent effects of conviction or incarceration, a high absconding or rearrest rate among defendants diverted from prosecution or detention, or ineffective or inappropriate referrals.

Types of Intervention

Not only are there many different possible points of intervention, but there are a variety of ways in which the intervention might occur. The level and restrictiveness of the intervention would depend on a number of factors including the types of programs available, the existence and quality of pretrial services in the jurisdiction, the characteristics of the defendant and nature of his drug problem, the perception of the level of risk posed by the defendant, the politics of the local community and criminal justice system, and the degree of interaction and cooperation of the different criminal justice agencies.

The types of intervention could include:

(1) mandatory enrollment in a community-based drug treatment program;

(2) civil commitment to a secure or non-secure residential treatment facility;

(3) mandatory periodic urine testing as a condition of release;

(4) enhanced pretrial supervision without treatment, which could include weekly or twice-weekly check-ins, participation in employment, training, or school, or restrictions on the defendant's movements;

(5) enrollment in community-based counseling program;

(6) intensive probation supervision; or

(7) mandatory incarceration with treatment.

The Lack of Treatment Facilities

During the early 1970s, when concern about the impact of drug abusers on the criminal justice system first crystallized into major policy innovations such as TASC, there was a rapid expansion of drug treatment programs using federal and state funds. The Comprehensive Drug Abuse Prevention and Control Act of 1970 provided expanded funding for drug treatment programs, especially methadone maintenance and residential drug-free programs. During this period the major drug of concern was heroin, and there were a number of programs set up to identify and divert arrested heroin users into treatment.

Traditional drug treatment modalities include residential programs, therapeutic communities, inpatient short-term detoxification, outpatient detoxification, outpatient counseling, and methadone maintenance. There are currently no proven effective treatment modalities for cocaine or crack abuse, although some success has been claimed using acupuncture to detoxify crack abusers. Many experts feel that long-term residential treatment is necessary, but these types of programs are expensive, have limited capacity, and are not appropriate for many defendants. Further, the drive to establish new treatment programs, even where the political and financial support exists, is often stalled or blocked by community opposition to the establishment of new facilities (the NIMBY phenomenon -- "not in my back yard").

As treatment resources have become more limited, and the nature of the drug abuse problem has changed over the past few years, the situation today is considerably different. The core of the problem lies in the overall lack of sufficient treatment slots, including methadone maintenance and therapeutic community programs and the lack of effective treatment modalities for cocaine and crack abuse, especially in the inner city. In New York State, for example, while there are a total of about 42,000 treatment slots including 34,000 for methadone maintenance and 8,000 drug-free, there are an estimated 200,000 heavy narcotics users in New York City alone (many of whom also use cocaine and other drugs), an estimated 49,000 heavy cocaine or crack abusers, and an additional 85,000 abusers of other drugs. Thus, it is not surprising that treatment programs in New York City typically have waiting lists up to six months long.

Although the 1988 anti-drug abuse legislation enacted by Congress includes provisions for expanded federal support of treatment and education/prevention programs, there are no assurances that sufficient money will actually be allocated to support these efforts. Even if effective modalities for treating cocaine or crack abuse were developed, the ability of states and cities to support the number of treatment slots necessary to have an impact on the cycle of drug use and crime is probably limited without greater federal funding.

Case Processing Initiatives

Faced with a huge influx of drug cases and limited resources, courts have had to consider various techniques and strategies for efficiently processing drug cases and limiting their impact on the administration of justice. Aside from the issues related to the effective handling of drug defendants discussed above, there are court management and other policies that have been put into place to reduce the backlog of drug cases (Hall et al., 1985). For example, New York City and New Orleans have established special narcotics divisions to expedite the processing of drug felonies. These divisions are designed to hear cases just prior to grand jury proceedings, with the goal of inducing defendants to accept plea bargain offers that are better than would be expected if the case proceeded through the grand jury. For example, prosecutors might offer a low-level felony plea with a short jail sentence or probation, or even a misdemeanor plea if the original felony charges were not serious or the defendant were a first offender. With this early intervention in the case, the New York City courts have been able to dispose of thousands of drug felonies per year in a much shorter time.

In the early 1970s New York State experimented with the establishment of special Narcotics Courts through which all drug cases were to be adjudicated. With the passage of the so-called Rockefeller Drug Laws, it was felt that these special courts would provide more efficient and expert processing of these cases using judges who were familiar with drug abuse, drug distribution, and drug enforcement techniques. Eventually these courts began to accept non-drug cases as a result of the exigencies of caseload pressures on the regular courts. The special Narcotics Courts appear to be, in part, a return to the notion that drug cases are different from other criminal cases and require special processing.

A number of jurisdictions have established special narcotics prosecutor offices to handle the prosecution of some or all drug cases. Again, the assumption is that a specially-trained group of experienced officials is better able to effectively prosecute drug cases and understand the medical and psychological processes of addiction and drug abuse, the types and quality of community-based treatment programs, and the legal and constitutional issues often arising from undercover and street drug enforcement efforts. Similarly, public defenders and defense counsel associations, as well as probation departments, have begun to set up drug offender bureaus as the number of drug cases rises and the pressure to develop alternative processing policies intensifies.

SUMMARY AND POLICY ISSUES

A number of policy issues and potential problems arise out of consideration for the various intervention options discussed above. These include:

Effects on Case Delay

The screening, assessment, and diversion requirements for drug offenders could delay the processing of cases, which is already a problem in many jurisdictions. By requiring additional adjournments or time for assessment of a defendant's drug problem or treatment needs, diversion to a treatment or other supervision program would mean longer processing time. Also, additional hearings might be required for the court to monitor the defendant's progress. Since many programs require, and treatment success often depends on, a minimum period of treatment, the case may continue for much longer than it would if there were no special intervention.

Net-widening Problems

The history of programs to divert certain groups of offenders from the criminal justice system, or to create enhanced supervision options as an alternative to incarceration, is filled with examples of responses by the system that widen the restrictive net over defendants (Hillsman, 1982). There is always a strong tendency, especially in a more conservative environment, to use these types of interventions to place additional restrictions and reporting requirements on defendants who, in the absence of such programs, would have been handled much more leniently (Schneider, 1988). By placing release conditions on defendants that may be difficult to fully adhere to (such as abstention from any drugs for an addict or heavy user), there becomes a high probability of failure and the subsequent revocation of release, or imposition of additional sanctions that have nothing to do with the original criminal event. On the other hand, those for whom an alternative to detention or jail might be appropriate continue to be placed in custody. Clearly, for the criminal justice system to be able to deal with the enormous influx of drug cases, alternative ways of handling drug-involved offenders must be tried in a way that will reduce the pressures on court caseloads and jail facilities, not make them worse.

Due Process and Constitutional Issues

There are several key constitutional issues about drug testing in the criminal justice setting that have not yet been resolved. A recent review by Rosen and Goldkamp (1988) concluded that, when used as part of the bail-setting decision, urine testing fits the definition of *search* under the Fourth Amendment, and therefore it may be important to establish individualized suspicion of drug use before imposing the test. However, the information that would enable this decision could render the urine test unnecessary.

The state is mandated to find the least intrusive way of fulfilling its obligations. Assuming that preventing absconding and pretrial crime are legitimate goals for the criminal justice system, the constitutional issue becomes: Is drug testing or other special supervision or restrictions on particular defendants the least intrusive ways of achieving these goals? If they are not the least intrusive, are they so superior to existing, less intrusive or restrictive methods, so as to justify their intrusiveness and potential for abuse? The answers to these questions depend on whether use of drugs is a useful predictor of failure to appear and rearrest, whether that information can be effectively used to reduce these problems, and whether urine testing in these applications is superior to other information already known about the defendant to override any constitutional concerns.

Further, the more that a system relies on technological or other screening measures to determine which defendants receive special handling, the more that errors in this screening process would engender due process concerns. For example, a less than ideal urine testing operation, or one without confirmatory tests, could result in higher-than-expected false positive rates and adversely effect a defendant's liberty or reputation. There is also concern about whether the drug test results or other drug use information gathered after the arrest and as part of the intervention process would be used for decisions unrelated to the original intent. This type of knowledge could lead to a higher likelihood of conviction or sentence to incarceration, other things equal. Although not formally specified for use in evidentiary, disposition, bail-setting, or sentencing hearings, judges and prosecutors would be aware of the drug test results or a defendant's pretrial drug use behavior, and may be influenced by the information.

Cost Issues

In most jurisdictions, the enhancement of services or supervision requirements for drug offenders, and screening/assessment for drug abuse, would command financial resources that are not readily available. While the cost of establishing and maintaining a urine test screening and monitoring program would vary across jurisdictions, the costs of maintaining an expanded support staff, as well as purchasing and using primary and secondary drug-testing equipment, would be considerable. In addition, there is the danger that, in the rush to deal with the drug offender, funds would be diverted from other basic services. A urine test alone does not provide information about a person's level of use, addiction status, or need for treatment (Wish et al., 1988); further diagnostic screening is necessary, albeit rather costly in terms of staff, money, and time.

Treatment Availability

As discussed earlier, perhaps the key problem currently faced by the criminal justice system in developing policies for dealing with the drug-using offender is the lack of suitable treatment facilities. With the emergence of powdered cocaine and crack as major drugs of abuse among arrestees, and the existing treatment facilities primarily experienced in treating heroin addiction, new types of programs must be developed. As of yet, there are very limited treatment facilities available for these drugs, and too few slots available generally for any drug treatment. The huge numbers of drug-involved arrestees entering the criminal justice system in the last few years has helped to quickly overwhelm current capacity. Those programs that do claim to offer effective treatment for cocaine or crack abuse are either geared toward middle- and upper-class clients, or are filled to capacity with non-criminal justice system clients. More generally, there are few other diversion or alternatives-to-incarceration programs in most jurisdictions, and those that do exist tend to have very limited capacity.

Often, jurisdictional conflicts mitigate against treatment program expansion. In New York, there has been an ongoing debate about the extent to which New York City or New York State should pay for treatment. At this point, the City has refused to provide any funding for drug treatment, claiming that this is solely the State's responsibility, as it has been in the past. New York State claims, in turn, that its fiscal problems preclude sufficient expansion of these programs, and that the City must therefore assist.

Another type of jurisdictional dispute affects the smooth establishment of a criminal justice system-drug program link. The Court and treatment systems are usually operated by entirely different entities, have different funding sources, different constituencies, and often vastly disparate goals. While the Court's interest may be primarily in reducing its caseloads, alleviating jail overcrowding or diverting defendants from prosecution (while minimizing pretrial absconding and rearrest), treatment programs have a primary concern in reducing their clients' dependence on drugs and establishing a more stable lifestyle. These interests and goals can easily conflict.

Also, with the amount of treatment funding currently limited relative to demand, and the apparent growth in the number of drug users seeking treatment, programs can easily fill their slots without criminal justice referrals, reducing their incentive to accept clients they may see as less reliable or amenable to treatment. In addition, there are usually additional reporting and supervision requirements imposed on programs by the courts when referring defendants, which adds to the programs' costs. During the early 1970s, when the criminal justice system-treatment link was being firmly established, the expansion of treatment programs and fewer potential clients than there are today meant competition for clients and a greater willingness to accept criminal justice system referrals (NIDA monograph).

Finally, an effective treatment-criminal justice system link would require that the courts (or their designees) be able to accurately identify offenders who are in need of and might benefit from treatment, but would not present an undue risk to the community (Hall et al., 1985). With the diversity of drug users entering the criminal justice system (Chaiken & Johnson, 1988) and the variety of possible types of treatment and other community-based supervision, the challenge of matching the defendant to the appropriate program is difficult, especially since the factors which predict treatment success are not always reliably identifiable *a priori*.

The effects of current drug enforcement and sanctioning policies will reverberate for a number of years. The ever-increasing number of drug arrests together with limited diversion options, higher likelihood of detention or sentence to incarceration, mandatory sentencing laws for repeat felons, and relatively high recidivism rates for drug offenders virtually assure continuing overcrowding problems for the nation's courts, jails, and prisons, and the spending of hundreds of millions of dollars on expansion of correctional facilities. Despite the large volume of arrests and convictions, however, it is clear that the ability of the courts or police to reduce the drug problem is limited: the demand for drugs and the economic rewards of drug dealing are too great. The rise in enforcement activity and prison admissions in recent years has not been accompanied by a reduction in drug supplies or drug use; there are simply too many illicit drug users for the criminal justice system to ever realistically absorb or control. Nor is there any evidence that crime levels have been reduced overall as a result. The implicit assumption that drug abusers are responsible for a disproportionate share of non-drug crime, and that if drug use can be curtailed and drug users or sellers incapacitated, non-drug crime rates will decrease, has not been adequately tested.

Conspicuous by its absence in the debate about drugs and their impact on the criminal justice system has been alcohol, a legal drug whose relationship to violent crime and deleterious impact on the health of those who enter the system is probably substantially greater than that of illicit drugs. If the system becomes better able to reduce the demand for illegal drugs and more effectively handle drug offenders, alcohol abuse may very well remain with its attendant effects on criminal behavior. Concern over the use and abuse of drugs in the defendant population should therefore not overshadow a very real alcohol problem, and the need to screen for this drug and to develop and utilize systems for reducing its impact on crime.

So the challenge to the system, given the likelihood that anti-drug enforcement policies will continue, is to more effectively absorb drug cases while improving the identification and diversion of those drug offenders who might benefit from treatment or other community supervision, and who do not represent an undue threat to public safety. This balance between a public safety and public health/rehabilitative approach is a difficult one to achieve but necessary in order to avoid the indiscriminate overloading of the system (without adequate measures to break the cycle of drug abuse and criminal activity) that has occurred in recent years (Nurco, 1987).

Developing a more balanced policy would require several important changes:

(1) The recognition that illicit drug users vary in many important ways and that appropriate interventions differ greatly depending on the type of drug, the level of use, prior treatment experience, social stability, and psychological factors.

(2) Creating the resources to identify drug users at appropriate points in the adjudication process and assess their level of use and impairment in order to identify alternatives to prosecution or incarceration.

(3) Acknowledging the importance of expediting the processing of nonviolent drug offenders through innovative court management techniques, without sacrificing due process or constitutional protections.

(4) Rebuilding the treatment/criminal justice system interactions of the 1970s in order to more effectively match defendants with appropriate types of program interventions.

(5) Improving the level of training of all system personnel (judges, prosecutors, defense attorneys, probation and parole officers, corrections officials) pertaining to drug abuse, mental health, and treatment issues.

Despite the conservative trend of the 1980s, there is evidence that support remains for enhanced drug treatment facilites and the goal of rehabilitation, at least for certain drug offenders. The leadership of criminal justice officials in lobbying for more processing options can help to expand community-based treatment programs and other alternatives (Metropolitan Court Judges Committee, 1988). Increased funding for research on treatment of cocaine and crack abuse is obviously an important priority as well. Efforts to reduce the demand for illicit drugs through effective community prevention and education programs should increase, although the efficacy of such programs is unclear. Finally, it is clear that jail- and prison-based treatment programs should be routinely offered to inmates, with early parole for successful completion of the program requirements.

REFERENCES

Anderson, D.C. (1988). "New York's Criminal Justice System and Crack: A Case Study in Crisis Management." New York, NY: *The Record of the Association of the Bar of the City of New York*, 43(5):519-540.

Anglin, M.D. (1988). "The Efficacy of Civil Commitment in Treating Narcotics Addiction." In C.G. Leukefeld & F.M. Tims (eds.) *Compulsory Treatment af Drug Abuse: Research and Clinical Practice*. Rockville, MD: National Institute on Drug Abuse.

Anglin, M.D. & G. Speckart (1988). "Narcotics Use and Crime: A Multi-sample, Multivariate Analysis." *Criminology*, 26(2):197-233.

Austin, J., B. Krisberg & P. Litsky (1985). "The Effectiveness of Supervised Pretrial Release." *Crime and Delinquency*, 31(4):519-537.

Belenko, S. & J.A. Fagan (1988). "The System Gets Tough: The Adjudication of Crack Arrestees in New York City." Paper presented at the annual meeting of the American Society of Criminology, Chicago, IL.

Belenko, S. & I. Mara-Drita (1987). "Drug Use and Pretrial Misconduct: The Utility of Prearraignment Drug Testing as a Predictor of Failure-to-Appear." New York, NY: New York City Criminal Justice Agency.

Belenko, S. & M.F. Schiff (1984). "Lower East Side Narcotic Arrests and the Politics of Pretrial Release." Paper presented at the annual meeting of the Academy of Criminal Justice Sciences, Chicago, IL.

Bureau of Justice Assistance (1988). *Treatment Alternatives to Street Crime: Program Brief*. Washington, DC: U.S. Department of Justice.

Bureau of Justice Statistics (1987). *Imprisonment in Four Countries*. Washington, DC: U.S. Department of Justice.

Bureau of Justice Statistics (1988a). *Drug Law Violators, 1980-1986*. Washington, DC: U.S. Department of Justice.

Bureau of Justice Statistics (1988b). *Tracking Offenders, 1984*. Washington, DC: U.S. Department of Justice.

Bureau of Justice Statistics (1988c). *Prisoners in 1987*. Washington, DC: U.S. Department of Justice.

Bureau of Justice Statistics (1988d). *Jail Inmates, 1987*. Washington, DC: U.S. Department of Justice.

Bureau of Prisons (1987). *Statistical Report, Fiscal Year 1986*. Washington, DC: U.S. Department of Justice.

Camp, G.M. & C.G. Camp (1988). *The Corrections Yearbook - 1988*. South Salem, NY: Criminal Justice Institute.

Carver, J.A. (1986). "Drugs and Crime: Controlling Use and Reducing Risk through Testing." *NIJ Reports*. Washington, DC: National Institute of Justice.

Chaiken, M. & B.D. Johnson (1988). *Characteristics of Different Types of Drug-Involved Offenders: Issues and Practices*. Washington, DC: National Institute of Justice.

Church, T.W., A. Carlson, J. Lee & T. Tan (1978). *Justice Delayed: The Pace of Litigation in Urban Trial Courts*. Williamsburg, VA: National Center for State Courts.

Church, T.W. (1982). *Examining Local Legal Culture: Practitioner Attitudes in Four Criminal Courts*. Washington, DC: U.S. Department of Justice.

Committee on Corrections (1987). "New York State Probation's Intensive Supervision Program: A Reform in Need of Reform." New York, NY: *The Record of the Association of the Bar of the City of New York*, 42(1):75-100.

Cullen, F.T., J.B. Cullen & J.F. Wozniak (1988). "Is Rehabilitation Dead?: The Myth of the Punitive Public." *Journal of Criminal Justice*, 16:303-317.

De Leon, G., M. Andrews, H.K. Wexler, J. Jaffe & M.S. Rosenthal (1979). "Therapeutic Community Dropouts: Criminal Behavior Five Years After Treatment." *American Journal of Drug & Alcohol Abuse*, 6:253-271.

De Leon, G. & S. Schwartz (1984). "The Therapeutic Community: What Are the Retention Rates?" *American Journal of Drug & Alcohol Abuse*, 10:267-284.

Department of Justice (1981-1988). *Crime in the United States*. Washington, DC: Federal Bureau of Investigation.

Department of Justice (1988). *Sourcebook of Criminal Justice Statistics - 1987*. Washington, DC.

Division of Criminal Justice Services (1988a). *New York State: Trends in Felony Drug Offense Processing 1983-1987*. Albany, NY: New York State Division of Criminal Justice Services.

Division of Criminal Justice Services (1988b). *Crime and Justice: Annual Report, 1987*. Albany, NY: New York State Division of Criminal Justice Services.

Erwin, B.S. & L.A. Bennett (1987). *New Dimensions in Probation: Georgia's Experience with Intensive Probation Supervision. Research in Brief*. Washington, DC: National Institute of Justice.

Gendreau, P. & R.R. Ross (1987). "Revivification of Rehabilitation: Evidence from the 1980s." *Justice Quarterly*, 4:349-407.

Glick, H.R. & G.W. Pruet, Jr. (1985). "Crime, Public Opinion, and Trial Courts: An Analysis of Sentencing Policy." *Justice Quarterly*, 2(3):319-343.

Gottfredson, S.D. & R.B. Taylor (1983). *The Correctional Crisis: Prison Populations and Public Policy*. Washington, DC: U.S. Department of Justice.

Hall, A., D.A. Henry, J.J. Perlstein & W. Smith (1985). *Alleviating Jail Crowding: A Systems Perspective*. Washington, DC: National Institute of Justice.

Hillsman, S.T. (1982). "Pretrial Diversion of Youthful Adults: A Decade of Reform and Research." *Justice System Journal*, 7(3): 361-387.

Hubbard, R.L., J.J. Collins, J.W. Rachal & E.R. Cavanaugh (1988). "The Criminal Justice Client in Drug Abuse Treatment." In C.G. Leukefeld & F.M. Tims (eds.) *Compulsory Treatment of Drug Abuse: Research and Clinical Practice*. Rockville, MD: National Institute on Drug Abuse.

Hunt, D. (1987). *Crack*. New York, NY: Narcotic and Drug Research, Inc.

Inciardi, J.A. (1986). "Exploring the Drugs/Crime Connection." Presented at the Workshop on Drugs and Crime. Atlanta, GA: National Research Council and National Institute of Justice.

Inciardi, J.A. (1988). "Some Considerations on the Clinical Efficacy of Compulsory Treatment: Reviewing the New York Experience." In C.G. Leukefeld & F.M. Tims (eds.) *Compulsory Treatment of Drug Abuse: Research and Clinical Practice*. Rockville, MD: National Institute on Drug Abuse.

Innes, C.A. (1988). *Profile of State Prison Inmates, 1986*. Washington, DC: Bureau of Justice Statistics, U.S. Department of Justice.

Japha, A. (1978). "The Nation's Toughest Drug Law: Evaluation of the New York Experience." Final report of the Joint Committee on the New York Drug Law Evaluation. Washington, DC: National Institute of Law Enforcement and Criminal Justice.

Johnson, B.D., A. Hamid & E. Morales (1987). "Critical Dimensions of Crack Distribution." Paper presented at the annual meeting of the American Society of Criminology. Montreal, Canada.

Kleiman, M.A.R., W.E. Holland & C. Hayes (1984). Report to the District Attorney for Essex County: Evaluation of the Lynn Drug Task Force. Cambridge, MA: Harvard University, John F. Kennedy School of Government.

Kleiman, M.A.R. (1986). "Bringing Back Street-Level Heroin Enforcement." Presented at Workshop on Drugs and Crime. Atlanta, GA: National Research Council and National Institute of America.

Maddux, J.F. (1988). "Clinical Experience with Civil Commitment." In C.G. Leukefeld & F.M. Tims (eds.) *Compulsory Treatment of Drug Abuse: Research and Clinical Practice*. Rockville, MD: National Institute on Drug Abuse.

McGlothlin, W.H., M.D. Anglin & B.D. Wilson (1977). An Evaluation of the California Civil Addict Program. Rockville, MD: National Institute on Drug Abuse, Services Research Monograph Series.

Metropolitan Court Judges Committee (1988). *Drugs - The American Family in Crisis: A Judicial Response*. Reno, NV: National Council of Juvenile and Family Court Judges.

Musto, D. (1981). "Review of Narcotic Control Efforts in the United States." In J.H. Lowinson & P. Ruiz (eds.) *Substance Abuse: Clinical Problems and Perspectives*. Baltimore, MD: Williams and Wilkins.

Nadelmann, E.A. (1988). "United States Drug Policy: A Bad Export." *Foreign Policy*, 70:83-108.

National Commission on Marihuana and Drug Abuse (1973). *Drug Abuse, Drug Use in America: Problem in Perspective*. Washington, DC: U.S. Government Printing Office.

National Institute of Justice (1988). *Drug Use Forecasting*. Washington, DC: U.S. Department of Justice.

National Institute on Drug Abuse (1978). *Criminal Justice Alternatives for Disposition of Drug Abusing Offender Cases*. Rockville, MD: Criminal Justice Branch, Division of Resource Development, National Institute on Drug Abuse.

New Jersey Administrative Office of the Courts (1985).   Intensive Supervision Program. Trenton, NJ.

Newsweek (1988). "Crack: The Drug Crisis." New York, NY: November 28, 1988.

New York City Criminal Justice Agency (1984). "Operation Pressure Point: Final Report on Arrest Characteristics and Court Outcomes." New York, NY.

New York City Police Department (1981-1989). *Statistical Report: Complaints and Arrests*. New York, NY: Office of Management Analysis and Planning.

New York Times (1989a). "Washington Drug Crisis Dominates Local News." April 14, 1989.

New York Times (1989b). "Number of Mothers in Jail Surges with Drug Arrests." April 17, 1989.

Nickerson, G.W. & P.A. Dynia (1988). "From Arrest to Jail: Arraignment Processing and the Detention Population." New York, NY: New York City Criminal Justice Agency, Brief Report.

Nurco, D.N. (1987). "Drug Addiction and Crime: A Complicated Issue." *British Journal of the Addictions*, 82:7-9.

Nurco, D.N., T.E. Hanlon, T.W. Kinlock & K.R. Duszynski (1988). "Differential Criminal Patterns of Narcotics Addicts Over an Addiction Career." *Criminology*, 26(3):407-423.

Pompi, K.F. & J. Resnick (1987). "Retention of Court-ordered Adolescents and Young Adults in the Therapeutic Community." *American Journal of Drug and Alcohol Abuse*, 13(3):309-325.

Press, A. (1988). "Piecing Together New York's Criminal Justice System: The Response to Crack." New York. NY: *The Record of the Association of the Bar of the City of New York*, 43(5):541-569.

Price, A.C., C. Weber & E. Perlman (1983). "Judicial Discretion and Jail Overcrowding." *Justice System Journal*, 8(2):222-238.

Rosen, C.J. & J.S. Goldkamp (1988). "The Constitutionality of Drug Testing at the Bail Stage." Proceedings of the annual meeting of the National Association of Pretrial Services Agencies, San Francisco, CA.

Schneider, A. (1988). "A Comparative Analysis of Juvenile Court Responses to Drug and Alcohol Offenses." *Crime and Delinquency*, 34(1):103-124.

Sells, S.B. & D.D. Simpson (1976). *Effectiveness of Drug Abuse Treatment.* Cambridge, MA: Ballinger.

U.S. News and World Report (1989). "Dead Zones." Washington, DC: April 10, 1989.

U.S. Sentencing Commission (1987). Supplementary Report on the Initial Sentencing Guidelines and Policy Statements. Washington, DC.

Ward, D.A. (1982). "Use of Legal and Nonlegal Coercion in the Prevention and Treatment of Drug Abuse." *Journal of Drug Issues*, 12:1-4.

Wexler, H.K., D.S. Lipton & B.D. Johnson (1988). A Criminal Justice Strategy for Treating Cocaine-heroin Abusing Offenders in Custody. Washington, DC: National Institute of Justice, Issues and Practices.

Wish, E.D. & B.D. Johnson (1986). "The Impact of Substance Abuse on Criminal Careers." In A. Blumstein, J. Cohen, J.A. Roth & C.A. Visher (eds.) *Criminal Careers and Career Criminals, Volume II*. Washington, DC: National Academy Press.

Wish, E.D., E. Brady & M. Cuadrado (1986). *Urine Testing of Arrestees: Findings from Manhattan*. New York, NY: Narcotic and Drug Research, Inc.

Wish, E.D., M.A. Toborg & J.A. Bellassai (1988). *Identifying Drug Abusers and Monitoring Them During Conditional Release*. Washington, DC: National Institute of Justice, Issues and Practices.

Yezer, A.M.J., R.P. Trost, M.A. Toborg, J.A. Bellassai & C. Quintos (1988). "Periodic Urine Testing as a Signaling Device for Pretrial Release." Monograph #5 of Assessment of Pretrial Urine Testing in the District of Columbia. Washington, DC: Toborg Associates.

Zimmer, L. (1987). *Operation Pressure Point: The Disruption of Street-Level Drug Trade on New York's Lower East Side*. New York, NY: Center for Research in Crime and Justice, New York University School of Law.

4

An Overview of Drug-Related Misconduct of Police Officers:

Drug Abuse and Narcotic Corruption*

David L. Carter

Michigan State University

Like in other occupations, the problem of employee drug abuse has emerged in law enforcement. While problems associated with alcohol abuse have been well documented as they relate to occupational life, scrutiny of drug effects other than alcohol have been less pervasive (See Shahandeh, 1985; Hore & Plant, 1981; Van, 1981; Dishlacoff, 1976). The obvious distinction between alcohol and illicit substances which faces police users is the illegal nature of the latter. Not only must concern be directed toward the behavioral effects associated with drug use, but also the abrogation of duty and trust in the officer who has violated the law through drug possession. Furthermore, concern must be given to the threat posed by the officer's association with drug dealers. Because of these factors, this paper focuses only on police officer involvement with narcotic and non-narcotic controlled substances.

While evidence exists indicating sporadic officer involvement with illicit drugs since the 1960s, it has emerged in substantially increasing numbers in the past half-decade.[1] The recent dramatic increase in officer drug use appears to be attributable to several factors. First, greater public attention

* The author thanks Robert Trojanowicz and Karen Carter for their time and constructive input in reviewing earlier drafts of this chapter.

about the problem via media accounts contributed to greater awareness of the problem. Second, this increased awareness has resulted in deeper inquiry into the extent of police drug involvement through proactive forensic and investigative tactics. Third, some police drug use cases involving extensive corruption, such as in Miami and New York, amplified the presence and extent of the problem.

A fourth reason is that increased drug use among the general population -- notably increasing in the late 1970s -- has also affected the police (See: Bureau of Justice Statistics, 1988; Jamieson & Flanagan, 1987). Particularly influential were the lower levels of social condemnation of drug use, curiosity about the drugs' psychoactive effects, and, in some cases, the symbolic nature of drugs (notably cocaine) as a trapping of an upwardly mobile social class. A final factor is that, in the past 15 years, police departments have increasingly employed people who have admitted experimentation with drugs. Whereas past standards totally excluded applicants who admitted any form of drug use, current standards typically will permit employment of persons who are not "chronic" or "recent" users of marijuana or cocaine. It is reasonable to conclude that some persons who have used drugs in the past may again do so if they are in social circumstances conducive to drug involvement. Based on the author's research, these factors serve as keystones to the current visibility of the problem.

This chapter presents an overview of the author's research findings on police drug use. Specifically, a model will be discussed describing the events wherein police departments typically discover a drug abuse problem among officers. This will be followed by discussions of the "recreational" drug user, drug corruption, environmental factors influencing the problem, and, finally, discussion of critical policy issues.[2]

RESEARCH METHODS

In light of the nature and sensitivity of the problem, predominantly qualitative research methods were used in this study. Several techniques were employed to obtain as much information as possible while maximizing the validity and reliability of that information. At the onset, a literature review of drug use and police misconduct was done to serve as a research foundation. Newspaper-clipping files were maintained and analyzed for content to identify law enforcement agencies with apparent drug-related problems among personnel and to gain insight into the specific nature of those problems.

Based on the author's previous research and available agency contacts, 13 law enforcement agencies were identified wherein personnel could be in-

terviewed concerning experiences with employee drug problems. All persons
interviewed were either of a management level or assigned to Internal Affairs
and were interviewed with an agreement of confidentiality. The law enforcement organizations included eight municipal departments, one sheriff's
department, two state agencies, and two federal agencies. Agency sizes
ranged from about 50 sworn personnel to several thousand officers. The
geographic distribution of the agencies was fairly balanced, with the exception of the northwest United States. The degree of drug problems in the departments varied as did the public knowledge of the problem ranging from
extensive publicity to only negligible media attention.

The interviews were supplemented with a review and content analysis of
Internal Affairs reports, statements, and/or depositions of officers (although
the specific types of materials available for review varied between agencies).
In addition, the author interviewed three officers who had been involved in
drug use and/or drug-related corruption. Supplemental reviews were made
of departmental policies, reports, and other documents which addressed officer drug use and any form of corruption.[3] Finally, the author obtained incidental information on drug problems from a wide range of departments as a
result of other work with the agencies. The supplemental information typically reinforced what was learned from the targeted departments. All information was synthesized into behavioral factors and patterns for comparison
in order to develop a profile of police drug involvement and policy issues.

DISCOVERING THE DRUG ABUSE PROBLEM

An interesting facet which emerged from the research was that a consistent
pattern existed in the manner in which officer drug involvement was discovered
-- or at least acknowledged -- by the organization. As depicted in Figure 4.1,
there were three distinct stages in the discovery process, each with three events,
which represented reactions to the problem. While the intensity of the events
tended to vary between the departments, the fundamental patterns remained
intact.

Stage 1: Discovery

In this stage, evidence of officer drug use begins to sporadically emerge
during the *Initiation* event. Typically, the problem is brought to attention as a
result of some circumstance associated with drug use. For example, an officer is involved in a shooting or a traffic accident and evidence of drug use is
found during the course of a routine follow-up investigation. In other cases,

departments have learned of drug involvement as a result of informant tips --
information which was initially disregarded due to the source, but eventually
shown to be valid. During the initiation event, drug use problems are generally handled as individual, spurious incidents rather than being viewed as a
potential systemic problem.

Figure 4.1
Organizational Discovery Model of Police Drug Involvement

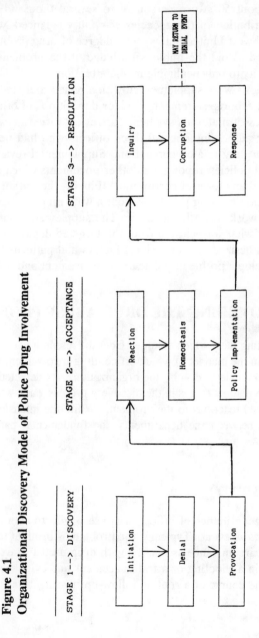

The next event is *Organizational Denial*. At this point, officer drug use cases have surfaced in sufficient numbers or magnitude to indicate that a systemic problem exists. However, administrators tend to deny this, expressing the belief -- both internally and externally -- that while numerous incidents have occurred, no "problem" really exists. Rather, they rationalized that the various cases occurred independently. It is important to emphasize that during this event there does not appear to be overt evidence that departments are "covering up" the problem with their denial. Rather, the denial is a function of disbelief: Police administrators cannot accept the fact that officers are using drugs. When asked about drug corruption, comments from police administrators were "I can't believe it", "I can't understand it", and, "The allegations can't be true". One administrator commented...

> The last problem I ever thought I'd face is my officers using drugs
> and drug dealers. I mean, the reports are here -- it's in black and
> white -- but my mind just can't accept it. I don't know if I let [the
> officers] down or they let me down. Something definitely went
> wrong in the system somewhere. This is further complicated in that
> many users are officers who have no history of disciplinary prob-
> lems and are frequently viewed as being "good cops".

Another element of denial is a product of generational differences between administrators and officers whose socialization concerning drugs differed significantly. On this subject a captain, who was a 24-year municipal police veteran, stated, "I guess I'm just from another generation -- I just don't understand [police officers using drugs]." Not surprisingly, generational differences most likely influence one's perception of drugs. Considering many police commanding officers and management officers grew up in a generation when drug use was not as prevalent among the "general society," officer involvement in drugs must appear particularly confounding.

The final first-stage event is *Provocation*. When a systemic drug use problem exists, a high profile, prominent incident generally occurs which attracts the attention of city administrators or the media, resulting in pressure to examine the problem in greater detail. In one city, there was the revelation that a group of drug-involved officers hired a contract killer to "hit" a prosecution witness. In another city, news stories told of on-duty officers robbing "crack" houses of both drugs and money. And in yet another locale, an off duty officer was killed outside of a "crack house" under "unusual" circumstances. Incidents such as these provoke calls for police action to aggressively investigate the problem, thus beginning a transition into the next discovery stage.

Stage 2: Acceptance

With this stage police organizations begin to accept the presence of the problem. They struggle with understanding the nature and extent of drug involvement and what to do about it. Most departments were administratively unprepared to deal with officer drug abuse. The *Reaction* event is when the department accepts that a problem exists and immediately implements procedures to deal with it. Because of the administrative trauma experienced during the discovery stage, reactions tend to be spontaneous and emotional rather than planned and rational. Administrators feel anger, embarrassment, betrayal, and distrust toward the offending officers. As a result, they permit these feelings to dictate policy -- sometimes policy which cannot be enforced. One department, during the reaction event, made a public announcement that they were ordering *all* officers to be drug tested or to face disciplinary action. Following the announcement, the department learned that not only did there appear to be Fourth Amendment problems with the order, but also that the order violated a provision in the collective bargaining agreement with the Police Officers' Association. Furthermore, the testing program would cost the department an estimated $100,000 for a one-time test for all employees -- an amount which was not readily available in the budget. Embarrassed administrators then had to retreat from their position and develop alternate plans.

The reaction event tends to evoke aggressive, frequently unworkable, responses, which forces administrators to look at the problem anew from a more rational perspective. This leads to the next event, *Homeostasis*. During homeostasis administrators begin to manage, rather than force, the issue thereby regaining control of the organization's response. Planning and research occurs to understand the issues and options with sound strategies developed for consideration. During this event it becomes apparent that the department understands the problem and will deal with it in a legal and fair manner, serving the best interests of the organization, employees, and the community.

The acceptance stage ends with the *Policy Implementation* event. Based on planning outcomes, administrators implement policies, procedures, and rules to deal with the drug-related issues. This signifies that they have accepted the existence of the problem and have implemented affirmative measures to deal with it.

Stage 3: Resolution

In some ways, this stage takes on a systemic character as the extent and types of actual drug involvement are directly addressed. Armed with the background research and newly implemented policies, the department transcends into the *Inquiry* event. Here, systematic investigations are conducted, frequently proactively, into allegations of officer drug use. The problem is examined from new perspectives in an attempt to identify signs of drug-related involvement. Comprehensive investigations are performed and both deterrence and preventive programs are typically introduced at this time.

As a result of the comprehensive, organized examination of drug use, departments typically enter the next event: *Corruption*. Discoveries are made that drug involvement is not only consumption, but includes the use of one's position for personal gain or benefit. Corrupt activities will range from converting seized drugs for personal use to robbery of drug traffickers. Since corruption will be discussed in detail later, suffice it to note that most departments which have experienced officer drug use, also experience some drug related corruption. This sometimes causes regression to the discovery stage, and particularly the denial event, with the cycle starting again as related to corrupt acts.

The final event, *Response*, signifies that rational programming is in place to deal with drug involvement. Some departments implement various drug testing programs as both a preventive and investigative tool.[4] Other programming including training sessions on drug involvement, special supervisory training for detecting drug involvement, an option within the Employee Assistance Program to deal with drug users, and the use of different investigative and inspection techniques to detect drug use or corruption.[5]

Observations on the Discovery Model

This model represents a common pattern in the discovery of police drug involvement. The events are not mutually exclusive; they represent a series of ongoing occurrences experienced by the organization, not individual police administrators. The transitions between states and events occur as continuous, rather than discrete, periods of change. While all organizations in this study experienced each element of the model, the duration of each stage and event varied. Interestingly, even though more police departments are discovering an officer drug misconduct problem, they still appear to go through each event of the model -- notably present are the denial and reaction events. However, research during the homeostasis and policy implementation events go much faster as a result of experiences by other law enforcement agencies.

"RECREATIONAL" POLICE DRUG USE

Police drug use results in some unusual problems which must be addressed by administrators. Some officers are simply "recreational" users of drugs. Others are unquestionably involved in drug corruption, while still others are somewhere in the middle -- their primary impetus is drug use, yet their behavior involves some corrupt acts. Understanding these factors with their attendant policy issues is an essential management responsibility.

"Recreational" use of drugs is a somewhat broad characterization. Admittedly, it is a term which may not be completely inclusive of all drug use, particularly in cases of addiction. For this study, recreational drug use was operationally defined as drug use that does not involve corruption and where use was initially a product of the desire to experience the expected exhilaration, psychoactive effects, and/or mood changes associated with drug consumption. Under this definition, drug use may include both on-duty and off-duty use of illicit narcotic and non-narcotic controlled substances as long as corruption was not involved.

On-Duty Drug Use

The extent of on-duty drug use by officers is simply not known. An intuitive assumption is that some on-duty use occurs; however, it does not appear to be extensive. When it does occur, the potential ramifications are widespread. The most serious implications are that the officer may use deadly force or be involved in a traffic accident while under the influence. Other effects of on-duty use include poor judgment in the performance of official duties, increased liability risks, misfeasant or nonfeasant behavior, having a negative influence on co-workers, and having a negative influence on community relations.

In one case of on-duty drug use, a patrol officer in one of the nation's major municipal police departments was discovered to be using cocaine on duty. During the internal affairs investigation, the officer admitted he had regularly used cocaine on duty for a little over a year. One would assume that the officer's behavior while under the influence would be a signal to co-workers that the officer was "high". However, the officer stated that after each time he "snorted" cocaine he would "chase it" with whiskey. He knew co-workers would "cover" for him if they thought he was an alcoholic, therefore, he masked the cocaine's behavioral influences with the odor of alcohol. This experience, which provides insight into the occupational culture of policing, serves as evidence of how substance abuse during working hours can occur without being discovered.

On-duty drug use can also occur if the problem becomes systemic within the work group. In one moderate-sized midwestern city, about 30 officers were identified as being involved in a "user's ring" (not all of whom used drugs on duty). Drug use became so pervasive that there was tolerance for its use even on duty. While some officers in the group did not like the on-duty use, they would not inform on those who used drugs while working because of the strong implication they would be discovered as a drug user, albeit during off-duty hours. One could conclude from this experience that, in light of the systemic and subcultural variables, if off-duty use becomes prevalent then the likelihood of on-duty use appears to increase among officers involved.

In perhaps the only study of the subject, Kraska and Kappeler (1988) serendipitously discovered on-duty drug use during the course of working with a police department on another project. Through the use of "unstructured self report interviews, departmental records and researcher observations, ... [they found that] 20 percent of the officers in the department used marijuana while on duty twice a month or more" [1988:12-14]. Another four percent had used marijuana at least once while on duty. Furthermore, 10 percent of the officers reported they had used non-prescribed controlled substances (defined in the study as including hallucinogenics, stimulants, or barbiturates) while on duty. (This may not be an additional 10%; it may include some of the marijuana users.) Most of the officers involved in on-duty drug use were between the ages of 21 and 38, and had been on the job 3 to 10 years.

Despite some methodological limitations of the study discussed by Kraska and Kappeler, the findings are sound -- and somewhat surprising. One may hope that the high incidence of on-duty drug use found in this study was an exceptional occurrence. If not, the problem may be greater than we believe. Furthermore, when one envisions the on-duty drug use problem there is a tendency to conclude it would be a problem found only in the nation's larger police agencies. This study, and the experience of this author, suggest that may not be the case.

These illustrations show that on-duty drug use does occur, at least to some extent. It is also reasonable to assume that those agencies which have had more serious drug related problems, such as corruption, have also experienced on-duty drug use by officers. A police administrator must assume the potential for on-duty drug use exists and take steps to address the problem.

Drugs of Choice by Police Officers

In cases where drug abuse has been documented, there are indications that officers have a "drug of choice." Not surprisingly, marijuana appears to be the most common drug used. Information gained from the research indicated the preference for marijuana because of its comparatively minor addictive nature, its limited long-term effects, the ease of obtaining it, its comparatively low cost, and, importantly, the lesser social stigma associated with the use of marijuana when compared with other drugs.

Cocaine use is clearly the second most frequently used drug and appears to be fairly prevalent. The best explanation for this seems to be its availability, its prevalent use in the general society, and, to some extent, greater exhilaration from cocaine compared to marijuana. Findings in an internal investigation in one of the cities found that far and above other substances, the drug of choice was "crack." The reasons given by the officers (during the course of *Garrity* interviews) was that the drug was very inexpensive and could be obtained easily without going to the same dealer.[6] The officers reasoned that if they could obtain a drug from different dealers, they were less likely to be discovered, thus lessening the chance for being blackmailed.

Finally, there was some evidence of abuse of non-prescribed or falsely prescribed pharmaceutical substances. Amphetamines and barbiturates fall into this category typically where officers have used the drugs as a way of coping with various personal problems. In some cases, stimulants have been used to help keep officers "alert" (or awake) when they have been working excessive hours in a second job or going to school. This form of substance abuse appears to have different dynamics than the marijuana or cocaine use. Interestingly, peer officers showed greater tolerance for protecting officers who used amphetamines and barbiturates as opposed to other controlled substances, despite the fact the use of those substances are illegal. There were no indications of a significant problem with synthetic hallucinogenic drugs or heroin.[7]

As a final note, some police administrators expressed concern that an increasing number of officers may be using illicit anabolic steroids. Their concern, while somewhat focused on the illegal use, was primarily directed toward the reported behavioral effects of steroids. Specifically, some research has indicated that regular steroid users become violent and aggressive. The implications of these effects in law enforcement are obvious. Interestingly, new police programming may indirectly contribute to this problem. With more departments participating in the Police Olympics; which include weight lifting, karate, running, and similar clubs; and rewarding physical fitness, the appeal of the conditioning effects of steroids is powerful. Any policy planning for development of an internal drug control program should include exploration of the anabolic steroid issue.

Substance Abuse as a Job-Related Condition

In cases of recreational drug abuse by police officers, the question has been posed of whether such use may be a job-related condition. There are two primary arguments that have been offered for this claim: stress and job assignment.

Those who advance the argument that drug use is a function of occupational stress state that, because of the high levels of stress in law enforcement, some officers have resorted to drug use as a coping mechanism. The author does not agree. In fact, it is argued that the opposite situation could conceivably occur. That is, an officer who is abusing substances could possibly experience *more* stress since the discovery of this behavior is likely to result in disciplinary action or termination.[8]

If stress was, in fact, a major causal factor in drug abuse among police officers, then it is likely that more significant levels of drug use would have surfaced in the last 15 years. Moreover, in cases where drug abusing officers have been disciplined or involved in plea bargaining and/or arbitration, the evidence suggests that job stress was not a facet of the drug abuse. Nevertheless, no empirical support has been found either for or against the drug/stress hypothesis in police work.

The second job-related issue is that substance abuse may be a product of job assignment. Some argue that officers who are working in an undercover capacity with frequent or ongoing exposure to narcotics and drugs may become socialized in the "drug culture." That is, constant interaction with the drug environment reduces the negative socio-moral implications of drug usage and concomitantly reinforces both the frequency and permissibility of drug usage.

Again, no research is available to substantiate or disclaim this argument. Instances were reported during the research where narcotics officers had been found to be abusing drugs both on- and off-duty. Particularly in the case of narcotic officer drug use, it may conceivably be argued that occupational socialization contributed to the abuse.

As one illustration, the author spoke with an undercover narcotics officer about the practice of "simulation" -- that is, pretending to smoke marijuana during the course of an undercover assignment as a means to help "legitimize" one's role as a "player." The officer reported that...

> Simulation is crap -- any user knows if you're smoking or faking and you can bet they're watching the new guys to see if you're taking a real hit. If I'm at a deal and I try to simulate I might as well be wearing a sign that says "COP". ...so you've got to take a real hit to

sell yourself. Anyway, it's just a hit of marijuana -- it's got less bite than tequila.

This officer went on to report that he, along with another undercover narcotics officer, had smoked some marijuana while off duty that they had picked up during their undercover activities. Perhaps what was most striking about the officer's statements was that he admitted his actions openly, apparently not recognizing the impropriety of his acts. In fact, he inferred that his department should permit undercover narcotics officers to smoke marijuana during the course of investigations to help maintain their credibility. The officer's occupational environment appears to have contributed to his misconduct; however, one cannot assign a causal weight to the environmental factors. When this quotation was told to a police supervisor from another agency, who formerly worked undercover narcotics, the supervisor stated, "That guy's got a problem. He's been in too long without anybody keeping an eye on him."

The implications for this are: (1) preventive procedures should be developed for high-risk assignments to help avoid (or at least minimize) this potential problem, and (2) procedures should be established to deal fairly with officers who may have abused substances as a result of occupational socialization. These decisions are very difficult and the literature provides little direction because of the relative contemporary nature of the problem.

THE PATHOLOGY OF DRUG CORRUPTION

When examining the problem of police drug involvement, the issue of corruption inevitably surfaces. Police corruption is generally defined as the use of an officer's authority or official position for personal benefit or gain. The benefit or gain may involve money, goods, services, or special preference which is either forthcoming immediately or in the future (See Barker & Carter, 1986; Barker, 1977; Goldstein, 1975). In light of this definition and the experiences of the departments in this study, drug-related corruption typically included:

* Accepting bribes from drug dealers/traffickers in exchange for "tip" information regarding drug investigations, undercover officers, drug strategies, names of informants, etc.

* Accepting bribes from drug dealers/traffickers in exchange for interference in the justice process such as non-arrest, evidence tampering, perjury, etc.

* Theft of drugs by the officer from property rooms or laboratory for personal consumption of the drug or for sale of the
  drug.

* Street "seizure" of drugs from users/traffickers without an accompanying arrest with the intent of converting the drug to
  personal use.

* Robbery of drug dealers of profits from drug sales and/or the
  drugs for resale.

* Extorting drug traffickers for money (and sometimes property
  such as stereos, televisions, etc.) in exchange for non-arrest or
  non-seizure of drugs.

Reviews of depositions and discussions with both internal affairs investigators and officers involved in these corrupt acts led the author to conclude
that there are two distinct cycles -- not necessarily mutually exclusive -- underlying drug-related corruption.

User-Driven Cycle

In these cases the officer started as a "recreational" user of drugs typically buying the substances from a dealer just as most users. Officer behavior
appears to evolve to a threshold wherein he/she decides rather than buy the
drugs they can be "confiscated" from the users/dealers or taken from the police property process. This decision appears to be the product of several in-
teractive factors. One is the increasing cost of drug use and/or the impact of
long-term expenditures for drugs on the officer's personal finances. A
second factor is the opportunity structure for seizure of drugs. That is,
through the work environment the officer has various opportunities to seize
drugs and convert them to personal use with minimal jeopardy of discovery.
Finally, officers begin to worry that their dealers may discover they are police
officers (if not already known) and blackmail the officer in some manner. As
a result of these concerns, the officer looks for optional ways to obtain the
drugs and reduce the dependency on the dealer.

From officer interviews, and inferences in depositions/statements, it appears that the progression from use to corruption is evolutionary, and that
will eventually affect most drug abusing officers to some degree. Furthermore, it appears that the probability of being involved in corruption linearly
increases with the length of time an officer uses drugs since his/her police
employment. While other variables intervene in this cycle, most typically the
corruption involves confiscation of drugs for personal use. One officer com-

mented on his taking drugs from street users for personal use, "I really didn't think about it. It just seemed like a natural thing to do." (Carter, forthcoming)

Figure 4.2
Police Drug Corruption

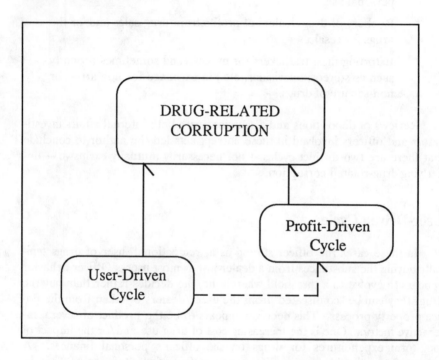

While recognizing such behavior is "wrong" (typically citing violation of department rules rather than criminal laws) officers did not view this behavior as "corrupt" since it did not involve an exchange of money between the officer and a drug trafficker. Furthermore, in explaining the behavior officers commonly referred to it as "not putting the drugs in the property room" rather than "taking drugs from a user/dealer." The subtle distinction is indicative of rationalizing one's behavior as a means of legitimizing the actions.

Some evidence showed instances wherein the corrupt user became involved in fairly aggressive profit-driven corruption. However, no discernible pattern was discovered. It appears that most user-driven corrupt officers did not involve themselves in profit-driven corrupt activities.

Figure 4.3
Drug and Corruption Probability

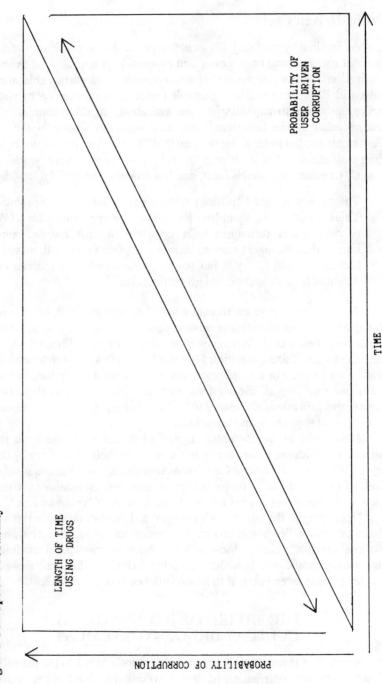

Profit-Driven Cycle

As implied by the label, the intent of profit-driven corruption was purely proprietary (involving both money and property). It appears that the primary motivation was the vast amount of unaccountable and untraceable money involved in illicit drug trafficking coupled with the opportunity, by virtue of police authority, to capitalize on the availability of these monies. This is compounded by the fact that illegal acts were the source of the monies. Comments tended to be along the line that "it's not fair" or "it's not right" that drug traffickers had more money than the officers who were "working for a living." Commenting on this facet, one law enforcement official stated,

> The money involved [in drug trafficking] is hard to comprehend. Think about it: An agent [or officer] sees the opportunity for a take of cash, either through a bribe or a rip-off, that involves more money than the agent may make in a year, five years, hell, maybe a lifetime. I hate to say it, but you've got to admit that you can understand how an agent could go on the take.

To give perspective on the amounts of money involved, one former undercover narcotics investigator now assigned to a task force to investigate drug corruption stated, "When you're looking at ongoing [drug] deals of even medium to small size quantities, $100,000 is a small score for a bribe in drug trafficking today." In another case, ten officers from one police department made two robberies of cocaine from drug traffickers. In just these two robberies, the officers made over $16 million among them. The amounts of money are staggering -- and tempting.

Most incidents of corruption identified in this study were not through bribes by traffickers, rather it was in the form of theft or robbery by the officers. While some bribery cases were identified, involving relatively large sums of money, the most frequent corrupt acts were "shakedowns" from drug users and street-level dealers followed by robberies of "crack houses."

Interestingly, the officers who committed thefts and robberies of drug dealers viewed officers who accepted bribes or committed extortions as being the "real corrupt" officers. Most officers who were involved in stealing drugs and money would not consider accepting bribes -- this was viewed as a greater offense, even betrayal to fellow officers, compared to theft.

THE MILIEU OF OCCUPATIONAL CULTURE DRUG INVOLVEMENT

Analysis of the various drug use and corrupt acts led to the identification of six constructs contributing to drug involvement. First is the *opportunity structure.* Through the situations afforded the officer via his/her position, the opportunities exist to exploit them for "profit". Barker (1977) observed that the opportunity structure provides the police officer with many situations to observe and/or participate in a wide range of activities. In addition, the police come into contact with many deviant actors during their normal work routine under conditions of little or no supervision. Kraska and Kappeler observed that ...

> Three variables related to the opportunity structure of policing add to the police officer's vulnerability [in drug cases]: 1) the duration and intensity of exposure to the drug using element of society; 2) the police officers' relative freedom from supervision; and, 3) the availability of illegal drugs (1987-88).

The drug-involved officer is one who exploits these elements.

The second construct (*rationalization* of behavior) is manifested in several ways. Most commonly officers would observe that "it's just drug money," inferring that there is a different standard for theft of illegally earned money compared to lawful profits. Another common rationalization theme was that the corruption "was not hurting anyone." Again, with the inference that there is a different standard of equity or justice applied to drug traffickers than other persons. Drug-abusing officers also rationalize their actions that "everyone uses drugs." Obviously, the fallacy in rationalization is the lack of introspection to recognize one's own failure or indiscriminate behavior.

The third construct is the *invulnerability factor*. Essentially, this was the perception that, because of the officer's position and authority, he/she could stay segregated from the misconduct (i.e., not implicated). Easy access to information, camaraderie, and the power to influence the behavior of drug users/dealers were contributory characteristics of this. Perhaps the epitome of this factor can best be illustrated in one officer's statement which was purportedly agreed with by others: "Who's going to take the word of a junkie over a cop?" It appears that the invulnerability factor is most pervasive in the profit-driven cycle of corruption.

Fourth is the *abrogation of trust*. Based on the literature of police ethics and values, the experiences of police departments with off-duty responsibilities of officers, labor arbitrations, and case law, it is clear that there is a higher standard of integrity required of police officers than of the "average citizen" (Carter, 1988). The essence of that standard lies in the officer's oath of office and the concomitant trust the people place in police officers in light of their unique authority. On the matter of corruption, Klockars emphasizes that, "What is corrupted in police corruption is the special trust police enjoy by virtue of their occupation" [1983:334]. Similarly, in recreational drug use by officers, our trust that officers will obey the law has been misplaced.

A fifth construct which compounds the drug-involvement problem is the so-called *Blue Code of Secrecy.* The literature has thoroughly discussed this "Code of Secrecy" which exists within the police culture (See Barker & Carter, 1986; Blumberg & Niederhoffer, 1985; Stoddard, 1983; Kennedy, 1977). The "code" is a cultural norm which prohibits discussion of occupational "secrets" and behaviors to those outside of the defined social group. The social group may vary depending on the nature of the secrets. The group's parameters may be defined by shift, assignment, rank, or simply employment by a police organization. The parameters may also be defined on the basis of one's participation with the occupational group. That is, an officer who does not subscribe to the code or adhere to its rules may be ostracized from the group. The influence of peer pressure to "belong" and the social sanctions associated with ostracism make the "code" a powerful cultural dynamic.

Despite the seriousness of police drug use, the author has found a reluctance of police officers to report fellow officers if the use was limited to off-duty instances. The "code" also influenced on-duty drug use in that drug abusing police officers may be ostracized by the peer group yet, somewhat surprisingly, there appears to still be some reluctance to inform on such officers.[9] Similarly, when corruption occurred there was a tendency to disassociate from the officers, but not turn them in. Interestingly, an officer who informed on a fellow officer may be labeled as a "rat" who could not be trusted, and might experience more ostracism than the officer(s) involved in the corrupt behavior (See McAlary, 1987; Knapp Commission, 1973). In one city, an officer who was not involved in drug use or any other form of misconduct, observed another officer taking a bribe. Yet, the "straight" officer did not turn in the bribe, nor did he say anything about it until he was interviewed by Internal Affairs during an investigation of the corrupt officer. When asked why the officer had not come forward, the investigator stated...

> ...he didn't fear getting shot, he didn't fear getting hurt [on the job]; he *did* fear the repercussions of turning in a fellow officer even under these circumstances. (Emphasis in original statement.)

The final construct is that *both cycles are difficult to break.* Even with the threat of investigation and the self-recognition of behavioral impropriety, it appears extraordinarily difficult for the officer to become extricated from the cycle. Following this line of thought, Goldstein notes what he calls the "addictive element." "Once an officer has agreed to accept the [personal gain] of corruption, he usually becomes addicted to the system" [1975:27]. This has a systemic reinforcing effect in that the officer must further rationalize his/her behavior when the opportunity exists for the improper act. Similarly, because of the difficulty of breaking out of the cycle, the feeling of invulnerability must be heightened.

POLICY ISSUES FOR POLICE EMPLOYEE DRUG CONTROL

An important aspect of this research was to address pragmatic concerns of police administrators in dealing with drug involvement. In this regard, three central policy areas were identified as the most complex: *identifying the drug user, disposition of the drug user, and dealing with the police union/Police Officer Association (POA)*. Critical decisions must be made before any internal drug control program can be promulgated. The following discussions highlight some of the issues involved in these areas.

Identifying the Drug User

Controversies exist in the philosophy, legal standards, and approaches to identifying police drug users. A synthesis of the various identification methods is presented to provide perspective on the issues.

Informant Information

One method of identifying drug involvement is through the use of complaints and informant information. Sources in this category may include suspicious officers, citizens observing "unusual" officer behavior, rumors in "the grapevine," and statements of persons arrested for drugs particularly when there is a conflict with the officer's statements. In one case reviewed in this study, a follow-up investigation on an overheard conversation between a narcotics officer and another individual resulted in the discovery of a major drug abuse and corruption problem in the unit. A degree of skepticism is reasonable; however, information should not be dismissed simply because the complaint may come from a "criminal" or someone else outside of the department.

Supervision

Supervisory observations are an important source of identifying drug misconduct. To be effective, supervisors must be trained to be cognizant of indicators which point to a potential drug abuse problem. Without the appropriate training it is difficult for the supervisor to identify the substance abuser. Not only are observations of drug use symptoms important, but also greater attention to supervisor/officer contacts. It was noted that an important contributing factor to officer drug involvement (as well as other forms of misconduct) is the lack of vigilant supervision. Police departments in general must ensure that effective supervision is occurring, to more effectively deal with misconduct problems.

Polygraph

Some agencies, in the course of drug use investigations, have relied on the polygraph for identification of drug involvement. It was found in the research that some departments, during the reaction event of discovery, used the polygraph as a screening tool. Investigators were searching for a tool to help deal with the problem, however, they were not using this tool in the most effective manner. For the polygraph to be most useful there must first be other indicators of a drug-related problem to serve as the grounds for further investigation. The polygraph's value as a means of user identification is limited by the evidentiary restrictions found in court rules and arbitration procedures. In addition, the polygraph cannot conclusively determine the presence of drugs as can a forensic analysis of blood or urine. In sum, the polygraph should not be used as the initial screening mechanism to determine if an officer is using drugs. If used in any form, it should be relied upon as an investigatory tool just as it would in any other form of internal investigation.

Self-Reports

One means of user identification often overlooked is the self-report. There are different reasons why an officer may report his/her substance abuse. Among these reasons are:

(1) The officer may feel the drug use is getting "out of control" -- too much time is spent on financing, obtaining, and using drugs;

(2) The officer may feel substances are ruining his/her life (personally and/or physically);

(3) The officer may feel drugs are pulling him/her toward corruption or some other compromising situation;

(4) The officer may feel his/her drug use is about to be discovered and hopes that self-reporting the problem, before being "charged" with it, will mitigate any penalty.

Should these different motives for the self-report affect the type and severity of disposition the officer receives? The answer to this question lies largely in the management philosophy of the chief with influence from the prevailing community standards.

One major department, faced with ongoing discovery of officer drug use, declared an "amnesty" period for officers. During the amnesty, officers could report their use of marijuana or cocaine and were guaranteed there would be no prosecution or disciplinary action against this as long as they were not involved in any corruption. Instead, the officers had to agree to go through a drug rehabilitation program sanctioned by the department. Those officers who admitted cocaine use were placed on unpaid suspension until they successfully completed the program. However, officers who admitted marijuana use were simply reassigned. The reassignments were not just to desk jobs, but to full law enforcement positions. This program was mandated during the Stage 2 Reaction Event. At this writing, the effect or ramifications of the amnesty period are not known. The wisdom of this self-report system is subject to debate. As one Lieutenant in the department stated, "We've been catching a lot of heat in the [media]. I'm afraid that instead of grasping for solutions we have grasped for some straws."

Drug Testing

The most effective and most controversial method of identifying drug users is through forensic drug testing. There has been debate on the forensic reliability of drug tests, the legality of mandatory testing, and administrative questions concerning the circumstances wherein drug tests should be given. While these issues are beyond the scope of the current paper, the different policy ideologies concerning drug testing are worthy of note.

The Police Executive Research Forum (PERF), in an attempt to better understand the concerns of police executives on drug testing, surveyed its member police chiefs on a variety of police drug use issues. Among the findings associated with drug testing were:

* 89.7%   Supported drug testing if reasonable grounds existed to suspect an officer was using drugs.

* 76.4%   Favored drug screening of police applicants.

* 66.1%   Favored regular drug testing of officers during the probationary period.

* 64.7%   Favored random screening of officers in "sensitive" assignments.

* 50.0% Favored a mandatory universal random drug-screening program.

* 42.6% Favored the drug testing of officers after they had been involved in a "serious incident" (Olson, 1988).

It is safe to say that the police chiefs desired to have a drug-free workplace, however, they differed on their standards and approaches to deal with the issue. In a debate on drug testing, Houston Police Chief, Lee Brown, argued in support of mandatory drug testing stating that an aggressive program is the best possible deterrent against drug use. Conversely, Kansas City Police Chief, Larry Joiner, argued against such programs. His rationale was that after recruiting, testing, investigating, selecting, training, and supervising police officers, departments should presume officers are drug-free unless evidence is presented otherwise to show reasonable cause exists to believe an officer is using drugs. At that point, drug tests should be administered (Carter & Stephens, 1988).

The lack of clear guidance from court cases and labor arbitrations coupled with the diversity of police chief opinions, is important evidence to show there remains a significant amount of planning and experimentation needed to resolve the dilemmas of the drug-testing issue.

Disposition of Drug-Abusing Employees

Just as identifying employee drug involvement presents a number of difficult policy decisions, so does the disposition of drug abusing officers. The problem cannot be easily resolved with the "fire 'em" approach. As in most management decisions, there are aggravating and mitigating circumstances which should be addressed in the planning and research process before policy is established. The debate on disposition centers on whether officers abusing drugs should simply be punished or whether attempts should be made to rehabilitate them. Although many chiefs currently favor termination, once again there is no clear consensus.

Termination and Discipline Short of Termination

When police departments began discovering substance abuse among police officers, the initial reaction was to terminate the officer. However, in some cases -- notably union departments -- the agency found that they did not have proper policies, procedures, or rules to support this decision (particularly when no criminal charges had been filed).

In one city, 13 officers (including two sergeants) were indicted by a federal grand jury for possession and/or distribution of controlled substances. All of those indicted eventually pleaded guilty on a plea negotiation to misdemeanor possession charges and were subsequently placed on federal probation. Five of the officers resigned from the department. The remaining eight officers, who were on unpaid suspension, opted to take their cases to labor arbitration in an attempt to get reinstated. In the department's efforts to terminate the officers, it found that there were inadequate policies, procedures, and rules in place to deal with officer drug use. The department reacted somewhat "arbitrarily" in the suspensions and the handling of the cases, resulting in a binding arbitrator's decision to reinstate the officers with partial salary reimbursement. In another city, the department opted not even to bring disciplinary charges against some drug-using officers because of "holes" in the disciplinary process which were part of the provisions in a collective bargaining agreement.

The lesson from these examples is that policy review and planning are essential for the disciplinary processes to be functional. The nature and severity of discipline may be dependent upon factors such as whether use was on or off duty, the type of substance which was used, factors on the job which may have contributed to the drug use, the officer's service and personnel record, and aggravating or mitigating factors unique to the individual officer's circumstances.

In making policy on discipline for drug use, agencies may also consider the investment that has been made in recruitment, selection, and training of the officer. As a management decision, the investment should be realistically balanced with the harm done to the organization and the ability of the officer to perform the job. When discipline is used as a disposition alternative, the agency must promulgate formal written policies, procedures, and rules to help ensure officers are aware of the department's expectations.

Rehabilitation

Some police departments have explored a rehabilitation alternative for substance-abusing personnel. Those in support of rehabilitation base their argument on the department's investment in the officer, the possibility that the job may have contributed to the problem, a recognition that drug use is a social problem not limited to policing, and the organizational obligation to the employee (notably in organizations subscribing to the so called "Type Z" management philosophy).

At the outset, it must be recognized that rehabilitation should only be an *option* to deal with substance abuse -- it cannot be viewed as an inherent employee right. This option carries with it many important policy questions that a police administrator must carefully evaluate and answer. Among the more critical questions are:

* To whom would the program be open? All officers; only those self reporting a drug problem; only marijuana users; only those *using* drugs, not dealing? How will past misconduct involving actions *other* than drug use be considered?

* What will be the officer's assignment and/or status during rehabilitation?

* Will the officer be on probation *after* the treatment period? Will the officer return to the assignment held when the problem was identified?

* What will the department's position be if the officer subsequently uses drugs after the rehabilitation? Is subsequent drug use the "failure" of the departmentally-sanctioned program or the officer?

* What are the criteria to be evaluated in a rehabilitation program to determine if the officer is "fit for duty"? Will the department have any input to determine if the rehabilitation has been accomplished, or is this solely a therapeutic/treatment decision?

* Who pays for the rehabilitation program? Police department? Officer? Union? Standard health insurance? Special insurance policy?

* Do any unique liability problems arise for the officer or department if an officer who has admitted drug use and has gone through a rehabilitation program returns to a law enforcement position? (i.e., Can the department be deemed negligent if it retains an officer who has admitted drug use?)

* Will there be any credibility problems for the officer in criminal trials if the defense counsel learns that the officer testifying in a criminal case (particularly a drug case) was an admitted drug abuser who has gone through a rehabilitation program? (Carter, 1987).

There are no easy answers to these questions. The manner in which the police administrator addresses these issues will be dependent on social, political, economic, and ideological variables. Clearly, implementation of a rehabilitation program, or at the least an Employee Assistance Program for drugs, requires significant thought and planning.

Criminal Prosecution

A final disposition alternative, obviously tied to discipline, is criminal prosecution. Like other criminal offenses, all aspects of police officer drug use must be examined. Does sufficient evidence exist? Would a case of this type be pursued if it were not an officer? Is the case only for possession or is corruption involved? What is the likely impact of prosecution on the individual and the department? For possession of small amounts for recreational use, departmental sanctions may be sufficient punishment. However, for drug related corruption this author argues that every effort should be made to prosecute the officer.

Union Issues

On the matter of substance abuse, labor leaders and police administrators agree that they both want a drug-free workplace. However, Police Officer Associations (POAs) have emphasized two important points: (1) They do not want a drug-free workplace at the expense of employee rights, and (2) they want employee drug use policies to support the rehabilitation model.

The central issue is employee rights -- the interpretation of which labor and management disagree upon. For example, both agree that internal investigations should incorporate minimal due process rights, however, they disagree on which specific rights are included on the "minimal due process" standard. The union sentiment was summarized by one Fraternal Order of Police (FOP) national official speaking to a group of police managers: "If you're going to get one of our members, you've got to get him *right*" (emphasis in original), (Possumato, 1987).

A major issue in the employee rights arena is drug testing. POAs have been outspoken critics of drug testing programs, generally arguing that drug testing of tenured employees violates their rights and improperly sets them apart (on a Fourth Amendment basis) from other citizens. According to Possumato (1987), POAs view drug testing programs, *per se*, as being a disciplinary action, not a preventive program. The logic used is that drug testing is a Napoleonic approach tantamount to a presumption of guilt until the officer "proves" his/her innocence through a negative urinalysis.

On the matter of testing, unions support testing police applicants, drug tests as part of personnel physical examinations (although not enthusiastically), "for cause" testing, and drug screening prior to assignment to a "sensitive position" (although the definition of a "sensitive position" is a source of debate). There are conflicting union opinions about the testing of probationary officers. In general, if a probationer is not covered by a contract/collective bargaining agreement, the union will not argue against drug testing.

Union representatives have generally not supported testing after critical incidents such as a traffic accident or a shooting. They argue that it taints the officer and there are no grounds to believe the officer used drugs simply because of involvement in an incident of this nature. Without question, most unions vehemently oppose random drug testing programs, although some notable exceptions have occurred.

With respect to the disposition of drug abusing officers, unions tend to support discipline, even termination, of an officer who is corrupt. However, for recreational users, the POAs strongly support the rehabilitation model. In this regard, two major components of the union argument are: (1) The policing occupation contributed to the drug use as a result of stress and occupational socialization, and (2) the organization has an obligation to its employees.

To state the obvious union and management must establish a dialogue on their differences to meet the mutual goal of a drug-free workplace. Both must have empathy for each other's advocacy responsibilities and be willing to resolve differences for the betterment of the department and the community.

CONCLUSION

Recently, it was reported that some 400 drug cases will be dropped in the District of Columbia because D.C. Metropolitan Police officers may have been involved in the theft of drugs and money during drug arrests (*USA Today*, 1987:3A). An officer on leave from the Pontiac, Michigan Police Department who refused to take a drug test before returning to duty was finally allowed to return to work without the test because the drug screening was not a matter of policy and there was no reason to suspect the officer had been using drugs (*MAP*, 1987:5-7). A Florida Deputy Sheriff who had been decertified for "gross misconduct" by the Criminal Justice Standards and Training Commission because he had admitted using marijuana two years earlier, had his case reversed. The Florida Court of Appeals held that the act did not amount to gross misconduct as required by the Florida decertification statute, *McClung v. Criminal Justice Standards and Training Commission*, 458 So. 2d 887 (Fla. Dist. Ct. App. 1984). These cases were variously aggravated because the agencies did not fully understand the nature of the drug problem nor did they have adequate planning, policy, or supervision to specifically address drug use.

How serious is the problem in law enforcement? Based on the research from this study, anecdotal information, and incidental data collected, the author will go out on a limb. In light of the collective findings, it is intuitively estimated that at least 30 percent of the nation's police officers have had some form of involvement with illicit drugs since becoming employed in law enforcement. While some may feel this percentage is high, the author feels it is conservative. Whether or not this constitutes an "epidemic" is arguable; but it certainly represents a pervasive problem. Consequently, police departments must accept the fact that officers become involved with drugs. With this acceptance, effective drug control programming may then be implemented.

Any internal drug control program must have both preventive and disciplinary components. As observed by Koehler (1986), the objective of personnel drug programs is prevention, not punishment. Policies prohibiting drug use and prescribing sanctions for violations should be viewed primarily as a preventive tool with invocation of the disciplinary process as a secondary role when prevention does not occur. Philosophically, when this approach is taken, the program presumes the innocence (rather than the guilt) of officers on the matter of drug use. Moreover, when the drug control program is viewed by management as a preventive mechanism, there will likely be reduced anxiety and less animosity among employees.

Because of the limited direction afforded to administrators on police officer drug abuse, the first step in planning for an effective drug-control program is to look back. Policies and procedures relating to misconduct need to be assessed, the nature of the drug problem within the agency must be analyzed, and mistakes from the past must be scrutinized. One must be particularly cognizant of omissions, applicability, comprehensiveness, fairness, clarity, propriety, and functionality of the policies and procedures as related to their goal.

Once police managers understand the current status of the problem, they must then decide the desired philosophy and consequent policies they hope to implement. A drug control program must be the product of critical introspection and consideration of what is best for the total organization as well as the community. The watchwords for an effective drug control program are *functional, comprehensive, realistic, fair,* and *legal.*

Epilogue

As is evident, this research was conducted from a policy perspective. While it was exploratory in nature, surprising consistency was found in the issues to the extent that cautioned generalizations were made. The characteristics of police drug involvement will likely change as departments become more accustomed to the problem and as social change occurs. Perhaps one of the more important findings of this study was not the dynamics of drug involvement, but the inability of police departments to effectively deal with the problem. The inference from this conclusion is that police departments must constantly be involved in proactive planning and research which examines social trends that have implications for police organizations. Based on their findings the departments must be willing to develop policy and innovative programming which facilitates prevention and affirmative problem-solving rather than reactionary responses.

During the course of another project, the author was in the office of a police chief discussing the need for comprehensive planning with a "futures orientation" in policy development. The chief stated, "In the two years I've been in this job, it seems like I spend most of my time putting out fires. For once I'd like to prevent one." About that time the phone rang and the chief was informed that an off-duty police captain was involved in a traffic accident. The captain had been drinking and was in his departmental car. The chief looked up and said, "Shit, I've got to put out another fire." To quote news commentator, Linda Ellerbee, "And so it goes."

NOTES

1   For example, see: "125 Detroit Officers Suspected of Crack Ties," *Detroit Free Press* (5 MAY 88:1A); "Corruption Among Drug Enforcers Startling," *The [Raleigh, NC] News and Observer* (17 APR 88:13A)' "Deputy Sheriff Jailed for Selling Cocaine," *The Lansing [MI] State Journal* (15 MAR 88:4B); "Drug Corruption Claims Growing Number of Miami Cops," *Law Enforcement News* (8 DEC 87:1); "State Drug Officer Arrested for Larceny of Drug Money," *The Lansing [MI] State Journal* (5 SEPT 87:1A); "400 Cases Will be Dropped Because D.C. Cops Stole Drugs," *USA Today* (17 Sept 87:3A); "13 New York Cops Charged With Shaking Down Drug Dealers," *The [MI] State News* (7 NOV 86:2); "Drug Use and Dealing with Cops Increasing," *The Detroit News* (28 MAR 86:A1-A6); "Grand Jury Indicts Flint Police Sergeant," The Flint [MI] Journal (22 JAN 86:A1).

2   It is emphasized that this paper is an overview of the research findings intended to highlight key factors of interest to both researchers and policymakers. Greater detail of the issues is presented in Carter and Stephens (1988) and Carter (forthcoming).

3   Four agencies had a "formal" internal review of drug use or corruption problems. These generally consisted of a short synopsis of the perceived extent of the problem and policy options for dealing with the problem.

4   There are legal, forensic, and ideological debates on drug testing that go beyond the scope of this chapter. Drug testing programs in police departments include random mandatory drug testing for all personnel, random testing for probationary officers, testing programs for persons in "sensitive" assignments, testing prior to promotion or reassignment, and testing during annual physicals.

5   Investigative and inspection techniques include integrity tests, interviews with persons arrested on drug charges, reconciliation of recorded drug seizures in the police property room with arrestee reports, and unobtrusive observations of changes in officers' lifestyles.

6   A "*Garrity* interview" is an internal affairs interview or deposition of a police officer accused of some misconduct for which the officer could be criminally prosecuted. Based on the case of *Garrity v. New Jersey*, the police department can compel an officer to testify against him/herself, however, the fruits of that testimony can only be used in departmental disciplinary proceedings (including a labor arbitration) but not as evidence in a criminal prosecution.

7   It bears repeating that the most common drug abuse problem among police officers is still alcohol.

8   There is some precedence for this in other forms of police/constituent interaction such as gambling, prostitution, and minor forms of corruption (See Barker & Carter, 1986).

9   There appear to be different standards for different drugs. Marijuana showed less consequence for peer group rejection than did cocaine or crack. Abuse of alcohol and prescription drugs had virtually no peer group rejection; in fact, these users typically would experience "protection" from the code of secrecy so the department would not learn of the problem. In these cases, officers appear to rationalize that the job contributed to the substance abuse, hence the officers deserved the protection. Instances of heroin use, or synthetic substances such as PCP, LSD, or designer drugs were not discovered in this study.

REFERENCES

Barker, T. (1977). "Peer Group Support for Police Occupational Deviance." *Criminology*, (November)15:3.

Barker, T. & D.L. Carter (1986). *Police Deviance*. Cincinnati: Anderson Publishing Co.

Blumberg, A.S. & E. Niederhoffer (eds.) (1985). *The Ambivalent Force* 3rd. Ed. New York: Holt, Rinehart, and Winston.

Bureau of Justice Statistics (1988). *Report to the Nation on Crime and Justice* 2nd. Ed. Washington, DC: U.S. Government Printing Office.

Carter, D.L. (1987). *Policy Issues in Police Drug Abuse*. Training Document for the Police Executive Research Forum. Washington, DC.

Carter, D.L. (1988). "Controlling Off-Duty Behavior: Higher Standards of Integrity for the Police." A paper presented at the annual meeting of the Academy of Criminal Justice Sciences. San Francisco.

Carter, D.L. (forthcoming). "Drug-Related Corruption of Police Officers: A Contemporary Typology." Internal policy paper in preparation as a journal article.

Carter, D.L. & D.W. Stephens (1988). *Drug Abuse by Police Officers: An Analysis of Critical Policy Issues*. Springfield, IL: Charles C Thomas, Publisher.

Commission to Investigate Allegations of Police Corruption and the City's Anti-Corruption Procedures. (Knapp Commission) (1973). New York: George Braziller.

Dishlacoff, L. (1976). "The Drinking Cop." *The Police Chief*, (43:5)9-18.

Goldstein, H. (1975). *Police Corruption: A Perspective on its Nature and Control*. Washington, DC: Police Foundation.

Hore, B.D. & M.A. Plant (eds.). *Alcohol Problems in Employment*. London: Crom Helm.

Jamieson, K.M. & T.J. Flanagan (eds.). *Sourcebook of Criminal Justice Statistics - 1986*. Washington, DC: Bureau of Justice Statistics.

Kennedy, D.B. (1977). *The Dysfunctional Alliance*. Cincinnati: Anderson Publishing Co.

Koehler, R.J. (1986). Chief of Personnel, New York City Police Department. Comments at conference on "Substance Abuse: The Dilemma of Law Enforcement", John Jay College of Criminal Justice. New York, NY. May 30.

Klockars C. (ed.) (1983). *Thinking About Police: Contemporary Readings*. New York: McGraw-Hill.

Kraska, P. & V. Kappeler (1983). "Police On-Duty Drug Use: A Theoretical and Descriptive Examination." *American Journal of Police*, (7:1)1-28.

McAlary, M. (1987). *Buddy Boys: When Good Cops Turn Bad*. New York: G.P. Putnam's Sons.

Michigan Association of Police (1987). "A Roundup of Other MAP 'Battles' in Pontiac." *News n' Views*, (Issue 1) pp. 5-7.

Olson, R. (1988). "Police Administrators' Perceptions of Drug Testing Law Enforcement Personnel." In D.L. Carter and D.W. Stephens (eds.) *Drug Abuse by Police Officers*. Springfield, IL: Charles C Thomas, Publisher.

Possumato, T. (1987). "Labor-Management Issues: The Union Point of View on Drug Testing." Presentation at the Police Executive Research Forum Program, *Police Drug Abuse and Testing: Issues and Information*. Arlington, Virginia (April 9-10).

Shahandeh, B. (1985). "Drug and Alcohol Abuse in the Workplace: Consequences and Countermeasures." *International Labour Review*, 124:233-247.

Stoddard, E.R. (1983). "Blue Coat Crime." In C. Klockars (ed.) *Thinking About Police: Contemporary Readings*. New York: McGraw-Hill.

Van, R. (1981). "Alcohol as a Problem Among Officers." In G. Henderson (ed.) *Police Human Relations*. Springfield, IL: Charles C Thomas, Publisher.

5

The Unmentionable Alternative:
The Need for, and the Argument Against, the Decriminalization of Drug Laws*

Peter B. Kraska
Kent State University

INTRODUCTION

According to recent opinion polls, illegal drugs are among the top political issues. This implies that for most Americans, our "intolerable" drug situation is as troublesome as the deficit, terrorism, poverty, and the growing AIDS epidemic. This perception either reflects an unfounded state of hysteria, or a legitimate social crisis justifying a "war-like" response to the problem. Those who see the problem as "drug-hysteria" are quick to cite election-year posturing by candidates and sensational media coverage of drug-related stories to support their position. They cite the finding that the overall use of illegal drugs has actually decreased in the last ten years -- especially among our youth (White House Drug Abuse, 1987). Furthermore, advocates of the "drug-hysteria" position point out that the social harm caused by illegal drugs is minimal when compared with other factors such as alcohol and tobacco.

* Support for this study was provided by a contributor who wishes to remain anonymous. Small sections of this chapter are also contained in a research study supported by the National Institute of Justice Research Fellowship Program (grant 88-IJ-CX-0017). I would like to thank Ralph Weisheit for his helpful comments and suggestions.

They go on to recommend treatment, education, and community program policies as the most appropriate methods to curtail drug usage.

Those advocating a "war on drugs," on the other hand, argue that new drugs and changes in the "drug culture" call for strong-handed measures in response to the drug problem. The emergence of the dangerous drug "crack", the untimely deaths of celebrities, and the apparent rise in drug-dealing gangs, gang warfare, and gang-related deaths are cited by these advocates in support of their declaration of a "war" on drugs. This group advocates "get tough" measures to combat the drug problem, including the use of the military, capital punishment for convicted dealers, and stiff penalties for anyone connected with drug usage.

It is obvious which perspective dominates in America today. The familiar litany of phrases reflects current thinking: "The War on Drugs," "Zero-Tolerance," "Drugs More Threatening Than Communism," "Just Say 'No'," "Crack Epidemic," and "The Death Penalty for Pushers" (Trager, 1986). Republicans and Democrats seem to agree on this hard-line approach. Anything less is unmentionable -- heretical.

As with any war, however, there are losses which must be acknowledged. In our battle against drugs, the losses continue to grow. When taken into perspective alongside our insignificant gains in this fight, old solutions must be questioned setting the stage for new proposals to arise. For many critics, the "war" has become too costly. New solutions are needed. Perhaps the most controversial solution (bordering on heresy to some) is to decriminalize/legalize many drugs currently proscribed under criminal statutes. Several television specials and a recent cover story by *Time* on legalization, "Thinking the Unthinkable," and *Newsweek*, "Should Drugs Be Legal?," all illustrate the recent interest in the issue (Morganthau, 1988; Koppel, 1988; Church, 1988). As with the war approach, both conservatives and liberals have joined together in support of this alternative, making the rationale in support of the decriminalization movement complex and varied.

This chapter will work through these complexities by first offering a simplified definition of the concept of "decriminalization." This definition is followed by a brief review of the history, relevant arguments, and empirical research related to decriminalization of drugs. It is important to note that there is very little research focusing upon the actual effects of the decriminalization of drugs. Inciardi's (1981) cost/benefit model is used to organize the discussion. The three sections include:

(1) the costs of criminalization,
(2) the potential benefits of decriminalization, and
(3) the potential costs of decriminalization.

It must be recognized that the argument for decriminalization will be more detailed and exhaustive only because of its novelty -- not necessarily its superiority.

DEFINING "DECRIMINALIZATION"

The terms "decriminalization" and "legalization" are often confused. Decriminalization is the reduction in severity of a criminal offense and the penalty associated with that offense (Morris & Hawkins, 1969; Packer, 1968). Marijuana possession, for instance, might be decriminalized from a felony offense to a misdemeanor. Legalization, on the other hand, is exactly what the word implies: removing or repealing statutory proscriptions entirely. To wit, possessing marijuana, once a criminal offense, becomes legal under the rubric of legalization. This chapter will intentionally coalesce the two concepts, and define decriminalization as any movement in the direction of their legalization. Legalization, thus, will be included within the term "decriminalization."

Fusing the concepts is necessary because of the misleading nature of the term, "legalization." Upon hearing the word, critics begin to conjure up images of all drug laws being repealed, a governmental approval for drug use, and the commercialization of marijuana, cocaine, and heroin by private business. As is illustrated, this is far from accurate: most advocates in support of the "legalization movement" only want to legalize certain drugs and tightly regulate the production and sale of those legalized. Decriminalization, thus, is simply a less threatening term.

THE HISTORY OF DECRIMINALIZATION

Prior to the 1900s, people were generally free to sell, buy, and use the narcotic of their choice. Social and personal control, not governmental, were the primary means of regulating its use. Although drugs like opium were as available and inexpensive as aspirin is today (Bakalar & Grinspoon, 1984; Trebach, 1982; Musto, 1973), narcotics generally were not perceived as a significant social problem. How did we get from this permissive state of affairs, only 80 years ago, to our current "all-out war on drugs"?

Americans tend to think that our drug problem is unique to our present generation. We often hear from certain political leaders that our current drug crisis is due to the permissive sixties' generation. They might be surprised to discover that historians estimate that early in this century, one individual out of every 400 people in the country was physically dependent on opium or its derivatives (Ray, 1983). Inciardi (1985) found that, "In the 1897 edition of the Sears Roebuck catalog, hypodermic kits, which included a syringe, two needles, two vials and a carrying case were advertised...." These were used for the injection of morphine.

This widespread addiction to, and overall use of, drugs at the turn of the century stemmed from three factors. First, the popularity of morphine among soldiers during the Civil War produced an increase in its use. Second, the influx of Chinese immigrants working on the nation's railroads created a natural increase in its use since the Chinese had a predilection for smoking opium. This form of recreation quickly gained popularity among many Americans (Morgan, 1982; Musto, 1973). And finally, the most influential factor contributing to the growth of the drug-using population was the "health tonic" industry. These patent medicines were claimed to cure everything from in-grown toenails to a weak heart; most were a concentrated mixture of cocaine, opium, and/or alcohol (Ray, 1983).

It was a conflict between the health tonic industry and the medical community that generated the first significant attempt by the government to regulate drugs in our society. In 1906, because of the medical community's influence, and Upton Sinclair's work, *The Jungle*, Congress passed the Pure Food and Drugs Act of 1906. This act required patent medicine manufacturers to clearly state the percentage of alcohol, morphine, marijuana, and heroin contained in their tonics. Because of the effectiveness of this law, Congress enacted a more stringent law on opium, making it illegal to import except for medical purposes.

The most important piece of legislation to be passed into law during this period was the Harrison Act of 1914 (Musto, 1973). The law called for the strict regulation of those people dispensing morphine, cocaine, and marijuana (physicians, dentists, and surgeons). By cutting off any legal means for obtaining drugs for purely recreational use, the Harrison Act cultivated a germinating illicit drug market. During this same time period, the U.S. Supreme Court decided that there should be no legal means for addicts to obtain drugs in order to support their addiction (U.S. 1919, 1922). The illegal drug market grew proportionately.

In an effort to reverse this enormous growth of the illicit drug market, Congress then passed a series of laws from 1922 to 1930 requiring even tougher sentences and fines for drug dealers. These laws brought the user into the purview of the criminal justice system by considering mere possession sufficient grounds for a "distribution" conviction. Most public officials had great faith in the efficacy of this hard line, criminal law approach (cited in Inciardi, 1985:17):

Snow Parties, which are said to have become so prevalent as to menace American civilization, will be made impossible by the

Jones-Miller bill governing the manufacture, importation and ex-
portation of habit forming drugs, which has been passed by
Congress and signed by President Harding. By striking at the
source of supply, the bill goes to the root of the evil, and, in time,
will eliminate it altogether.

This faith in the criminalization approach guided drug legislation into
the early 1970s. After World War II, Congress reacted to a widespread belief
that illegal drug addiction was increasing. In 1951, they passed the Boggs
Act, introducing stiff mandatory sentences for narcotic offenders (Musto,
1987). In 1956, Congress passed the Narcotics Drug Control Act that mandated a two- to ten-year prison sentence for the possession of marijuana.
States followed the U.S. Congress's punitive example, taking their precedence to an extreme. For example, in 1971, "In Virginia, the minimum
penalty for possessing more than 25 grains (about one-half teaspoonful) of
the drug (marijuana) is twenty years -- that is the same as the minimum
penalty for first degree murder" (Mills, 1971:68). During the same time period, a person in North Dakota could receive 99 years of hard labor for the
mere possession of marijuana. By this time, "the United States had adopted
one of the strictest narcotics control policies in the world" (Weissman,
1978:120).
    What fomented such harsh measures? The answer would not be com-
plete without mentioning Harry J. Anslinger. Anslinger was the commissioner of the Bureau of Narcotics from its inception in 1930 until 1962. He is
best known for his influence in the passage of the Marijuana Tax Act of 1937
and the Narcotic Drug Control Act of 1956. His entire career was devoted to
exposing the "criminogenic effect" of illegal drugs by relaying anecdotal accounts of the horrors of drugs (Inciardi, 1985; Trebach, 1982; Weissman,
1978; Musto, 1973; Lindesmith, 1968). His propaganda techniques were
quite effective in shaping public and legislative opinion:

An entire family was murdered by a youthful addict in Florida.
When officers arrived at the home, they found the youth staggering
about in a human slaughter-house. With an ax he had killed his
father, mother, two brothers, and a sister. He seemed to be in a
daze. He had no recollection of having committed the multiple
crime. The officers knew him ordinarily as a sane, a rather quiet
young man; now he was pitifully crazed. They sought the reason.
The boy said that he had been in the habit of smoking something
youthful friends called "muggles", a childish name for marijuana
(Inciardi, 1985:22).

Accounts of this type were often generalized to the entire nation. One report estimated that 50 percent of all crime in urban areas and 25 percent of all crimes were caused by the illicit drug addiction. The report also claimed that promoting drug addiction was one of the primary ways Communist China would destroy the core values of the United States (The Senate Committee, 1956). Drugs, drug dealers, and drug users became the moral scapegoats of the day.

Considering the punitive nature of drug laws in the 1950s and 1960s, a case could be made that widespread "decriminalization" of drug laws has already taken place (Brownell, 1988). A gradual decrease in the punitiveness of drug laws began in the early 1970s with the passage of the Comprehensive Drug Abuse Prevention and Control Act of 1970. The Act completely reconstructed the federal drug laws. Although the Act contained some punitive features, it did allow for probation for first-time drug offenders, and significantly reduced many of the penalties for dealers and users. Education and rehabilitation were encouraged as viable responses to the drug problem; little support was given to increases in the law enforcement response (Trebach, 1982).

Perhaps the most surprising outcome of the Controlled Substance Act was its stance on marijuana: a conservative commission studying the issues of marijuana recommended, "...that federal and state laws be changed so that private possession of small amounts of marijuana for personal use, and casual distribution of small amounts without monetary profit, would no longer be offenses..." (Farnsworth, 1972:1-2).

Shortly after this report, a wave of events signified the radical change in attitude with regard to marijuana. First, the National Organization for the Reform of Marijuana Law (NORML) began to gain political power and significantly influenced many politicians on the need for decriminalization of marijuana (Wisotsky, 1986). Second, the Canadian government issued a report in 1972, entitled the LeDain Report, strongly recommending that possession of marijuana be legalized in that country (Ray, 1983). Even the American Medical Association publicly voiced their support for eradicating criminal penalties for small amounts of marijuana, claiming, "there is no evidence supporting the idea that marijuana leads to violence, aggressive behavior, or crime (Lyons, 1972). Finally, William Buckley, one of the most conservative editorial columnists in America, publicly voiced his support for the decriminalization of drug laws (Ray, 1983).

This shift in thought had a tangible effect on the law. By the mid-1970s, 11 states had decriminalized the possession and use of marijuana (Slaughter, 1988). Oregon, Maine, Alaska, and Nebraska resorted to civil fines for possession of small amounts of marijuana. California, Minnesota, Mississippi, Colorado, Ohio, New York, and North Carolina simply reduced the original penalties to small fines. Eventually in Alaska, it became legal for anyone to grow and consume marijuana for their own personal use. It seemed the country was on its way to a "vice" approach to handling drugs in our society. The "vice" approach is similar to the method used during Prohibition where the burden of criminal sanction falls on the manufacturers and distributors rather than the consumers.

In 1978, President Jimmy Carter put into place an educational and rehabilitation-oriented approach to illegal drugs. He and his wife even publicly supported the decriminalization of marijuana laws (Ray, 1983). It is interesting to note that their son was discharged from the Navy because of marijuana use. Carter's influence eventually waned and the decriminalization movement suddenly died. Most attribute this death specifically to Congress' failure to pass legislation decriminalizing marijuana on the federal level (Inciardi, 1985). During this same period, the use of marijuana began to decline -- from 50 million Americans in the late 1970s reporting its use to only 25 million Americans in the mid-1980s (Hamoway, 1987).

The move towards our current hard-line approach to illicit drugs was inevitable -- it developed within the conservative whirlwind that swept the country in the early 1980s. As President Reagan asserted, "The mood towards drugs is changing in this country and the momentum is with us. We're making no excuses for drugs, hard, soft, otherwise. Drugs are bad and we're going after them" (Reagan, 1982). Almost immediately after his election, Reagan outlined a seven-step plan to eradicate drugs from society. This included a diversion of 708.8 million dollars from educational, treatment, and research programs to law enforcement programs. An additional 127.5 million dollars were appropriated for increased prison space, and to increase the personnel of the Drug Enforcement Administration and the Federal Bureau of Investigation. The old war on drugs was resurrected once again. To date, the war itself and the rhetoric about the war have constantly escalated. Some see gains in the battle; others see hysteria and counterproductive measures.

The Utility of History

History can serve two distinct and diametrical purposes. First, an understanding of the history of our nation's drug laws can be a tool for realizing the possibility for changing these laws. As we become more enlightened to the realization that mainstream thinking about our drug problem is the result of past decisions influenced more by hysteria and political struggles, than by empirical findings, we may discover that more reasonable decisions could have been made. Realizing that our official reaction to the drug problem is the result of questionable decisions and motives will move us beyond an acceptance of our current situation as a "natural" state of affairs (reification). From here, we can reconceptualize, research, and enact constructive alternatives to our current approach. Stated simply: an understanding of the past aids us in realizing the possibility and direction of change in the future.

For those comfortable with the mainstream approach, however, an historical understanding acts as a descriptive affirmation of how, in the end, the "best" approach prevailed even though there were interesting conflicts and struggles along the way. History, from this perspective, is a tool for affirming the superiority of the status quo. Unfortunately, the history of drug regulation can be interpreted either way. Historical perspective, therefore, although invaluable in some respects, has limitations in convincing others on the need for change.

THE NEED FOR DECRIMINALIZATION

In going beyond the limitations of an historical awareness of our drug laws, the next step is to discuss the arguments on the need for decriminalization. In order to detangle the various contentions, the discussion will be split into first, the unintended, negative consequences of our current war on drugs; and second, the advantages of decriminalizing drug laws. Inciardi (1981), makes this helpful distinction between a critique of the old and advantages of the new through his cost/benefit model. In borrowing Inciardi's method of analysis, this section is split into: (1) the "costs" of the war on drugs (a critical analysis of the present approach), and (2) the "benefits" of decriminalization.

The Costs of the War on Drugs

Our current "war on drugs" has many serious consequences that we usually do not think about, or assume as a "necessary price we have to pay." These consequences present costs which directly affect our youth, the police, and the poor in our country. Furthermore, our principles of liberty and justice are often called into question as we wage war on the drug problem. And finally, the current, war-like approach to this problem represents direct and obvious economic costs to our nation. It is the argument by those who advocate decriminalization that these costs are too extensive and counterproductive to rationalize as necessary casualties in the war on drugs.

The War On Our Youth

Nancy Reagan, at the beginning of her crusade against drugs, claimed, "We're in danger of losing our whole next generation" (cited in Trebach,

1987:135). Trebach (1987), discusses the destructive consequences of Nancy Reagan's type of extremist campaign against our youth and drug use. He claims that the rhetoric of Nancy Reagan and the various parent groups that support her perspective are not only far to the right of the facts, they have created unfounded hysteria. The unintended effects of this hysteria include:

(1) frequent violations of children's rights,
(2) the insular and dangerous stance that all of our youth's problems stem from, or are created by drug use,
(3) exaggerating information about the dangers of drugs by providing extreme information that often contradicts our youths' actual experiences, and
(4) labeling our young people as a "rotten, satanic, dying generation of youth" (Trebach, 1987:25).

As an example of their distortion of the facts, the parent's groups continually point to the astronomical growth of illegal drug use by today's youth (Trager, 1986); when in fact, almost all the credible research suggests exactly the opposite. For instance, the daily use of marijuana by high school students has decreased from 10.7 percent in 1978 to only 4.9 percent in 1985. Even the use of hallucinogens has dropped. An often cited governmental study comparing drug use from 1978 to 1985 found, "The most dramatic change between 1982 and 1985 was a drop of nearly half -- from 21.1 to 11.5 percent -- in the number of young adults who had ever used hallucinogens" (White House Drug Abuse, 1987). This downward trend began in 1977-78, before our most current war on drugs.

Trebach (1987) also argues that, contrary to what the mainstream position asserts, decriminalization will not significantly increase marijuana use among our youth. He cites research in Alaska and in Holland that have found that marijuana use has not increased once legalized. In Alaska, Dr. Segal of the University of Alaska demonstrates in his research that compulsive marijuana use among Alaska's youth is actually significantly *lower* than the rest of the nation. Moreover, Inciardi (1978:117) states that, "on the whole, where cannabis is tolerated, as in California and Oregon, its use has tended to drop." Brownell (1988) cites research findings in California that the daily use of marijuana dropped dramatically after the state decriminalized the drug. Although claiming that decriminalization caused these decreases would be going beyond the limits of the research, the fears that decriminalization would create an epidemic of drug use never materialized.

The final, and perhaps most destructive, consequence of the war approach on our youth is how the tremendous profit-motive brings lower-class youth into the realm of drug dealing and crime (Bakalar & Grinspoon, 1986; Ray, 1983; Gooberman, 1974). The tighter the drug market is squeezed by tougher law enforcement, the more lucrative dealing in illicit drugs becomes (Musto, 1987; Inciardi, 1985; Weismann & DuPont, 1982; Gooberman, 1974). While most of the law enforcement community argues that these crackdowns diminish supply, they must also recognize that such practices encourage youth to deal with illicit drugs, as they have the advantage of being handled by the more lenient juvenile justice system if caught. Gooberman's (1974) in-depth study of the effects of "Operation Intercept" (a massive governmental effort to curb the importation of marijuana across the Mexican-American border), confirms the unanticipated efforts of this "get-tough" policy on the youth population. He stresses that two unintended consequences of this supply-side effort were first, an increase in the number of youth dealing marijuana. And second, more youth were forced from the use of marijuana to the more potent and available drug, hashish. Whether decriminalization is the answer or not, introducing the juvenile into the illegal drug business is an unfortunate consequence of the war on drugs.

The Police

Other, but not often thought about, victims in our drug war are the sol-diers themselves -- the police. Law enforcement officers must risk the lethal dangers of battling powerful black-market organizations and gangs which are involved in the profitable drug industry (Trebach, 1987; Inciardi, 1985). They also have to resist the corrupting pressures of huge monetary gains by either becoming involved in, or turning the other cheek to, illegal drug dealings (Manning & Redlinger, 1986). Finally, they must battle the psychological pressures of waging a war against the same behavior that at least one-fourth of the nation participates in, and the constant realization that their efforts are, at best, a small Band-Aid on an infectious wound.

As in the days of alcohol prohibition, the lure of hopping on the prof-itable bandwagon of the illegal drug market is too seductive for many police and governmental officials to pass up. Practically every major city has had a corruption scandal involving illegal drugs (Trager, 1986). In Miami, an ex-ternal investigation of corruption and drug use by police officers has resulted in the indictment of 12 patrol and vice officers, with many more expected. All of those indicted are charged with the sale and possession of marijuana, various forms of cocaine, and Quaaludes (Kraska & Kappeler, 1988). After extensive research on the corrupting effects of the illicit drug market, Barnett (1987:98-99) states:

As I have observed elsewhere, the social consequences of the wholesale corruption of our legal system by the large amounts of black market money to be made in the drug trade have never been adequately appreciated. The extremely lucrative nature of the illicit drug trade makes the increased corruption of police, prosecutor, and judges all but inevitable.

The Constitution

Packer (1967:333) foresaw another type of corruption as the most disturbing danger of the drug war:

> A disturbing large number of undesirable police practices -- unconstitutional searches and seizures, entrapment, electronic surveillance -- have become habitual because of the great difficulty that attends the detection of narcotics offenses.

Barnett (1987) places the blame on the "victimless status" of legal prohibition of drugs. Using the concept "victimless" in a very limited sense, he argues that the police commit many constitutionally questionable practices because there is no victim to testify that a crime had actually occurred, or that the specific offender committed the crime. What the police have to resort to, then, is "systematic surveillance." They actually have to become the witnesses -- even if this means eavesdropping on private residences. As Barnett (1987:90) states, "the enormous interference with individual liberty that such surveillance would cause is quite obvious."

This basic difficulty has led to a considerable amount of frustration among narcotic control officers. Narcotic vice department investigations have revealed widespread violations of the constitutional rights of those already convicted in several major cities. The difficulty of "enforcing unenforceable laws" often requires the police to view constitutional rights as an unnecessary evil (Wisotsky, 1986; Hellman, 1976).

The Offenders

Most people would be a little short on sympathy for the big-time drug traffickers that are the end recipients of these constitutional violations. But many argue that we do need to consider the effect the drug war has on users and small-time dealers. Criminologists have long urged restraint in using criminal sanctions. One of the primary reasons is the destructive power of labeling someone a "criminal." This label can act as a self-fulfilling prophecy, through the label itself, and by closing the doors of employment opportunities for ex-offenders (Erickson, 1980). Moreover, research has shown that, for many, correctional institutions are a naturally corrupting environment, often assimilating inmates into the criminal subculture (Johnson, 1987). Bakalar and Grinspoon (1984) point out that if drug laws are intended to protect potential users from the dangerous effects of drugs, it is ironic that drug laws seem to harm users of drugs far more than the actual drug use. An undercover vice cop in Brian/College Station, Texas, best sums up the dilemma: "We're always setting up turds (term for small-time dealers) and sending them to jail or T.D.C. [Texas Department of Corrections]; it's kind of a waste. Many of them are alright guys, they have decent jobs, families...fortunately, I don't have to see what happens to their lives after the arrest" (Kraska, 1987).

The War On Our Poor

Stuart Mills (1971) noted in the early 1970s that one of the most serious negative consequences of the war on drugs was discriminatory law enforcement against society's "undesirables" (he primarily meant "hippies" and "beatniks"). A strong argument can be made that the same is happening today with our poor.

Criminologists agree that the bulk of law enforcement efforts at fighting crime is directed towards the lower class. This is justified by the finding that statistically, the majority of "garden-variety" crimes (i.e., robbery, burglary, assault) are committed by this lower-income group. Although many criminologists disagree with the validity of these statistics, the figures continue to be used to explain away what appears to be a class-differentiated law enforcement response to most crimes.

Now, suppose that some "crimes" were committed across all social classes. The justification for differential law enforcement across class boundaries would be refuted. An exclusive war-like approach towards either the rich or poor, excluding other criminal groups, would clearly be seen as discriminatory. Do such crimes exist? Certainly. Research has proven that illegal drug use occurs in all sectors of society including doctors, lawyers, police officers, celebrities, and sport stars (Kraska & Kappeler, 1988; Shahandeh, 1985; Ray, 1983). With over 24 million admitted marijuana smokers and 12 million cocaine users, hardly anyone would disagree that drugs had spread into the mainstream of society (Wisotsky, 1986). Illegal drug use knows no class boundaries.

The controversial question seems obvious: Is it "just" to wage the war on drugs only against the poor -- a relatively powerless class of people in our society? And, why is it that we immediately think "treatment" for the upper class, or celebrity addict, when prison seems the proper place for a lower-class heroin or "crack" addict? Similarly, we think nothing of the police raiding lower-class homes and neighborhoods in the justified pursuit of illegal drugs, drug dealers, and drug users. At the same time, however, we are aghast at the Coast Guard's "Zero-Tolerance" program of searching and seizing equipment and boats from middle- to upper-class citizens on the coastal states. The Coast Guard's tactics, common practices in the lower-class sections of the cities, were quickly curtailed.

One of the negative consequences of our war on drugs, therefore, is a discriminatory criminal justice response against the poor. Those advocating decriminalization believe that this argument must be taken seriously for two reasons. First, tunneling most of our energies in a downward direction towards the lower and under classes inhibits us from looking upward. In other words, law enforcement efforts seldom focus on the banks and real estate agencies that support and make enormous amounts of money from the illegal drug industry. As Long (1986:12) explains, banks and real estate agencies collaborate with drug suppliers by, "...assisting traffickers in moving large numbers of dollars from one country to another and in laundering those dollars through legitimate investments."

Second, as we become desperate for solutions to the drug problem, disturbing policy recommendations directed specifically at the poor are being made. For instance, Kaplan (1988:45) recommends "taking the drug problem seriously" by implementing selective enforcement in lower-class urban areas in order to "...drive much of the dealing indoors where a large percentage of potential customers are afraid to go." Again, our solution is to arrest, process, and incarcerate the poor, overlooking more just, and imaginative alternatives.

Besides the injustice of a discriminatory law enforcement response, we are also sending a negative message to the American people about the administration of justice in this country, fomenting disrespect for the law as a legitimate social institution.

Disrespect for the Law

The criminal law approach to our nation's drug problem breeds disrespect in other ways as well. An argument often voiced in the late 1960s by many prestigious legal scholars is that illegal drug laws themselves generate disrespect for the law (Morris & Hawkins, 1969; Packer, 1968; Kadish, 1967; Allen, 1964). Their argument is that the scope of the criminal law has been seriously overextended. Criminal laws that attempt to criminalize activities that affect a person's health or morality place the seriousness of the criminal sanction in jeopardy. The criminal law must be reserved for only our most serious social harms. Both the lack of a direct victim, and a lack of societal consensus about the crime, render the use of the criminal law and its machinery overextended, outside the realm of their inherent limits.

A Step Towards Big Brotherism

Thomas Szaz (1987), perhaps the most "progressive" decriminalization advocate, raises even more fundamental issues about the criminalization of drug use. He focuses on the rights of Americans to partake in whatever food or mind-altering substance they wish, as long as they understand the dangers involved. He notes that prior to 1914, with the passage of the Harrison Act, we had the fundamental right to "self-control" our diets and drugs. He blames the deterioration of this basic right on the medical community. He sees today's society as therapeutic, as the medieval Spanish society was theocratic. While the Spaniards believed that the masses needed to be protected from select books and ideas, so does "Big Brother" feel today that it must forbid a drug like marijuana while promoting the tobacco and alcohol industry. Szaz's (1986:344) point is made clear in this passage:

> The argument that people need the protection of the state from dangerous drugs, but not from dangerous ideas, is unpersuasive. No one has to ingest any drug he does not want, just as no one has to read a book he does not want. Insofar as the state assumes control over such matters, it can only be in order to subjugate its citizens -- venting them from assuming self-determination over their lives, as befits an enslaved population.

Szaz sees repressive measures to control the use of illegal drugs as an extreme overextension of the medical communities, and the government's control in people's private affairs. He especially fears the increasingly "warlike" measures taken and advocated by those who propagandize the evils of drugs. Although Szaz' position may seem hyper-critical on the surface, his fears may have some basis.

The mayor of New York City, Ed Koch, and the Commissioner of Customs, Von Raab, both advocate a rather distressing drug-reduction proposal (Koppel, 1988). In attempting to diminish the "demand" side of our drug problem, they propose to boost efforts at detecting, apprehending and prosecuting the largest consumer group of illegal drug users in this country -- the "casual," otherwise law-abiding user. Once prosecuted and found guilty, this large group of citizens (comprised of all occupational groups and social classes) would have to be punished severely enough to send a "zero-tolerance" message to the users themselves and to the rest of the American people. We could not, of course, place them in our already burgeoning prisons and jails, so Von Raab and Koch advocate a war-time tactic: sentence and detain the "users" of illegal drugs in state-operated "work camps." These work camps, ostensibly designed to detain large numbers of American citizens in an unpleasant place of confinement, would stress the virtues of "hard work."

Von Raab and Koch did not clarify the specific meaning of "work camp." However, envisioning the consequences of such a proposal -- millions of American citizens detained in prison camps across the country -- should invoke fear in the minds of anyone with an awareness of the use of "work camps" in our world's history. From Szaz' perspective, this extreme type of proposal illustrates the alarming steps towards "Big Brotherism" that some influential political and agency officials are willing to take in our war against drugs.

The Black Market

With the government attempting to protect us from the dangers of illicit drug use, an ironic situation has arisen. It almost seems to be a contradictory statement: the stringent criminalization of drugs greatly contributes to the power and influence of the illicit drug market. In other words, the solution is a significant part of the problem. There are many reasons for this. The simplest is that, despite enormous increases in funding and manpower, law enforcement officials only manage to stop around 10 percent of illegal drugs imported to, and manufactured in, the United States (Hamoway, 1987; Trebach, 1987; Inciardi, 1985). Even the most zealous law enforcement efforts have had little significant impact on this percentage (sometimes as high as 15 percent) (Wisotsky, 1986). In the meantime, tougher enforcement causes the price of the related illegal narcotic to increase dramatically. Higher prices mean enhancing the profit-incentive to deal in illegal drugs, and providing the black market with even more investment capital. Escalating the war on drugs, therefore, only escalates the depth and width of the black market. Supply-side control has been a dismal failure (Reuter, 1988; Slaughter, 1988; Nadelmann, 1988; Wisotsky, 1986; Gooberman, 1974).

The consequences of this illicit drug market are well known. For instance, the emergence of drug gangs in our inner cities and violence and crime associated with these gangs is beginning to receive more attention. Many cities have reported a dramatic increase in gang- and drug-related murders and other violent crimes (Morganthau, 1988).

The Economic Costs Of The War On Drugs

The dollar is the bottom line for most policy decisions. This is why decriminalization advocates quickly point out that the Drug Enforcement Administration has an annual budget of over $1 billion a year. Overall, we spend more than $10 billion a year trying to suppress the supply of drugs into and within this country (Bakalar & Grinspoon, 1984). What are the benefits of these enormous costs? As mentioned above, about 10 percent of illicit drugs are seized (Wisotsky, 1986).

Now, consider the effects of decriminalization. Research by Aldrich and Mikuriya (1988) in California examined the economic effects of the passage of the Moscone Act, which significantly reduced the penalties for many marijuana offenses. By adding up the savings from reduced arrest costs, court costs, prison costs, and parole costs, California has saved nearly $100 million a year, or a total of $1 billion since 1976. Moreover, decriminalizing these laws did not cause an increase in marijuana use (Mandel, 1987). Conversely, the extremely punitive "Rockefeller" laws, passed in New York in the early 1970s, had two primary effects. First, they immediately over filled the courts and jails (Pekkanen, 1980). Second, the laws introduced juveniles into the illegal drug business (Ray, 1983). The intended effect of reducing drug dealing and drug use rates was never achieved (Hamoway, 1987; Ray, 1983; Pekkanen, 1980).

Criminalization is simply not economically feasible. Decriminalization not only has the potential to save billions through cutting criminal justice costs, it could also generate huge revenues through governmental taxation of those drugs decriminalized. The revenues generated combined with those saved, could be applied to education, community, treatment, and social programs.

Criminalization Doesn't Work

To recap, decriminalization advocates argue that there are too many social and economic costs -- with very few gains -- to justify the continuance of our current approach. The police, drug users and small-time dealers, our youth, the poor, our Constitution, and our freedom are all victims in the war on drugs. Moreover, the war on drugs is counterproductive to its own goals. The situation has reached crisis proportion. The mainstream, hard-line approaches have failed throughout history, and there seems little chance that they will fare any better today or in the future. Some alternatives must be considered.

The Benefits of Decriminalization

In light of the above negative consequences, some ask: "Are the costs of criminalization worth the benefits?" and "What alternatives are there?" According to decriminalization advocates, reducing many drug offenses and legalizing others, will diminish or eliminate many of the aforementioned costs.

Unfortunately, decriminalization advocates are at this time long on criticisms and short on focused literature and/or research specifically outlining the overall benefits and methods of decriminalization. Criticizing the mainstream approach, though, exposed a few obvious benefits of decriminalization. These include:

(1) Regaining a respect for criminal laws and the criminal justice system as a means, not for regulating peoples morality, but rather preventing and responding to our most serious social harms;

(2) Helping to curb the extreme intrusion the police and government must employ to be even marginally effective in the war on drugs; and,

(3) Clearing the smoke-filled air from the war on drugs so that alternative ways of dealing with the problem can be envisioned and discussed.

The remainder of the benefits to accrue from decriminalization must be discussed more thoroughly.

Additional Resources

Decriminalization of drugs would generate additional revenues through two sources. The most obvious is the money that would be saved by reducing the role that the federal, state, and local police, courts and prisons have in combating the war on drugs. Recall that, in California, a simple reform in marijuana laws and police practices has saved approximately $1 billion. The second source would be the revenues generated through the taxation of drugs similar to alcohol and tobacco. Combined, an enormous amount of money could go towards effecting the demand side of illicit drugs. Most decriminalization advocates recommend better and more realistic educational programs, comprehensive treatment programs, and community-based prevention programs (Szaz, 1987; Trebach, 1987; Wisotsky, 1986; Ray, 1983; Hellman, 1975).

Diminish the Illicit Drug Market

No systematic research exists that supports or refutes the contention that decriminalization of drug laws will, in turn, diminish the illicit drug market. In recalling the history of decriminalization, though, we noted the cause of the emergence of the black market -- namely, the lack of any legal means to obtain sought-after illicit drugs. Does this mean the reverse is true? De-criminalization advocates assume it is: decriminalization will subdue the ille-gal narcotic market. By making certain drugs legally available, buyers will be channeled toward legitimate sources, like the government. The overall power and destructive consequences of the illegal market would crumble, even though some of the market would always remain in tact.

Norval Morris (1969:9) summarizes their claim well:

> The one certain way totally to destroy the criminal organizations engaged in the narcotics trade and to abolish addict crime would be to remove the controls and make narcotics freely available to ad-dicts. We do not propose the abolition of all controls over impor-tation, manufacture, and distribution of drugs, nor the abolition of penalties against those unauthorized persons who trade in drugs for profit; but we are convinced that if addiction were treated as a medical matter, this would undercut the illicit traffic and largely eliminate the profit incentive supporting that traffic.

A Reduction in Crime

The war on drugs has historically been justified on the grounds that drugs cause crime. This argument is also frequently heard today. As is noted below, research does show a link between illegal drugs and crime (Speckart & Anglin, 1988; Wish, 1987; Anglin & Speckart, 1986; McBride & McCoy, 1982). It is ironic then, that decriminalization advocates justify the abolition of many drug laws on the basis that the drug *laws* cause crime. The question arises, what is responsible for the high amount of drug-related crimes -- the drugs or the drug laws? This question, when taking into consideration the voluminous literature on the link between drugs and crime, is not easily answered. However, decriminalization advocates assert that this answer is not needed for their purposes. Part of their argument revolves around their thesis that decriminalization would crumble the black market and presumably the violence and crime associated with the illicit drug organi-zations and gangs. This would be the primary crime reduction effect associ-ated with decriminalization. Additionally, decriminalization would diminish crimes motivated by the need to support an expensive illegal drug addiction. Decriminalization would lower the costs of the drugs and, in some cases, make them available on an outpatient basis. The best example of this is the practice of dispensing heroin to addicts. The reasoning here is that heroin addicts' high involvement in property crimes, in order to support their habits, is diminished (Trebach, 1982; Kaplan, 1978). The advantage of this approach is two-fold: it allows for the treatment of the addicts and at the same time keeps them out of trouble.

THE COSTS OF DECRIMINALIZATION

Advocates of decriminalization have a slight advantage: the historical gift of hindsight. They can scrutinize the negative consequences of the get-tough approach *ex post facto*. Advocates of the war approach, however, can only speculate as to what might be the negative consequences of decriminalization. They cannot be certain that their predictions are accurate, but a few of the more popular speculations are definitely noteworthy.

Increased Usage

Opponents to decriminalization believe that criminalizing illicit drugs has two primary effects that curb the extent of drug usage in society. The first is that law enforcement efforts diminish the availability of illegal drugs to the average person. A potential user has to overcome many obstacles such as high prices, the risk of detection, and the inconvenience of finding a supplier. Second, the prevention or discouragement of crime through fear -- induced by sanctioning drug offenders (deterrent effect) -- is assumed. Legalizing drugs would neutralize both these constraining forces, thereby opening the door for a literal epidemic of illicit drug usage. Accordingly, the number of problems and costs associated with illegal drug use -- more addicts, more crime, and more youthful users -- will also increase. Overall, Kaplan (1988) believes that we would experience enormous public health costs as a result of decriminalizing drug laws.

More Crime

Inciardi's (1979:335) well-known research on 356 heroin addicts concludes that, "the data on current criminal activity clearly demonstrate not only that most heroin users were committing crimes, but also that they were doing so extensively and for the purpose of drug use support." A more recent article by Speckart and Anglin (1988:226) concludes, "both current and earlier works cited, we believe, present strong evidence that there is a strong causal relationship, at least in the United States, between addiction to narcotics and property crime levels." Although the issue will always be debated, it is reasonable to assume that there is a relationship (whether or not it is causal is questionable) between drugs and crime. Opponents of decriminalization, in believing the usage of drugs will dramatically increase, also believe that crime will increase proportionally. Additionally, this link also justifies handling drug offenders as criminals -- not just people with a drug problem, or poverty-stricken victims driven by the lucrative drug business.

Moral Deterioration

Robert Cole, a Harvard psychiatrist, claims that legalization would be a "moral surrender of far-reaching implication about the way we treat each other" (Church, 1988:16). His fear: rampant hedonism. Many perceive illicit drugs as simply wrong. "Drugs are not bad because they're illegal. They're illegal because they're bad" (Church, 1988:16). The same could be said of prostitution; although prostitution laws will not eliminate the behavior, they serve at least a partial function in officially recognizing the immorality of the act. In the same way, many argue that drug laws were created and now are supported on the belief that taking mind-altering substances for recreational purposes is immoral. Drugs are seen as an evil; a seductive force from which the American people must be sheltered. The widespread use of drugs signifies a deterioration of the core values of American society. Legislating morality in this instance is, therefore, justified -- the American people must be protected.

"Drugs Are Okay"

What would be the effect, then, of "de-legislating morality" (decriminalizing drug laws)? The message from the American government would be clear: we have lost the war on drugs and now concede that taking illicit drugs is okay. Regardless of how many cautions about the dangers of drug use that were tagged on to the decriminalization legislation, the American people would still interpret this move as a governmental endorsement for taking illicit drugs.

HINDRANCES TO THE
DECRIMINALIZATION MOVEMENT

The "Drugs are Okay" argument, although not that imposing on the surface, is probably one of the greatest hindrances to the decriminalization of drug laws. Americans have become highly reliant on the law to delineate moral boundaries. For better or worse, the law as a social institution is increasingly becoming America's omnipotent regulator, organizer, controller, and teacher. One effect of the breadth and depth of the law is a blending (or some would argue confusing) of unethical/immoral behavior and illegal behavior (Lieberman, 1981). The prevailing attitude, thus, is that if a particular behavior does not break any laws, then that behavior is not wrong. Related to decriminalizing drug laws, the opponents have a strong argument: if decriminalized, a message would be sent to the American people that drug use is not illegal, therefore, it is not wrong. It is highly unlikely that lawmakers will pass any new legislation in this direction unless the message is clear that such legislation does not imply a "pro-drug" stance. This would require fundamental changes in the thinking of the American people and the role the law plays in representing our morals.

Another hindrance to decriminalization requiring fundamental change is discussed by Wisotsky (1986:174) who states, "public criticism does not occur very often because seven decades of Government propaganda about the evils of drugs have deprived the public of the power of critical thought respecting drugs and cowed it into silence." This is precisely the reason this chapter is entitled, "The Unmentionable Alternative." The information that we receive every day from the media (and indirectly from criminal justice agencies) is skewed towards the 326 deaths a year involving cocaine (Wisotsky, 1986); or the quite rare cases of violence caused by PCP (Inciardi, 1985). Of course, these cases are tragic. However, when compared to the 50,000 to 200,000 deaths each year caused by alcohol (Institute of Medicine, 1980), and the fact that 350,000 people will die next year of cigarette-caused lung disease (Buckley, 1988), we can begin to put the problem into perspective, and more rationally prioritize our concerns. Because of our war approach we seldom hear from the majority of drug-using Americans who lead productive, and otherwise law-abiding lives (Trebach, 1987; Bakalar & Grinspoon, 1984). The point here is not that we must condone drug-using behavior, but rather, that the current approach deprives the American people and their representatives the necessary balanced information for reasonable decision-making. Until a more balanced discourse is realized, the argument for decriminalization will fall on deaf ears.

With these limitations in mind, it is interesting to note that recently the debate has opened up tremendously. Besides the feature article in *Time*, which focused mainly upon the "pros" of the decriminalization debate, Phil Donahue, host of one of the nation's most popular daytime television talk shows, recently gave some of the country's most respected proponents of decriminalization a chance to discuss the issue. Then, in September of 1988, Ted Koppel, the host of the television news show *Nightline*, aired a prime time special on "The Legalization of Drugs." The show's panel included a distinguished panel of both political and intellectual heavyweights. According to the politicians, the U.S. Congress will begin debating this issue in the next few months. Whether these developments are an indication of more open thinking, or mere desperation, the "can of worms" is open. It seems that in the near future, advocates of decriminalization will come out of the closet and begin to mention the unmentionable.

In order for this more open discussion to yield anything constructive, however, advocates of decriminalization must streamline their arguments. As evidenced in Table 5.1, there are a number of diverse criticisms of the mainstream approach and potential benefits of decriminalization. Although impressive in breadth, the discussions are, with a few exceptions, vague, un-refined, and disparate. If decriminalization arguments are to have any effect, they must be clearly stated with specific recommendations for policy. Until this task is undertaken, discussions of decriminalization will probably stay confined to the more esoteric sectors of the academic community -- having little effect on our current approach in handling our drug problem.

Table 5.1
Decriminalizing Drug Laws

Costs of Current Approach	Benefits of Decriminalization
Youth as Victims	Regaining Respect for the Law
Offenders as Victims	Reduction in Big Brotherism
Police as Victims	Clearing the Air for Alternatives to the War on Drugs
The Erosion of Constitutional Rights	Generating and Saving Revenue Rights through Taxation and Reduced CJ Response
The War On Our Poor	Diminishing the Black Market and Drug Gangs
Breeding Disrespect for the Law	Reduction in Crime
A Step Towards Big Brotherism	
The Creation and Escalation of the Black Market	
The Enormous Economic Costs	
The Ineffectiveness of the Criminal Law Approach	

REFERENCES

Aldrich, M.R. & T. Mikuriya (1988). "Savings in California Marijuana Law Enforcement Costs Attributable to the Moscone Act of 1976 -- A Summary." *Journal of Psychoactive Drugs*, 20(1), 75-81.

Allen, F.A. (1964). *The Borderland of Criminal Justice*. Chicago, IL: Chicago University Press.

Anglin, M.D. & G. Speckart (1986). "Narcotics Use, Property Crime and Dealing: Structural Dynamics Across the Addiction Career." *Journal of Quantitative Criminology*, 153-170.

Anglin, M.D. & G. Speckart (1988). "Narcotics Use and Crime: A Multisample, Multimethod Analysis." *Criminology*, 26(3), 197-233.

Bakalar, J.B. & L. Grinspoon (1984). *Drug Control in a Free Society*. New York: Cambridge University Press.

Barnett, R.E. (1987). "Curing the Drug-Law Addiction: The Harmful Side Effects of Legal Prohibition." In R. Hamoway (ed.), *Dealing With Drugs: Consequences of Governmental Control*. San Francisco: Pacific Research Institute for Public Policy.

Brownell, G.S. "Marijuana and the Law in California: A Historical and Political Overview." *Journal of Psychoactive Drugs*, 20(1), 71-74.

Buckley, W.F., Jr. (July 11, 1988). "Prescriptions for Drug Problem." *Houston Post*.

Buckley, W.F., Jr. (December 18, 1972). "Pot, Legalization of, Conservative Division." *New York Times*.

Church, G.J. (May 30, 1988). "Thinking the Unthinkable." *Time*.

Erickson, P.G. (1980). *Cannabis Criminals: The Social Effects of Punishment on Drug Users*. Ontario: Best Printing.

Farnsworth, D.L. (1972). "Summary of the Report of the National Commission on Marijuana and Drug Abuse." *Tracks*, 9, 1-2.

Gooberman, L.A. (1974). *Operation Intercept: The Multiple Consequences of Public Policy*. New York: Pergamon Press.

Hamoway, R. (1987). *Dealing With Drugs: Consequences of Governmental Control*. San Francisco: Pacific Research Institute for Public Policy.

Hellman, A.D. (1975). *Laws Against Marijuana: The Price We Pay*. Champaign: University of Illinois Press.

Inciardi, J.A. (1979). "Heroin Use and Street Crime." *Crime and Delinquency*, 25, 335-346.

Inciardi, J.A. (1981). Marijuana Decriminalization Research: A Perspective and Commentary. *Criminology*, 19(1), 145-159.

Inciardi, J.A. (1985). *The War On Drugs: Heroin, Cocaine, Crime, and Public Safety*. Palo Alto, CA: Mayfield Press.

Institute of Medicine (1980). *Alcoholism, Alcohol Abuse and Related Problems: Opportunities for Research*. Washington, DC: National Academy Press.

Johnson, R. (1987). *Hard Time: Understanding and Reforming the Prison*. Monterey, CA: Brooks/Cole Publishing Company.

Kadish, S.H. (1967). "The Crisis of Overcriminalization." *The Annals of the American Academy of Political and Social Science*, 374, 157.

Kaplan, J. (1988). "Taking Drugs Seriously." *The Public Interest*, 2(92), 32-65.

Kaplan, J. (1983). *The Hardest Drug: Heroin and Public Policy*. Chicago, IL: University of Chicago Press.

Kaplan, J. (1970). *Marijuana -- The New Prohibition*. New York: World, 160.

King, R. (1972). *The Drug Hang-up: America's Fifty Year Folly*. New York: W.W. Norton and Company.

Koppel, T. (Host) (Sept. 13, 1988). *The Legalization of Drugs* [Television Documentary]. American Broadcasting Company.

Kraska, P.B. (1987). Notes from field interviews with an undercover narcotic agent.

Kraska, P.B. & V. Kappeler (1988). "Police On-duty Drug Use: A Theoretical and Descriptive Examination." *American Journal of Police*, VII(1).

Lieberman, J.K. (1981). *The Litigious Society*. New York: Basic Books.

Lindesmith, A.R. (1968). *The Addict and the Law*. Bloomington, IN: Indiana University Press.

Long, R.E. (1986). *Drugs and American Society*. New York: H.W. Wilson Company.

Lyons, R.P. (June 21, 1972). "AMA Would Drop Serious Penalties." *New York Times*.

Mandel, J. (1987). "Are Lower Penalties a Green Light for Drug Users?" *Journal of Psychoactive Drugs*, 19(4), 383-385.

Manning, P.K. & L.J. Redlinger (1986). "Invitational Edges of Corruption: Some Consequences of Narcotic Law Enforcement." In T. Barker & D.L. Carter (eds.) *Police Deviance*. Cincinnati: Anderson Publishing Co.

McBride, D.C. & C.B. McCoy (1982). "Crime and Drugs: The Issues and the Literature." *Journal of Drug Issues*, 12, 137-152.

Mills, S.L. (1971). *Crime, Power, Morality: The Criminal-Law Process in the United States*. Scranton, OH: Chandler Publishing.

Morgan, P.A. (1982). "History of Legal Controls." In J. Weissman (ed.) *Criminal Justice and Drugs: The Unresolved Connection*. New York: Associated Faculty Press.

Morganthau, T. (May 30, 1988). "Should Drugs Be Legal?" *Newsweek*, 36-38.

Morris, N. & G. Hawkins (1969). *The Honest Politicians Guide to Crime Control*. Chicago, IL: University of Chicago Press.

Musto, D.F. (1973). *The American Disease: Origins of Narcotic Control.* New Haven, CT: Yale University Press.

Musto, D.F. (1987). "The History of Legislative Control Over Opium, Cocaine, and Their Derivatives." In R. Hamoway (ed.) *Dealing with Drugs: Consequences of Governmental Control.* San Francisco: Pacific Research Institute for Public Policy.

Nadelmann, E.A. (1988). "The Case For Legalization." *The Public Interest,* 2(92), 3-31.

Packer, H.L. (1968). *The Limits of the Criminal Sanction.* Stanford, CA: Stanford University Press.

Pekkanen, J.R. (1980). "Drug Law Enforcement Effects." In *Drug Abuse Council: The Facts About Drug Abuse.* New York: Free Press.

Ray, O. (1983). *Drugs, Society, and Human Behavior.* St. Louis, MO: The C.V. Mosby Company.

Reagan, R. (1982). Presidential Speech in October, 1982.

Reuter, P. (1988). "Can The Borders Be Sealed?" *The Public Interest,* 2(92), 51-152.

Shahandeh, B. (1985). "Drug and Alcohol Abuse in the Workplace: Consequences and Countermeasures." *International Labour Review,* 124(2), 137-152.

Slaughter, J.B. (1988). "Marijuana Prohibition in the United States: History and Analysis of a Failed Policy." *Columbia Journal of Law and Social Problems,* 21(4), 417-474.

Szaz, T. (1987). "The Morality of Drug Controls." In R. Hamoway (ed.) *Dealing With Drugs: Consequences of Governmental Control.* San Francisco: Pacific Research Institute for Public Policy.

Trager, O. (1986). *Drugs in America: Crisis or Hysteria?* New York: Facts on File Publication.

Trebach, A.S. (1982). *The Heroin Solution*. New Haven, CT: Yale University Press.

United States v. Behrman, 258 U.S. 280 (1922).

Webb v. United States, 249 U.S. 96, 99 (1919).

Weissman, J.C. (1978). *Drug Abuse: The Law and Treatment Alternatives*. Cincinnati: Anderson Publishing Co.

Weissman, J.C. & R.L. DuPont (1982). *Criminal Justice and Drugs: The Unsolved Connection*. New York: Associated Faculty Press.

Wepner, R.S. & J.A. Inciardi (1978). "Decriminalizing Marijuana." *International Journal of Offender Therapy and Comparative Criminology*, 22(2), 115-126.

White House. (1984). "Drug Abuse Policy Office, Office of Policy Development." *National Strategy for Prevention of Drug Abuse and Drug Trafficking*. (Washington, DC: U.S. Government Printing Office.)

White House. (1987). *Drug Abuse and Drug Abuse Research*. The Second Triennial Report to Congress from the Secretary, Department of Health and Human Services.

Wish, E.D. (1987). "Drug Use Forecasting: New York, 1984-1986." *Research in Action*. National Institute of Justice, U.S. Department of Justice.

Wisotsky, S. (1986). *Breaking the Impasse in the War on Drugs*. New York: Greenwood Press.

Section II

DRUG USE AND CRIME

Few dispute that drugs and crime are related, but the nature of that relationship is complex. There are drug-intoxicated individuals who commit crimes because they have lost their natural inhibitions while under the influence. However, these crimes constitute only a fraction of the offenses which can be attributed to drugs, and even for these cases there is dispute about whether the influence of the drugs caused crime or merely provided a rationalization for it. There are also crimes which stem from the drug business (e.g., fights during the course of drug deals) and crimes which arise from economic necessity, because users need money to purchase more drugs. Broader discussions of these issues are available elsewhere. In this section of the book, the authors focus on specific topics related to the drugs-crime connection.

In the opening chapter of this section, Duane C. McBride and James Swartz consider the link between drug use and violence. They describe how the image of this relationship has changed over time, from the origins of the drug problem in the United States to the present. While the pharmacological effects of a particular drug are relevant, the link between drugs and violence is also shaped by social patterns of use and by economic factors. McBride and Swartz argue that the link between crack cocaine and violence is not merely an illusion created by the media. Crack-related violence is cause for particular concern because of the convergence of particular social, economic, and pharmacological factors.

Henry Brownstein and Paul Goldstein utilize police records to develop "A Typology of Drug-Related Homicide." Their work suggests that Goldstein's typology (psychopharmacological, systematic, and economic-compulsive) of motivators for drug-related violence is a useful way to categorize drug-related homicides. Surprising to many will be their finding that most drug-related homicides were psychopharmacological, that is, the killing arose as a result of long- or short-term drug use. Over half of the cases fit this category. Only about 20 percent of the cases were homicides which arose as a result of participation in the drug business, and only a few cases arose because of the economic desperation produced by a drug lifestyle.

139

In the next chapter, Bruce Johnson, Mitchell Kaplan, and James Schmeidler focus on heroin users on the street who also engage in drug distribution activity; and when the users engaged in such activities, they were most likely to serve as brokers between buyers and sellers, rather than engaging in direct sales. Surprisingly, drug thefts were relatively rare. Although on active days these users often engaged in numerous transactions, their drug distribution activities yielded them an average of only about $45 per day of activity. From these findings, the authors raise a series of social policy questions regarding the street-level sale of drugs.

Next, Helene White examines "The Drug Use-Delinquency Connection Among Adolescents." White not only pulls together the extensive and often contradictory literature on the topic, but uses new data to further explore problem areas. It is concluded that drug use and delinquency are not causally related among adolescents. Regardless of the extent to which they use drugs, most users have little involvement in serious delinquency. Further, while adolescents vary widely in their delinquency and substance use, peer group influences are among the best predictors of both drug use and delinquency. Finally, it is suggested that studying minor drug use among normal populations of adolescents has not been very fruitful. Instead, it is suggested that future research focus on those adolescents who are heavily engaged in the use of hard drugs.

In the final chapter of this section, Larry Gould and Doris MacKenzie consider the link between driving while intoxicated (DWI) and crime. Utilizing data from Louisiana, they find that compared with other drivers those arrested for DWI have far more extensive criminal histories. While the prior arrests of DWI offenders are likely to be for violent crime, such as assault or battery, these offenders also have more extensive histories of such nonviolent offenses as theft or burglary. DWI offenders are also five times more likely to have prior arrests for drug offenses, suggesting that alcohol, drugs, and crime may all be interrelated. This chapter again highlights the value of broadly defining "drugs" when we seek to understand the drugs-crime connection. There is a great deal to be learned about how the social and legal response to alcohol might inform policies regarding illicit drugs. Like illicit drug users, DWI offenders place a tremendous burden on the criminal justice system. Not only is it the single most frequent offense listed in the Uniform Crime Reports, but informal conversations with probation officers suggest that in some local jurisdictions as many as two-thirds of probationers are DWI offenders.

6

Drugs and Violence in the Age of Crack Cocaine*

Duane C. McBride
Andrews University
Institute of Alcoholism and Drug Dependency Research Center

James A. Swartz
Illinois Treatment Alternatives for Street Crime

INTRODUCTION

The relationship between criminal and drug-using behavior is one of the most thoroughly examined relationships in criminology. In the decades of analysis, researchers have found that illicit drug users comprise a large proportion of arrestees, that drug use does appear to increase and sustain criminal behavior, and that overall, drug use is probably involved in a considerable proportion of criminal activity (Research Triangle Institute, 1976; Speckart & Anglin, 1976; Gandossy et al., 1980; McBride & McCoy, 1982; Leukefeld, 1985; Inciardi, 1986). One aspect of the drugs-crime nexus that has received a great deal of attention from the general public, policymakers and researchers is the link between drug use and violent crime. It was the concern about violent crime that was used to justify drug laws and the imprisonment of users (see Federal Strategy, 1975). It was the fear of violence, particularly street crime, that was used in arguments for establishing a National Institute on Drug Abuse. And in this age of crack cocaine, it is the continued fear of

---

* The preparation of this chapter was supported in part by a grant from the National Institute on Drug Abuse Grant No. R18 D905349.

violence (which now seems to be escalating out of control) that plays a major role in drug enforcement, treatment, and other policy discussions including arguments against the legalization of drugs (see Inciardi & McBride, 1989).

It is the purpose of this chapter to briefly examine the issues, observations, and data surrounding the relationship between drugs and violence within the context of a number of different topics:

* The perceived relationship between drugs and violence in the early part of this century.

* The drug epidemic of the late 1960s and early 1970s, and the burgeoning research interest in drugs and crime.

* Drugs, violence and the emergence of a street drug culture.

* Violence and drug use in the late twentieth century.

* A framework for understanding and interpreting violence and the use of crack cocaine according to a confluence of factors:
  - psychopharmacology
  - the saturation of cocaine use by street criminals
  - distribution and market instability
  - macro-societal trends

THE PERCEPTION OF THE RELATIONSHIP BETWEEN DRUGS AND VIOLENCE IN THE LATE NINETEENTH AND EARLY TWENTIETH CENTURIES

Much of the historical literature around the turn of the century and over the next few decades approached drug use from the perspective of an assumed causal relationship to violence. In many instances, there was a tendency to portray the violent drug user as an exaggerated stereotype. This tendency seemed to be driven by fear and ideology as opposed to careful observation. The stereotypical drug fiend engaging in bizarre, unpredictable, violent behavior was a staple of the popular press (*New York Times*, 1927), and of articles and books written by government officials (Anslinger & Ousler, 1961). An extreme example of this type of characterization is the classic film *Reefer Madness*, which depicted the use of marijuana as causing bizarre, sexually aggressive, and violent behavior, (Sloman, 1979). The professional literature was prone to similar distortion. However, at least one author did seem to take into consideration the type of drugs used. Kolb (1925a) saw opiate use as being related to less violence because of its sedative effect as compared to cocaine which is a strong stimulant. The discussion of drugs and violence in the late nineteenth and early twentieth centuries took place within the context of a general concern over the prevalent use of narcotics, cocaine, and marijuana in American society.

At this time, America was a country experiencing rapid social, legal, and physical change. There were mass movements of people to the west, a devastating civil war, the end of slavery, large numbers of immigrants from all over the world with accompanying ethnic conflict, and rapid industrialization. Another major part of the milieu of nineteenth-century America was patient medicines which, actually, were usually unpatented. These were commercial pharmaceutical products that were available over the counter, through the mail, or off the back of the frontier and rural traveling medicine wagon.

While the manufacturers often did not disclose the contents of these "medicines," many such preparations contained opiates, barbiturates, or cocaine (Inciardi, 1986).

The widespread availability of narcotics and other drugs is illustrated by the mail-order catalogs of that era. The 1897 Sears and Roebuck mail-order catalog included prominently featured advertisements for a variety of medicines that contained opiates and/or barbiturates. Perhaps the strongest evidence of the commonality of hard drug use in this time period, in this "middle America" consumer journal, are the ads for complete hypodermic kits, including a syringe, needles, vials, and attractive carrying cases.

Near the turn of the century the American establishment became more conservative and began reacting against the social changes of the late nineteenth century, including the influence of foreigners who were perceived as evil, and the widespread use of narcotics. Somehow, these two distinct phenomena came to be viewed as inextricably intertwined; solving the drug problem meant cracking down on foreigners. In a powerful series of essay's, in Collier's magazine, Samuel Adams decried the common, unregulated sale and use of powerful drugs that destroyed the body and turned young men into criminals and young women into prostitutes (Young, 1961). The increasing public fear of the consequences of narcotics use was combined with both the demand for government controls on food production and distribution (resulting from Sinclair's exposé of the meat-packing industry), and with a reaction against immigrants who, from the public's perspective, were highly associated with the "foreign" drugs they purportedly had introduced to this country. Also, the development of these social attitudes took place concurrently with the movement for prohibition, which was calling America back to its puritan, hardworking, sober, English and Calvinist Scotch-Irish roots. Thus, a crucial part of the interpretation of the relationship between drugs and violence in the early twentieth century took place within the context of a mixture of clinical observation and a distrust of the foreigners who were perceived as overwhelming America with their undesirable behavior and values.

Interestingly, a crude typology arose that linked the abuse of a specific drug with a particular ethnic group. For example, even though the use of patent medicines containing narcotics was quite widespread in general society (Terry & Pellens, 1970), opiate use was seen as being uniquely associated with immigrant or laborer Chinese populations. Similarly, marijuana use was viewed as a part of the dangerous behavior of Mexicans (Inciardi, 1986). Further, shortly after the turn of the century, a number of articles appearing in newspapers and medical journals specifically linked cocaine use to violent attacks by black men on southern white women (Siegel, 1984).

This amalgam of fear, irrationality, and a nostalgic desire to return to simpler times, along with a justifiable concern over the unregulated use of potent drugs, provided a significant portion of the impetus for the 1914 Harrison Act. While the Harrison Act appeared to be just a tax issue, in that a government tax stamp was required before the included drugs could be distributed, in reality, because the tax stamp was never issued, the distribution of opiates, cocaine, and other substances became illegal.

Once the bureaucracy of drug regulation and enforcement was created by the Harrison Act, the combination of knowledge and myth about drug use and its violent behavioral consequences was propagated by the new government bureaucracy. This bureaucracy was more often interested in preserving its own existence and expanding its power and budget, than in studying and accurately portraying drug abuse problems.

For a time, the anti-drug social reform movement focused on marijuana use and its associated evils, particularly its relationship to violence. Here again, the image of the drug user as an out-of-control maniac was brought to the forefront. American media and the new Director of the Bureau of Narcotics, Harry J. Anslinger, seemed to delight in printing and telling stories of insanity, suicide, rape, and murder all caused by marijuana use. Sloman's (1979) work on the history of marijuana use in America, documents the horror file that the government built and disseminated to an ingenuous media and public. These stories included sordid descriptions of ax murders and gang rapes, which carefully noted that the victims were white and the marijuana users was Mexican or black. This portrayal of the effects of marijuana resulted in the 1937 passage of a Marijuana Tax Act that classified marijuana as a narcotic.

This same perspective persisted through the 1950s, with the American anti-narcotic establishment and the popular press emphasizing the purported, seemingly exclusive link between drug use and disvalued groups, and the drug-induced attacks of these groups on innocent, real, (i.e., white), American youth. Thus, the drug addict continued to be portrayed as an American menace committing wanton violence (Pittman, 1974).

Characterizations of drug use by the popular press and an ideologically rigid bureaucracy aside, reactions to drug users since the passage of the Harrison Act in 1914, and the Marijuana Tax Act in 1937, have varied dramatically in different parts of American society. The debate was complex and included elements of medical management and support of use, the mental health movement, social and economic reform, along with the dominant law enforcement perspective. The law enforcement perspective, which emphasized that drug use was illegal and, feeding on the fear of violence from the user, generally (and successfully) argued that users should be incarcerated and the public protected from their bizarre behavior and violence. While the dominant views of the drug abuser did not go unchallenged, during the 1950s American society was not yet prepared to accept alternative perspectives.

Between the passage of the Harrison Act in 1914 and the Marijuana Tax Act of 1937, and the 1950s, there is little epidemiological evidence about the impact of the anti-narcotic legislation, law enforcement, and media efforts. There is evidence that, prior to the passage of the Harrison Act, the use of narcotics, because of their availability, was widespread. Except for the interruption of trade routes during World War II, there is very little evidence that the narcotics trade was significantly impacted by U.S. government policy (Inciardi, 1986). By removing narcotics and other drugs from over-the-counter and mail-order trade, there does appear to have been a change in the populations that used the now-illegal drugs. Working- and middle-class populations that appeared to make up a large proportion of turn-of-the-century users, virtually disappeared from identified user groups by the end of the 1950s and, increasingly, opiate use was identified as occurring almost exclusively in the rapidly growing urban inner-city neighborhoods (Ball, 1965).

THE DRUG EPIDEMIC AND VIOLENCE

There is evidence that in the late 1960s and early 1970s, American society experienced a drug epidemic. This evidence includes a variety of data obtained from a number of statistical reporting systems. For example, during this time there were reported increases in drug overdoses and drug-related deaths (Inciardi et al., 1978), the numbers of drug treatment admissions (Dupont, 1973) and drug use by arrestees (McBride, 1976; Gandossy et al., 1980). As a result of these types of data and particularly of the apparent relationship between drugs and crime, President Nixon, in his message to Congress on June 17, 1971, declared that the drug abuse problem in the United States had reached the dimensions of a "national emergency." Attempting to launch a counterattack, he created the Special Action Office on

Drug Abuse Prevention (SAODAP), and a few years later, the National Institute on Drug Abuse (NIDA).

Of particular concern in this era was the heroin user who was portrayed as the street criminal the public should fear most. While the new image of the violent drug addict was somewhat more realistic than earlier depictions, it still involved a degree of exaggeration and inaccuracy. The explanation of violent criminal behavior now began to shift away from being based purely on physiological changes induced by the drug (i.e., the drug caused violence by virtue of altering the user's mental and physical status to produce uncontrolled attacks) to one which ascribed a degree of purposefulness to the drug addict as well. Violent acts were now seen as being committed by predatory drug addicts who were in desperate need of obtaining a fix and who would rob and murder innocent citizens in order to acquire the money to do so (Inciardi, 1986). Heroin users were implicated because of the chronic nature of their drug habit and the expense involved in maintaining such a habit over an extended period of time (McBride & McCoy, 1982). Combined with widespread press coverage of the 1960's and 1970's drug culture, this portrayal had enough intuitive appeal to cause a great deal of alarm and apprehension among the general public. Surveys in the early 1970s found that fear of crime and drug users were two of the public's major concerns (Inciardi, 1986).

This renewed, though certainly less simplistic, description of the criminally violent addict portrayed by federal agencies resulted in a flurry of new research activity. Unlike the situation in the early part of the century when the view of the violent, drug-crazed criminal went relatively uncontested, the research efforts initiated during this time were geared towards examining the reality of this portrayal by looking carefully at the research data. These efforts began to elucidate a different picture of the opiate addict.

In the mid-1970s, the newly-created National Institute on Drug Abuse (NIDA) organized a panel consisting of experts on crime and drugs, and investigators with ongoing relevant research projects, to review the issues and analyze the existing data (Research Triangle Institute, 1976). The resulting discussions and review of the data did not support the government's view of the simple linear relationship between drug use and crime. The group simply would not conclude that the initiation of drug use, particularly heroin use, turned non-criminals into extensive and violent offenders.

The panel found that a preponderance of studies conducted between the 1950s and early 1970s concluded that prior to the initiation of heroin use, a large proportion of users reported extensive criminal activity (e.g. see Stephens & McBride, 1976). Thus opiate addiction was not seen as causing one to become a criminal *per se* but rather seemed to potentiate criminal activity in a person already prone in that direction (Inciardi, 1986). Moreover, the types of crimes committed by opiate addicts were not found to be more violent than those committed by non-drug using criminals. In an excellent descriptive study on the effect of the initiation of heroin on a street group, Finestone (1957), reported that as the group initiated and increased heroin use, they decreased their violent crimes and focused their activity on manipulation and con-like behavior that would yield cash or property that could be used to purchase drugs. Survey research data in the early 1970s supported Finestone's earlier observations and indicated that heroin users were over-represented in property crime categories, and under-represented in crimes against persons (Inciardi & Chambers, 1972; Kozel et al., 1972; Barton 1976; McBride, 1976).

Ethnographic researchers were also portraying the heroin user not as a violent, irrational criminal, but rather as someone who focused all criminal activities in a very rational, even status-conscious manner, to obtain heroin. These efforts consisted of conning and hustling for the purpose of obtaining drug money and were not random, aimless acts of violence (Preble and Casey, 1969; Agar, 1973). Thus, the work of these researchers did not support the portrayal of the violent narcotized offender.

The work of Lindesmith (1967), and Schur (1969), further undermined the violent stereotype. As Lindesmith pointed out, the relationship between crime and drugs, and its associated violence, can be viewed as a socially created artifact resulting from drug laws and their enforcement. From this perspective, laws that make heroin illegal result in exorbitant prices for heroin, and because of the nature of addiction, force heroin users to engage in criminal activity to acquire funds to purchase heroin, create a criminal network to supply heroin, and create violence associated with the distribution of heroin or violent activities of those seeking to obtain the drug.

These ideas, data, and conclusions were not exactly what the federal government wished its expert panel to conclude. Adding to the government's consternation was the fact that the report's executive summary was not clear and maintained a number of points denying a causal linkage between crime and drugs while specific papers in the report tended to emphasize the complexity of the crime-drug relationship rather than to deny its existence (Research Triangle Institute, 1976). Clayton and Tuchfeld (1983) argued that the major problem in the debate about the crime-drug relationship was the failure to understand the meaning of causality. In any case, published or not, conceptually clear or not, the conclusions reached by this panel and by other similar research projects (e.g., Gandossy et al., 1980) shifted the image of the opiate addict away from that of being a violent predator to that of a rather pathetic con man prone towards a life of crime from the start, who became further compelled to commit petty and cowardly acts of thievery to support a consuming addiction. The narcotic drugs, because of their sedative effect, were thought, if anything, to reduce the likelihood that a user would commit a violent crime.   Other work conducted around this same time, though, was beginning to suggest that the pendulum had now swung too far in the other direction; narcotics addicts were not crazed and malicious maniacs but neither were they strangers to aggressive acts and violent crimes.

DRUGS, VIOLENCE, AND THE EMERGENCE OF A STREET DRUG CULTURE

While data derived from studies conducted in the early part of the 1970s did not *generally* support a relationship between hard drug use and violence, a number of contradictory observations were emerging that did suggest the daily life of the heroin addict was becoming, or was already, increasingly violent. As noted by Agar (1973), the context of the heroin buy takes place within a milieu of suspicion and potential violent reaction. The dealer is attempting to sell the lowest quality at the highest prices, and the buyer is attempting to purchase the best quality at the lowest prices. The buyer fears getting "burned" (of getting poor quality) and the dealer fears getting "ripped off" (having his drugs stolen by the user). Fiddle (1976) saw this setting as creating the context for inter-addict violence. Thus, studies initiated in the mid-1970s to early 1980s began finding that violence was a common part of the world of the street drug user.

Researchers reported that homicides were a major cause of death among drug treatment program clients (Fitzpatrick, 1974) as well as street users (McCoy et al., 1978). McCoy and his colleagues found that two-thirds of the deaths of street drug users awaiting entry to treatment in Miami, Florida were due to homicide, and police records indicated that the homicide took place within the context of a drug deal. Other investigators such as Monforte and Spitz (1975) found that community homicide rates were significantly impacted by the extent of violence among drug users. They reported that during the early 1970s, two-thirds of the homicide victims in Wayne County (Detroit), Michigan were involved in illegal drug use or drug dealing.

How then can these more recent findings of violent behavior among narcotics addicts be reconciled with the earlier, seemingly contradictory reports? Are narcotics addicts more or less prone to violence than non-drug using offenders by virtue of their addictions? As with many questions concerning complex social issues, the answer does not appear to be a simple yes or no. With a few qualifications and additional considerations, it appears that narcotics addicts have been somewhat less prone towards violent crime than their non-addicted counterparts, but not to the extent previously thought.

Moreover, it also seems to be the case that those criminals who developed addictions since the 1970s are more violent than previous cohorts; the ones studied by earlier researchers.

First, the view that the main, or sole, psychopharmacological effect of narcotics is sedative and thereby suppresses aggressive impulses is an over-simplification. While it is true that this class of drugs has a sedative effect shortly after administration, the withdrawal period (which is not an infrequent event for street drug users) is anything but sedate and is punctuated by discomfort, irritability, and a strong craving to get a "fix." It is during this time of drug withdrawal that the direct physiological effects of the drug may induce the addict to commit a violent act (see Goldstein, 1979). Even though the direct physiological effect of any given drug probably accounts for only a small portion of the violent crimes committed (Goldstein, 1985; Inciardi, 1986), any analyses should take into account the full range of effects a drug might have, not simply those immediately following administration of the drug.

Second, a number of studies of the relationship between heroin addiction and crime did not include robbery as a violent crime (Inciardi, 1986) but instead include it as a property crime. Anyone who has been the victim of robbery, particularly armed robbery, will probably attest to the fact that it is indeed a violent act. When robbery is classified as a violent crime, the discrepancy between drug users and non-drug users diminishes (e.g., Eckerman et al., 1976). Thus, the perception that narcotics addicts are non-violent may depend, in part, on how one defines the term.

Irrespective of definitional issues however, there have been a number of indications that the street drug use culture in the 1970s was changing in the direction of increased violence. Data reported by Zahn and Bencivengo (1974), and Stephen and Ellis (1975), suggested that heroin users who initiated use in 1970, and later, represented a different cultural cohort of users. This new generation of users was seen as more willing and likely to engage in violent crimes and violence against each other.

Evidence for this increasing violence comes from a late-1970s study of South Florida arrestees. It was found that heroin and dilaudid users, while comprising about 16 percent of all arrestees, were responsible for about one-third of all serious crimes against persons (McBride, 1981). These findings were the reverse of previous results from an earlier time period (McBride, 1976) and from most of the similar research in the early 1970s. It may be, then, that the overall milieu of the narcotics addict, perhaps as a reflection of society in general, was becoming more violent during the 1970s. The result was that compared to drug users who began in the 1950s and 1960s, younger addicts were enculturated into a system where violence was more accepted, and perhaps even necessary, in order to survive. Compared to later studies, research carried out prior to and during the early 1970s would have likely sampled addicts who initiated their drug use in a milieu that was less violent and who were consequently less inclined than younger addicts to commit violent acts of crime. The effect of a cultural promotion of violent behavior has received some support in broad-based sociological studies (Messner, 1988).

Another explanation for the increased violence found in successive cohorts is that, beginning in the 1970s, opiate addicts showed a greater tendency than older generations to be poly-drug abusers (Inciardi, 1986). Poly-drug abuse has been found to be a factor associated with a higher probability of committing violent crimes (Chaiken & Chaiken, 1982; Ellinwood, 1971). Related to this same point is the fact that cocaine use was just beginning to increase in the early 1970s. It is probable that as this trend continued escalating over the following decade, cocaine became one of the more frequently used combination drugs. If, as seems reasonable to suppose, cocaine use leads to increased violence, it could be that another reason opiate addicts were becoming more violent was simply due to the fact that they were using more and more cocaine in conjunction with or in lieu of narcotics.

Finally, a sad but significant trend over the past 20 years is that the age of first drug use and, subsequently, the age at which addiction occurs are both declining (Inciardi, 1986). The National High School Senior Survey (Johnston et al., 1988) indicates that, nationwide since 1978, there has been a decrease in the age of alcohol and drug use initiation. Another recent report, based on data gathered as a part of the National Drug Use Forecasting Project (Wish & O'Neil, 1989), revealed that arrestees who had turned 21 on or after 1983 had, on average, begun using alcohol, cocaine, and heroin at earlier ages than a group of older addicts (National Consortium of TASC Programs, 1990). These data also suggested that the time between first drug use and the development of an addiction for a given drug was shortening, thereby further decreasing the average age of addicted arrestees. Since younger age is a factor that has been associated with a greater tendency towards aggressiveness and violence, the steady increases in violent, drug-related crime may be partially due to the younger age of the addicted criminal population.

Thus, younger addicts, enculturated into a climate of greater overall violence and prone to opportunistically using multiple drugs, either successively or in combination (e.g., speedballs), have shown less reluctance to turn to violent crime as a way of generating income, settling scores or demarcating territorial rights. Within this increasingly volatile and violent mix, the emergence of cocaine, and particularly crack and free base cocaine, along with the proliferation of a powerful arsenal of weaponry, seems to have wrought a quantum change in the degree and lethality of street violence.

DRUGS AND VIOLENCE
IN THE LATE TWENTIETH CENTURY

For most of this century concerns and questions about the connection between drugs and violence focused on heroin users. The expense of heroin use, the reported and estimated large number of heroin users, and the type of population that used heroin were all thought to contribute to the extent of crime among heroin users. By the early 1980s a variety of epidemiological data began to show a general, societal, downward trend in heroin use, and actually almost all types of illegal drug use (Clayton et al., 1988; Johnston et al., 1988). These data indicated that heroin use never spread to general society and that there was decreasing support for illegal drug use. These and other data, however, also revealed the increasingly widespread use of a heretofore rarely used drug, cocaine (Johnston et al., 1988; Gawin & Kleber, 1988;). In many areas of the country, perhaps with Miami on the cusp, cocaine has replaced heroin as the street drug of choice for IV drug users and non-IV drug users alike (Hall, 1987). While the use of cocaine in and of itself is hardly a new phenomenon, the degree and rapidity with which its use became so widespread among the criminal community was novel.

Possibly the most significant evidence of the changes in street drug use patterns comes from research directed by Eric Wish (Wish & O'Neil, 1989). Wish reports urinalysis results from a selected population of jail inmates in 21 cities across the United States (Drug Use Forecasting, 1989). The population selected and procedures employed are similar to those used in a variety of surveys of drug use patterns conducted in the 1970s (Research Triangle Institute, 1976; Gandossy et al., 1980). Generally, these earlier studies found current heroin use among 16-35 percent of those arrested or in jail (McBride & McCoy, 1982). Wish's data, however, indicate that cocaine use has virtually saturated criminal justice populations. He found that across the United States, the majority of males who had been arrested and jailed had used cocaine within 24 to 48 hours of their arrest. Manhattan had the highest rate of cocaine use among arrestees, with about 82 percent testing positive, with many of the other participating sites reporting similarly high rates (Drug Use Forecasting, 1989). In contrast, it should be noted that the highest proportion of opiate use in any city was 25 percent. In fact, in one city (Miami) only 1 percent of the sampled arrestees had used opiates.

This latter finding is sharply divergent from the situation in 1974 when 16 percent of all Miami felony arrestees tested positive for opiates (McBride, 1976). All tolled, these data illustrate how the world of the street drug user has changed; cocaine has become the most frequently used drug on the streets. Thus, an examination of the current relationship between drugs and violence must place emphasis on the predominant role that cocaine now plays in the world of the drug-abusing criminal.

The extent of cocaine use in street populations has caused considerable difficulties for the substance abuse treatment system that, in turn, exacerbates and perpetuates the problem. A large proportion of treatment services and their underlying theoretical base are derived from research on and clinical experience with heroin users. The treatment regimen that serves the largest number of heroin addicts (methadone maintenance) has no equivalent for cocaine users. Except for some attempts to utilize antidepressants or lithium, there are not as yet any established pharmaceutical treatment protocols for cocaine users (Siegel, 1985). While traditional outpatient and residential programs have attempted to expand their conceptions of addiction and provide services to cocaine users (cf., Gawin & Kleber, 1988), the lack of any successful large-scale treatment programs probably contributes to the high numbers of users who remain addicted to cocaine and on the streets.

Not only has there been an apparent increase in cocaine use in general society and particularly among street criminal groups, there has also been a major change in the form in which cocaine is ingested. Since the Harrison Act and until the late 1970s, cocaine was a relatively expensive drug of often unstable availability (Gawin & Kleber, 1988). It was considered either as a secondary drug in a street culture that primarily used opiates, or perhaps as the drug of choice among the affluent. By the early 1980s a variety of reports indicated a significant price decline in cocaine and a change in the form of the drug and its use. Instead of being sold as a powder and consumed by insufflation or injection, cocaine was being produced and nationally distributed in a crystalline form called "rock" or "crack" (Inciardi, 1986). In this form it can be smoked in a pipe resulting in more potent effects that have been described as comparable to those achieved with intravenous use (Siegel, 1984).

This change in form and ingestion patterns probably played a major role in increasing the use of cocaine. Price decreases made cocaine more readily available to even the poorest segments of American society and smoking became a much more acceptable means of drug use than injection. Users who previously had been reluctant to shoot-up to attain a more intense effect, could now achieve the same result by lighting a water pipe. Moreover, since the smokable forms of the drug, free base and crack, are much more addictive than the snorted cocaine-hydrochloride powder, a higher proportion of users developed more severe addictions in shorter periods of time (Gawin & Kleber, 1988).

Changes in price, availability, the addictive potential of free base and crack cocaine, the lack of a comprehensive treatment model and available treatment beds, and the vast amounts of money to be made distributing and selling cocaine, have all served to increase its use dramatically in the past few years, especially among poor minorities, street criminal populations and gangs. Ironically, the increase in use among these groups has occurred at a time when illegal drug use in the middle class is declining. The general issue of a cocaine "epidemic" and how to manage it through treatment and interdiction efforts has been cause enough for great public concern. However, very recently, at least in the popular press, the focus has been more on another aspect of the cocaine problem: its apparently strong relationship to violence.

Cocaine-related violence, particularly in conjunction with gang activities, has become a familiar part of the modern urban scene (Virgil, 1988). Some of the most common headlines in major metropolitan newspapers today involve reports of innocent bystanders shot, of dealers gunned down in disputes, and of gang warfare based on access to and distribution of crack cocaine. In Washington, D.C., homicides, presumably related to the street crack cocaine trade, became so commonplace during the first half of 1989 that it earned the unenviable sobriquet of the "Murder Capital." The eruptive occurrence of violence in the world of the criminal cocaine user has become so routine that it has warranted its own street name, "tweaking". As described by an emergency room physician who frequently deals with the after-effects of tweaking, "Women get fists and feet, men get tire irons and guns" (*New York Times*, August 6, 1989).

Beyond anecdotal evidence, existing data and reports indicate that increased use of cocaine is highly correlated with the current higher rates of violence in our society. A study in Miami (McBride et al., 1986), and New York found that cocaine was the most frequently identified illegal drug in the bodies of homicide victims. Analyses conducted by the Research Triangle Institute concluded that about 10 percent of assaults and homicides across the United States are drug related, with cocaine playing a major role (Harwood et al., 1984). Other researchers have also reported a relationship between assaults and cocaine use (Goldstein & Hunt, 1984).

If, in fact, the vast influx and use of crack cocaine has elevated and perhaps accelerated the trend towards violent criminality in this country, the question of how it has brought on this effect still remains. As succinctly stated by Massing, "The crack trade is far more violent than that for any other drug, but we don't understand why" (*New York Review of Books*, March 30, 1989). At present, there is little hard data from which any definitive answers to this question can be drawn. However, in the absence of such, it might prove worthwhile to speculate about the nature of this relationship with the hope that such speculation proves fruitful in guiding current and future research efforts.

A FRAMEWORK OF INTERPRETATION

In discussing the association between cocaine and violence, it is helpful to use a conceptual framework. Goldstein (1985) has suggested that the crime-drugs relationship can be understood using a tripartite model consisting of the psychopharmacological effects of the drug, the economic aspects, and what he calls the systemic component. Since it was first proposed, this paradigm has proven to be a very useful way of examining and understanding how drug use and distribution influence crime. Below, each of the components of the model, as each pertains to our present understanding of cocaine, is discussed.

The Psychopharmacology of the Drugs-Violence Relationship

Perhaps in reaction to the blatantly distorted presentation of the violent behavior of drug users in the first half of this century, researchers have been skeptical about the direct psychopharmacological impact of drugs on violent behavior. Most of the early research on the impact of heroin use on behavior, as already noted, concluded that the drug's sedative effect increased the probability of non-violent, non-confrontational property crime (Dai, 1937; Finestone, 1967; Kramer, 1976). As was also mentioned though, the experience of withdrawal from narcotics has been associated with increased violent behavior (Goldstein, 1979). In either case, the type and amount of crime committed as a direct result of the psychopharmacology of narcotic drugs has been thought to be small (Inciardi, 1986).

Past research on drugs and violence has focused primarily on strong hallucinogenic drugs such as LSD and PCP, and stimulants like amphetamines. When LSD and PCP had a higher prevalence of use there were a variety of case reports that indicated that the perceptual distortion that resulted from the use of these drugs could result in very violent behavior. The violence did not, however, appear to be a systematic, reflexive result induced directly by the drug, but rather a very idiosyncratic and complex response that seemed to occur in particular individuals at unpredictable times (Tinklenberg & Woodrow, 1974; Burns & Lerner, 1976). There have also been numerous accounts, mostly in the form of case studies, of the psychopharmacological link between amphetamine use and violence. For example, in an analysis of 13 individuals who committed homicides while under the influence of amphetamines, Ellinwood (1971), concluded that amphetamine use led to paranoid thought patterns and delusions, and consequently to violent behavior directed toward perceived persecutors. Other research during this same time further suggested that amphetamine use was involved in creating a violent subculture marked by stereotypic behavior patterns (Smith, 1972; Asnis & Smith, 1978).

Though the impact of hallucinogenic drugs and amphetamines is an important aspect of the drugs-violence relationship, the use of these drugs has almost always been found to be relatively rare in the general population, and even in high risk, criminal populations. The reason for elaborating on some of these earlier studies, particularly those involving amphetamines, is that cocaine has similar psychopharmacological effects and, hence, is likely to influence criminal behavior in the same way. Additionally, given the unprecedented dominance of crack cocaine use by street groups, its direct psychopharmacological impact on violent behavior may be much more significant than any of these other drugs.

Like the amphetamines, cocaine is pharmacologically classified as a sympathomimetic and a powerful central nervous system stimulant (Fischman et al., 1976). Unlike amphetamines, cocaine also has local anesthetic properties, though it remains unclear whether these play any role in its psychological effects. Recreational, intermittent use produces a number of immediate psychological and physiological effects; the former include euphoria, increased alertness, and self-confidence while the latter consists of tachycardia, pupillary dilation, psychomotor agitation, etc. (Fischman et al., 1976; Siegel, 1984; Gawin & Kleber, 1986, 1988).

Early reports based on observations of humans erroneously concluded that psychological dependence developed with chronic cocaine use but not physical dependence. These conclusions were based primarily on the absence of gross symptomatology similar to those seen during withdrawal from opiates or alcohol (Gawin & Kleber, 1988). Such reports may have been partially responsible for the general perception that cocaine was a relatively safe drug. Animal research has shown that cocaine is powerfully addictive owing to its strength as a potent reinforcer (Balster, 1988; Johanson, 1988). Given open access, animals will use cocaine until they become exhausted or die from its effects (Johanson et al., 1976). More recent studies of human behavior have also suggested that chronic cocaine users, especially those who use the smokable forms of the drug, do experience withdrawal symptoms (Hasin et al., 1988). Some researchers now believe that these cocaine withdrawal symptoms indicate sustained neurophysiological changes and hence are evidence for "physical" addiction (Gawin & Kleber, 1988). Whether or not cocaine addiction is more correctly classified as psychogenic or physiological seems relatively unimportant when one considers the number of users who seem unable either to stop or to control their use of the drug. Moreover, the time it takes for the development of an addiction to cocaine seems to have been shortened by free base and crack, sometimes to a period as brief as a few weeks (Gawin & Ellinwood, 1988).

With chronic use, and the development of dependency and tolerance, larger doses of the drug are consumed more and more frequently (Gawin & Kleber, 1988). In extreme cases, the smoking of free base cocaine at parties organized for that purpose, has been reported to last as long as 96 hours or more ("base binges"), concluding only when the supply has run out or the participants are exhausted (Siegel, 1984). Psychological changes of a more insidious nature also develop with repeated use. The initial "rush" of warmth and euphoria, if experienced at all, becomes briefer and less intense. Instead, to varying degrees but especially during "crashes" or periods of withdrawal, depression, anhedonia, anergia, anxiety, irritability, paranoia, and aggressiveness become regular aspects of the cocaine user's emotional profile (Siegel, 1984; Gawin & Ellinwood, 1988). Research and clinical reports indicate that cocaine use, because of its rapid metabolism, also produces rapid mood swings. (For a description of cocaine users' perceptions of themselves, see Morningstar & Chitwood, 1984).

Thus, while the use of cocaine makes individuals feel alert and aggressive, rapid in their perceptions and action, on top of the world and invincible, it also induces alternative feelings of depression irritability, suspicion and paranoia. The combination of suspiciousness, paranoia, and a feeling of aggressive invulnerability, can certainly result in the tendency to define situations or interactions as threatening, to be willing to be aggressive in those situations and to feel that the aggressive confrontation can be won. The identification of cocaine in a large number of autopsies of Miami homicide victims (McBride et al., 1986), and the multiple wounds to those individuals, suggests that cocaine use may have operated on both sides of the equation. The murderer may have been under the influence of cocaine at the time the act was committed and was thus driven towards committing a particularly brutal murder. The victim, possibly feeling a sense of invulnerability, may have miscalculated the risk that was being taken in the encounter.

In and of themselves, violent acts are complex behavioral phenomena that are most likely caused by a confluence of factors: cultural, situational and dispositional. It is, therefore, difficult to tease out the specific impact made by a given drug's psychopharmacology. Drug use does not occur in a vacuum. But, for heuristic purposes, it may be worth conjecturing that it is the *interaction* of the psychopharmacological effects induced by chronic cocaine use with a milieu that encourages suspicion and aggressiveness that synergistically potentiates such a high degree of violent behavior. The seamless meshing of the psychopharmacology of crack cocaine with an environment that is partially produced by and that, in turn, enhances these effects, may be an element unique to cocaine and to present conditions on the street, compared to previous times.

Economics, Drugs and Violence

The concept of economically driven violence is derived from the observation that the compulsive nature of drug use, particularly heroin and cocaine use, coupled with the expense of these drugs and the fact that a significant proportion of users does not have a large amount of easily accessible, disposable cash, results in criminal activities to obtain money for drugs (Ball et al., 1983, 1986). Research on the contribution of the economics of drug cost to violence is limited. Most studies in this area have focused on property acquisitive crime. Consistently over the last 60 years (Kolb, 1925a; Johnson et al., 1985), researchers have concluded that the high cost of drugs and the compulsive nature of many drug use patterns encourages users to focus on profitable, economically rewarding crime rather than on assaults or other violent crime that increases their personal risk in the confrontation.

Within this framework, violence may occur due to the emotional state of an addict desperate to obtain drugs. Because crack and free base cocaine are so strongly addictive, and the time between one administration and the need for the next is so short compared to heroin (Siegel, 1984), it is possible that cocaine addicts are more frequently in a state of requiring the "next fix." This would mean that more and more money would be needed to support the addiction. And, as Speckart and Anglin (1986) have shown with respect to opiate addiction, the greater the cost of a drug habit, the more likely that high-risk crimes (i.e., crimes against the person, such as robbery) will be committed to support the addiction. By extrapolation, these findings may mean that if supporting an addiction to crack or free base becomes an extremely expensive proposition over time, the probability of a violent, income-producing crime being committed to sustain the addiction increases. Also, the fact that supplies may need to be replenished more often (because of the shorter course of action of the drugs) means that income producing crime must also occur more frequently.

There are some additional considerations with respect to economics, violence, and crack cocaine. Wide availability has tended to drive down prices at all levels of distribution, thereby making cocaine less costly to the user. However, chronic abuse continues to require large sums of money to maintain the habit, and the fact that the market is so large means that the profits associated with cocaine distribution are still enormous, even at the lower rungs of the distribution ladder. Teenagers have reported daily incomes of $2,000 or more (*New York Times*, August 6, 1989). Thus, the sight of youths in otherwise poor urban areas wearing leather jogging suits, driving expensive cars, and carrying electronic beepers to support their businesses is fairly common. In this light, the economic impact of cocaine on violence, like the psychopharmacological impact, may be one that potentiates rather than causes violence. Large profits mean much is at stake. For minors and adults, particularly those from poor minorities, with no or few opportunities for low-paying legitimate work, may feel that establishing and maintaining their drug trade *at any cost*, is worth it; their only chance in life to escape poverty and be somebody. From this perspective, cocaine dealing is a high-risk, high-gain proposition. If the risk of violence is a necessary, and possibly exciting and status-enhancing, part of keeping the dream of wealth and sense of power and importance alive, then it may seem worth it.

Perhaps the biggest impact of the economics of drugs on violent behavior may lie in the unsettled market distribution of cocaine. Because large scale cocaine use is relatively recent in America, there are few stable, local distribution networks. This instability, the high demand for cocaine, and therefore the huge profits that can be made all result in considerable violence surrounding market access and control. These market conflicts exist at all levels, from international trade to the local street corner.

An important part of understanding the relationship between cocaine and violence lies in an examination of the market violence issues that exist on an international scale. Cocaine is probably the most economically valuable agricultural product in the world. Because of the nature of the coca tree itself, it can only be grown in a fairly narrow range of climate, elevation, and soil conditions.

Currently, coca is grown primarily in South American countries that have poorly developed legitimate economies. As Craig (1988) has documented, the cocaine trade produces up to $1 billion of hard currency annually in countries such as Bolivia, Peru, and Colombia. Given the high U.S. demand for cocaine, there is simply no other product or service that can be produced in those countries that even comes close to the economic worth of coca leaves (see also "How to Fight the Drug War" in *The Atlantic*, July, 1989 for a fuller discussion of this issue).

The international cocaine trade may be the most significant transfer of wealth between affluent and less economically developed countries in the world today. This transfer of wealth has apparently capitalized large criminal enterprises whose power, wealth and demonstrable willingness to use lethal violence has resulted in an intertwining of cocaine, political and even revolutionary power. Increasingly, cocaine distributors are acting like revolutionary groups with emerging populist rhetoric and declarations of war against governments. By the end of 1989, this was readily evident in the assassination of Colombian officials and politicians, the intimidation and resignation of large numbers of judges, and in declarations of war within the democratic government of Colombia (*New York Times*, August 27, 1989).

The economic strength of coca, the recency and strength of demand, and thus the developing network of international, national, local, and street-corner distribution of this incredibly valuable agricultural commodity provides a significant economic base to cocaine-related violence. The potential for profits is so high, and the alternative economic options in developing countries and in the streets of American inner cities are so few, that growers, refiners, and distributors at every level appear to be extremely willing to engage in any type of violence necessary to retain access to the profits available.

Many users of crack cocaine, including dealers, undoubtedly commit many crimes (some violent) to support their habits. In this respect, there is not much difference between the sources of economically-related violence in the past and the present. And violence associated with maintaining territorial rights to the lucrative illicit drug trade is at least as old as the days of Al Capone and prohibition. But again, what is unique about crack cocaine is the size of the market, the amounts of money to be made, and the fact that so many competing factions (including street gangs already prone towards violence) have created such an unstable market situation.

The Systemic-Lifestyle-Nature of the Drugs-Violence Relationship

It has been well documented that violence, or the potential for violence, is an integral part of being a street drug user (Preble & Casey, 1969; Agar, 1973), and that drug users often reside in areas characterized by a high degree of violence (McBride & McCoy, 1981; Goldstein, 1985). The face-to-face interaction of the drug buy with the dealer attempting to sell poor quality drugs at the highest price, and the buyer attempting to obtain the best quality drugs at the lowest price, produces a situation that easily can become violent. For example, users will often employ violence against dealers who overcharge them or sell them poor quality drugs, or they will simply assault a dealer or each other to get supplies of drugs. Similarly, dealers will routinely use violence as a management tool to maintain accurate accounting and return on investment with those that work for them in distribution networks (for extensive descriptions of the routine violence inherent in the daily life of the street drug user, see *Newsday* Staff & Editors, 1974, and Hanson et al., 1985).

Ecological analysis has shown that street drug users engage in the use and buying and selling of drugs in the neighborhood context of a subculture that values violence (McBride & McCoy, 1981). The subculture of violence has been described as existing against the general background of young males with limited economic opportunities and limited skills whose status and position are often determined by their willingness and ability to use violence to control others or to obtain what they want from others (Wolfgang, 1967). Seen from this perspective, the violence surrounding interactions between drug users is not unique, but rather is systemically a part of a broader context of violence.

The individual interaction and neighborhood systemic aspect of the relationship between drugs and violence also takes place within macro international and national trends towards greater violence. As Loftin (1986) has shown, in the last few decades the United States has experienced a rapid increase in violence. As a society, we seem to be more violent in our interactions and in our use of violence to deal with conflicts. The subculture of violence appears increasingly to have become a part of the values and behavior patterns of many groups. Additional evidence of this trend comes from the flourishing gun trade in this country.

Americans, as a people, appear to have an almost mystic relationship to weapons. The sense of independence from oppressors and the tradition of self-preservation on the frontier has left many Americans with a high regard for the value of armed citizens. Since 1960, Americans have increased the rate of licensed handgun possession (Loftin, 1986). Many of the violent weapon assaults committed in urban areas are by robbery victims, not offenders. In fact, Rose and Deskins (1980) found that, in Detroit, more robbers were killed than the store owner/employee victims. It appears that Americans are very willing, today, to use lethal weapons in situations that they perceive as threatening.

In addition to a willingness to use lethal weapons, in the 1980s there has been a significant increase in the lethality of the weapons used. The widespread availability and use of machine guns and semi-automatic weapons significantly increases the level and scope of violence. Today the weapons of choice in pharmacological, economic or systemic-based violence are routinely of a lethality unknown in previous decades. At some point, it would seem that it is necessary to recognize that, to commit to readily available, very lethal weaponry, will inevitably produce a high level of societal violence and a particularly high level of violence in confrontational, criminal activities. The relationship between drugs and violence cannot be addressed apart from weapons availability and the control of availability.

The high lethality weapons trade appears to be a major part of international economics and even U.S. foreign policy. To this extent, the perceived level of the relationship between cocaine and violence may well reflect an increasing relationship between drug distribution and international political violence and terrorism. As Craig (1988) has discussed, coca growing and co-

caine distribution in Central and South America has become increasingly intertwined with political revolutionary movements. The cocaine trade helps
fund radical groups and provides an alliance between revolutionaries and the
peasant farmers who grow the most valuable agricultural commodity in the
world.

CONCLUSION

Extensive data on cocaine and violence does not yet exist and in fact is
confounded by these societal changes and contexts discussed. The interpretation of the relationship between cocaine and violence must take place
within the recognition that there is a broad and committed market demand
from cash-rich countries for cocaine that can only be met by a commodity
produced in severely economically depressed and politically unstable geographic areas, and that the combination of addiction, psychopharmacology,
and huge profit potential to groups with few other economic options, results
in a willingness to use the level of lethal weapons readily available to access
and control the cocaine marketplace. Intervention attempts cannot consist
solely of treatment for the individual user. The systemic violence appears to
be so driven by economics that any hope of successful intervention has to be
international in scope with a primary focus on economic development and
opportunity from the Andes Mountains to the inner cities of America. Fundamental issues of education and economic justice are crucial.

Demand reduction through treatment and interdiction efforts can only
be effective if the developed world is willing to make the commitment to provide economic opportunities for their own citizens and for developing countries that include options other than coca growing and cocaine distribution.
Perhaps a major focus of national and international drug policy should also
include attention to international gun control, and the willingness of rich
countries to freely distribute heavy, mobile weapons as extensions of their
foreign policy. Because these weapons and the world's various revolutionary
and counter-revolutionary movements have become so intertwined with the
cash-rich cocaine trade, cocaine-related violence must be dealt with not only
on the individual, local and national levels, but also as a crucial aspect of the
broadest issues of worldwide political justice and peace.

REFERENCES

Agar, M. (1973). *Ripping and Running: A Formal Ethnography of Urban Heroin Addicts*. New York: Academic Press.

Anslinger, H.J. & W. Ousler (1961). *The Murderers: The Shocking Story of Narcotics Gangs*. New York: Farrar, Straus and Cudahy.

Asnis, S. & R. Smith (1978). "Amphetamine Abuse and Violence." *Journal of Psychedelic Drugs* 10, 317-377.

Ball, J.C. (1965). "Two Patterns of Narcotic Addiction in the United States." *Journal of Criminal Law, Criminology and Police Science*, 56, 203-211.

Ball, J.C., L. Rosen, J.A. Flueck & D.N. Nurco (1983). "The Day-to-Day Criminality of Heroin Addicts in Baltimore - A Study in the Continuity of Offence Rates." *Drug and Alcohol Dependence*, 12, 119-142.

Balster, R.L. (1988). "Pharmacological Effects of Cocaine Relevant to its Abuse." In Clouet, D., K. Asghar & R. Brown (eds.) *Mechanisms of Cocaine Abuse and Toxicity*, (NIDA Research Monograph #88. DDHS Pub. No. (ADM) 88-1588), Washington, DC: Supt. of Docs., U.S. Government Printing Office, 1-13.

Barton, W.D. (1976). "Heroin Use of Criminality: A Survey of Inmates of State Correctional Facilities." In *Drug Use and Crime* (National Technical Information Service). Springfield, VA.

Burns, S.R. & S.E. Lerner (1976). "Perspectives: Acute Phencyclidine Intoxication." *Clinical Toxicology*, 9, 477-501.

Chaiken, J.J. & M.R. Chaiken (1982). *Varieties of Criminal Behavior: Summary and Policy Implications*. The RAND Corporation: Santa Monica, Ca.

Clayton, R.R. & B.S. Tuchfeld (1982). "The Drug-Crime Debate: Obstacles to Understanding the Relationship." *Journal of Drug Issues*, 153-166.

Clayton, R.R., H.L. Voss, L. LoSciuto, S.S. Martin, W.F. Skinner, C. Robbin & R.L. Santos (1988). *National Household Survey on Drug Abuse. Main Findings 1985, Alcohol, Drug Abuse, & Mental Health Administration*. DDHS Pub. No. (ADM) 88-1586), Washington, DC: Supt. of Docs., U.S. Government Printing Office.

Craig, R.B. (1988). "Illicit Drug Traffic: Implications for South American Source Countries." *Inter-American Studies and World Affairs*, 29, 1-34.

Dai, B. (1937). *Opium Addiction in Chicago*. Montclair: Patterson Smith.

Dupont, R. (1973). "The Dynamics of a Heroin Epidemic." *Science*, 181, 716-722.

Eckerman, W.C., W.K. Poole, J.V. Rachal & R.L. Hubbard (1976). "Insights Into the Relationship Between Drug Usage and Crime Derived from a Study of Arrestees." In Research Triangle Institute, *Appendix to Drug Use and Crime: Report of the Panel on Drug Use and Criminal Behavior*, Research Triangle Park, NC, 387-407.

Ellinwood, E.H. (1971). "Assault and Homicide Associated with Amphetamine Abuse." *American Journal of Psychiatry*, 127(9), 1170-1175.

Federal Strategy for Drug Abuse Prevention (1975). Washington, DC: U.S. Government Printing Office.

Federal Strategy for Drug Abuse and Drug Traffic Prevention (1975). Washington, DC: U.S. Government Printing Office.

Fiddle, S. (1976). "Sequences in Addiction." *Addictive Diseases*, 2, 553-568.

Finestone, H. (1957). "Cats, Kicks and Color." *Social Problems*, 5, 3-13.

Finestone, H. (1967). "Narcotics and Criminality." *Law and Contemporary Problems*, 22, 60-85.

Fischman, M.W. (1984). "The Behavioral Pharmacology of Cocaine in Humans." In Grabowski, J. (ed.) *Cocaine: Pharmacology, Effects, and Treatment of Abuse*, (NIDA Research Monograph #50. DDHS Pub. No. (ADM) 84-1326), Washington, DC: Supt. of Docs., U.S. Government Printing Office, 72-91.

Fischman, M.W., C.R. Schuster, L. Resnekov et al. (1976). "Cardiovascular and Subjective Effects of Intravenous Cocaine Administration in Humans." *Archives of General Psychiatry*, 33, 983-989.

Fitzpatrick, J.P. (1974). "Drugs, Alcohol and Violent Crime." *Addictive Diseases*, 1, 353-367.

Gandossy, R.P., J.R. Williams, J. Cohen & H.J. Harwood. *Drugs and Crime: A Survey and Analysis of the Literature*. Washington, DC: U.S. Department of Justice, National Institute of Justice, U.S. Government Printing Office.

Gawin, F.H. & E.H. Ellinwood (1988). "Cocaine and Other Stimulants." *New England Journal of Medicine*, 18, 1173-1182.

Gawin, F.H. & H.D. Kleber (1986). "Abstinence Symptomatology and Psychiatric Diagnosis in Cocaine Abusers." *Archives of General Psychiatry*, 43, 107-113.

Gawin, F.H. & H.D. Kleber (1988). "Evolving Conceptualizations of Cocaine Dependence." *The Yale Journal of Biology and Medicine*, 61, 123-136.

Goldstein, P.J. (1979). *Prostitution and Drugs*. Lexington, MA: Lexington Books.

Goldstein, P.J. (1985). "The Drugs/Violence Nexus: A Tripartite Conceptual Framework." *Journal of Drug Issues*, 13, 493-506.

Goldstein, P.J. (1986). "Homicides Related to Drug Traffic." *Bulletin of the New York Academy of Medicine*, 62, 509-516.

Goldstein, P.J. & D. Hunt (1984). "Health Consequences of Drug Use." Report to the Carter Center of Emory University and the Center for Disease Control: Atlanta, GA.

Hall, J.N. (1987). *Drug Use in Miami (Dade County), Florida in Patterns and Trends of Drug Abuse in the United States and Europe*. Proceedings of the Community Epidemiology Work Group. National Institute on Drug Abuse.

Hanson, B., G. Beschner, J.M. Walters & E. Bovelle (1985). *Life With Heroin: Voices from the Inner City*. Lexington, MA: Lexington Books.

Harwood, H., D. Napolitano, P. Kristiansen & J. Collins (1984). *Economic Costs to Society of Alcohol, Drug Abuse, and Mental Illness*. Final report to the Alcohol, Drug Abuse and Mental Health Administration.

Hasin, D.S., B.F. Grant, J. Endicott & T.C. Harford (1988). "Cocaine and Heroin Dependence Compared in Poly-drug Abusers." *American Journal of Public Health*, 78(5), 567-569.

Inciardi, J.A. (1986). *The War on Drugs*. Palo Alto, CA: Mayfield Publishing Co.

Inciardi, J.A. & C.D. Chambers (1972). "Criminal Involvement of Narcotics Addicts." *Journal of Drug Issues*, 2, 57-74.

Inciardi, J.A. & D.C. McBride (1989). "Legalization: A High-risk Alternative in the War on Drugs." *American Behavioral Scientist*, 32, 259-289.

Inciardi, J.A., D.C. McBride, A.E. Pottieger, B.R. Russe & H.A. Siegal (1978). *Legal and Illicit Drug Use: Acute Reactions of Emergency Room Populations*. New York: Praeger Publishers.

Johanson, C.E. (1988). "Behavioral Studies of the Reinforcing Properties of Cocaine." In Clouet, D., K. Asghar & R. Brown (eds.) *Mechanisms of Cocaine Abuse and Toxicity*, (NIDA Research Monograph #88. DDHS Pub. No. (ADM) 88-1588), Washington, DC: Supt. of Docs., U.S. Government Printing Office, 107-124.

Johanson, C.E., R.L. Balster & K. Bonese (1976). "Self-administration of Psychomotor Stimulant Drugs: The Effects of Unlimited Access." *Pharmacological Biochemical Behavior*, 4, 45-51.

Johnson, B.D., P.J. Goldstein, E. Preble, J. Schmeidler, D.S. Lipton, B. Spunt & T. Miller (1985). *Taking Care of Business: The Economics of Crime by Heroin Users*. Lexington, MA: Lexington Books.

Johnston, L.D., P.M. O'Malley & J.G. Bachman (1988). *Illicit Drug Use, Smoking, and Drinking by America's High School Students, College Students, and Young Adults 1975-1987, Alcohol, Drug Abuse and Mental Health Administration,* (NIDA DDHS Pub. No. (ADM) 89-1602), Washington, DC: Supt. of Docs., U.S. Government Printing Office.

Kolb, L. (1925a). "Drug Addiction and its Relation to Crime." *Mental Hygiene*, 9, 74-89.

Kolb, L. (1925b). "Pleasure and Deterioration from Narcotic Addiction." *Journal of Mental Hygiene*, 9, 699-724.

Kozel, N., R. DuPont & B. Brown (1972). "Narcotics and Crime: A Study of Narcotic Involvement in an Offender Population." *International Journal of the Addictions*, 7, 443-450.

Kramer, J.C. (1976). "From Demon to Ally: How Mythology Has and May Yet Alter National Drug Policy." *Journal of Drug Issues*, 6, 390-406.

Leukefeld, C.G. (1985). "The Clinical Connection: Drugs and Crime." *The International Journal of the Addictions*, 20, (6 & 7), 1049-1064.

Lindesmith, A.F. (1967). *The Addict and the Law.* New York: Vantage Books.

Loftin, C. (1986). "Assaultive Violence as a Contagious Social Process." *Bulletin of the New York Academy of Medicine*, 62, 550-555.

McBride, D.C. (1976). "The Relationship between Type of Drug Use and Arrest Charge in an Arrested Population." In *Drug Use and Crime.* National Technical Information Service. Springfield, VA.

McBride, D.C. (1981). "Drugs and Violence." In *The Drugs Crime Connection* (105-123). Beverly Hills, CA: Sage Publications.

McBride, D.C., C. Burgman-Habernehl, J. Alpert & D.D. Chitwood (1986). "Drugs and Homicide." *Bulletin of the New York Academy of Medicine*, 62, 497-508.

McBride, D.C. & C.B. McCoy (1981). "Crime and Drug Using Behavior: An Areal Analysis." *Criminology*, 19, 281-302.

McBride, D.C. & C.B. McCoy (1982). "Crime and Drugs: The Issues and the Literature." *Journal of Drug Issues*, 12, 137-152.

McCoy, C.B., D.C. McBride, J.E. Rivers & B.R. Russe (1978). "The Assessment of Social Cost Savings." Final report to the National Institute of Drug Abuse, Grant #271771217.

Messner, S.F. (1988). "Research on Cultural and Socioeconomic Factors in Criminal Violence." *Psychiatric Clinics of North America*, 11(4), 511-525.

Montforte, J.R. & W.U. Spitz (1975). "Narcotic Abuse Among Homicides in Detroit." *Journal of Forensic Sciences* 20:186-190.

Morningstar, P.J. & D.D. Chitwood (1984). "Cocaine Users' View of Themselves: Implicit Behavior Theory in Context." *Human Organization*, 43, 307-318.

National Consortium of TASC Programs (1990). *Implications of Drug Use Forecasting Data for TASC Programs*, Bureau of Justice Assistance. Monograph forthcoming.

National Drug Control Strategy (1989). Office of National Drug Control Policy. Executive Office of the President: Washington, DC.

National Technical Information Service (1976). *Drug Use and Crime.* Springfield, VA.

Newsday Staff & Editors (1974). "The Heroin Trail." New York: Holt, Rinehart, and Winston.

New York Times, July 6, 1927. "Mexican Family Goes Insane." p.10.

New York Times, Sunday August 27, 1989. "Colombia Welcomes Aid: Long Struggle Seen." J.B. Treaster, p. 25; "Threats Terrorize Colombia's Courts." J. Brooke, p. 24.

Pittman, D.J. (1974). "Drugs, Addiction and Crime." In D. Glaser (ed.) *Handbook of Criminology.* (pp. 209-232). Chicago: Rand McNally.

Preble, E. & J. Casey (1969). "Taking Care of Business: The Heroin User's Life on the Street." *The International Journal of the Addictions*, 4, 1-24.

Research Triangle Institute (1976). Report of the Panel on Drug Use and Criminal Behavior. Springfield, VA: National Technical Information Service.

Rose, H.M. & D.R. Deskins, Jr. (1980). "Felony Murder: The Case of Detroit." *Urban Geography*, 1, 1-21.

Schur, E. (1969). *Our Criminal Society.* Englewood Cliffs, NJ: Prentice-Hall.

Siegel, R.K. (1984). "Cocaine Smoking." *Journal of Psychoactive Drugs*, 14, 271-359.

Siegel, R.K. (1985). "Treatment of Cocaine Abuse: Historical and Contemporary Perspectives." *Journal of Psychoactive Drugs*, 17, 1-9.

Sloman, L. (1979). *Reefer Madness: A History of Marijuana in America.* Indianapolis: Bobbs-Merrill.

Speckart, G. & M.D. Anglin (1986). "Narcotics Use and Crime: An Overview of Recent Advances." *Contemporary Drug Problems*, 741-769.

Stephen, R. & R.D. Ellis (1975). "Narcotics Addicts and Crime: Analysis of Recent Trends." *Criminology*, 12, 474-488.

Stephens, R.C. & D.C. McBride (1976). "Becoming a Street Addict." *Human Organization*, 35, 87-94.

Terry, C.E. & M. Pellens (1970). *The Opium Problem.* Montclair, NJ: Patterson-Smith.

Tinklenberg, J.R. & K.M. Woodrow (1974). "Drug Use Among Youthful Assaultive and Sexual Offenders." In S.H Frazier (ed.) *Aggression: Proceedings of the 1972 Annual Meeting of the Association for Research in Nervous and Mental Disease.* Baltimore: Williams and Wilkins.

U.S. Department of Justice (1989). *Drugs Use Forecasting (DUF) Third Quarter, 1988.* Washington, DC: U.S. Government Printing Office.

Virgil, J.D (1988). *Barrio Gang: Street Life and Identity in Southern California.* Austin, TX: University of Texas Press.

Wish, E.D. & J. O'Neil (1989). *Cocaine Use in Arrestees Refining Measures of National Trends by Sampling the Criminal Population.* Proceedings at the National Institute on Drug Abuse Technical Review Session on Cocaine Use, Washington, DC, April 4, 1989.

Wolfgang, M.E. (1967) (ed.) *Studies in Homicide.* New York: Harper & Row.

Young, J.H. (1961). *The Toadstool Millionaires: A Social History of Patent Medicines in America before Federal Regulation.*   Princeton, NJ: Princeton University Press.

Zahn, M. & M. Bencivengo (1974). "Violent Death: A Comparison Between Drug Users and Non-Drug Users." *Addictive Diseases*, 1, 283-296.

7

A Typology of
Drug-Related Homicides*

Henry H. Brownstein
New York State Division of Criminal Justice Services

Paul J. Goldstein
Narcotic and Drug Research, Inc.

TYPES OF DRUG-RELATED HOMICIDE

Homicide is a phenomenon that is both difficult to understand and difficult to explain (cf. Wolfgang, 1958; Swigert & Farrell, 1976; Nettler, 1982; Wolfgang & Ferracuti, 1982; Wolfgang & Zahn, 1983; Loftin, 1986). Nonetheless, homicides need to be, and have been, classified for both scientific and practical reasons (cf. Boudouris, 1974; Nettler, 1982; Jason et al., 1983). This chapter offers a classificatory framework for a particularly troubling subcategory of homicides, those that are drug related. Drug-related criminal homicides are classified both by type of homicide and by the nature of the relationship between the homicide and drugs.

---

* The research on which this report is based has been supported by a grant from the National Institute of Justice, number 85-IJ-CX-0052. The encouragement and critical faculties of Bernard Gropper are warmly acknowledged. Additional support has been made available by the New York State Division of Criminal Justice Services and by Narcotic and Drug Research, Inc. However, opinions and points of view expressed herein do not necessarily reflect or represent the positions or policies of the U.S. Government, the State of New York or any of its divisions, nor of the Narcotic and Drug Research, Inc., and no official endorsement should be inferred.

171

THE CLASSIFICATION OF HOMICIDES

Nettler suggests that there is "no taxonomy adequate for a science of mortal fighting" given the complexity of the phenomenon and the "morally infused criteria by which we classify homicide" (1982:6). Still, he argues that a taxonomy of homicide is needed for students of criminal homicide to be able to conduct scientific analyses. He wrote, "If we cannot neatly define classes of acts, we cannot count them reliably; and if we cannot reliably count the events of interest, there is no ground on which to build scientific explanation" (1982:5).

Depending upon their purpose, social scientists and criminal justice practitioners have classified homicide in a variety of ways. For purposes of law enforcement, criminal killings are distinguished from those that are non-criminal by "the intention to kill or to inflict harm upon the victim" (Wolfgang & Ferracuti, 1982:188) and by the extent of recklessness and forethought related to the action that resulted in the killing (Dykes, 1912; Wolfgang, 1958; Wolfgang & Zahn, 1983). For scientific or research purposes, classifications focus on the distinguishing characteristics of the event, the participants in the event, and the relationship between the participants.

Event characteristics that have been used to distinguish homicides include things such as motive, circumstance, and location. In an early attempt to classify homicides by motive, Tennyson argued that murder "groups itself naturally" into six divisions: gain, revenge, elimination, jealousy, lust, and conviction (1924:13). Later, Wolfgang and Ferracuti distinguished pre-meditated killings from those committed "in the heat of passion" (1982:189) and Loftin distinguished "robbery-circumstance" homicides from all others (1986). Messner (1983) used region and Centerwall (1984) used "immed-iate environment" (residence or not) as distinguishing factors of location.

In terms of the actors involved in the killing (victim and perpetrator) and their relationship, Guttmacher (1960) wrote from his experience as a psychiatrist who examined 175 accused murderers for court cases. He proposed ten types of murderers, ranging from the "normal," to the "sociopathic," the "avenging," and "passive-aggressive," and the "sadistic." Maxson and her associates studied data from over 700 homicide investigations and concluded that homicides involving larger groups of people, specifically gangs, are different from those not involving gangs (1985). Christoffel studied homicides involving children and consequently described variations of what happens when the relationship between parent and child disintegrates in the extreme (1983). Others who have studied homicide have classified cases by the relationship between victim and perpetrator in terms of things like race (Wolfgang, 1958; Gary, 1986; Hewitt,

1988) and level of intimacy or interaction (Boudouris, 1974; Riedel & Zahn, 1985; Hewitt, 1988; Williams & Flewelling, 1988).

Each of the classificatory schemes noted above is unidimensional in that it classifies homicides primarily in terms of one aspect of the killing or its participants. That is, none of them adequately recognizes the complex nature of homicide. Consequently, their utility for classification of homicides is limited.

A more comprehensive classification of homicide cases was proposed by Smith and Parker (1980). They suggested two types of criminal homicide, each emphasizing the relationship between the victim and the perpetrator, but also incorporating elements of circumstance, motive, and location. A homicide, according to Parker and Smith, may be primary or non-primary. About primary homicides, which Smith and Parker identify as the "most frequent type," they wrote, "(these) homicides tend to occur in the context of interpersonal relationships with intimates, and are often acts of passion" (1980:139). Non-primary homicide, they wrote, "usually occurs in the course of another crime, such as robbery or rape, but also includes murders committed by snipers and hired assassins. Generally, offenders and victims have no prior relationship" (1980:139). In contrasting the types, they concluded, "non-primary homicides are more instrumental in nature, involve at least some degree of premeditation by the offender, and are less likely to be precipitated by the victim" (1982:139).

In their effort to categorize homicides for public health purposes, Jason et al. (1983) improve upon the homicide classificatory scheme proposed by Smith and Parker. First, they clarify and provide empirical support for the distinction between primary and other homicides. In addition, they suggest a substantive categorization of what Smith and Parker call non-primary homicides that recognizes them as more than simply not primary. Proposing that homicides may be classified as primary or secondary, they wrote, "Specifically, a homicide was 'primary' when it was the main reason for the offender's assault; it was 'secondary' when the offender's primary intent was to commit some other crime and the homicide occurred secondary to this activity" (1983:310). After analyzing homicide cases included in the FBI's Supplementary Homicide Report file for the years 1976-79, they conclude that the distinction between primary and secondary homicides is empirically grounded (1983:317).

THE DRUGS AND HOMICIDE NEXUS

While past research has shown there to be a strong relationship between drugs and homicide or other types of violence (Zahn & Bencivengo, 1974;

Monteforte & Spitz, 1975; Stephens & Ellis, 1975; Preble, 1980; McBride, 1981; Ball et al., 1983; Felson & Steadman, 1983; Goodman et al., 1986), efforts to identify types of drug-related homicide have been limited by their focus of study. For example, much of the research has concentrated on the drug use of the victim, depending upon data collected by medical examiners (Zahn, 1975; Haberman & Baden, 1978; Felson & Steadman, 1983; Goodman et al., 1986; Abel, 1987). Other research has limited attention to "homicides as an aspect of drug trafficking systems" (Heffernan et al., 1982:3). We have not found any studies with typologies that consider drug-related homicide in terms of the variety of ways that drugs can be related to the killing.

A tripartite conceptual framework developed by Goldstein (1982; 1985; 1986) provides a comprehensive model for classifying drug-related violence. It suggests that drugs and homicide (as a form of violence) can be related in three different ways. Their relationship can be psychopharmacological, it can be economic-compulsive, or it can be systemic; or, it can contain more than one of these dimensions.

According to the psychopharmacological explanation, violent behavior resulting in a killing can be the consequence of short- or long-term ingestion of specific substances by the perpetrator of victim of the event (cf. Shupe, 1954; Wolfgang, 1958; Senay & Wettstein, 1983). The ingestion of substance may result in one or both of the actors becoming excitable, irrational, and violent. Or, the ingestion of drugs might target an individual as a docile victim for violent predators.

The economic-compulsive explanation purports that some drug users participate in economically-oriented violence in order to support costly drug use (cf. American Bar Association, 1972; Voss & Stephens, 1973; Petersilia et al., 1978). Under some circumstances, a robbery to obtain money for drugs may become a homicide.

When a homicide is the outcome of the traditionally aggressive patterns of interaction within the system of drug use and distribution, the relationship between the killing and the substance is considered systemic (cf. Zahn, 1980; Heffernan et al., 1982; Adler, 1985; Lewis at al., 1985; Ricks, 1986). Systemic homicide would include murders committed within dealing hierarchies as a means of enforcing normative codes, robberies ending in the death of a drug dealer and the consequent fatal retaliation by the associates of the dealer, elimination of informers, killings resulting from disputes between drug dealers over territory, disputes over drugs or drug paraphernalia, punishment of dealers for selling adulterated or phony drugs, punishment for failing to pay one's debts, and so on.

Given the complex nature of drug-related criminal homicide, such murders cannot always be categorized in terms of one explanatory type. Some cases have two or more dimensions, no one predominating, and need to be classified as multidimensional. For example, a drug dealer may murder a rival dealer while "high" on cocaine. Such an event includes both psychopharmacological and systemic dimensions.

HOMICIDE DATA FROM NEW YORK STATE

According to the Uniform Crime Report statistics, there were 1,777 criminal homicides (murder and non-negligent manslaughter) committed in New York State in 1984. Data were collected in 1986 from existing police records for 1,768 cases that occurred in 1984. (The small discrepancy in the total number of cases appears to be the result of double counting between police agencies whose jurisdictions overlap.) Of those, 309 were committed outside of New York City, 1,459 in the city. The data used for this analysis are from all drug-related criminal homicides committed in New York State, but outside of New York City in 1984. (For the New York City data, there was not enough detail about each of the cases to include them in this analysis.) Included are the 129 cases (41.7%) of the non-New York City homicides that were identified as drug-related.

For each of these homicides, data were collected about the characteristics of the event, the victim, and the perpetrator. Included is information about circumstance, motivation, location, means used, victim/perpetrator relationship, and so on. Also included is specific information about the drug-relatedness of the case, such as whether the victim or perpetrator was a known alcoholic or a drug user; whether either was using or trafficking in drugs or drug paraphernalia at the time of the killing; what types of drugs if any were being used; whether or not the victim or perpetrator was high on alcohol or drugs, or sick and in need of drugs, at the time of the killing; whether either was known to be a drug trafficker; and so on.

THE CLASSIFICATION
OF DRUG-RELATED HOMICIDES

For purposes of analysis, the 129 drug-related homicide cases are classified in two ways. First by the tripartite conceptual framework and then by the primary/secondary typology.

The classification of the 129 cases by the tripartite conceptual framework was accomplished in two stages. First, two separate investigators independently reviewed the characteristics of each case and subjectively classified each in terms of the categories of the framework. Then a third investigator was added and the three together reviewed all of the cases. In most instances, the three agreed about the appropriate classification; when they did not, the known characteristics of the case were reviewed further and a consensus was reached. Table 7.1 shows the percent and number of cases placed in each category of the framework.

The 129 drug-related homicide cases were also categorized as primary or secondary. The work of Jason et al. (1983) was used as a basis for this typology. Following their definition (1983:310), when the main reason for the action or interaction was to kill (or at least seriously harm) the victim, the homicide was defined as primary. A drug-related homicide was considered to be secondary when the killing was not the main reason for the action or interaction, but rather was instrumental to some other purpose, such as another crime.

Table 7.1
Tripartite Conceptual Framework

Primary Categorization	Number	Percent
Psychopharmacological	76	58.9
Systemic	27	20.9
Economic Compulsive	4	3.1
Multidimensional	18	14.0
Other	4	3.1
Total	129	100.0

Cases were classified for the primary/secondary typology with the aid of a free-form, text-oriented data base management computer program (McKinney, 1985). Text-based narratives of each case were analyzed for the occurrence in the text of particular items or combinations of items. For example, cases were distinguished in terms of victim/perpetrator relationship, type of dispute, and particular type of other crime. Then those cases in which the killing (or at least serious harm that might reasonably result in death) was the primary objective of the perpetrator were distinguished from those in which the killing was a means to another end. Of the 129 drug-related homicides, 91 (70.5%) were classified as primary and 38 (29.5%) were classified as secondary.

Primary homicides predominated among the psychopharmacological (85.5%) and multidimensional (77.8%) cases, and secondary homicides were most common among the systemic (57.3%), economic compulsive (100.0%), and other drug-related (75.0%) cases. Similarly, psychopharmacological cases clearly predominated among the primary homicides (71.4%) and systemic cases were most common among the secondary homicides (42.1%). Table 7.2 shows the distribution of cases by both the tripartite conceptual framework and the primary/secondary typology.

Table 7.2
Classification of Drug-Related Homicide Cases

Tripartite Conceptual Framework Category			Primary/Secondary Category		
	Primary		Secondary		Total
	N	%	N	%	N
Psychopharmacological	65	50.4	11	8.5	76
Systemic	11	8.5	16	12.4	27
Economic Compulsive	0	0.0	4	3.1	4
Multidimensional	14	10.9	4	3.1	18
Other	1	0.8	3	2.3	4
Total	91	(70.6)	38	(29.4)	129

Given the table above, there are theoretically a possible ten different types of drug-related homicide. For example, a drug-related homicide might be primary/psychopharmacological or it might be secondary/systemic. Using examples from the 129 homicides of this analysis, detailed descriptions of cases from each category follow.

TYPES OF DRUG-RELATED HOMICIDE

Primary Homicides

Primary/Psychopharmacological

Of the 129 drug-related homicide cases, 65 (50.4%) were classified as both primary and psychopharmacological. Simply, the killing or the actions that led to the killing were in themselves the primary reason for the fatal interaction between the victim and the perpetrator and one or both actors was behaving in this violent or violence-producing manner as a result of drug ingestion.

Four of these cases involved child abuse. In such cases an adult, generally a parent, participated in the killing of his or her own child while under the influence of drugs or alcohol. For example:

In March, 1984, a 19-year-old white female participated with her boyfriend, a 20-year-old male, in the killing of her 2-year-old son. The boyfriend gave the child marijuana, then beat him and put him in a clothes dryer. The police believe that both perpetrators were regular users of drugs such as PCP, LSD, and marijuana and that they were "smoking pot" at the time of the killing. The mother was convicted of endangering the welfare of a child. Her boyfriend was convicted of 2nd degree manslaughter and sentenced to 5 to 15 years in prison. (#0173)

Thirteen cases involved the killing of a spouse, common-law spouse, or boy/girlfriend. Generally, these were domestic disputes during a time of drug ingestion. For example:

During December, 1984, a 19-year-old black female killed her long-term boyfriend, age 21. She was sitting in a bar, drinking enough to be high, when she saw him walking by. She ran out onto the street after him. They struggled. She stabbed him, he stabbed her; he died. According to the police, her daughter had been raped the day before, and she believed that he had had something to do with the rape. She was arrested that same day and eventually sentenced to 1 1/2 to 4 1/2 years in prison. (#0202)

Four cases involved disputes between other family members or relatives. For example:

In May, 1984, a 55-year-old black man was killed by his son, age 24. The killing took place in a residence where on previous occasions neighbors had heard the son threaten his father with death. When he was killed, the man had been drinking, though probably was not drunk. His son was high on both alcohol and marijuana. A dispute spontaneously broke out, and the son stabbed his father to death. He was arrested that same day. (#0106)

Seven of the cases in this subcategory involved the killing of a friend. All of these cases were related to a dispute. For example:

In June, 1984, a 32-year-old white male killed two white males age 52 and 50. The victims lived together as lovers. They brought the perpetrator, a friend, into their home as a favor. But they found him to be "a slob." He worked in a fish market and each day came home smelling of fish. One day, one of the older men complained to him about the fish smell. An argument followed, and the younger man stabbed him to death. The other victim, who had been sleeping, awoke. He saw what had happened but before he could respond, he too was stabbed to death. Both victims were known to have been alcoholics, the perpetrator a user of both alcohol and opiates. At the time of the killing, the perpetrator had been high on heroin, and perhaps alcohol as well. He was arrested that same day. (#0252)

Three cases involved neighbors. Like the other cases in this category, the killings followed an altercation that took place at a time when one or more of the participants was considered to have been high on drugs or alcohol. For example:

In July, 1984, a 24-year-old white male killed his neighbor, a 19-year-old white male. In what the police called a "love triangle," the victim found his girlfriend in bed with the perpetrator. The perpetrator grabbed a loaded shotgun and a struggle ensued. During the struggle, the shotgun discharged, striking the victim in the chest. At the time, both were believed to have been drinking alcohol, and the perpetrator was smoking marijuana as well. (#0127)

In 21 cases, the victim and perpetrator were acquaintances but not neighbors or relatives. Like most of the other cases in this category, the killing was related to a dispute. For example:

During July, 1984, two black men, one 27 and the other 28 years old, long term acquaintances, sat together in a bar drinking to the point of drunkenness. A dispute broke out when the older man spilled the younger man's drink. The younger man drew a knife and held his drinking partner at knife point. They settled down and the older man left, soon to return with a handgun with which he shot and killed his acquaintance. (#0110)

In September, 1984, a 51-year-old black man killed his long term acquaintance, a black man of the same age. Both has been farm laborers together. One night, a dispute took place when one accused the other of "making too much noise." At the time, they were both drinking heavily. The victim was stabbed with a butcher knife; he bled to death from a single wound in his left cheek. The perpetrator was sentenced to 4 to 12 years in prison. (#0142)

Finally, 13 primary/psychopharmacological cases involved strangers. For example:

> On a January night in 1984, a 38-year-old white man was "causing a lot of problems" in a local bar. He had been kicked out repeatedly. After the fourth time, he returned with a handgun and fired shots into the bar. A 27-year-old white man, an innocent bystander who had been drinking but probably not high, was shot and killed. Before he returned to the bar and fired the shots, the perpetrator too had been drinking and also smoking marijuana. When he was arrested later that day, he was found with cocaine, hashish, marijuana, alcohol, and drug paraphernalia on or near him. Police believe he was high at the time of the killing. (#0104)

Primary/Systemic

Of the 129 drug-related homicide cases, eleven (8.5%) were classified as both primary and systemic. That is, killing or inflicting great harm was the primary intention of the killer and the killing was a product of the violence inherent in the world of drug trade and trafficking.

Two types of cases were included among these eleven. Seven of the cases were drug-related executions. Generally, little is known about these cases, other than that the victim was known by the police to have been involved in drug trade or trafficking and that his or her body was found dead from an "execution style" slaying. For example:

> In April, 1984, the body of a 22-year-old black man was found. He had been shot "execution style" with a .38 caliber handgun through the head. Police identified him as a man known to have been a user of opiates and other drugs, and a high level drug dealer. There were several suspects, all young black men known to be involved in drug selling, gun selling, and arson-for-hire. But there was never enough evidence to arrest anyone. (#0144)

The remaining four cases in this subcategory involved disputes related to drug business. Included were cases of revenge, sometimes in response to an earlier theft. For example:

> A 37-year-old white male was killed by a 24-year-old white male in October, 1984. They were both low level drug dealers who shared an apartment. Apparently, the perpetrator had one day stolen both

money and drugs from his roommate. The roommate became angry and a fight ensued. During the scuffle, the perpetrator shot his roommate with a shotgun. According to the police, neither was using drugs or alcohol at the time. But, .5 grams of cocaine and five ounces of marijuana, along with assorted fireworks, were found on or near the victim. The perpetrator was arrested, convicted of 2nd degree manslaughter, and sentenced to prison. (#0159)

Primary/Economic Compulsive

Of the 129 cases, none were classified as both primary and economic compulsive. That is, of the cases that involved killing for the sake of killing, none involved offenders acting only out of compulsive need to obtain money to support costly drug use.

Primary/Multidimensional

Fourteen (10.9%) of the 129 drug-related homicides were both primary and multidimensional. The killing was the main objective of the killer and the relationship to drugs was multifaceted.

Seven of these cases involved disputes over the theft of drugs or money for drugs. Previous to the killing, the victim or perpetrator or both were involved in stealing or deceiving others to obtain drugs or money to purchase drugs. For example:

Early in May, 1984, a 15-year-old white male killed a 13-year-old white female. He brutally beat and cut her, almost to the point of severing her head. At a party in the victim's home, they were both drinking heavily, smoking marijuana, and taking amphetamines. After the party, in an open field adjacent to her home, they argued. According to the police, the victim's father had been selling marijuana from his home. The perpetrator had previously burglarized the victim's home, stealing money and drugs. In the open field, the victim threatened to tell her father. So the perpetrator, a long time acquaintance, killer her. (#0178)

Two cases involved disputes that ended in death because one person would not share his or her drugs with the other. For example:

In September, 1984, a 15-year-old white male killed his cousin, a 12-year-old white female. Just prior to the killing, they were sitting together smoking marijuana and getting high. The police also found alcohol near the victim's body. Apparently, they argued and he killed her with a garden hose. When asked, he said that she had always "hogged the marijuana." He was arrested a few days later. (#0122)

Three other primary homicides related to drugs in a multidimensional way involved disputes over the proposed sale or purchase of drugs. For example:

Late in February, 1984, a 22-year-old black female killed a 60-year-old black male, her live-in lover. They were sitting at home drinking to the point of being high. Based on prior criminal records, both were believed to have been low level drug dealers and users of opiates as well as other drugs. She asked him for money. He told her he would not give her any more money "to get shot up." A dispute followed and she stabbed him with a butcher knife. She was arrested that same day. (#0170)

The remaining two homicides in this subcategory were also disputes involving drugs. But the precise nature of these disputes was undetermined.

Primary/Other

There was one other primary homicide among the 129. This was drug-related but not in a way that permitted it to be classified by the tripartite conceptual framework of drug relatedness. It involved a man and his girlfriend as follows:

In January, 1984, a 52-year-old white male killed his 45-year-old girlfriend, a white female. He believed she was trying to poison him, to kill him with drugs, so he began to beat her. With a blunt instrument, he beat her to death. No drugs or other poisons were found at the scene, but the man had cleaned up before the police arrived. No one could ever prove she had tried to kill him with drugs. He attempted to plead insanity, but failed and was found guilty of the murder. (#0101)

Secondary Homicides

Secondary/Psychopharmacological

Eleven (8.5%) of the 129 drug-related homicides were both secondary and psychopharmacological. That is, the killing was incidental or instrumental to something else, such as another crime, and was committed by an offender who was acting violently due to the ingestion of drugs.

Of the eleven cases in this subcategory, six specifically involved a robbery or burglary. For example:

Early in January, 1984, two young white men, both age 22, killed a 68-year-old white man, a neighbor who knew neither one of them. They had been drinking and smoking marijuana, getting high, when they decided to break into the older man's home. Their intention was to commit burglary. When they saw the older man at home, they killed him using a knife or cutting instrument, another blunt instrument, and physical force. After killing him, they tried to conceal their crime by setting fire to his house. In the fire that ensued, one of the young men was consumed and died along with his victim. The other young man was arrested later that day. (#0034)

Four of the remaining cases that were both secondary and psychopharmacological involved a forcible sex crime. For example:

In September, 1984, a 16-year-old white female was killed by a 23-year-old white male. They were strangers. The event began as a forcible sex crime in a residential backyard. At the time, the young man was in the area having just visited someone else known to be a drug user. According to the police, he was high on at least alcohol, so was acting irrationally when the sex crime turned into a killing. He was arrested a few days later. (#0032)

The one other case in this category involved a fight between rival gangs as follows:

Late in February, 1984, two young white males, age 16 and 20, killed another young white male, age 17. They were strangers when they found themselves in confrontation during a fight between rival gangs in the parking lot of a neighborhood bar. The victim was stabbed with a knife or some other cutting instrument. Both perpetrators, if not the victim as well, were believed by the police to have been high on alcohol at the time of the killing. A few days later both were arrested. (#0312)

Secondary/Systemic

Of the 129 drug-related homicides in New York State but outside of New York City in 1984, 16 (12.4%) were both secondary and systemic. The killing was instrumental and was related to the violence inherent in drug trade and trafficking.

Of the 16 cases, nine began as the robbery of a drug dealer and ended as a killing. For example:

> In May, 1984, a 27-year-old white female was killed. It began with the robbery of her boyfriend, who police believed was on the "fringe" of organized crime. He ran an auto body shop and from there operated a high level drug dealing operation. Another man arranged to purchase a large quantity of cocaine from him. Preparations were made for the cocaine to be at the body shop. The other man and three associates, one of whom was a woman, were setting up a robbery. The first man made the arrangements, the other two men would commit the robbery, and the woman provided the stocking masks to be worn during the crime. When the two men showed up at the body shop, there was apparently some resistance. They began shooting. The operator of the shop was shot and wounded, his girlfriend was hit by a shot from a handgun and killed. All four perpetrators were arrested a few weeks after the event. (#0179)

Four other of these cases involved the rivalry between drug dealers over territory. Killing was used as a means of dispute or conflict resolution. For example:

> In August, 1984, two unknown perpetrators killed a 31-year-old black male. He was a drug dealer's accomplice and they were believed to have been some of his drug business acquaintances. He was shot with a handgun in an open area near a "bank" where drugs were being stored. According to the police, the killers were resolving a dispute over the exclusive use of a particular area for the purpose of trafficking in drugs. (#0256)

The remaining three cases in this subcategory were related to the collection of a drug-related debt. For example:

> A 31-year-old black male was killed by two Hispanic people in March, 1984. They were all drug business acquaintances. The black man was given money by the two other men to buy some kind of pills for them. He took the money, but instead of buying the pills, he kept it. They pursued him, found him in a public area, and shot him with a handgun. (#0100)

Secondary/Economic Compulsive

All four (3.1%) of the 129 drug-related homicide cases that were economic compulsive were secondary as well. That is, in each killing that was motivated solely be the compulsive need to support a costly drug habit, killing was not the main intention of the killer. In fact, every one of the four cases started out as a robbery. For example:

> In September, 1984, a 24-year-old black woman was killed by a 48-year-old black man, a man she believed to be her friend. The police believed him to be a low-level drug dealer who needed money to make a drug purchase. He chose to rob and then rape a woman he knew. Overpowering her with his own physical force, he stabbed her to death. A few weeks later he was arrested and eventually convicted of 2nd degree murder. (#0065)

Secondary/Multidimensional

Four (3.1%) of the 129 cases were both secondary and multidimensional. The killing was not the primary purpose of the killer and the relationship to drugs was multifaceted.

Three of these cases specifically involved a robbery or burglary. For example:

> On an April day in 1984, a 28-year-old white female was sitting in her apartment, known to be a drug sales location. She had ingested enough alcohol, tranquilizers, barbiturates, and marijuana to fall into a stupor. While she was unconscious, two white males one age 37 and the other age 29, one of whom knew her, entered her home. Both were high on drugs and alcohol and were there for the purpose of burglarizing the residence. When they took what they

wanted, they set fire to the apartment and left. The woman died of smoke inhalation. (#0176)

The other case in this subcategory involved the collection of a drug-related debt as follows:

One day in November, 1984, in the hallway of a municipal housing project, a 31-year-old black man was selling drugs to two other black men, one age 20 and the other 19. They were recent casual acquaintances previously involved in drug business transactions. At the time, all three were high on alcohol and heroin. A dispute broke out. The police believe it involved the selling of bad drugs, probably an old debt as well. What began as a drug sale became a homicide. The dispute ended with the older man dead, stabbed and beaten with a blunt instrument. Both perpetrators were arrested the next day. (#0257)

Secondary/Other

Three cases (2.3%) of the 129 drug-related homicides, all from the same event, were both secondary and related to drugs in a way that did not fit the tripartite conceptual framework. The three victims were all killed in an occurrence that began as arson as described below:

One night in September, 1984, a 22-year-old man had an argument with another man in a bar. In his anger, he decided to get revenge on the man by burning the building in which be believed the man's drug dealer lived. He located what be believed was the appropriate building, set fire to it, and watched it burn from across the street. In fact, the drug dealer did not live there. Nonetheless, three residents of the building, all strangers to the arsonist, died in the fire from asphyxiation. The victims included a 56-year-old man and two women, ages 44 and 45. When he was arrested, the young man showed no remorse, admitting to having previously set eight other fires. (#0154, 0155, 0321)

SUMMARY AND CONCLUSION

Homicide is a complex phenomenon and therefore difficult to understand and explain. Given this complexity and the problems it presents for the scientific study and legal processing of homicides, adequate and realistic typologies of homicide are needed for both research and policy purposes. Based on a study of homicides committed in New York State in 1984, this paper proposes a typology for the classification specifically of drug-related homicides.

While a number of homicides nationwide has not been increasing dramatically in recent years (Jamieson & Flanagan, 1987), there has been growing concern about the extent to which homicides are drug-related (Gropper, 1984; 1985; Graham, 1987). Of the 1,459 homicides committed in New York City in 1984, 23.8 percent were identified as drug-related; of the 309 homicides committed elsewhere in the State that year, 41.8 percent were identified as drug-related. However, these percentages are probably underestimates; of the remaining cases, 13.4 percent of those in New York City and 18.5 percent of those from the remainder of the State lacked sufficient information to identify them as either drug-related or not. Also, the New York City data set did not include information about the extent to which alcohol was involved in homicide cases.

For this analysis, homicides were categorized in two ways: by type of homicide and by the nature of their relationship to drugs. By type of homicide, they were classified as primary or secondary. By their relatedness to drugs, they were classified as psychopharmacological, systemic, economic-compulsive, or as related to drugs through more than one of these dimensions.

The works of Smith (1979) and Parker (1980) and Jason et al. (1983) were used to define primary and secondary homicide categories. This distinction was selected particularly for its comprehensiveness. Distinguishing cases where killing or at least recklessly endangering the lives of others was the primary intention from those where killing was secondary to some other intention, this classification scheme incorporates an emphasis on the relationship of the victim and perpetrator with elements of circumstance, motive, and location.

Derived from the works of Goldstein (1982; 1985; 1986), the tripartite conceptual framework from classifying the relationship between drugs and violence was also used to distinguish the homicides of this study. With this framework, it was possible to categorize the study cases relative to their drug relatedness in a variety of ways, encompassing the various types of relatedness posited in earlier studies. For example, homicides related to drugs due to the drug ingestion of the victim or perpetrator could be classified, as could homicides related to drugs through their links to a drug trafficking system.

This analysis demonstrates the complex nature of drug-related homicide. Ten different types of drug-related homicide were identified and empirical evidence of the existence of nine of these was provided. The predominant type was the primary/psychopharmacological, with 50.4 percent of the cases. Next was the secondary/systemic type with 12.4 percent of the cases, and the primary/multidimensional type with 10.9 percent.

For criminal justice researchers and policymakers, these findings suggest that multifaceted strategies are needed to appropriately understand, explain, and respond to the problem of drug-related homicide. What works in some instances will not work in others, and the typology presented here will assist researchers and policymakers who must determine what approach to use in a given situation.

REFERENCES

Abel, E.L. (1987). "Drugs and Homicide in Erie County, New York." *The International Journal of the Addictions*, 22:195-200.

Adler, P. (1985). Wheeling and Dealing: *An Ethnography of an Upper-Level Dealing and Smuggling Community*. New York: Columbia University Press

American Bar Association (1972). *New Perspectives on Urban Crime*. Washington, DC.

Ball, J.C., J.W. Schaeffer & D.W. Nurco (1983). "The Day-to-Day Criminality of Heroin Addicts in Baltimore -- A Study in the Continuity of Offense Rates." *Drug and Alcohol Dependence*, 12:119-142.

Boudouris, J. (1974). "A Classification of Homicides." *Criminology*, 11:525-540.

Centerwall, B.S. (1984). "Race, Socioeconomic State and Domestic Homicide, Atlanta, 1971-72." *American Journal of Public Health*, 74:813-815.

Christoffel, K.K. (1983). "Homicide in Childhood: A Public Health Problem in Need of Attention." *American Journal of Public Health*, 74:68-70.

Dykes, D.O. (1912). "Classification of Homicide -- A Study of Comparative Law." *Juridical Review*, 24:177-184.

Felson, R.B. & J.J. Steadman (1983). "Situational Factors in Disputes Leading to Criminal Violence." *Criminology*, 21:59-74.

Gary, L.E. (1986). "Drinking, Homicide, and the Black Male." *Journal of Black Studies*, 17:15-31.

Goldstein, P.J. (1986). "Homicide Related to Drug Traffic." *Bulletin of the New York Academy of Medicine*, 62:509-516.

Goldstein, P.J. (1985). "The Drugs/Violence Nexus: A Tripartite Conceptual Framework." *Journal of Drug Issues*, Fall, 493-506.

Goldstein, P.J. (1982). "Drugs and Violent Behavior." Paper presented at the annual meeting of the Academy of Criminal Justice Sciences, Louisville, KY.

Goodman, R.A., J.A. Mercy, F. Loya, M.L. Rosenberg, J.C. Smith, N.H. Allen, L. Vargas & R. Kolts (1986). "Alcohol Use and Interpersonal Violence: Alcohol Detected in Homicide Victims." *American Journal of Public Health*, 76:144-149.

Graham, M.G. (1987). "Controlling Drug Abuse and Crime: A Research Update." U.S. Department of Justice, *NIJ Reports*, SNI 202, March/April.

Gropper, B.A. (1985). "Probing the Links Between Drugs and Crime." U.S. Department of Justice, *Research in Brief*, February.

Gropper, B.A. (1984). "Probing the Links Between Drugs and Crime." U.S. Department of Justice, *NIJ Reports*, SNI 188, November.

Guttmacher, M.S. (1960). *The Mind of the Murderer*. New York: Farrar, Straus and Cudahy.

Haberman, P.W. & M.M. Baden (1978). *Alcohol, Other Drugs and Violent Death*. New York: Oxford University Press.

Heffernan, R., J.M. Martin & A.T. Romano (1982). "Homicide Related to Drug Trafficking." *Federal Probation*, 46:3-7.

Hewitt, J.D. (1988). "The Victim-Offender Relationship in Homicide Cases: 1960-1984." *Journal of Criminal Justice*, 16:25-33.

Jamieson, K.M. & T. Flanagan (eds.) (1987). *Sourcebook of Criminal Justice Statistics, 1986*. U.S. Department of Justice, Bureau of Justice Statistics, NCJ-105287.

Jason, J., L.T. Strauss & C.W. Tyler, Jr. (1983). "A Comparison of Primary and Secondary Homicides in the United States." *American Journal of Epidemiology*, 117:309-319.

Lewis, R., R. Hartnoll, S. Bryerl, E. Daviaud & M. Mitcheson (1985). "Scoring Smack: The Illicit Heroin Market in London, 1980-1983." *British Journal of Addiction*, 80:281-290.

Loftin, C. (1986). "The Validity of Robbery-Murder Classification in Baltimore." *Violence and Victims*, 1:191-204.

Maxson, C.L., M.A. Gordon & M.W. Klein (1985). "Differences Between Gang and Non-Gang Homicides." *Criminology*, 23:209-222.

McBride, D.C. (1981). "Drugs and Violence." In J.A. Inciardi, (ed.) *The Drugs-Crime Connection*. 105-124. Beverly Hills: Sage Publications.

McKinney, M.H. (1985). *askSam*. Corpus Christi, TX: Seaside Software, Inc.

Messner, S.F. (1983). "Regional Differences in the Economic Correlates of the Urban Homicide Rate." *Criminology*, 21:477-488.

Molotsky, I. (1988). "Capital's Homicide Rate Is at a Record." *The New York Times* (October 30).

Monteforte, J.R. & W.U. Spitz (1975). "Narcotic Abuse Among Homicides in Detroit." *Journal of Forensic Sciences*, 20:186-190.

Nettler, G. (1982). *Killing One Another*, Vol. 2 of *Criminal Careers*. Cincinnati: Anderson Publishing Co.

Parker, R.N. & M.D. Smith (1979). "Deterrence, Poverty, and Type of Homicide." *American Journal of Sociology*, 85: 614-624.

Petersilia, J., P. Greenwood & M. Lavin (1978). *Criminal Careers of Habitual Felons*. National Institute of Law Enforcement and Criminal Justice, Washington, DC.

Pitt, D.E. (1988). "New York City Nears Record for Slayings." *The New York Times* (November 22): B1, B2.

Preble, E. (1980). "El Barrio Revisited." Paper presented at the Annual Meeting of the Society of Applied Anthropology.

Reidel, M. & M.A. Zahn (1985). *The Nature and Patterns of American Homicide*. U.S. Department of Justice, National Institute of Justice, Research Report.

Ricks, T.E. (June 30, 1986). "The Cocaine Business." *The Wall Street Journal* (June 30): 1, 16.

Senay, E.C. & R. Wettstein (1983). "Drugs and Homicide: A Theory." *Drug and Alcohol Dependence*, 12:157-166.

Shupe, L.M. (1954). "Alcohol and Crime: A Study of Urine Alcohol Concentration Found in 882 Persons Arrested During or Immediately After the Commission of a Felony." *Journal of Criminal Law, Criminology, and Police Science*, 44:661-664.

Smith, M.D. & R.N. Parker (1980). "Type of Homicide and Variation in Regional Rates." *Social Forces*, 59:136-147.

Stephens, R.C. & R.D. Ellis (1975). "Narcotic Addicts and Crime: Analysis of Recent Trends." *Criminology*, 12:474-488.

Swigert, V.L. & R.A. Farrell (1976). *Murder, Inequality, and the Law*. Lexington, MA: Lexington Books.

Tennyson, J.F. (1924). *Murder and its Motives*. London: William Heinemann, Ltd.

Voss, H.L. & R.C. Stephens (1973). "Criminal History of Narcotic Addicts." *Drug Forum*, 2:191-202.

Williams, K.R. & R.L. Flewelling (1988). "The Social Production of Criminal Homicide: A Comparative Study of Disaggregated Rates in American Cities." *American Sociological Review*, 53:421-431.

Wolff, C. (1988). "As Drug Trade Rises in Hartford, So Does Violent Crime." *The New York Times* (December 16): B1, B2.

Wolfgang, M.E. (1958). *Patterns of Criminal Homicide*. Philadelphia: University of Pennsylvania.

Wolfgang, M.E. & F. Ferracuti (1982). *The Subculture of Violence--Towards an Integrated Theory in Criminology*. Beverly Hills: Sage Publications.

Wolfgang, M.E. & M.A. Zahn (1983). "Homicide: Behavioral Aspects." In S.H. Kadish (ed.) *Encyclopedia of Crime and Justice*, 849-855. New York: Free Press.

Zahn, M.A. (1980). "Homicide in the Twentieth Century United States." In J.A. Inciardi and C.E. Faupel (eds.) *History and Crime*. Beverly Hills, CA: Sage Publications.

Zahn, M.A. (1975). "The Female Homicide Victim." *Criminology*, 13:400-416.

Zahn, M.A. & M. Bencivengo (1974). "Violent Death: A Comparison Between Drug Users and Non-Drug Users." *Addictive Diseases*, 1:283-296.

8

Days with Drug Distribution:
Which Drugs?
How Many Transactions?
With What Returns?*

Bruce D. Johnson
Narcotic and Drug Research, Inc.

Mitchell A. Kaplan
Narcotic and Drug Research, Inc.
and American Foundation for AIDS Research

James Schmeidler
Mount Sinai School of Medicine

The sale and distribution of illegal drugs is thought to be one of the most frequently committed and economically lucrative crimes in American society today. However, contrary to this popular belief, research on heroin addicts by Johnson et al. (1985) and others shows that drug dealers spend only a small fraction of their time engaged in actual drug distribution activities and only receive small amounts of cash and other income for their labors. The

---

* The material in this chapter was supported by the Economic Behavior of Street Opiate Users Project with funding from the National Institute on Drug Abuse (1 R01 DA01926-07). Additional support was provided by the New York State Division of Substance Abuse Services and Narcotic and Drug Research, Inc.

The material in this chapter was written while these authors were employed by New York State Division of Substance Abuse Services. Points of view or opinions in this document do not necessarily represent the official position or policies of the U.S. Government, New York State Division of Substance Abuse Services, or Narcotic and Drug Research, Inc.

purpose of this article is to examine more closely than previous research, the day-to-day patterns of drug distribution and returns of street-level heroin dealers.

National surveys of youths and young adults (Elliott & Huizinga, 1985; O'Donnell et al., 1975; Kaplan, 1987) show that approximately 10 percent of these populations report sale of some drug, usually marijuana, and about half of these sellers report sale of some other illicit drugs (pills, cocaine, heroin, hallucinogens) during the past year. These and related studies (Carpenter et al., 1988; Waldorf et al., 1977; Waldorf, 1987; Adler, 1985) also reveal several important facts about drug sales:

(1) Virtually all sellers are users of drug(s) sold.

(2) The more frequent the use of a specific drug, the higher the probability of selling it and selling it at high rates.

(3) Regular sellers frequently consume some of the drug(s) sold; they "earn" (and use) drugs so they do not need to raise cash for drug purchases.

(4) Probably less than 20 percent of all sellers make over 50 sales per year, but such high-rate sellers account for over two-thirds (or more) of all sales (Kaplan, 1987).

Recent studies of criminal offenders (Chaiken & Chaiken 1982; Chaiken, 1986; Chaiken & Johnson, 1988; Blumstein et al., 1986) and of heroin abusers (Ball, Shaffer & Nurco, 1983; Inciardi, 1979, 1986; Hanson et al., 1985; Johnson et al., 1985; Johnson & Wish, 1986, 1987; Mieczkowski, 1986; Speckart & Anglin, 1986, 1988) reveal extremely high rates of drug selling and other distribution activity (defined below). Among the majority of criminals and heroin abusers who sell, most sellers average hundreds or more sales per year, and a minority report a thousand or more sales per year.

The above studies of selling have two major drawbacks. Sales of all substances are typically combined. That is, no published study has presented (because most have not collected) data for drug-specific rates of selling and dollar returns. Thus, marijuana and pill sales are counted equally with heroin or cocaine sales.

Likewise, most prior studies implicitly assume that all forms of drug distribution are direct sales or include various distribution roles (such as steering or copping) as sales. Yet ethnographic data suggest that persons may engage in a wide variety of distribution roles other than sales (see below). Thus, it is important to disaggregate various forms of distribution activity, and not assume that it is "selling."

Studies of the economic returns from drug distribution are less well documented than rates of offending. With one exception (Johnson et al.,

1985 -- see below), reports (McGlothlin, Anglin & Wilson, 1977; Anglin, 1986; Speckart & Anglin, 1986, 1988; Collins, Hubbard & Rachel, 1985; Mieczkowski, 1986) presenting data about economic returns from selling are based upon self-reports covering a month or year period, and as such may be subject to considerable under- or over-reporting by sellers simply because they do not accurately remember what they did day-by-day. [Additional literature by economists (Simon & Witte, 1982) and policymakers (Presidents Commission on Organized Crime 1985) --not further considered here) attempts to estimate the aggregate economic value of illicit drug sales.]

Economic Behavior Project

In the early 1980s, the National Institute on Drug Abuse (NIDA) funded a major research project to study the Economic Behavior of Street Opiate Users in New York City. This study was designed to collect detailed data about daily patterns of criminal and drug-using behavior. One central finding was how extensive and important various forms of drug distribution were to the lifestyles of heroin abusers. Heroin distributors in New York were found to engage in a complex set of distribution roles which are documented in Johnson et al. (1985).

In the current paper, analytic attention will be directed towards three forms[1] of drug distribution: direct sales, steer-tout-cop, and drug thefts, as defined below.

A. Direct *selling* (sales) involves exchanges of money for drugs between two persons (buyer and seller) who generally meet face-to-face.

B. Many heroin abusers engage in related distribution roles: A *steerer* (*steering*) refers a customer to a seller. A *tout* (*touting*) locates customers for a particular seller. *Cop men* (*copping*) transport money and drugs between sellers and buyers who rarely meet. Steering, touting, and copping are frequently interchangeable roles which cannot be easily differentiated by offenders, thus we shall refer to *steer-tout-cop* or *STC* in the remainder of this paper.

C. *Drug thefts* occur when an offender gains a supply of drugs from a seller during a robbery, burglary, or theft. While a sale did not occur, an illegal transaction did and the drugs have a known economic value.

Persons may frequently shift from role to role and engage in both sales and STC on the same day. The terms "drug business" or "drug distribution" describe all three forms of transactions, regardless of specific substance(s) involved.

How much do distributors gain from their activities? Gross business refers to the total dollar value of drug(s) which the person sells or helps distribute; but generally over half of this amount must be returned as cash to the supplier to obtain another set of supplies.

Many laymen assume that persons who distribute drugs receive mainly *cash income*. Ethnographic studies of sellers (Blum, 1972; Carpenter et al., 1988; Waldorf et al., 1987; Adler, 1985; Hanson et al., 1985; Johnson et al., 1985) indicate that many distributors consume substantial proportions of their supplies while selling and thus receive "payments" as drug income (Johnson et al., 1985). Thus, *economic returns* from distribution consists of the sum of cash plus drug income.

Data from the Economic Behavior study shows that about half of 201 heroin abusers engaged in direct sales, but did so on less than 8 percent of the time and had annualized returns of about $1,400 from drug sales. Over three-quarters of heroin abusers engaged in steer-tout-cop, about 12 percent of the time, and had annual returns of $2,200 from STC (Johnson et al., 1985:234-5).

Like other studies, these findings do not separate various drugs, the types of drug business transactions, or economic returns. Aggregate data such as those shown here also include those persons who do not distribute drugs, or who have many days without sales/STC.

Daily Patterns of Drug Business Activity

This chapter describes more closely than previous research the day-by-day patterns and returns from the drug business. Johnson et al. (1985: Ch. 6) suggest considerable daily variability in drug business activity. Annualized data based upon individual subjects regarding their drug business participation, days active, number of transactions, and returns are provided elsewhere (Johnson et al., 1985: Appendix B). Vignette 8.A illustrates the variety of transaction types, substances, and types of returns of one individual across a week.

Vignette 8.A
Drug Distributors at Work

ILLUSTRATION 1
STEER-TOUT-COP MEN

Ephram S. (Hispanic male, age 30) was a daily heroin user engaged in a variety of low-level distribution activities. For example, in a four-day period he reported the following activities:

7/6/81   Copped about $200 worth of coke and $200 worth of heroin for two neighborhood people and three white guys from New Jersey; earned $15 and $40 worth of heroin (but no cash) from STC.

7/7/81   Helped a house connection. It was a slow day. I stayed in the street and talked to drug buyers. They gave me money to go up and cop from the house dealer. Got $82 cash, $70 worth of heroin and $5 worth of coke for STC.

7/8/81 Bought three half quarters for $20, sold them for $25, Bought three $10 bags of heroin for $7 and sold them for $10 each. Earned $25 cash from heroin sales.

ILLUSTRATION 2
ROLE DIVERSITY IN THE DRUG BUSINESS

Neville E. (black male, age 32) was a daily heroin user working for a dealer. A buyer who wanted a quarter of heroin gave $50 to a cop man, who in turn gave it to Neville, who counted the money to be sure it was correct. He gave the money to the dealer, who gave him the quarter. Neville gave the drugs to the cop man, who returned it to the buyer. He did ten to forty such transactions per day.

Neville earned $50 a day for STC from his dealer. But in addition, he stole some of the money he received for the dealer ($20 to $50 a day). He also tapped the bags before returning it to the cop man, stealing $20 to $50 worth of drugs, thefts of drugs, which he consumed. He also bought drugs with cash from this dealer, paying $35 per quarter (instead of $50). If a buyer approached him directly, Neville would earn $15 cash from the sale.

This chapter focuses upon the daily activity and returns from the drug business by addressing the following questions:

1. What proportion of days involve distribution?
2. What drugs are involved?
3. How many transactions occur on days with distribution?
4. Do subjects sell directly or engage in STC (steer-tout-cop)?
5. How much do they earn in drugs and cash from their drug business activities?

So little is known about the frequency and returns from the drug business that careful description and statistical averages about days with drug distribution will provide important new information. The implications of these data will be provided in the concluding section.

This paper continues the analysis of drug distribution presented in Johnson et al. (1985), but provides a much more detailed picture of daily drug business activities among heroin abusers.

METHODS

The subjects, methods of recruitment, and repeated daily interviews with subjects are described elsewhere (Johnson et al., 1985); only brief descriptions of the methodology are provided here. During 1980-1982, 201 active heroin users were recruited from the streets of Harlem and East Harlem (Manhattan); they consumed heroin primarily by intravenous injection, and with a relatively high frequency of use. Subjects were primarily blacks and Puerto Ricans, with less than high school education, unstable family ties, and rarely employed. They were selected by street recruiters to reflect the diversity in lifestyles of street heroin abusers. While no claims of representativeness can be made, their demographic and lifestyle characteristics are quite similar and perhaps typical of heroin abusers entering drug treatment programs and those arrested in Manhattan (Johnson et al., 1985; Wish, Brady & Cuadrado, 1984).

The data were collected several years before crack (free base cocaine sold in vials) became widely available (about 1986). The data below reveal infrequent sales, STC, and thefts of cocaine; these findings should be considered conservative. While many more persons were selling and using powdered cocaine (but not selling heroin), they were specifically excluded from this study which was primarily focused on heroin abusers.

Unit of Analysis: Person-Days and Active Days

The findings reported below shift the unit of analysis from the individual to the person-day. The person-day (PD) is defined as a 24-hour period, ending at midnight. The data collection procedure was that each individual subject was interviewed about drug use, purchase, sale, distribution, non-drug crimes, income, and expenditures for each separate day (the person-day) for at least 33 (usually) consecutive days during 9 different interviews. About one-third of the 201 subjects were reinterviewed about 3-6 months later for a second cycle of 28 days; about 20 subjects had a third or fourth cycle of 28 days. A total of 11,470 person-days of data were collected. For each person-day, respondents were asked to sum up all events of a given type (e.g., direct sales of heroin) and report the total number of transactions, their cash earnings, drug earnings, and the gross value of drugs distributed during that 24-hour period.

Active Days (*AD*) are those days on which a specific combination of drug and transaction occurred (e.g., one or more STC transactions of cocaine was reported).[2] The number of active days may vary dramatically for specific drugs and transactions. The averages presented below are to be interpreted as pertaining to the amounts involved on days that the persons did the particular activity and had known dollar returns.

In the analyses below, we focus primarily on the following questions: What percent of all days have specific forms of transactions (Participation)? How many drug business transactions occur (Frequency)? Which drug(s) are involved and how many transactions? Which forms of distribution occur and how many transactions? What gross amount of drug(s) did the respondent help distribute? How much cash and drug income was obtained? What total economic returns were gained?

FINDINGS

This section presents descriptive results about drug distribution based upon person-days as the unit of analysis.

Participation in Drug Business

Participation in the various forms of drug business and specific drugs are shown in the first column of Table 8.1. The data are presented for three distinct categories of distribution: direct sales, steer-tout-cop (STC), and drug thefts. The combined transactions are shown in the bottom section of Table 8.1.

Table 8.1

Participation and Frequency of Transactions plus Gross Business Amounts, via Drug Sales, Steer-Tout-Cop, Drug Theft, and All Transactions Combined, by Specific Drug(s)

Drug(s)	For Specific Drug(s) and Transaction Type at Left			Base Ns: No. AD[a]		
	Average Cash Income per AD with $1+ of Cash	Average Drug Income per AD with $1+ of Drugs	Average Returns per AD with $1+ Cash/Drugs	Cash Income (Col.1)	Drug Income (Col.2)	Average Returns (Col.3)
	DIRECT SALES of:					
Any Illicit Drug	$38.36	$54.35	$43.74	858	97	873
Heroin	67.90	64.31	86.37	191	71	203
Cocaine	34.90	33.79	44.30	40	19	46
Methadone	23.56	.00	23.56	303	0	303
Marijuana	29.28	2.33	29.30	262	15	263
Pills	30.63	4.83	30.87	122	6	122
Alcohol	10.00	.00	10.00	1	0	1
	STEER, TOUT, COP of:					
Any Illicit Drug	19.91	33.19	36.46	850	1328	1673
Heroin	19.32	33.50	36.97	666	1149	1389
Cocaine	14.04	18.54	21.21	230	280	397
Methadone	10.64	10.00	10.63	39	1	40
Marijuana	13.17	8.10	11.61	18	41	49
Pills	9.26	4.89	9.57	19	9	23
Alcohol	.00	3.00	3.00	0	1	1
	DRUG THEFTS of following:					
Any Illicit Drug	*	118.98	118.98	*	86	86
Heroin	*	150.70	150.70	*	54	54
Cocaine	*	86.92	86.92	*	13	13
Methadone	*	19.00	19.00	*	2	2
Marijuana	*	38.33	38.33	*	3	3
Pills	*	57.93	57.93	*	14	14
Alcohol	*	12.00	12.00	*	1	1
	COMBINED (Sale+STC+Theft) Transactions:					
Any Illicit Drug	30.33	40.36	44.84	1643	1476	2440
Heroin	30.61	40.76	48.17	844	1256	1599
Cocaine	17.13	22.83	25.99	270	305	446
Methadone	22.42	16.00	22.43	337	3	339
Marijuana	28.34	8.31	27.24	279	58	308
Pills	28.15	31.57	33.31	139	28	144
Alcohol	10.00	7.50	12.50	1	2	2

a - AD: Active Days--On the given day, the subject
    reported $1 or more dollars from transaction(s) of
    this type for specific drug(s) indicated. Columns 3-6 are
    denominators for amounts given in columns 1-3, respectively.
* - No cash income from "drug thefts" is obtained.
NOTE: Alcohol is not included in "Any Illicit" Drug.

Drug Sales

Reading down the first column of Table 8.1 shows that direct sales activity occurred on 8 percent (PD = 873) of all person-days (only rounded figures are given in the text below). Direct sales of heroin occurred on 2 percent (PD = 203) of all person-days. The sale of cocaine occurred on less than 1 percent (PD = 46), methadone on 3 percent (PD = 303), marijuana sales on 2 percent (PD = 263) of the person-days, pills on 1 percent (PD = 122) of the person-days; alcohol sales rarely occurred (only 1 PD).

Steer-Tout-Cop

This behavior occurred on 15 percent (PD = 1,673) of all person-days. STC behavior involving heroin occurred on 12 percent (PD = 1,389) and cocaine on 3 percent (PD = 397) of all person-days. STC of methadone (PD = 40), marijuana (PD = 49), pills (PD = 23), alcohol (PD = 1) occurred on less than 1 percent of all person-days.

Drug Thefts

This behavior occurred on less than 1 percent (PD = 86) of all person-days; heroin was the drug most commonly stolen (PD = 54).

Combined Transactions

Some type of drug business activity occurred on 21 percent (PD = 2,440) of all person-days (bottom of Table 8.1). Subjects reported participating in some form of (combined) drug business for heroin on 14 percent (PD = 1,599) of the person-days, 4 percent (PD = 446) for cocaine, 3 percent (PD = 339) for methadone, 3 percent (PD = 308) for marijuana, and 1 percent (PD = 144) for pills.

In short, some kind of drug business occurred on about one-fifth of all person-days, but with much variation by specific drug and type of distribution. Steer-tout-cop of heroin was the most common behavior (12% of person-days), followed by STC of cocaine (3% of all person-days). The direct sales of heroin (2%) and cocaine (0.40%), was much less common than STC among these heroin abusers. The direct sales of methadone (3%) and marijuana (2%) was relatively less common when compared with STC of heroin.

Frequency of Transactions per Active Day

Table 8.1 also shows the frequency of various types of drug transactions on active days. Frequency is defined here as the number of self-reported transactions per day with at least one act of participation in that activity on a given day.

Direct Sales

The first row of Table 8.1 shows that 873 person-days had some type of direct sales. Subjects reported an average of 12 direct sales during days with one or more direct sale transactions involving any of the five illicit substances. There were 17 transactions on days with heroin sales, 40 transactions on days with cocaine sales, 1 transaction on methadone sale days, 15 transactions on marijuana sale days, and 5 transactions on days with pill sales.

Steer-Tout-Cop

Subjects reported an average of five STC transactions per day with STC activity for any substance. There were 5 STC acts per day for heroin, 3 for cocaine, 3 for illicit methadone, 2 for marijuana, and 4 for pills.

Drug Thefts

Subjects reported only one drug theft transaction per day with some theft of drugs. This did not vary by type of drug.

Combined Transactions

Subjects in the sample reported an average frequency of 8 transactions per day with any form of distribution activity (bottom section of column 3, Table 8.1). The frequencies of combined transactions per AD was 6 for heroin, 7 for cocaine, 13 for marijuana, 5 for pills, and 4 for alcohol.

In summary, these data show that while relatively few days involved direct sales, on days when subjects sold heroin or cocaine, they reported sizable numbers of drug transactions (17 and 40 transactions respectively). While subjects had many more days with STC transactions of heroin and cocaine, the average number of STC transactions was much lower for heroin and cocaine (5 and 3 respectively).

Due to relatively low penalties (marijuana possession and sale of small amounts typically result in fines) and the low value of retail units of marijuana and pills (joints and pills sell for under a dollar), the number of days and frequencies of direct sales of marijuana and pills is considerably higher than for STC of these drugs.

Gross Business on Active Days

The fourth column of Table 8.1 shows the dollar value of gross business per day with one or more known transactions of specific drugs and types of distribution activity. *Gross business* is defined as the approximate economic value of drugs which subjects helped to distribute on a given person-day. Thus, gross business is greater than the subject's cash or drug income (see Table 8.2), since much of money is returned to the supplier and/or shared with others who may assist in drug business activity.

Drug Sales

On the 873 days with any direct sales activity, subjects made average gross sales of $103 per AD. The gross business per AD was highest from the sale of heroin ($257) and cocaine ($390). Gross business amounts were considerably less for methadone ($24), marijuana ($16), pills ($27), and alcohol ($5) on days when direct sales of these substances occurred.

Steer-Tout-Cop

On person-days with STC transactions, the gross business averaged $154 per AD, regardless of the drug. Gross business was highest on days with heroin STC ($160), and less for other: cocaine ($68), methadone ($48), marijuana ($53), and pills ($31).

Drug Thefts

Gross business amounts from drug thefts were not computed because the thief generally consumed the drugs and did not resell them. Such stolen drugs are included as "drug income" and are reported below.

Combined Transactions

Finally, on days with combined (sale, STC, theft) drug business activity, subjects reported average gross business amounts of $143 per AD, which varied by specific drug: heroin ($176), cocaine ($107), methadone ($26), marijuana ($22), pills ($27), and alcohol ($6).

Thus, the highest gross business values per AD involved direct sales of heroin ($257) and cocaine ($390). The lowest gross business amount per AD involved marijuana sales ($16).

In short, on the average day when they engaged in some type of drug distribution, subjects reported helping to sell or actually selling illicit drugs with a gross value of over $140 per AD. Subjects received less than one-third of this figure as their "income," as discussed in the next section.

Table 8.2

Average Cash and Drug Income and Combined Returns in Drug Selling, Steer-Tout-Cop, Drug Theft, and Combined Returns on Active Days with Specific Transactions Involving Indicated Substance, by Drugs

Drug(s)	For Specific Drug(s) and Transaction Type at Left Average Cash Income per AD with $1+ of Cash	Average Drug Income per AD with $1+ of Drugs	Average Returns per AD with $1+ Cash/Drugs	Base Ns: No. AD[a] Cash Income (Col.1)	Drug Income (Col.2)	Average Returns (Col.3)
	DIRECT SALES of:					
Any Illicit Drug	$38.36	$54.35	$43.74	858	97	873
Heroin	67.90	64.31	86.37	191	71	203
Cocaine	34.90	33.79	44.30	40	19	46
Methadone	23.56	.00	23.56	303	0	303
Marijuana	29.28	2.33	29.30	262	15	263
Pills	30.63	4.83	30.87	122	6	122
Alcohol	10.00	.00	10.00	1	0	1
	STEER, TOUT, COP of:					
Any Illicit Drug	19.91	33.19	36.46	850	1,328	1,673
Heroin	19.32	33.50	36.97	666	1,149	1,389
Cocaine	14.04	18.54	21.21	230	280	397
Methadone	10.64	10.00	10.63	39	1	40
Marijuana	13.17	8.10	11.61	18	41	49
Pills	9.26	4.89	9.57	19	9	23
Alcohol	.00	3.00	3.00	0	1	1
	DRUG THEFTS of following:					
Any Illicit Drug	*	118.98	118.98	*	86	86
Heroin	*	150.70	150.70	*	54	54
Cocaine	*	86.92	86.92	*	13	13
Methadone	*	19.00	19.00	*	2	2
Marijuana	*	38.33	38.33	*	3	3
Pills	*	57.93	57.93	*	14	14
Alcohol	*	12.00	12.00	*	1	1
	COMBINED (Sale+STC+Theft) Transactions:					
Any Illicit Drug	30.33	40.36	44.84	1,643	1,476	2,440
Heroin	30.61	40.76	48.17	844	1,256	1,599
Cocaine	17.13	22.83	25.99	270	305	446
Methadone	22.42	16.00	22.43	337	3	339
Marijuana	28.34	8.31	27.24	279	58	308
Pills	28.15	31.57	33.31	139	28	144
Alcohol	10.00	7.50	12.50	1	2	2

a - AD: Active Days--On the given day, the subject reported $1 or more dollars from transaction(s) of this type for specific drug(s) indicated. Columns 3-6 are denominators for amounts given in columns 1-3, respectively.
*--No cash income from "drug thefts" is obtained.
NOTE: Alcohol is not included in "Any Illicit" Drug.

Returns from Drug Business Activity

This section analyzes how much was "earned" on days with distribution activity. Since many distributors consume substantial proportions of their supplies while selling, they receive much of their "earnings" as *drug income*. Less often do they receive "cash income" (money payments). On some days they receive both cash income and drug income, sometimes for different drugs or for different behaviors (selling and STC). Earnings from distribution activities are given as cash income, drug income, and combined returns (cash and drug income together).

Table 8.2 shows the average daily cash income as it would appear to the drug user-distributor on days when he was active. The average dollar returns given in columns 1-3 of Table 8.2 are based upon active days (columns 4-6) which meet all three of the following characteristics:

(a) one or more dollars of cash or drug income was earned,
(b) from the specific type of drug business (sales, STC, thefts, or combined),
(c) for the drug(s) specified in each row.

The dynamics of earnings from drug business crimes can be better understood by comparing the number of active days (Base Ns) with the average amounts earned on those days.[3]

Drug Sales Per AD

On the days with direct sales, subjects reported an average of $38 on 858 days with cash income and $54 of drug value on 97 days with drug income. The returns (cash + drug income) were $44 on the 873 days with any drug sales. The corresponding average cash income, drug income, and returns from heroin sales were somewhat higher than for any drug sales. The returns ($86) during 203 days with heroin sales were almost twice as great as the returns ($44) on 46 days with cocaine sales. Methadone, marijuana, and pills are almost always sold and rarely used to gain drug income (amounts are small when gained).

Steer-Tout-Cop Per AD

On days with STC activity, an average of $20 on 850 days with cash income and $33 from 1,328 days with drug income provided average returns of $36 on 1,673 days with STC. Most of income from STC came from heroin.

Drug Thefts Per AD

Drug thefts do not generate cash income, but were the most lucrative way to obtain large drug incomes. Returns from drug thefts were substantial only for heroin ($150). Thefts of cocaine and pills occurred much less frequently and with lower returns than heroin. Thefts of methadone and marijuana were very uncommon.

Combined Transactions Per AD

On the days with combined drug transactions, subjects reported an average of $30 on 1,643 days with cash income and $40 of value on 1,476 days with drug income. The average returns (cash + drug income) were $45 on the 2,440 days with any drug business activity. The average returns for combined transactions are dominated by the large number of days with heroin activity relative to other drugs.

The average returns ($48) on 1,599 days with heroin distribution were about twice as high as the returns ($26) on 446 days with cocaine distribution and the returns from marijuana, methadone, and pill distribution activity ($22-$33).

CONCLUSIONS

This study of 201 heroin abusers is one of the first to obtain detailed daily information about various types of drug distribution. Data presented elsewhere (Johnson et al. 1985) shows that the average heroin abuser in this study is very active in drug distribution crimes; they annually commit over 360 drug sales, and over 500 steer-tout-cop transactions, but receive relatively low economic returns (about $1,000 in cash and $2,000 as drug income annually). The data presented in this paper further specifies information about days with drug distribution crimes by these Northern Manhattan heroin abusers. Over one-fifth of all person-days involved some form of drug distribution, but with much variation by specific substance and type of transaction (Table 8.1). Direct sales were relatively less common than steer-tout-cop activity. While heroin was the favorite drug and used on a near daily basis by most subjects, only 2 percent of the person-days involved direct sales of heroin, while 12 percent of person-days had STC of heroin. For other drugs (cocaine, marijuana, methadone, and pills), less than 4 percent of person-days involved either direct sales or STC.

While days with drug selling or STC were a minority of all days, multiple transactions on active days were common. The average day with heroin sales involved 17 transactions, days with cocaine sales had 40 transactions, and days with marijuana sales had 15 transactions. Days with STC of heroin or cocaine were six times more common than direct sales. There were 5 heroin and 3 cocaine transactions per STC active day (Table 8.1).

The returns from drug business of heroin abusers averaged $45 per active day. Somewhat less than one-half came as cash income, and the remainder as drug income. Even when the returns were limited to active days and some income (Table 8.2), the returns were relatively modest. Even on days with an average of 17 heroin sales, the combined returns were only $86. The returns from other types of transactions and for other drugs were less than one-half this figure. Moreover, the average (mean) amounts provided here are greatly affected by a few person-days with very large returns. It is likely that more than 75 percent of the person-days with distribution activity had returns which were less than the averages presented in Table 8.3. In short, the median returns are well under $50 a day for all forms of drug business.

Implications

The patterns of drug distribution described above have important implications for social policy towards heroin abusers and their numerous drug business crimes. The heroin abuser studied here have characteristics very similar to persons arrested for drug sales and possession (Wish, Brady & Cuadrado 1984, 1986). The types of drug crimes these heroin abusers commit are very similar to the typical arrests made for heroin sale and possession. Although these subjects do not constitute a representative sample of this difficult-to-specify population, the large number of person-days collected and the findings above may help in suggesting future social policies towards heroin sales and related crimes (but not cocaine or crack distribution crimes). The central implications of findings above include:

(1) *Should drug laws be changed to recognize a distinction between direct sales and other similar crimes such as steer-tout-cop?* The evidence presented here shows that STC crimes by heroin abusers occur on many more days than direct sales. Days with STC of heroin or cocaine are 6-8 times more common than direct sales. While the average returns from heroin sales per active day exceed those from STC per AD (Table 8.2), the total dollar volume from STC exceeds sales of heroin or cocaine. Current laws and arrest practices by police, however, treat STC crimes as equivalent to drug sales (i.e., STC crimes are frequently charged as drug sales).

(2) *Should penalties and related legal sanctions be lower for STC crimes than for direct sales?* These data suggest that STC crimes could involve lesser sanctions than direct sales, since the offender is typically "assisting" in sales work, and not the direct transaction. In current practice, STC crimes may already receive lesser sanctions than direct sales. Many arrestees charged with "sales," but who have actually committed STC crimes, may already have their charges dismissed, reduced to possession, or otherwise obtain minor penalties. On the other hand, new penalties for STC crimes might be sanctioned more severely than simple possession because persons have been active participants in illegal transactions.

(3) *For drug sales involving small amounts and lower dollar returns, should non-incarcerative penalties be the primary sanctions?* One way to relieve jail overcrowding would be to impose nonpenal punishments upon user-dealers who commit numerous STC and sales transactions, but typically earn under $100 or its retail equivalent per day. For the vast majority of drug-related arrests, this is likely to be the *de facto* policy of the courts (if not penal law), simply because jail space is unavailable for large number of offenders charged with drug business crimes.

(4) *Should and can new nonpenal sanctions be developed which have the primary goal of effectively supervising the typical heroin abuser who engages in drug business while at liberty so they have less time to sell drugs or engage in STC?* The data presented above document widespread participation in a variety of drugs and types of illegal drug transactions. New social policies designed to reduce such involvements by half or more could mean substantial reductions in individual patterns of drug business activity. A supervision system needs to be designed to reduce both the frequency of use and the sale or STC of heroin or cocaine by heroin abusers such as those in this study. While a description of such a supervision system is beyond the scope of this paper, several major themes for implementing such a system are available (Johnson, Lipton & Wish, 1986; Wexler, Lipton & Johnson, 1988).

Regardless of the particular social policies pursued by police and other authorities, a major policy implication flowing from this chapter and research is as follows: Heroin abusers commit a variety of drug distribution crimes involving several drugs, particularly heroin, cocaine, and marijuana. Virtually all these drug crimes occurred without any contact with police. Most distribution crimes occur during a relatively small number of days, but involve several transactions per day from which relatively limited returns in cash are realized. Most transactions are "paid" in drugs which the person consumes. Such frequent, but small, drug transactions by heroin abusers at the street level have become the major crime problem in New York City and many other cities in America. Since solutions to the problem of preventing numerous small transactions by low-level users and distributors are nowhere evident, new efforts to greatly improve enforcement practices and make treatment widely available to drug abusers are badly needed.

NOTES

[1] Johnson et al. (1985: Ch. 6) also delineates other supportive roles in drug distribution such as lending or renting works, holding or testing drugs, guarding or looking out for sellers, running a shooting gallery, etc. Such roles generally do not involve illegal drug transactions which may be counted (as with sales, STC, or thefts). Moreover, persons performing such roles are typically paid for their time, but not on a transaction basis. Detailed data on economic returns from such activities were not obtained during the study.

[2] While the data were carefully coded, missing information was frequently encountered. For example, a respondent recalled 8 heroin sales and selling marijuana, but couldn't remember the number of marijuana transactions. This was counted as 9 transactions (8 heroin and at least 1 marijuana). If the subject recalled making 5 STC transactions, but couldn't recall which drugs, this was excluded from the active day pool. When the respondent reported a distinct number of transactions, but could not remember the dollar amounts, a value of $1 was assigned (although it was probably greater in most cases). Thus, the number of transactions and dollar amounts reported herein are conservative estimates of distribution behavior on active days.

[3] On a minority of person-days, subjects earned both cash income and drug income for selling a specific drug. Thus, the sum of active days (base Ns) in column 4 + 5 of Table 8.2 are generally larger than the number of days given in column 6. The dollar values, however, are accurately summed, but weighted by the number of active days.

REFERENCES

Adler, P.A (1985). *Wheeling and Dealing: An Ethnography of Upper Level Drug Dealing and Smuggling Communities*. New York: Columbia University Press.

Anglin, M.D. & W.C. McGlothlin (1984). "Outcome of Narcotic Addict Treatment in California. In F.M. Tims & J.P. Ludford (eds.) *Drug Abuse Treatment Evaluation: Strategies, Progress, and Prospects*, 106-128. Research Monograph Series 51. Rockville, MD: National Institute on Drug Abuse.

Ball, J.C. (1986). "The Hyper-Criminal Opiate Addict." In B.D. Johnson & E. Wish (eds.) *Crime Rates Among Drug Abusing Offenders*. Final Report to National Institute of Justice, 81-104. New York: Narcotic and Drug Research, Inc. July.

Ball, J.C., L. Rosen, E.G. Friedman & D.N. Nurco (1979). "The Impact of Heroin Addiction upon Criminality." In L. Harris (ed.) *Problems of Drug Dependence, 1979*. Research Monograph 27, Rockville, MD: National Institute on Drug Abuse: 163-169.

Ball, J.C., L. Rosen, J.A. Flueck & D.N. Nurco (1981). "The Criminality of Heroin Addicts When Addicted and When Off Opiates." In J.A. Inciardi (ed.), *The Drugs-Crime Connection*, 39-65. Beverly Hills, CA: Sage.

Ball, J.C., L. Rosen, J.A. Flueck & D.N. Nurco (1982). "Lifetime Criminality of Heroin Addicts in the United States." *Journal of Drug Issues* 3:225-239.

Ball, J.C., J.W. Shaffer & D.N. Nurco (1983). "The Day-to-Day Criminality of Heroin Addicts in Baltimore: A Study in the Continuity of Offence Rates." *Drug and Alcohol Dependence* 12(1):19-142.

Blum, R. (1972). *The Dream Sellers*. San Francisco: Jossey-Bass.

Blumstein, A., J. Cohen, J.A. Roth & C.A. Visher (eds.) (1986). *Criminal Careers and "Career Criminals."* Washington, DC: National Academy Press.

Carpenter, C., B. Glassner, B.D. Johnson & J. Loughlin (1988). *Kids, Drugs and Crime*. Lexington, MA: Lexington Books.

Chaiken, J.M. & M.R. Chaiken (1982). *Varieties of Criminal Behavior*. Santa Monica, CA: The RAND Corporation.

Chaiken, J.M. & M.R. Chaiken (1983). "Crime Rates and the Active Offender." In J.Q. Wilson (ed.) *Crime and Public Policy*, 11-29. New Brunswick: Transaction Books.

Chaiken, M.R. (1986). "Crime Rates and Substance Abuse Among Types of Offenders." In B.D. Johnson & E. Wish (eds.), *Crime Rates Among Drug Abusing Offenders*. Final Report to National Institute of Justice, 12-54. New York: Narcotic and Drug Research, Inc. July.

Chaiken, M.R. & B.D. Johnson (1988). *Characteristics of Different Types of Drug-Involved Offenders*. Washington, DC: National Institute of Justice. Issues and Practices.

Collins, J.J., R.L. Hubbard & J.V. Rachal (1985). "Expensive Drug Use and Illegal Income: A Test of Explanatory Hypotheses." *Criminology*, 23(4):743-764.

Elliott, D.S. & D. Huizinga (1985). "The Relationship between Delinquent Behavior and ADM Problems." Proceedings of the ADAMHA/OJJDP Research Conference on Juvenile Offenders with Serious Drug Alcohol, Mental Health Problems. Washington, DC: OJJDP.

Hanson, B., G. Beschner, J.M. Walters & E. Bovelle (1985). *Life with Heroin: Voices from the Inner City*. Lexington, MA: Lexington Books.

Harwood, H.J., D.M. Napolitano, P.L. Kristiansen & J.J. Collins (1984). *Economic Costs to Society of Alcohol and Drug Abuse and Mental Illness: 1980*. Research Triangle Institute, Research Triangle Park, North Carolina, 1-12.

Hubbard, R.L., J.V. Rachal, S.G. Craddock & E.R. Cavanaugh (1984). "Treatment Outcome Prospective Study (TOPS): Client Characteristics and Behaviors Before, During, and After Treatment." In F.M. Tims & J.P. Ludford (eds.) *Drug Abuse Treatment Evaluation: Strategies, Progress, and Prospects*, 42-68. Research Monograph Series 51. Rockville, MD: National Institute on Drug Abuse.

Inciardi, J.A. 1979. "Heroin Use and Street Crime." *Crime and Delinquency* (July):335-346.

Inciardi, J.A. (1984). *Criminal Justice*. Orlando, FL: Academic Press.

Johnson, B.D. (1978). "Once an Addict Seldom an Addict." *Contemporary Drug Problems*, Spring: 35-53.

Johnson, B.D., B. Glassner, J. Loughlin & C. Carpenter (1986). *Drugs and Alcohol in Adolescent Delinquency*. Final Report to the National Institute of Justice. New York: Interdisciplinary Research Center and Narcotic and Drug Research, Inc.

Johnson, B.D., P. Goldstein, E. Preble, J. Schmeidler, D.S. Lipton, B. Spunt, & T. Miller (1985). *Taking Care of Business: The Economics of Crime by Heroin Abusers*. Lexington, MA: Lexington Books.

Johnson, B.D., D.S. Lipton, & E.D. Wish (1986). *Findings about Drug Abusing Offenders: Alternatives to Incarceration*. Summary report to the National Institute of Justice.

Johnson, B.D. & T. Williams (1986). "Economics of Dealing in a Nonmonetary Labor Market." Paper presented at the International Conference on Drug Abuse and Addiction, Amsterdam, April.

Johnson, B.D. & E.D. Wish (1986a). *Crime Rates Among Drug Abusing Offenders*. Final Report to National Institute of Justice, 10-54. New York: Narcotic and Drug Research, Inc. July.

Johnson, B.D. & E.D. Wish (1986b). *Highlights from Research on Drug and Alcohol Abusing Criminals*. Summary report to the National Institute of Justice.

Johnson, B.D. & E.D. Wish (1987). *Criminal Events Among Seriously Criminal Drug Abusers*. New York: Narcotic and Drug Research, Inc.

Johnson, B.D., E.D. Wish & B. Glassner (1986). *Disaggregating Drugs-Alcohol to Crime Relationships: Highlights of Studies Among Youths in the General Population*. Summary report to the National Institute of Justice.

Kaplan, M.A. (1987). "The Relationship Between Drug Use, Drug Sales, and Non-drug Related Criminal Behavior in a National Sample of Youth." Doctoral Dissertation in Sociology, City University of New York Graduate Center.

McGlothlin, W.C., M.D. Anglin & B.D. Wilson (1977). *An Evaluation of the California Civil Addict Program.* Rockville, MD: National Institute on Drug Abuse.

Mieczkowski, T. (1986). "Geeking Up and Throwing Down: Heroin Street Life in Detroit." *Criminology*, 24(4): 645-646.

Nurco, D.N., J.C. Ball, J.W. Shaffer & T.E. Hanlon (1985). "The Criminality of Narcotic Addicts." *Journal of Nervous and Mental Disease*, 173(2): 94-102.

O'Donnell, J.A., H.L. Voss, R.R. Clayton, G.T. Slatin & R.G.W. Room (1976). *Young Men and Drugs: A Nationwide Survey.* Rockville, MD: National Institute on Drug Abuse.

President's Commission on Organized Crime (1986). *The Impact: Organized Crime Today.* Washington, DC: U.S. Government Printing Office.

Speckart, G. & M.D. Anglin (1986). "Narcotics Use and Crime: An Overview of Recent Research Advances." Presentation to Drugs, Alcohol, and Crime Conference, sponsored by National Institute of Justice, San Francisco, CA, May.

Speckart, G. & M.D. Anglin (1988). "Narcotics Use and Crime: A Causal Modeling Approach." *Journal of Quantitative Criminology*, 2:3-28.

Simon, C.P. & A.D. Witte (1982). *Beating the System: The Underground Economy.* Boston: Auburn House.

Waldorf, D., S. Murphy, C. Reinarman & B. Joyce (1977). "An Ethnography of Cocaine Snorters." Washington, DC: Drug Abuse Council.

Waldorf, D. (1987). "Business Practices and Social Organization of Cocaine Sellers." Presented at the American Society of Criminology, Montreal Canada, November.

Wexler, H.K., D.F. Lipton & B.D. Johnson (1988). A Criminal Justice Strategy for Treating Cocaine-heroin Abusing Offenders in Custody. *Issues and Practices*. Washington, DC: National Institute of Justice.

Wish, E.D. (1982). "Are Heroin Users Really Nonviolent?" Paper presented at Academy of Criminal Justice Sciences, Louisville, Kentucky.

Wish, E., E. Brady & M. Cuadrado (1984). "Drug Use and Crime in Arrestees in Manhattan." Paper presented at the 47th Meeting of the Committee on Problems of Drug Dependence, New York, Narcotic and Drug Research, Inc.

Wish, E.D., E. Brady & M. Cuadrado (1986). "Urine Testing of Arrestees: Findings from Manhattan." New York: Narcotic and Drug Research, Inc.

Wish, E.D., M. Cuadrado & J.A. Mortorana (1986). *Estimates of Drug Use in Intensive Supervision Probationers: Results from a Pilot Test*. New York: Narcotic and Drug Research, Inc.

Wish, E.D., B.D. Johnson, D. Strug, M. Chedekel & D.S. Lipton (1983). "Are Urine Tests Good Indicators of the Validity of Self-Reports of Drug Use?" Paper presented at the American Society of Criminology, Denver, Colorado.

Wish, E.D., K.A. Klumpp, A.H. Moorer & E. Brady (1980). *An Analysis of Crime among Arrestees in the District of Columbia*. Institute for Law and Social Research. Springfield, VA: National Technical Information Services.

9

The Drug Use-Delinquency Connection in Adolescence[*]

Helene Raskin White
Center of Alcohol Studies
Rutgers, The State University of New Jersey

The relationship between drug use and criminal behavior is the source of continuing speculation and debate. Researchers probing the links between drug use and crime for the past 50 years have produced an abundance of contradictory findings. These disparities have paved an erratic course for social policy. Although American drug control and crime control strategies assume that an important connection exists between drug use and crime (Watters, Reinarman & Fagan, 1985; Clayton, 1981a), the precise nature of the relationship between drug use and crime remains elusive. About the only area of agreement is that substance use and crime are somehow linked (Gropper, 1985).

Much of the literature supporting the drug-crime connection has been drawn from studies of criminality among narcotic addicts (cf. Inciardi, 1979; Ball, Rosen, Flueck & Nurco, 1981; Nurco, Schaeffer, Ball & Kinlock, 1984; McGlothlin, Anglin & Wilson, 1978) or alcoholics (Collins, 1981) or studies of drug use among criminal offenders (Barton, 1976; Bureau of Justice Statistics, 1983a, b). This research supports the notion that alcohol use is associated with violent crime (see Collins, 1981, 1988; Pernanen, 1976, 1981)

---

[*] The author would like to express appreciation to Dr. Jeffrey Fagan for his substantial contributions to this manuscript, and to Drs. Marsha Bates, Richard Catalano, and Randy LaGrange for their comments and suggestions on earlier drafts. Preparation of this chapter was supported, in part, by grants from the National Institute on Drug Abuse (#DA-03395) and the National Institute on Alcohol Abuse and Alcoholism (#AA-05823).

while other drug (especially heroin) use is associated with a high proportion of property crime (see Ball et al., 1981; Nurco et al., 1984; McGlothlin et al., 1978).   Proponents of the alcohol-violence model emphasize the psychopharmacological effects of alcohol intoxication as the cause for violent behavior (Collins, 1988; Pernanen, 1981). The drug-property crime model is based principally on the notion that heroin (and other drug) addicts commit crimes in order to secure money for drugs (Ball et al., 1981; Nurco et al., 1984; McGlothlin et al., 1978). Interestingly, proponents of the alcohol-violence model do not give weight to the fact that a substantial proportion of inmates convicted of property crimes were under the influence of alcohol at the time of the offense (Bureau of Justice Statistics, 1983a, b). Similarly, drug-property crime model proponents have only recently given weight to the fact that heroin-addicted individuals often are involved in violent crimes, typically committed over drug possession and sale (see Goldstein, 1985). In advancing these separate views, some researchers have ignored the fact that distinctions between property and violent crime are often blurred. For example, some robberies have begun as property crimes purely for economic gain and have resulted in a person being hurt, thus changing categories from property to violent crime.[1] They also have included drug-related crimes (from possession and dealing, to murder resulting from a bad drug deal) in their analyses, which inflates the associations between drug use and crime.

The value of these studies examining the drug-crime nexus in addict and criminal samples lies in their ability to detect a high degree of overlap among persons heavily involved in both behaviors. But the question still remains as to the degree of association between drug use and criminal behavior in the general population. All studies of "normal" (i.e., noncriminal, non-drug ad-dicted) individuals have been conducted on samples of adolescents and young adults. Clearly, the drug-crime connection in the adolescent population is of interest because adolescents account for a large proportion of criminal be-havior. The purpose of this chapter is to review the literature on the drug-crime (delinquency) nexus among adolescents. Given that several excellent reviews have previously been written (e.g., Elliott & Ageton, 1976a; Watters et al., 1985), I will not attempt to replicate these efforts, but rather highlight important conclusions from these reviews. I will also add some recent find-ings from several large studies of adolescents that have not been brought to-gether in previous reviews. First, I will discuss the methodological issues in studying the drug-crime connection. Then I will present general models of the drug-crime connection and specifically discuss the spurious model among adolescents. Finally, I will describe recent results from three studies focusing on the drug-delinquency nexus in adolescence.

METHODOLOGICAL ISSUES

Definitions

In order to fully understand the data bearing on the relationship be-tween drug use and delinquency, there are several methodological issues that need to be addressed. The first issue has to do with definitions of drug use and delinquency and the extent to which they represent two distinct types of deviant behavior. There is a history of including drug use in the early scales of delinquent behavior (see for example Gold & Reimer, 1975; Hindelang, 1972). In a recent issue of *Criminology*, Hill and Atkinson (1988), for exam-ple, included six categories of drugs, as well as two drug-related offenses among their list of 20 offenses that are combined to form a single scale of self-reported delinquency. On the other hand, several papers in this same journal reported research on drug use only (e.g., Johnson, Marcos & Bahr, 1987) or employed delinquency scales which did not include drugs (e.g., La-Grange & White, 1985).

Elliott, Huizinga, and Ageton (1985) included certain types of drug-re-lated offenses in their self-reported delinquency scale, such as buying liquor for a minor and dealing drugs, but excluded measures of personal use. Maintaining drug selling in a delinquency scale, however, can still artificially inflate the relationship between drug use and delinquency because it has been well accepted that almost all persons who sell drugs are also regular users of those substances (Goode, 1970; Johnson, 1973; Single & Kandel, 1978). In a recent interview study, Carpenter, Glassner, Johnson, and Loughlin (1988) found that virtually all adolescents who sold drugs were users of a wide variety of substances. They also found that as drug use in-creased, so did dealing. On the other hand, research on gangs and drug sell-ing suggests that not all persons who sell drugs are users. The recent re-search on gang members and other adolescents who are involved in drug selling organizations presents strong evidence that many adolescents avoid using drugs while dealing or avoid them altogether (see Fagan, 1989a).

Clearly illicit alcohol and other drug use fits the definition of delinquent behavior, which is generally defined as illegal acts committed by juveniles. In the basic texts on delinquency, drug use appears to be treated as a type of delinquency. For example, Jensen and Rojek (1980, p. 219) stated "An inter-esting finding concerning female delinquency is the influence of males on fe-male drug use." In his book on deviant behavior, Akers (1985, p. 68) wrote "...and one form of delinquency, underage drinking..." Akers (1985, p. 128) suggested how researchers in the drug-crime field should address this defini-tional problem: "Obviously, the possession and sale of illegal drugs are themselves criminal offenses, but what is the relationship between drug use and nondrug criminal behavior?"

In order to be able to clearly distinguish drug-taking behavior from criminal behavior, this chapter will focus on the connection between drug use (i.e., typical drug use patterns, as well as pattern of use at the time of commission of an offense) and *other non-drug* delinquent behaviors (i.e., excluding illicit drug use, possession, distribution, and importation, etc.).

Measures

Most of the survey research on the drug-crime connection has relied upon self-report data. Self-reports are generally accepted as a reliable indicator of delinquent behavior (Hindelang, Hirschi & Weis, 1981; Huizinga & Elliott, 1981) and alcohol and drug use (Single, Kandel & Johnson, 1975; Radosevich, Lanza-Kaduce, Akers & Krohn, 1980; Rouse, Kozel & Richards, 1985). In addition, self-reports provide a more direct, sensitive, and complete measure of various forms of deviant behavior than do measures based upon official law enforcement and institutional records (Elliott & Huizinga, 1989; Dunford & Elliott, 1984) and avoid the problem of false negatives (i.e., "hidden" cases) (Elliott, Huizinga & Menard, 1989). According to Elliott et al. (1989), the weight of the evidence suggests that self-reports of drug use and delinquency have good to excellent levels of reliability and acceptable levels of validity, as compared to other social science measures. (For a list of supporting studies, see Elliott et al., 1989).

Of course there are many caveats for using self-report data. First, delinquents are harder to contact than nondelinquents and when contacted are less likely to participate in research. In addition, delinquents are less likely than nondelinquents to give honest replies when they do participate (Hindelang et al., 1981). Further, there may be racial differences in reliability and validity of self-report data (Hindelang et al., 1981). According to Elliott et al. (1989), falsification is relatively rare, although there are some problems related to accuracy of recall, classification errors, and reporting of trivial events.

There also have been problems operationalizing variables. For example, in most research on the drug-crime relationship among adults, drug users have been defined as opiate addicts, and alcohol users have been defined as either alcoholics or persons who were intoxicated on alcohol at the time of the crime. For adolescents, however, a user often is anyone who has ever tried a particular substance, regardless of their frequency or extent of use. These types of contradictions have created problems for comparisons across studies. (See also McBride & McCoy, 1982 for issues in definitions and classification schema.)

In addition to failing to consider levels of drug use and delinquency, most researchers have also failed to distinguish among onset, continuation, and cessation of these behaviors. In fact, research on adolescents suggests that different factors contribute to the onset of drug use and delinquency than contribute to their continuation (Akers, 1985) and cessation (Hawkins & Farrington, 1988). Also, for many adolescents, behaviors such as drug use and delinquency are constantly changing, so measures tapping a static point may not represent the true behavior pattern (see Blumstein, Farrington & Moitra, 1985).

There are also issues of measurement in terms of using simple dichotomies or trichotomies which could mask subtle differences between groups. As Fagan, Hansen, and Jang (1983) have suggested, crude measures can obscure critical analytic distinctions and mask etiological distinctions between various behavior patterns. Questionnaires often contain terms which lead to arbitrary interpretation, such as "often" or "occasionally," thus making comparisons among subjects unreliable. In addition, researchers often truncate scales, thus obscuring discrimination at the high end. Elliott et al. (1989) have argued that trivial forms of delinquent activity are often overrepresented and serious forms are either underrepresented or omitted.

Further, aggregate scales are often used, which have both advantages and disadvantages. Some aggregate indices of drug use combine quantitative and qualitative aspects of drug use and are sensitive to multiple drug use (see Pandina, White & Yorke, 1981). However, the types of aggregate drug use scales typically used in the drug-delinquency literature are often operationalized as use of any drug other than alcohol or marijuana a certain number of times in the past year (e.g., Elliott et al., 1989). Use of this type of scale masks the unique relationship between certain drugs (e.g., crack or cocaine) and delinquency and also disregards multiple drug use in terms of concurrent use of alcohol or marijuana and another drug. Similarly all types of delinquency are often merged into one scale obscuring distinctions between property and violent crimes or between serious and nonserious crimes.

Samples

Researchers have relied upon captive samples in prisons or in treatment programs to study the drug-crime relationship. Such samples have the advantage of providing a pool of subjects who exhibit high frequencies of the behaviors of interest, but the relationships observed may not be generalizable to the general population (see Waldorf & Reinarman, 1975). At the same time, it may be these relationships that have the greatest relevance for drug control and crime control policies.

On the other hand, samples drawn from general populations have limited numbers of individuals engaging in drug use or delinquency. Drug use and delinquency are concentrated in urban areas, while some survey research is spread across wide geographic areas, hence, seriously underrepresenting these behaviors and possibly attenuating the relationships observed (Fagan, Weis, Cheng & Watters, 1987). Further, many general surveys are administered in schools and omit dropouts who are known to have higher rates of drug use (Fagan & Pablon, 1989) and delinquency (Fagan & Pablon, 1989; Thornberry, Moore & Christenson, 1985).

Analyses

Another problem in estimating the extent of overlap between drug use and delinquency results from differences in classification schema and analytic strategies. Researchers often fail to control for age in their analyses. Given that drug use and delinquency are age-dependent (Hirschi & Gottfredson, 1983; LaGrange & White, 1985), failure to take account of this phenomenon can lead to spurious findings. In addition, researchers use different analytic strategies (i.e., OLS, LISREL, path models), all of which involve differences in causal assumptions. There is conflict about whether to include Time 1 measures of the dependent variable in longitudinal models. Inclusion of these measures controls for the behavior at a prior time but also inflates the amount of variance explained (see Hirschi, 1987).

Clayton and Tuchfeld (1982) have argued that most researchers have failed to apply the appropriate standards of proof and criteria of causality: researchers' standards of proof of causality have been unreasonably high and rigid; they have misunderstood the criteria for causality; and they have been reluctant to make causal statements for fear of the policy implications. Instead, Clayton and Tuchfeld have suggested three criteria for causality: a statistical association between two variables must be established, the causal variable must precede the effect, and the relationship must not be spuriousness.

The issues raised here provide a sample of the many conceptual and methodological ambiguities that characterize the drug-crime literature and the following review should be interpreted within these limitations. In the next section, I will present four general models that have been employed to explain the association between drug use and crime.

GENERAL ASSOCIATIVE MODELS

Four different perspectives of the drug-crime connection have been predominant in the literature (Elliott & Ageton, 1976a; Watters et al., 1985). Each implies a different strategy for control policies. Here I will briefly discuss these four models and the literature on both adults and adolescents which supports or refutes each model.

Model 1 - the "drugs-cause-crime" explanation assumes that drug users need to generate illicit income to support their drug habit (economic motivation), and/or that the psychopharmacological effects of drugs increase the addict's propensity toward crime, and especially violent crime. This view has been the cornerstone of U.S. narcotic and treatment policies (McBride, 1981; Watters et al., 1985). Recent and impressive evidence of the economic motivation explanation for the drugs-cause-crime model comes from literature on heroin addicts which indicates that raising or lowering the frequency of substance use among addicts raises or lowers their frequency of crime (e.g., Anglin & Speckart, 1988; Ball et al., 1981; Nurco, et al., 1984; McGlothlin et al., 1978). Other studies demonstrate that criminal activity is significantly greater following addiction to drugs than before addiction (De Fleur, Ball & Snarr, 1969; Plair & Jackson, 1970). Heavily involved daily drug users, especially heroin users, account for a disproportionate share of criminal acts, and the containment of drug use through treatment and close supervision leads to dramatic reductions in both drug use and crime (Clayton & Tuchfeld, 1982).

On the other hand, the psychopharmacological explanation for the drugs-cause-crime model has largely been refuted in the literature with regard to heroin and marijuana, but has received strong support in the alcohol literature and occasionally for other drugs such as barbiturates, amphetamines, PCP, and LSD (Goldstein, 1985). This model suggests that the psychopharmacological effects (including disinhibition, cognitive-perceptual distortions, etc.) of intoxication, as well as situational factors accompanying occasions of intoxication, contribute to crimes of violence (Collins, 1981, 1988). (For greater detail on the link between violence and specific substances see Fagan, 1989b; Fagan et al., 1987; Gandossy, Williams, Cohen & Harwood 1980.)

The psychopharmacological approach, however, has received little support in the adolescent literature. While research on delinquents indicates that many have used drugs or alcohol prior to committing a crime, most youth deny that their criminal behavior is due to their substance use (Huizinga, 1986). For example, Carpenter et al. (1988) found that although teenagers reported being under the influence of alcohol or drugs when committing crimes, none attributed their behavior to the effects of the drugs. In fact, some youth used drugs so routinely that virtually all their activities also involved prior drug use. Among seriously delinquent drug users, the majority of drug-using episodes did not involve delinquency and the majority of delinquent events did not involve prior drug use. When drug or alcohol use occurred prior to a criminal event, subjects listed many reasons other than drug use as contributing factors. Subjects reported never being out of control from drug use when committing crimes and, in fact, they purposely regulated their drug use depending upon the nature of the crime (i.e., either to enhance an activity or to avoid interference with skillful execution of a crime) (Carpenter et al., 1988). It is also possible that many youth lack insights into the reasons for their behavior and, thus, do not necessarily perceive a direct connection between their drug use and delinquent behavior.

In contrast to a pharmacological explanation for the drugs-cause-crime relationship between heroin use and violent crime, Goldstein (1985) has identified a systemic violence model. He suggests that the system of drug distribution and use is inherently connected with violent crime. This model is probably not applicable to the majority of youthful drug users because few are involved in distribution at this level. In the Carpenter et al. interview study (1988), approximately 10 percent of all youths in their random sample and one-third of their whole sample reported selling drugs. With few exceptions, nearly all of the drug dealing occurred within a loosely structured circle of friends and relatives. Only six out of 100 subjects were intensely involved in dealing. However, research on drug dealing within youth gangs partially supports Goldstein's (1985) systemic violence model. That is, some violent incidents were found to be related to disputes over drug sales or selling territories, whereas, the majority of violent incidents were not drug related, but rather resulted from other issues, such as conflicts over status and "turf" (see Fagan, 1989a).

Similarly, the economic motivation explanation for the drugs-cause-crime model has not been supported among adolescents. Johnston, O'Malley and Eveland (1978) concluded their longitudinal study of adolescents by stating that nonaddictive use of illicit drugs does not appear to play a role in causing users to become more delinquent. In accord, a reanalysis of the National Youth Survey data indicated that intensive drug users and highly delinquent youth do not report committing property crimes to raise money for drugs (Johnson, Wish, Schmeidler & Huizinga, 1986). Instead, the money they get from crime is used for commodities other than drugs. In the Carpenter et al. (1988) study, most of the thefts took place for direct acquisition rather than for resale. While subjects attributed alcohol or drug use as the cause of crimes for other individuals, most denied that their own crimes were related to their drug use. Subjects reported committing crimes for fun, to obtain valued goods, or to get money. They claimed to be able to obtain drugs within their usual budgets and that other commodities were more important to purchase with the profits from crime.

Hence, there is little overall support for a drugs-cause-crime model in adolescent literature. Clearly, for those who are involved in delinquency and drug use, onset of delinquency generally precedes drug use, thus refuting any hypothesis that drug use leads to initial delinquent involvement (Elliott et al., 1989; Kandel, Kessler & Margulies, 1978). While it is probable that for some youths under some conditions, the use of illegal drugs leads to delinquent behavior, there is little convincing evidence that this happens for the majority of youths.

A second perspective is *Model 2 - "crime causes drug use."* According to this explanation, involvement in delinquency provides the context, the reference group, and definitions of the situation that are conducive to subsequent involvement with drugs (Bachman, O'Malley & Johnston, 1978; Elliott & Ageton, 1981). Collins, Hubbard & Rachal's (1985) analysis of individuals in cocaine treatment programs supports this model. They found that income generated from crime provides the individual with extra money to secure drugs, and places the individual in an environment which is supportive of drug use, rather than a need for cocaine compelling the individual to commit crimes (see also Goldman, 1981; Johnson, et al., 1985). Again, the evidence supporting this view is not conclusive. While it is indeed probable that crime leads to drug usage under certain conditions for certain persons, a direct causal path from crime to drugs is not likely to reflect the dominant pattern.

Model 3 - the reciprocal model has been suggested by Elliott and Ageton (1976a) and reintroduced by Watters and colleagues (1985). This model postulates that the relationship between drug use and delinquency is bidirectional, that is, that drug use and delinquency are causally linked and mutually reinforcing. Support for this perspective is derived from several recent studies of either drug use or delinquency which have found reciprocal relationships (see Ginsberg & Greenley, 1978; Reinarman, 1979; Thornberry & Christenson, 1984). This perspective has also been supported by Goldstein's (1981) ethnographic research in New York City. Goldstein (1981) suggested that the relationship between drug use and crime moves in both directions even for the same individuals. When a heroin addict has an easy opportunity to obtain money illegally, he will engage in the activity and then buy drugs with the money gained, not out of a compulsion but rather as a consumer expenditure. Conversely, when the need for drugs is great, users will commit crimes to get money to buy drugs. While reciprocity is only a recently developed area, it may hold promise in clarifying causal relationships.

A final model, *Model 4 - the spurious model*, is the perspective that is generating increasing research and theoretical support, especially among normal populations. Rather than being causally connected, the empirical link between drug use and crime is assumed to be spurious (Elliott & Ageton, 1976a; Elliott & Huizinga, 1989). Either the relationship between use and delinquency is coincident and both sets of behaviors may be elements in a concurrent cluster of other adolescent problem behaviors (Kandel, 1978; Jessor and Jessor, 1977), or, alternatively, drug-crime relationships may be explained by a "common cause," that is, both substance use and delinquent behavior are the result of the same factor or set of factors (Collins, 1981; Goode, 1972). "Common-cause" hypotheses identify a number of social and psychological factors seemingly shared by adolescent substance users and delinquents and postulate that similar causal processes exist for both forms of deviance. Alternatively, the "coincident" hypothesis assumes that drug use and delinquency cluster together as a result of experimentation with a wide range of behaviors during the adolescent stage in the life cycle.

The empirical evidence confirms that adolescent drug use and delinquent behavior are spuriously related, and in the following sections I will present this evidence within a three-part framework similar to the one suggested by Clayton and Tuchfeld (1982). The three sections are the *degree of association between drug use and delinquency, temporal ordering of the behaviors*, and *tests of spuriousness*.

THE ASSOCIATION BETWEEN DRUG-USE AND DELINQUENCY IN ADOLESCENCE: A SPURIOUS RELATIONSHIP

Degree of Association

Elliott and Ageton's (1976a) review of ten major studies exploring the drug-crime nexus among noninstitutionalized youthful populations suggested that involvement in delinquency and drug use are covariants, and the association holds for both serious and nonserious crimes. They concluded that the most plausible model for the drug-crime relationship among adolescents is a spurious model. A later review indicated that the correlations between drug use and delinquency reported in the literature generally range between .40 and .60 (e.g., Clayton, 1981b). Although these correlations are moderate, more than 60 percent of the variance is not shared.

Research by Kandel, Simcha-Fagan, and Davies (1986) supports the association between drug use and delinquency into young adulthood. Among subjects 24-25 years of age, they found a positive relationship between involvement in drug use and delinquency indicating that current users of harder drugs were more deviant than former users and those who have used only marijuana. They also found that among males, early delinquency predicted later drug use but early drug use did not predict later delinquency. For females they found that illicit drug use in adolescence predicted delinquency in adulthood. These data, thus, indicate that there are gender differences in the association between drug use and delinquency.

In examining the degree of association between delinquency and drug use, it must be recognized that there is only a small group of youth who are both serious delinquents and problem drug users. In a national representative sample of youth, it was found that less than 5 percent of all youth reported serious crimes and used hard drugs. This small group accounted for approximately 40 percent of all delinquencies, 60 percent of all index offenses, over 50 percent of all felony assaults, over 60 percent of all felony thefts, 75 percent of all robberies, over 80 percent of all drug sales, 30 percent of all marijuana use occasions, and 60 percent of all other drug use occasions (Johnson et al., 1986).

Violence, especially, is concentrated among only a few youth (Johnson et al., 1986, Carpenter et al., 1988). Most youth involved in felony assault and other felonies also commit several index offenses and many minor delinquencies per year and use drugs regularly (Johnson et al., 1986). Carpenter and colleagues (1988) found that those youth involved in violence were also more involved in delinquency and drug use than their peers. Not only were those heavily involved individuals more often perpetrators, but also they were more often victims of violence. The most frequent type of violence was fighting primarily to defend one's honor and to test others. More serious incidents of violence occurred in the distribution of drugs, gang battles, instances of racial or ethnic antagonism, and in acts of revenge. In all of these instances it was the most heavily involved drug users and the most criminally active youth who were engaged.

The data reviewed above indicate that there is a statistical association between drug use and delinquency in adolescence, but that serious drug use and delinquency are concentrated in a small segment of the adolescent population. More data regarding this association will be presented later in the section on recent empirical studies.

Temporal Order

Almost all empirical studies report that, among those who engage in both delinquency and drug use, delinquent behavior (both serious and nonserious) developmentally precedes the use of drugs (Elliott et al., 1989). Thus, considering the requirement of temporal sequencing (see Clayton, 1981b; Clayton & Tuchfeld, 1982), these findings do not support the "drugs-cause-crime" model.

A longitudinal analysis by Huizinga and Elliott (1981) indicated that, for the largest group of adolescents who were both users and delinquents, involvement in delinquency (especially minor offenses) preceded substance use. However, this research also identified groups of youths who displayed simultaneous initiation into drug use and delinquency and groups whose drug use preceded involvement in delinquent behavior. Only the offense of drug selling was almost always preceded by drug use (Huizinga & Elliott, 1981). Kandel et al. (1978) also found that participation in minor forms of delinquency preceded initiation into hard liquor use and marijuana use and that participation in major forms of delinquency preceded initiation into the use of other illicit drugs.

Information about whether delinquent behavior increases with the onset of substance use among adolescents is limited and contradictory. In general, onset of drug use is not associated with increases in delinquency (Kandel, 1978). The studies reviewed by Elliott and Ageton (1976a) clearly indicated that differences in delinquency between drug users and nonusers existed before the onset of drug use. Huizinga and Elliott (1981, p. 81) warned that "global generalizations about the drug use/delinquency relationship within the youth population are likely to be inaccurate" because of the existence of different temporal ordering of onset of both behaviors among different subgroups of youth. Their longitudinal analysis of the drug-delinquency connection led to the conclusion that for the large majority of youth, the use of drugs is not related to involvement in delinquent behavior. Whether the onset of drug use leads to increases in delinquency is dependent on the types of drugs, the quantity and frequency of use, and the subculture of the individual (Huizinga & Elliott, 1981).

In another longitudinal analysis, Johnston and colleagues (1978) demonstrated that drug users as compared to nonusers were substantially more delinquent before they began using drugs. Thus, they concluded that level of delinquency can hardly be attributed to drug use and, if a causal relationship exists, their data supported a delinquency-causes-drug use model. They suggested several alternative explanations for the covariation between drug use and delinquency: drug use may cause a short-term increase in delinquency, methodological artifacts may exist because the variables are measured simultaneously, drug use and delinquency may be explained by common causative factors, or other factors than drug use, per se, lead to increases in delinquency.

The literature on temporal ordering reviewed above refutes a causal model and, therefore, supports a spurious model. (More data related to this issue will be presented later.) The following section presents explanations offered to account for the spuriousness.

Tests of Spuriousness

Evidence supporting the spurious model frequently has been derived from adolescent samples where relatively nonserious forms of substance use (cigarette smoking, occasional alcohol use, or experimentation with marijuana) appeared to occur simultaneously with relatively minor and infrequent forms of delinquent behavior. This type of association led Jessor and Jessor (1977) to identify a problem behavior syndrome in which cigarette use, precocious sexual behavior, problem drinking, use of marijuana and other drugs, stealing, and aggression clustered together. This cluster of behaviors was explained by the same set of environmental and personality variables and was negatively related to conventional behavior. Donovan and Jessor (1985) provided additional support for their hypothesis of a single dimension of deviance proneness. They advised, however, that there are several possible explanations that could account for the strong correlations among all their problem behaviors. For example, each behavior could be an interchangeable means of achieving desired goals, the behaviors could be learned together and performed together, or there might be peer pressure when engaging in one behavior to also engage in the other.

The concept of a problem behavior syndrome has been supported by other research. Having engaged in premarital sexual intercourse (White & Johnson, 1989) and driving while intoxicated (Johnson & White, 1989) were both related to a high-risk profile delineated by high sensation-seeking needs and high levels of impulsivity. This same profile was also related to drug use (Bates, Labouvie & White, 1986) and delinquency (White, Labouvie & Bates, 1985b).

In a cluster analysis, Hindelang and Weis (1972) found that marijuana use loaded on a general delinquency scale with alcohol use and intoxication, theft, vandalism, truancy and cheating, but other drug use (i.e., LSD, mescaline, methedrine, glue, heroin) loaded on its own scale. The fact that marijuana, as compared to other drug use, was more strongly related to delinquency may have been a statistical artifact due to a lower variation in other drug use than in marijuana. This early study, thus, suggested that marijuana use is part of a general deviance syndrome. Elliott and Ageton (1976b) also concluded that marijuana use was part of a general deviance involvement, while sale of drugs and use of hard drugs were related to crime and not explained by a general involvement in delinquency.

Klein (1989) agreed that the relationship is spurious and argued that, except for drug use leading to drug selling, the relationship between delinquency and drug use is the result of a pattern of simultaneous deviant activity. He described most adolescent delinquency as cafeteria-style delinquency, meaning that most adolescents engage in a variety of delinquent behaviors rather than specialize in only one type. This style of delinquency is comparable to typical adolescent drug use patterns which often involve multiple drug use rather than use of a single substance. In fact, Klein argued that drug use is one component of cafeteria-style delinquency.

Kandel et al. (1986) identified several possible explanations for the co-occurrence of both behaviors; both behaviors could result from a common psychological trait, a common clinical disorder such as conduct disorder, a particular lifestyle, or common developmental processes. Similarly, Johnston et al. (1978) stated that the spuriousness of the relationship between drug use and delinquency may result from common personality characteristics, that is, drug users and delinquents are both deviance-prone individuals.

Common etiological roots for high rates of delinquency and drug use include: early antisocial behavior in elementary school, inconsistent parenting, lack of communication with parents, school adjustment problems, association with deviant peers, low degree of social bonding to prosocial individuals, positive attitudes toward drug use and delinquency, early onset (for drugs only), low self-esteem, high sensation-seeking, low attachments to school and family, having alcoholic parents, poor school performance, low IQ, and inadequate moral development (e.g., Carpenter et al., 1988; Hawkins, 1989; Hawkins, Lishner & Catalano, 1985; Huba & Bentler, 1984; Kaplan, Martin & Robbins, 1984; Loeber & Dishion, 1983; Zuckerman, 1979).

There are a few noteworthy applications of theoretical common cause models to substance use and delinquency. In studies of etiology, researchers have applied traditional deviance theories to explain delinquency and drug use. The most often-tested theories are control theory (Hirschi, 1969), differential association theory (Sutherland & Cressey, 1978) and integrations of the two (e.g., Elliott et al., 1985). For example, as predicted by control theory, adolescents who are not well-bonded to their parents, to their teachers, or to school are more likely to engage in delinquency (Agnew, 1985; La-Grange & White, 1985; Matsueda, 1982; Wiatrowski, Griswold & Roberts, 1981) and in substance use (Elliott et al., 1985; Massey & Krohn, 1986). At the same time, the deviance-inducing effect of deviant peers as postulated by differential association theory (Sutherland & Cressey, 1978) has been at least equally successful in explaining adolescent substance use (Akers, Krohn, Lanza-Kaduce & Radosevich, 1979; Jaquith, 1981; White, Johnson & Horwitz, 1986) and delinquency (LaGrange & White, 1985; Matsueda, 1982).

In addition, several researchers (e.g., Catalano, White, Hawkins & Pandina, 1985; Elliott et al., 1985; Johnson, 1979; Johnson et al., 1987; Marcos, Bahr & Johnson, 1986) have applied mixed or integrated theories combining differential association and control perspectives to both delinquency and drug use. They have argued that attenuated bonds to parents and school, in conjunction with bonding to deviant peers, predisposes one to both drug use and delinquency.

Hawkins and Weis' (1985) Social Development Model integrates social control and social learning theory stressing the importance of early antisocial behaviors, early experiences in the family, later experiences in school, and interaction with peers. Their model has been moderately successful in predicting adolescent marijuana use and delinquency (Catalano et al., 1985). Elliott et al. (1985) tested a social-psychological model incorporating elements of traditional strain theory, social control (bonding) theory, and social learning theory; the social learning aspect suggests that bonding to deviant persons provides the social rewards (motivations) for deviant behavior. They concluded that alcohol and marijuana use belong to a general deviance syndrome involving a wide range of minor criminal acts, and that they are predicted by a common set of causes. Their results, as well as the other tests of theory presented above, strongly support a common cause hypothesis.

On the other hand, there has been evidence which refutes common cause models suggesting that there be may independent causes for involvement in delinquency and involvement in drug use and that delinquency and drug use may represent distinctively different types of behavior (e.g., White, 1987; White, Pandina & LaGrange, 1987, see below). Elliott, Ageton, and Canter (1979) suggested that different causal paths could account for different types of delinquency. For example, a strain path might lead to instrumental forms of delinquency such as theft, while attenuated commitments might result in less instrumental types such as drug use.

Loeber's (1988) review of the literature on antisocial behavior also suggested that there are independent predictors of drug use and delinquency. After identifying four categories of antisocial outcomes: versatile offenders, exclusive violent offenders, exclusive property offenders, and exclusive substance abusers, he delineated the various paths to these outcomes suggesting that a history of aggressive or nonaggressive acts may determine the eventual outcome. Loeber concluded that nonaggressive rather than aggressive antisocial behaviors are predictive of later substance use or abuse, while aggression is more strongly predictive of other forms of delinquency.

Similarly, Kandel et al.'s (1986) research failed to support a common cause hypothesis. They tested a risk model combining variables from socialization, social learning, and social control theories, as well as sociodemographic variables and measures of commitment to adult roles. They compared the ability of this model to predict theft, interpersonal aggression, marijuana use, and illicit drug use among male and female young adults (24 to 25 years of age). These researchers concluded that their results were equivocal in regard to the ability of a common cause model to predict adult participation in delinquency and use of illicit drugs. Rather, they found that prediction depended upon the type of delinquency, the type of drug used, and sex of the individual. For males they found a common etiology between illicit drug use and theft, rather than between illicit drug use and interpersonal aggression. They also found that the same factors that predicted illicit drug use among female adults predicted delinquency among males.

Differences in developmental patterns of drug use and delinquency also provide evidence against a common cause hypothesis. It is generally well-accepted that most adolescents mature out of delinquency after the age of 16 or in late adolescence (Matza, 1964; Hirschi & Gottfredson, 1983). Some criminologists attribute this "maturation" to spontaneous cessation or developmental maturation. Others attribute it to the deterrent effect of perception of the differences in the criminal justice treatment of and sanctions for adolescent and adult offenders (Carpenter et al., 1988, see also Thornberry, 1987). On the other hand, for the majority of drug users, drug use persists into young adulthood. According to Chaiken and Johnson (1988), about two-thirds of drug-using delinquents continue to use drugs into adulthood, while close to one-half stop committing crimes.[2]

Another distinction between drug use and delinquency arguing against a common cause model has to do with the purpose of each behavior in the adolescent's lifestyle. In the study by Carpenter and her colleagues (1988), the majority of delinquent youth were heavily involved with marijuana and alcohol and also used other substances. This substance use was a major form of self-identity, commitment, and recreation. On the other hand, their involvement in delinquency was irregular and rarely part of their self-identity (see also Schwendinger & Schwendinger, 1985).

Most of the research reviewed above supports a spurious relationship between delinquency and drug use, but is contradictory as to whether a common cause hypothesis can account for this spuriousness. In the following section I will continue to explore these issues highlighting recent empirical research which focuses directly on the drug-crime nexus.

RECENT EMPIRICAL RESEARCH

This section of the chapter will focus on recent results from these research projects that have attempted to unravel the drug-delinquency nexus in adolescence. These include: the National Youth Survey (Elliott et al., 1989), the Urban Youth Study (Fagan et al., 1987), and the Rutgers Health and Human Development Study (Pandina, Labouvie & White, 1984). Although these three studies differ in terms of their samples, their general compatibility in respect to measures and types of analyses utilized makes comparisons across studies possible.

The National Youth Survey (NYS) is a longitudinal study collecting data from a national household probability sample which began in 1977 with subjects aged 11 through 17 years (N=1725) and has collected data annually through 1980 and again in 1983 and 1986 (13% attrition over the six surveys). The results reported below include data through the 1983 survey when subjects were ages 18-24 years old. (For greater detail on study design and sample, see Elliott & Huizinga, 1989.)

The Urban Youth Survey (UYS) collected data from youth (13-18 years old) in four inner city, high-crime neighborhoods in 1985. Subjects were either high school students (N=666) or dropouts identified through a snowball technique (N=196). Subjects were predominantly black, with a smaller proportion of Hispanic youth. Respondents most often lived with single parents. Students, as compared to dropouts, were younger and lived more often in intact families and less often alone. (For greater detail on study design and sample, see Fagan et al., 1987.)

The Rutgers Health and Human Development Study (HHDP) is a prospective longitudinal study of adolescents and young adults. A quota sample of New Jersey adolescents originally identified by a random telephone call were first studied in 1979-1981 at the ages of 12, 15, and 18 years old (N=1380). They have been retested every three years until the ages of 18, 21 and 24 years old (N=1270, 8% attrition over the three test occasions). These subjects are primarily white, working- and middle-class adolescents and are representative of the New Jersey population in terms of religion and family income. A large majority come from two-parent families. (For greater detail on the design and sample, see Pandina, Labouvie & White, 1984; White & Labouvie, 1989).

In the following sections of the chapter, I will compare findings across the three studies in terms of the same three areas reviewed above: the association between drug use and delinquency, the temporal ordering of drug use and delinquency, and tests of spuriousness.

Associations between Drug Use and Delinquency

One way to determine the association between delinquency and drug use is to examine the correlations between various measures of each behavior. Results from the HHDP cross-sectional and longitudinal analyses indicated that the drug-delinquency relationship is modest at best, with correlations generally ranging between .20-.40 (White et al., 1985a; White, Pandina & Labouvie, 1985c; Pandina & White, 1989). White et al. (1985a) found that cross-sectional correlations were strongest among the middle age group (age 15 at Time 1) as compared to the younger (age 12) and older (age 18) age groups. Further, they found that male subjects exhibited much stronger drug-delinquency relationships than did female subjects, and the significant relationships for females involved minor delinquency only (probably because of the small amount of variance in serious delinquency among females in the sample).

White, Pandina, and Labouvie (1985c) found similar patterns in their longitudinal analyses. The observed relationships between drug use and delinquency suggested that because adolescence is the period of initiation and experimentation with both drug use and various types of delinquent behavior, the drug-delinquency relationship may simply be the result of the synchronous occurrence of both behaviors during the same period in adolescence. The stronger association between delinquency and substance use in mid-adolescence (age 15), as compared to early (age 12) or later (age 18) adolescence, suggested an initial, but temporary equivalence in terms of possible common underlying functions and/or causes. In later adolescence and early adulthood (18- and 21-years-old), however, differentiation between the two behaviors became evident in terms of lowered correlations. Differential age trends and cross-lagged correlations suggested that more delinquency is rechanneled into substance use than vice versa (White et al., 1985c). Thus the research by White and her colleagues suggests that a coincident hypothesis as compared to a common cause hypothesis may be more applicable to adolescents.

Elliott et al. (1989) also reported relatively weak correlations between delinquency and drug use in the NYS sample. While all the correlations were positive, they accounted for only 1 to 12 percent of the shared variance.

In addition to correlational analyses, all three studies have used various typologies to examine the association between drug use and delinquency. Elliott et al. (1989) divided drug use into four types: nonuse, alcohol use, marijuana use, and polydrug use.[3] Similarly, the delinquency typology consisted of four categories: nondelinquents, exploratory delinquents, nonserious delinquents, and serious delinquents.[4] In their data there was a clear monotonic relationship between substance use and delinquency type at all three measurement occasions. Serious delinquents had, by far, the highest rates of consumption of marijuana and other drugs, as well as alcohol and drug problems, and the rates continued to decrease moving down the typology. Similarly, drug use types were clearly differentiated in terms of delinquency involvement. For virtually all offenses, polydrug users reported the highest prevalence rates, and non-users reported the lowest rates.

White, et al. (1985a) also examined the relationship between drug use stage (abstainer, alcohol user only, alcohol and marijuana user only, and alcohol, marijuana, and other drug user) and delinquency stage (no delinquency, minor delinquency only, and serious delinquency). They, in accord with Elliott et al. (1989), found that there was a high degree of synchrony in the progression through the stages of drug use and the stages of delinquency. Abstainers and alcohol-only users were most likely to be nondelinquents, those who used alcohol and marijuana as compared to only alcohol were more likely to be delinquent, and those who had progressed to the use of other drugs, as compared to those not involved with other drugs, were most likely to have also progressed to involvement in more serious forms of delinquency.

Fagan et al. (1987) used cluster analysis to develop a typology of substance use and delinquency. In terms of prevalence, they identified five distinct groups having varying combinations of high and low delinquency and substance use rates. With the exception of the group of subjects with low delinquency and low substance use, use of alcohol and marijuana did not differ significantly across groups, while use of harder drugs did. The fact that subjects who were high in delinquency had either high or low levels of substance use and also subjects who were high in substance use had either high or low levels of delinquency suggested that knowledge about substance use does not help predict involvement in delinquency and knowledge about delinquency does not help predict drug use. It also suggested that the drug-delinquency connection is relatively weak.

In terms of incidence clusters (taking into account the frequency of the behavior), five groups emerged:

(1) no delinquency, no substance use (90%),
(2) high opiate and other drug use, high property crime
      (less than 1%),
(3) moderate delinquency, low substance use (3%),
(4) low delinquency, low substance use (6%), and
(5) high delinquency, high substance use (less than 1%).

The incidence typology results, as compared to the prevalence typology results, supported a stronger relationship between drug use and delinquency. Those youth who were more frequently involved in serious crime were also more likely to be involved in serious alcohol and drug use. The most serious delinquent involvement was related to heroin use, although this pattern was relatively rare among the youth studied.

In these analyses, knowledge about extent of involvement in one area clearly contributed to knowledge about extent of involvement in the other. However, knowledge about delinquency was less informative about drug use than knowledge about drug use was informative about delinquency. The comparison of the prevalence and incidence clusters confirmed that differences in measures clearly lead to differences in conclusions regarding the extent of overlap between delinquency and drug use. In addition, there were significant differences among the clusters in terms of age, sex, race, and dropout status, suggesting that sociodemographic factors influence the joint occurrence of substance use and delinquency. The results of these cluster analyses indicated that there are several heterogenous groups of adolescents; for some, drug use and delinquency are closely related and for others they are independent of each other (see also White et al., 1987).

In a subsequent analysis of only the high school subsample from the UYS, Fagan, Weis and Cheng (1989) developed delinquency and substance use typologies similar to those reported above for Elliott et al. (1989). They found that alcohol and drug use was more frequent among more serious juvenile offenders. For males, marijuana was used more frequently than alcohol across all delinquency groups, but the level of use increased sharply for the most delinquent group. On the other hand, hard drug use did not increase linearly from one delinquency group to the next. Only 1.2 percent of the males and 0.3 percent of the females met the criteria for membership in both the most serious delinquency group and the most serious drug use group. It should be kept in mind that school dropouts and institutionalized youth were not included in the high school sample and, thus, these rates are conservative (Fagan et al., 1989).

Further, for those subjects in the serious substance use category it was just as likely that they engaged in serious delinquency as they engaged in no delinquency at all. These researchers identified an asymmetry between delinquency and drug use. That is, while high rate substance users were more prevalent among the most serious delinquents, the mean substance use level did not vary across delinquent groups. The results reaffirm earlier studies indicating that the association between substance use and delinquency depends on the severity of the delinquency and the types of substances used (Fagan et al., 1989).

In sum, the data from the typological analyses suggest that, in general, there is a linear relationship between level of drug use and level of delinquency. The relationship appears asymmetrical, that is, the majority of serious delinquents are drug users, but among serious drug users, level of delinquency is varied.

Temporal Ordering

Most of the information on temporal ordering comes from Elliott et al.'s (1989) study because their design allowed for the collection of yearly prevalence data from early adolescence through young adulthood. Their comparison of prevalence rates over time indicated that the dynamics of heavy drug use from adolescence to young adulthood are very different from those for serious delinquency. The rates for serious delinquency decreased by 70 percent as the sample aged from the 11-17 category to the 18-24 category. On the other hand, the rates for polydrug use increased 350 percent during this same time period. An age, cohort, and period analysis of these data also revealed discrepancies between substance use and other forms of delinquency. Both behaviors differed substantially in their age of maximum prevalence, and the presence of an increasing period trend was noted for substance use, but not for delinquency (see Elliott et al., 1989, for greater detail on this analysis and results).

When they compared yearly initiation and cessation rates, Elliott et al. (1989) again found that drug use and delinquency showed the opposite pattern. While prevalence rates of general delinquency declined from 1976 to 1983, initiation exceeded cessation for alcohol, marijuana, and polydrug use every year (except 1983), hence, prevalence increased every year. Similarly, cessation rates were lowest for alcohol use and lower for marijuana and polydrug use than for general delinquency or Index offenses.

In one analysis, Elliott et al. (1989) examined the temporal order between types of delinquency and drug use only among subjects who had initiated both behaviors. They found that minor delinquency almost always came first and, in fact, no one initiated marijuana or polydrug use before minor delinquency. Alcohol use came second, however, a substantial percentage of subjects initiated Index offenses prior to alcohol use. In general, however, after alcohol use came marijuana use, then Index-offending, and finally polydrug use. Among subjects who initiated both marijuana use and Index-offending, Index-offending was more likely to precede marijuana use than vice versa.

Elliott et al. (1989), in another analysis, determined how well they could predict different types of delinquency and drug use from one another. Despite the low correlations among the various behaviors, the researchers were able to make strong predictive statements about one type of behavior based upon knowledge of the other. Their strongest predictions occurred within one behavioral area, that is, either drug use or delinquency. For example, they were able to predict with almost perfect accuracy that a subject would not try marijuana or other drugs if they had never used alcohol.[5] One strong prediction across domains was that if an individual never committed a delinquent act, that individual would almost never use illegal drugs other than marijuana (92-93% accurate).

Based upon the results of their temporal analyses, as well as their prediction analyses, the authors concluded that:

(1) alcohol use is a necessary precursor of marijuana and other drug use,

(2) minor delinquency is a necessary precursor of Index-offending,

and, most relevant for the present review:

(3) minor offending is a necessary precursor of marijuana and other drug use among persons who engage in both behaviors.

They stated that their results indicate that, in terms of a causal relationship, the onset of minor delinquency leads to the onset of drug use and not vice versa. Besides alcohol use and minor delinquency, the relationship between delinquency and drug use was not very strong. Although they did note that while delinquency is more likely to influence the onset of drug use than the reverse, serious drug use (repeated polydrug use) is more likely to influence the maintenance of serious delinquency than the reverse. This result suggested the possibility that if drug use does influence delinquency, it may be by reducing the probability of terminating rather than by increasing the probability of initiating delinquent behavior.

Elliott et al. (1989) also examined drug immediately prior to the user's committing an offense. For most offenses, the rates were low and, hence, they concluded that their results offer little support for the idea that drug use leads to crime in either the long-term or immediate-time perspective. In contrast, they found a strong association between alcohol use immediately preceding an offense characterized by physical violence, but not by a profit motive. (For greater detail on alcohol and violence, see Collins, 1981, 1988; Fagan, 1989b; Pernanen, 1976; Tinklenberg, 1973).

Using the HHDP data, White, Pandina, and Labouvie (1985c) also examined the ability to predict delinquency and drug use over time. They were better able to predict Time 2 (T2) substance use with Time 1 (T1) overall delinquency involvement, than they could predict T2 delinquency with T1 substance use. They concluded that their data indicated that delinquency may lead to drug use, but that drug use does not necessarily lead to delinquency.

As with the earlier research, these data on temporal ordering do not support a causal relationship between initiation to drug use and initiation to delinquency nor between escalation in drug use and escalation in delinquency. In the following section I will examine tests of spuriousness within the three data sets to evaluate the ability of a common cause hypothesis to explain the spuriousness of the relationship between drug use and delinquency.

Tests of Spuriousness

Elliott et al. (1989) tested an integrated social psychological model, combining elements of strain theory, social control (bonding) theory, and social learning theory, separately for drug use and delinquency. Their recent results did not support a common cause model. They found that delinquency was influenced by delinquent peer-group bonding, sex, and the interaction between conventional and delinquent bonding. On the other hand, the only independent variable shared by both drug use (alcohol use, marijuana use, and polydrug use) and delinquency was delinquent peer bonding. They found that beliefs, age (for alcohol), and family involvement (for marijuana) had direct influences on drug use, although not on delinquency, and that neither sex nor the interaction between conventional and delinquent bonding were significant influences on drug use. Rather than a common etiology, their findings suggested that drug use and delinquency have separate but related etiological paths with only one direct influence (bonding to delinquent peers) and several indirect influences (e.g., sex, school strain, belief in conventional norms) in common.

Fagan et al. (1987) tested a social development model (Hawkins & Weis, 1985) by first examining incidence group differences (described earlier) on the independent variables. They found that the majority of variables drawn predominantly from control theory and differential association theory differed among groups in the expected direction. They then combined their 22 theoretical variables into seven factors: *family*, *peer*, *victimization*, *school attachment*, *neighbors' criminal involvement*, *conventional values*, and *delinquency influence in the neighborhood and school*. Univariate analyses of variance indicated that there were group differences among the four types of deviants (excluding the no-drug, no-delinquency group) in terms of these eight social domains. As found in most other studies, peer influences were the strongest predictors of both joint and separate occurrences of drug use and delinquency. The discriminate analyses were able to distinguish noninvolvement (no drug use, no delinquency group) from any level of involvement (the other four groups), but could not differentiate among levels of involvement (Fagan et al., 1987).

In a subsequent paper, Fagan et al. (1989) examined the same theoretical model among the subsample of high school students from the UYS. Overall, they found that the model significantly predicted seriousness and intensity of substance use and delinquency, although the amount of variance explained was relatively low. When they controlled for delinquency type, they found that the model was only powerful in predicting substance use for low-level delinquency, but not more serious delinquency. In accordance with Elliott et al. (1989), the authors concluded that the results of their study reinforce the fact that substance use and delinquency are explained by parallel but different processes.

In a recent study, White et al. (1987) also demonstrated that drug use and delinquency represent qualitatively different types of behaviors and that there are factors that distinguish those adolescents who turn to drug use from those who turn to delinquency. Their data indicated that serious drug use and delinquency are not necessarily concentrated in a homogeneous grouping of adolescents, but rather that each group represents a somewhat unique set of individuals whose levels of drug use and delinquency are distinct. Analyses also indicated that while a combination of differential association theory and control theory was useful in explaining deviance proneness among adolescents, there may be an additional set of intrapsychic predictors (such as autonomy, impulsivity, need for achievement, and harm avoidance) that differentiate "deviants" who will become serious delinquents from those who will become serious substance abusers.

As a result of that study, White (1987) undertook another analysis to examine the question of why some "deviants" primarily choose delinquency while others choose drug use. She tested an "independent cause" hypothesis predicting that there are different etiological factors that account for specific *modes* of deviant behavior. Rather than focusing on the similarities between delinquent and drug (marijuana) using adolescents, this study attempted to elucidate the peer group and personality differences between them to better understand the unique underlying processes involved in the development of each.

In order to examine differences between marijuana-using deviants and delinquent deviants, a cluster analysis technique was employed to develop independent groupings of subjects. Individuals' T1 and T2 scores on the delinquency and marijuana use measures were clustered to obtain distinct types of deviant and nondeviant adolescents separately for each age/sex group. Among younger (age 12 at T1) subjects, four clusters were retained:

(1) low on both measures at both times,
(2) low on delinquency at both times, but high on marijuana use at T2,
(3) low on marijuana use, high on delinquency at T1, but low on delinquency at T2, and
(4) low on marijuana use, low on delinquency at T1, but high on delinquency at T2. Note that the majority of this age group fell into group 1.

In addition to these four groups, a group high on both marijuana use and delinquency at both times emerged for the older subjects (age 15 at T1). The results of these longitudinal cluster analyses support Fagan et al.'s (1987) results indicating that there are several distinct groups of adolescents, some of whom are high in both drug use and delinquency, some of whom are low in both, and some of whom are high in one and low in the other.

Repeated measures analyses of variance were utilized to examine cluster group effects on the selected personality and peer variables. As hypothesized, the peer variables (especially the proportion of friends using marijuana and the relative proportion of marijuana-using friends to delinquent friends) clearly differentiated marijuana using deviants from delinquent deviants. An earlier study using these same data also demonstrated that while delinquents have friends who are delinquents and drug users have friends who are drug users, these deviant peer groups do not represent a single subsample but rather two distinct sets of individuals (White et al., 1985a; see also Fagan et al., 1987).

For the personality variables the findings were less consistent than those for the peer variables. Intensity of emotional outbursts, disinhibition, and impulsivity were significantly related to group membership across all age/sex groups (except impulsivity for younger females). While these variables were significantly related to cluster group membership, the mean comparisons indicated that there were no consistent marijuana-user versus delinquent differences. Also, subjects grouped by level of marijuana use and delinquency were not reliably differentiated in level of hostility, self-esteem, depression, or psychoticism.

The independent cause hypothesis, that certain peer and personality variables increase the likelihood of expressing deviance by delinquent behavior rather than by marijuana use, was only partially supported. The relative proportion of peers who engaged in one or the other activity clearly differentiated between these two types of deviants as did the actual proportion of marijuana-using friends in several comparisons. Thus, these data supported differential association theory's general prediction that peer behaviors are strongly related to adolescent behaviors (e.g., Akers et al., 1979) and further contribute to our understanding of the association. For example, Elliott and his colleagues (1985) reported that attachment to delinquent peers is strongly related to adolescent drug use. But White's (1987) findings suggested that it is the specific *type* of deviance that is engaged in by peers which helps predict the type of deviant that the adolescent will become, thereby confirming that marijuana users and delinquents are not necessarily an equivalent group of individuals, certainly in terms of their peer associations (see also White et al., 1985a).

On the other hand, the data did not confirm that these two distinct types of deviants differ in terms of any of the personality variables studied (see also White et al., 1987). While emotional outbursts might be a common occurrence among delinquents and impulsivity might be a salient characteristic of drug users, neither of these variables reliably differentiated between these types of deviants. Perhaps there are alternative personality variables which distinguish between deviants. Yet other analyses of these same data did not find a relationship of marijuana use or delinquency to several other intrapersonal variables including: achievement orientation, social orientation, anxiety, paranoid ideation, somaticism, interpersonal sensitivity, phobic anxiety, masculinity, femininity, or stress.

While the earlier tests of explanatory models provided equivocal findings in regard to common cause hypotheses, the recent findings from these three studies suggest that drug use and delinquency may be independent manifestations of a general pattern of deviant behavior and, thus, support a coincident spurious relationship between drug use and delinquency.

CONCLUSION

Across the studies described here, the findings are sometimes equivocal and sometimes outright contradictory. Several of these contradictions may be due to the differences in measures and in samples. Despite these differences there are several convergent views that emerge from the literature cited above:

(1) In adolescence, general forms of drug use and delinquency are not causally related but are spuriously related because they are both types of deviant activity in which adolescents engage.

(2) Adolescents are heterogeneous in terms of their levels of substance use and delinquency, and the co-occurrence of both behaviors.

(3) The majority of adolescents have no or only minor delinquency involvement regardless of the extent of their substance use.

(4) Peer group influences are the best predictors of delinquency and drug use.

J. Fagan (personal communication, March 29, 1989) feels that bonding to delinquent peers is the important theoretical and dependent variable in a developmental sequence leading to specific forms of deviance and that this sequence is dictated by group processes. Because groups are heterogeneous in their patterns of behaviors, the specific form of deviance may be determined by a particular group behavior, apart from anything that bonds the individuals to the group. In Fagan's opinion, the degree of immersion in the peer group, and the acceptance of its symbolic value, are critical for explaining bonding to deviant peers.

It must be kept in mind, however, that research has not established a clear causal link between peer deviance and adolescent deviance (see Elliott et al., 1985; Kandel, 1985). That is, it seems as likely that deviants would select a group of peers who reinforce their own behavior as that friends would "create" the original deviant behavior. If selection and socialization are reciprocal processes, then we still need to discover why one person chooses delinquents while another chooses drug users as his/her peer group (see Schwendinger & Schwendinger, 1985).

There are several other areas that have not been thoroughly addressed when exploring the drug-delinquency connection. For example, a possible explanation for why some adolescents become more involved in delinquency and others in drug use is differential opportunity (Cloward & Ohlin, 1960). One might speculate that demographic characteristics or neighborhood composition affect access to certain peer groups, to opportunities to learn certain behaviors, or to specific drugs. Research has demonstrated that the social ecology of urban areas influences gang participation and violence through its effect on the strengths of social controls on behaviors (see Fagan, 1989a). Thus, situational and ecological variables may interact to determine, first, the degree of attachment and commitment to conventional behaviors and, second, the available types of peer groups with whom adolescents can bond.

Another fruitful avenue for exploration may be found in the reinforcements derived from behaviors. That is, we may need to look more closely at personal motivations for using drugs and engaging in delinquency in order to gain a better understanding of the reasons why certain individuals are drawn to certain forms of deviance. While much research is emerging on expectancies of alcohol and drug use (e.g., Brown, Goldman, Inn & Anderson, 1980; Christiansen, Goldman & Inn, 1982), this area is relatively unexplored in relation to delinquent behavior (Agnew, 1988). We also need to examine the consequences that have been experienced as a result of engaging in each behavior. These include both the direct social reinforcement from peer acceptance for the behavior, as well as indirect social reinforcement, such as approval for one's new clothes purchased with stolen money.

We cannot overlook the nonsocial reinforcers. Drugs have psychopharmacological effects that distinguish their use from other forms of delinquent behavior. There may be a certain high from stealing for some individuals, and there is usually positive reinforcement when one buys a desired commodity, regardless of where the money originates. However, drugs allow individuals to alter their moods in a more precise and direct manner. The

coping functions of alcohol and drugs have been demonstrated to be a significant aspect of use (Labouvie, 1986, 1987). These pharmacological reinforcements and punishments are certainly important determinants of the
continued use of a drug (see Akers, 1985; White, Bates & Johnson, forthcoming). Hence, the mood-altering function of drug use cannot be dismissed
by researchers attempting to understand drug use among adolescents
(Labouvie, 1986).

Until recently, there has been little attention focused on the motivations
for and the expectations of delinquent behavior.[6] Social learning theory
(Akers, 1985) includes principles of reinforcement, yet most of its applications have operationalized only the social reinforcement from primary
groups. Delinquency researchers need to consider why adolescents engage in
delinquent behavior. As stated above, we need to consider both social and
nonsocial reinforcers. Watters et al. (1985) also highlighted the need to understand the setting, social context, and motivation of the event when studying drug use and delinquency. They found that violence, for example, involved several different motivations including impulsivity, instrumentality,
and compulsivity. Similarly, the reinforcements from drug use depended
upon psychological set, subcultural norms, and social setting and varied from
one drug to another.

In complement, a recent analysis by Agnew (1988) focused directly on
reasons for committing delinquent acts. He tested three theories as explanations for delinquent events: *strain theory, subcultural deviance theory*, and *social control/rational decision theory*. He found that different theories accounted for the commission of different delinquent acts. For example, strain
theory (i.e., anger/retaliation) best predicted violent behavior and running
away; property crime (except vandalism) was best explained by rational
choice theory (i.e., self-gratification/utilitarian need); and drug offenses were
best explained by subcultural theory (i.e., peer pressure/influence). More of
this type of research is needed.

Before concluding, I would like to comment on the most promising directions for studying the drug-crime nexus. After reviewing the data on the
drug-crime connection, Williams (1979) recommended that adolescents be
examined to better understand this connection. After ten years of additional
research in this area, however, this type of research has not proven to be as
insightful as Williams had thought. The studies of adult institutional samples
(e.g., drug treatment clients) (e.g., Ball et al., 1981) and the ethnographic
studies (e.g., Goldstein, 1981, Johnson et al., 1985) have provided more clues
as to the nature of the relationship between drug use and crime, than has the
adolescent literature. While the research on normal populations of
adolescents reviewed above has increased our understanding of developmental and etiological processes involved in drug use and delinquent behav-

iors, it may not be most relevant for the types of issues that face drug control and crime control policymakers. Rather than continue to examine the relationship between delinquency and the prevalence of use of the "softer" drugs, such as marijuana, in adolescent populations, attention should be focused on the more intensive use of "harder" drugs, such as crack, cocaine, and heroin. Fagan's (1989a) research on gangs and the recent longitudinal studies which oversample high-risk populations (based on census track characteristics, see Swain, 1988) exemplify the direction in which we need to move. This research focuses on the tail of the distribution, the point where serious delinquency and drug use are concentrated. Such research will also allow us to test whether well-accepted theories of deviance (e.g., control theory, social learning theory) have equivalent explanatory power across disparate populations and social areas.[7]

NOTES

[1]   The distinctions between violent and property crime are often arbitrary. Burglary is considered a property crime and robbery a violent crime. Yet both are acquisition crimes and in a sense would support an economic motivation theory as opposed to a psychopharmacological theory. Murder and robbery are linked together as personal or violent crimes, yet motivations for robbery are probably more similar to those for burglary than those for murder (unless the murder occurs during a robbery).

[2]   Those most likely to continue criminal activities into adulthood came from poor families, had other criminals in their family, did poorly in school, began using drugs and committing delinquent acts at an early age, used multiple drugs and committed frequent crimes, and had few opportunities for participating in rewarding activities.

[3]   *Nonuse* = no use of any drug 4 or more times; *alcohol use* = use of alcohol 4 or more times, but no other substance 4 or more times; *marijuana use* = use of marijuana 4 or more times, possible alcohol use, but no other substance 4 or more times; and *polydrug use* = use of other drugs 4 or more times.

[4]   *Nondelinquents* = fewer than 4 self-reported delinquent offenses and no Index offenses; *exploratory delinquents* = 4-11 total offenses, but no more than 1 Index offense, or 1 Index offense and fewer than 4 total offenses; *nonserious delinquents* = 12 or more total offenses, but no more

than 2 Index offenses, or 2 Index offenses and fewer than 12 total offenses; *serious delinquents* = at least three Index offenses.

[5]   The predictions within each behavioral area, especially substance use, are consistent with the concept of drug stages (see Kandel, 1975).

[6]   There are two basic reasons for this lack of attention:
   (1)   most studies of delinquent explanations were based on small, unrepresentative samples, and therefore not generalizable, and
   (2)   there have been serious questions regarding the validity of delinquent explanations (Agnew, 1988).

[7]   J. Fagan (personal communication, March 29, 1989) has questioned whether control theory or the various integrated theories would have equivalent explanatory power in lower-class inner cities as compared to upper-class suburbs and on behaviors as diverse as crack use and chronic marijuana use.   He has suggested that social and economic forces shape behaviors and that differences in these forces will affect the applicability of certain theoretical concepts.

REFERENCES

Agnew, R. (1985). "Social Control Theory and Delinquency: A Longitudinal Test." *Criminology*, 23, 47-61.

Agnew, R. (1988, November).   "The Origins of Delinquent Events: An Examination of Offender Accounts." Paper presented at the American Society of Criminology Meeting, Chicago, IL.

Akers, R. (1985). *Deviant Behavior*. Belmont, CA: Wadsworth Publishing Co.

Akers, R.L. M.D. Krohn, L. Lanza-Kaduce & M.J. Radosevich (1979). "Social Learning and Deviant Behavior: A Specific Test of a General Theory." *American Sociological Review*, 44, 636-655.

Anglin, M.D. & G. Speckart (1988).   "Narcotics Use and Crime: A Multisample, Multimethod Analysis." *Criminology*, 26, 197-233.

Bachman, J.G., P. O'Malley & L.D. Johnston (1978). *Youth in Transition.* Ann Arbor, MI: Institute for Social Research.

Ball, J.C., L. Rosen, J.A. Flueck & D. Nurco (1981). "The Criminality of Heroin Addicts When Addicted and When Off Opiates." In J.A. Inciardi (ed.) *The Drugs-Crime Connection*, 39-65. Beverly Hills, CA: Sage.

Barton, W.I. (1976). "Heroin Use and Criminality: Survey of Inmates of State Correctional Facilities, January 1974." In Research Triangle Institute, *Appendix to Drug Use and Crime: Report of the Panel on Drug Use and Criminal Behavior* (NTIS No. PB 259 167, pp. 419-440). Springfield, VA: National Technical Information Service.

Bates, M.E., E.W. Labouvie & H.R. White (1986). "The Effect of Sensation Seeking Needs on Alcohol and Marijuana Use in Adolescence." *Bulletin of the Society of Psychologists in Addictive Behaviors*, 5, 29-36.

Blumstein, A., D.P. Farrington & S. Moitra (1985). "Delinquency Careers: Innocents, Desisters, and Persisters." In M.H. Tonry and N. Morris (eds.), *Crime and Justice: An Annual Review of Research*, 7. Chicago University Press.

Brown, S.A., M.S. Goldman, A. Inn & L.R. Anderson (1980). "Expectations and Reinforcements from Alcohol: Their Domain and Relation to Drinking Patterns." *Journal of Consulting and Clinical Psychology*, 48, 419-426.

Bureau of Justice Statistics (1983a). *Prisoners in 1982* (NJC-86233). Washington, DC: U.S. Department of Justice.

Bureau of Justice Statistics (1983b). *Prisoners and Alcohol* (NJC-87933). Washington, DC: U.S. Department of Justice.

Carpenter, C., B. Glassner, B.D. Johnson & J. Loughlin (1988). *Kids, Drugs, and Crime.* Lexington, MA: Lexington Books.

Catalano, R., H.R. White, J.D. Hawkins & R.J. Pandina (1985, November). "Predictors of Initiation and Frequency of Alcohol Use, Drug Use and Delinquency: An Examination and Comparison of Relationships in Two Longitudinal Studies." Paper presented at the annual meeting of the American Society of Criminology, San Diego, CA.

Chaiken, M.R. & B.D. Johnson (1988). "Characteristics of Different Types of Drug-Involved Offenders." *Issues and Practices*. Washington, DC: National Institute of Justice.

Christiansen, B.A., M.S. Goldman & A. Inn (1982). "Development of Alcohol-Related Expectancies in Adolescents: Separating Pharmacological from Social-Learning Influences." *Journal of Consulting and Clinical Psychology*, 50, 336-344.

Clayton, R.R. (1981a). "Federal Drugs-Crime Research: Setting the Agenda." In J.A. Inciardi (ed.) *The Drugs-Crime Connection*, 17-38. Beverly Hills, CA: Sage.

Clayton, R.R. (1981b). "The Delinquency and Drug Use Relationship Among Adolescents." In D.J. Lettieri and J.P. Ladford (eds.) *Drug Abuse and the American Adolescent* (NIDA Research Monograph 38, pp. 82-103). Rockville, MD: National Institute on Drug Abuse.

Clayton, R.R. & B.S. Tuchfeld (1982). "The Drug-Crime Debate: Obstacles to Understanding the Relationship." *Journal of Drug Issues*, 12, 153-166.

Cloward, R. & L.E. Ohlin (1960). *Delinquency and Opportunity*. New York: Free Press.

Collins, J.J. (ed.) (1981). *Drinking and Crime*. New York: Guilford.

Collins, J.J. (1988). "Suggested Explanatory Frameworks to Clarify the Alcohol Use/Violence Relationship." *Contemporary Drug Problems*, 15, 107-121.

Collins, J.J., Jr., R.L. Hubbard & J.V. Rachal (1985). "Expensive Drug Use and Illegal Income: A Test of Explanatory Hypotheses." *Criminology*, 23, 743-764.

De Fleur, L.B., J.C. Ball & R.W. Snarr (1969). "The Long-Term Correlates of Opiate Addiction." *Social Problems*, 17, 225-234.

Donovan, J.E. & R. Jessor (1985). "Structure of Problem Behavior in Adolescence and Young Adulthood." *Journal of Consulting and Clinical Psychology*, 53, 890-904.

Dunford, F.W. & D.S. Elliott (1984). "Identifying Career Offenders Using Self-Report Data." *Journal of Research in Crime and Delinquency, 21*, 57-86.

Elliott, D.S. & A.R. Ageton (1976a). "The Relationship Between Drug Use and Crime Among Adolescents." In Research Triangle Institute, *Appendix to Drug Use and Crime: Report of the Panel on Drug Use and Criminal Behavior* (NTIS No. PB 259,167, pp. 297-320). Springfield, VA: National Technical Information Service.

Elliott, D.S. & A.R. Ageton (1976b). *Subcultural Delinquency and Drug Use.* Boulder, CO: Behavioral Research Institute.

Elliott, D.S. & S.S. Ageton (1981). *The Epidemiology of Delinquent Behavior and Drug Use Among American Adolescents, 1976-78.* Boulder, CO: Behavioral Research Institute. (NYS Report No. 14).

Elliott, D.S., S.S. Ageton & R.J. Canter (1979). "An Integrated Theoretical Perspective on Delinquent Behavior." *Journal of Research on Crime and Delinquency, 16*, 3-27.

Elliott, D.S. & D.H. Huizinga. "The Relationship Between Delinquent Behavior and ADM Problems." In C. Hampton & I. Silverman (eds.) *Drug Abuse, Mental Health and Delinquency.* Rockville, MD: ADAMHA (forthcoming).

Elliott, D.S., D.H. Huizinga & S.S. Ageton (1985). *Explaining Delinquency and Drug Use.* Beverly Hills, CA: Sage.

Elliott, D.S., D.H. Huizinga & S. Menard (1989). *Multiple Problem Youth: Delinquency, Substance Use and Mental Health Problems.* New York: Springer-Verlag (forthcoming).

Fagan, J. (1989a). "The Social Organization of Drug Use and Drug Dealing Among Urban Gangs." *Criminology, 27*(4), 633-667.

Fagan, J. (1989b). "Intoxication and Aggression." In J.Q. Wilson & M. Tonry (eds.) *Drugs and Crime (Crime and Justice: An Annual Review of Research, Vol 13)*, Chicago: University of Chicago Press (forthcoming).

Fagan, J.A., K.V. Hansen & M. Jang (1983). "Profiles of Chronically Violent Delinquents." In J. Kleugal (ed.) *Evaluating Juvenile Justice*, 91-119. Beverly Hills: Sage.

Fagan, J. & E. Pablon (1989). *Contributions of Delinquency and Substance Use to School Dropout Among Inner City Youths*. New York: John Jay College of Criminal Justice.

Fagan, J., J.G. Weis & Y.T. Cheng (1989).   Drug Use and Delinquency Among Inner City Students." *Journal of Drug Issues* (forthcoming).

Fagan, J., J.G. Weis, Y.T. Cheng & J.K. Watters (1987). *Drug and Alcohol Use, Violent Delinquency and Social Bonding: Implications for Intervention Theory and Policy*. San Francisco: The URSA Institute.

Gandossy, R.P., J.R. Williams, J. Cohen & H.J. Harwood (1980). *Drugs and Crime: A Survey and Analysis of the Literature*. Washington, DC: U.S. Department of Justice.

Ginsberg, I.J. & J.R. Greenley (1978).   "Competing Theories of Marijuana Use: A Longitudinal Study." *Journal of Health and Social Behavior*, 19, 22-34.

Gold, M. & D.J. Reimer (1975). "Changing Patterns of Delinquent Behavior Among American 13 to 16 year olds--1972." *Crime and Delinquency Literature*, 7, 483-517.

Goldman, F. (1981).   "Drug Abuse, Crime, and Economics: The Dismal Limits of Social Choice." In J.A. Inciardi (ed.) *The Drug-Crime Connection*, 155-181. Beverly Hills: Sage Publications.

Goldstein, P.J. (1981). "Alternatives to Predatory Crime Among Street Drug Users." In J.A. Inciardi (ed.) *The Drug-Crime Connection*, 67-84. Beverly Hills: Sage Publications.

Goldstein, P.J. (1985). "The Drugs/Violence Nexus: A Tripartite Conceptual Framework." *Journal of Drug Issues*, 15, 493-506.

Goode, E. (1972).   "Excerpts from Marijuana and Crime." In National Commission on Marijuana and Drug Abuse, *Marijuana--A Signal of Misunderstanding* (Appendix, Vol. 1).   Washington, DC: U.S. Government Printing Office.

Goode, E. (1970). *The Marijuana Smokers*. New York: Basic Books.

Gropper, B.A. (1985). *Probing the Links Between Drugs and Crime* (National Institute of Justice Reports). Washington, DC: National Institute of Justice.

Hawkins, J.D. "Drug Abuse, Mental Health, and Delinquency: Executive Summary." In C. Hampton & I. Silverman (eds.) *Drug Abuse, Mental Health and Delinquency*. Rockville, MD: ADAMHA (forthcoming).

Hawkins, J.D. & D.P Farrington (1988). *Prediction of Participation, Early Onset, and Later Persistence in Officially Recorded Offending: The Relevance of Social Development Model Constructs*. Seattle, WA: Social Development Research Group, University of Washington.

Hawkins, J.D., D.M. Lishner & R.F. Catalano (1985). "Childhood Predictors and the Prevention of Adolescent Substance Use." In C.L. Jones & R.J. Battjes (eds.) *Etiology of Drug Abuse: Implications for Prevention* (75-126). Washington, DC: National Institute on Drug Abuse.

Hawkins, J.D. & J.G. Weis (1985). "The Social Development Model: An Integrated Approach to Delinquency Prevention." *Journal of Primary Prevention*, 6, 73-97.

Hill, G.D. & M.P. Atkinson (1988). "Gender, Familial Control, and Delinquency." *Criminology*, 26, 127-147.

Hindelang, M.J. (1972). The Relationship Between Self-Reported Delinquency to Scales of the CPI and MMPI." *Journal of Criminal Law, Criminology and Police Science*, 63, 75-81.

Hindelang, M.J., T. Hirschi & J.G. Weis (1981). *Measuring Delinquency*. Beverly Hills: Sage.

Hindelang, M.J. & J.G. Weis (1972). "The BC-Try Cluster and Factor Analysis System: Personality and Self-Reported Delinquency." *Criminology*, 10, 268-294.

Hirschi, T. (1969). *Causes of Delinquency*. Berkeley: University of California Press.

Hirschi, T. (1987). "Review of Explaining Delinquency and Drug Use." *Criminology*, 25, 193-201.

Hirschi, T. & M. Gottfredson (1983). "Age and the Explanation of Crime." *American Journal of Sociology*, 89, 552-584.

Huba, G.J. & P.M. Bentler (1984). "Causal Models of Personality, Peer Culture Characteristics, Drug Use, and Criminal Behaviors Over a Five-Year Span." In D.W. Goodwin, K. van Dusen & S. Mednick (eds.) *Longitudinal Research in Alcoholism*, 73-94. Boston: Kluwer-Nijhof.

Huizinga, D.H. (1986). "The Relationship Between Delinquent and Drug Use Behaviors in a National Sample of Youths." In B.D. Johnson & E. Wish (eds.) *Crime Rates Among Drug Abusing Offenders*, 145-194. New York: Interdisciplinary Research Center, Narcotic and Drug Research, Inc.

Huizinga, D.H. & D.S. Elliott (1981). *A Longitudinal Study of Drug Use and Delinquency in a National Sample of Youth: An Assessment of Causal Order.* Report of the National Youth Survey Project, Report #16). Boulder, CO: Behavioral Research Institute.

Inciardi, J.A. (1979). "Heroin Use and Street Crime." *Crime and Delinquency*, 25, 335-346.

Jaquith, M. (1981). "Adolescent Marijuana and Alcohol Use: An Empirical Test of Differential Association Theory." *Criminology*, 19, 271-280.

Jensen, G.F. & D.G. Rojek (1980). *Delinquency: A Sociological View.* Lexington, MA: Heath.

Jessor, R. & S. Jessor (1977). *Problem Behavior and Psychosocial Development - A Longitudinal Study of Youth.* New York: Academic Press.

Johnson, B.D. (1973). *Marijuana Users and Drug Subcultures.* New York: Wiley.

Johnson, B.D., P. Goldstein, E. Preble, J. Schmeidler, D.S. Lipton, B. Spunt & T. Miller (1985). *Taking Care of Business: The Economics of Crime by Heroin Abusers.* Lexington, MA: Lexington Books.

Johnson, B.D., E. Wish, J. Schmeidler & D.H. Huizinga (1986). "The Concentration of Delinquent Offending: Serious Drug Involvement and High Delinquency Rates." In B.D. Johnson & E. Wish (eds.) *Crime Rates Among Drug Abusing Offenders*, 106-43. New York: Interdisciplinary Research Center, Narcotic and Drug Research, Inc.

Johnson, R.E. (1979). *Juvenile Delinquency and Its Origins: An Integrated Approach*. New York: Cambridge University Press.

Johnson, R.E., A.C. Marcos & S.J. Bahr (1987). "The Role of Peers in the Complex Etiology of Adolescent Drug Use." *Criminology*, 25, 323-339.

Johnson, V. & H.R. White (1989). "An Investigation of Factors Related to Intoxicated Driving Behaviors Among Youth." *Journal of Studies on Alcohol*, 50, 320-330.

Johnston, L., P. O'Malley & L.K. Eveland (1978). "Drugs and Delinquency: A Search for Causal Connections." In D.B. Kandel (ed.) *Longitudinal Research on Drug Use: Empirical Findings and Methodological Issues*, 137-156. New York: Wiley.

Kandel, D.B. (1975). "Stages in Adolescent Involvement in Drug Use." *Science*, 190, 912-914.

Kandel, D.B. (1978). "Convergences in Prospective Longitudinal Surveys of Drug Use in Normal Populations." In D.B. Kandel (ed.) *Longitudinal Research on Drug Use: Empirical Findings and Methodological Issues*, 3-38. New York: John Wiley.

Kandel, D.B. (1985). "On Processes of Peer Influences in Adolescent Drug Use: A Developmental Perspective." *Advances in Alcohol and Substance Abuse*, 4(3/4), 139-163.

Kandel, D.B., R.C. Kessler & R.Z. Margulies (1978). "Antecedents of Adolescent Initiation into Stages of Drug Use: A Developmental Analysis." In D.B. Kandel (ed.) *Longitudinal Research on Drug Use: Empirical Findings and Methodological Issues*, 73-100. New York: John Wiley.

Kandel, D.B., O. Simcha-Fagan & M. Davies (1986). "Risk Factors for Delinquency and Illicit Drug Use from Adolescence to Young Adulthood." *Journal of Drug Issues*, 16, 67-90.

Kaplan, H.B., S.S. Martin & C. Robbins (1984). "Pathways to Adolescent Drug Use: Self-Derogation, Peer Influence, Weakening of Social Controls, and Early Substance Use." *Journal of Health and Social Behavior*, 25, 270-289.

Klein, M.W. "Police Processing of Serious Juvenile Drug Abusers." In C. Hampton & I. Silverman (eds.) *Drug Abuse, Mental Health and Delinquency*. Rockville, MD: ADAMHA (forthcoming).

Labouvie, E.W. (1986). "The Coping function of Adolescent Alcohol and Drug Use." In R.K. Silbereisen, K. Eyferth & G. Rudinger (eds.) *Development as Action in Context*, 229-240. New York: Springer-Verlag.

Labouvie, E.W. (1987). "Relation of Personality to Adolescent Alcohol and Drug Use: A Coping Perspective." *Pediatrician*, 14, 19-24.

LaGrange, R.L. & H.R. White (1985). "Age Differences in Delinquency: A Test of Theory." *Criminology*, 23, 19-47.

Loeber, R. (1988). "Natural Histories of Conduct Problems, Delinquency, and Associated Substance Use." In B.B. Lahey & A.E. Kazdin (eds.) *Advances in Clinical Child Psychology*, Vol. 11, 73-124. New York: Plenum Press.

Loeber, R. & T.J. Dishion (1983). "Early Predictors of Male Delinquency: A Review." *Psychological Bulletin*, 94, 68-99.

Marcos, A.C., S.J. Bahr & R.E. Johnson (1986). "Test of a Bonding/Association Theory of Adolescent Drug Use." *Social Forces*, 65, 135-161.

Massey, J.L. & M.D. Krohn (1986). "A Longitudinal Examination of an Integrated Social Process Model of Deviant Behavior." *Social Forces*, 65, 106-134.

Matsueda, R.L. (1982). "Testing Control Theory and Differential Association Theory: A Causal Modeling Approach." *American Sociological Review*, 47, 498-504.

Matza, P. (1964). *Delinquency and Drift*. New York: Wiley.

McBride, D.C. (1981). *Drugs and Violence*. In J.A. Inciardi (ed.) *The Drugs Crime Connection*, 105-123. Beverly Hills: Sage Publications.

McBride, D.C. & C.B. McCoy (1982). "Crime and Drugs: The Issues in the Literature." *Journal of Drug Issues*, 12, 137-152.

McGlothlin, W.H., D. Anglin & B.D. Wilson (1978). "Narcotic Addiction and Crime." *Criminology*, 16, 293-315.

Nurco, D.C., J.W. Schaeffer, J.C. Ball & T.W. Kinlock (1984). "Trends in the Commission of Crime Among Narcotic Addicts Over Successive Periods of Addiction." *Journal of Drug and Alcohol Abuse*, 10, 481-489.

Pandina, R.J., E.W. Labouvie & H.R. White (1984). "Potential Contributions of the Life Span Developmental Approach to the Study of Adolescent Alcohol and Drug Use: The Rutgers Health and Human Development Project, a Working Model." *Journal of Drug Issues*, 14, 253-268.

Pandina, R.J. & H.R. White. "The Relationship Between Alcohol and Marijuana Use and Crime: Implications for Intervention and Prevention. In C. Hampton & I. Silverman (eds.) *Drug Abuse, Mental Health and Delinquency*. Rockville, MD: ADAMHA (forthcoming).

Pandina, R.J., H.R. White & J. Yorke (1981). "Estimation of Substance Use Involvement: Theoretical Considerations and Empirical Findings." *International Journal of the Addictions*, 16, 1-24.

Pernanen, K. (1976). "Alcohol and Crimes of Violence." In B. Kissin & H. Begleiter (eds.) *The Biology of Alcoholism: Vol. 4. Social Aspects of Alcoholism*, 351-444. New York: Plenum Press.

Pernanen, K. (1981). "Theoretical Aspects of the Relationship Between Alcohol Use and Crime." In J.J. Collins (ed.) *Drinking and Crime*, 1-69. New York: Guilford Press.

Plair, W. & L. Jackson (1970). *Narcotic Use and Crime: A Report on Interviews with 50 Addicts Under Treatment* (Research Report No. 33). Washington, DC: District of Columbia Department of Corrections.

Radosevich, M., L. Lanza-Kaduce, R. Akers & M. Krohn (1980). "The Sociology of Adolescent Drug and Drinking Behavior: A Review of the State of the Field." *Deviant Behavior*, 1, 145-169.

Reinarman, C. (1979). "Moral Entrepreneurs and Political Economy: Historical and Ethnographic Notes on the Construction of the Cocaine Menace." *Contemporary Crises*, 3, 225-254.

Rouse, B.A., N.J. Kozel & L.G. Richards (eds.) (1985). *Self-Report Methods of Estimating Drug Use: Meeting Current Challenges to Validity* (NIDA Research Monograph 57). Rockville, MD: NIDA.

Schwendinger, H. & J. Schwendinger (1985). *Adolescent Subcultures and Delinquency.* New York: Praeger.

Single, E. & D. Kandel (1978). "The Role of Buying and Selling in Illicit Drug Use." In A. Trebach (ed.) *Drugs, Crime, and Politics*, 118-128. New York: Praeger.

Single, E., D. Kandel & B. Johnson (1975). "The Reliability and Validity of Drug Use Responses in a Large Scale Longitudinal Survey." *Journal of Drug Issues*, 5, 426-433.

Sutherland, E.H. & D.R. Cressey (1978). *Criminology* (10th ed.). Philadelphia, PA: Lippincott.

Swain, P. (1988, November). "Progress in the Consortium of Studies on the Causes of Crime." Panel presented at the annual meetings of the American Society of Criminology, Chicago, IL.

Thornberry, T.P. (1987). "Toward an Interactional Theory of Delinquency." *Criminology*, 25, 863-891.

Thornberry, T.P. & R.L. Christenson (1984). "Unemployment and Criminal Involvement: An Investigation of Reciprocal Causal Structures." *American Sociological Review*, 49, 398-411.

Thornberry, T.P., M. Moore & R.L. Christenson (1985). "The Effect of Dropping Out of School on Subsequent Criminal Behavior." *Criminology*, 23, 3-18.

Tinklenberg, J.R. (1973). "Drugs and Crime." In National Commission on Marijuana and Drug Abuse, *Drug Use in America: Problem in Perspective* (Vol. 1, Appendix, 242-299). Washington DC: U.S. Government Printing Office.

Waldorf, D. & C. Reinarman (1975). "Addicts -- Everything but Human Beings." *Urban Life*, 4, 30-53.

Watters, J.K., C. Reinarman & J. Fagan (1985). "Causality, Context, and Contingency Relationships Between Drug Abuse and Delinquency." *Contemporary Drug Problems*, 12, 351-373.

White, H.R. (1987, November). *Drug Use and Delinquency: A Test of the 'Independent Cause' Hypothesis*. Paper presented at the annual meetings of the American Society of Criminology, Montreal, Quebec.

White, H.R., M.E. Bates & V. Johnson. "Social Reinforcers of Alcohol Consumption." In W.M. Cox (ed.) *Why People Drink: Parameters of Alcohol as a Reinforcer*. New York: Gardner Press (forthcoming).

White, H.R. & V. Johnson (1989). "Risk Taking as a Predictor of Adolescent Sexual Activity and Use of Contraception." *Journal of Adolescent Research*, 4, 317-331.

White, H.R., V. Johnson & C. Garrison (1985a). "The Drug-Crime Nexus Among Adolescents and Their Peers." *Deviant Behavior*, 6, 183-204.

White, H.R., V. Johnson & A. Horwitz (1986). "An Application of Three Deviance Theories to Adolescent Substance Use." *International Journal of the Addictions*, 21, 347-366.

White, H.R. & E.W. Labouvie (1989). "Towards the Assessment of Adolescent Problem Drinking." *Journal of Studies on Alcohol*, 50, 30-37.

White, H.R., E.W. Labouvie & M.E. Bates (1985b). "The Relationship Between Sensation Seeking and Delinquency: A Longitudinal Analysis." *Journal of Research in Crime and Delinquency*, 22, 197-211.

White, H.R., R.J. Pandina & E.W. Labouvie (1985c, August). "The Drug-Crime Nexus: A Longitudinal Analysis." Paper presented at the annual meetings of the Society for the Study of Social Problems, Washington, DC.

White, H.R., R.J. Pandina & R.L. LaGrange (1987). "Longitudinal Predictors of Serious Substance Use and Delinquency." *Criminology*, 25, 715-740.

Wiatrowski, M.D., D.B. Griswold & M.K. Roberts (1981). "Social Control Theory and Delinquency." *American Sociological Review*, 46, 525-541.

Williams, J.R. (1979). *Exploring the Drug Use and Criminal Behavior Nexus: A Research Agenda and Selected Research Designs*. Research Triangle Park, NC: Research Triangle Institute.

Zuckerman, M. (1979). *Sensation Seeking: Beyond the Optimal Level of Arousal*. Hillsdale, NJ: Lawrence Erlbaum Associates.

10

DWI: An Isolated Incident or a Continuous Pattern of Criminal Activity?*

Larry A. Gould
Louisiana State University

Doris Layton MacKenzie
*The National Institute of Justice
and Louisiana State University*

INTRODUCTION

"DWI is the crime most commonly committed by a noncriminal." (Joye, 1983). This statement raises an interesting research question concerning the actual prior histories of persons arrested by police for driving while intoxicated (DWI).

For the courts, researchers, and policymakers one of the critical, but often overlooked, questions in evaluating those charged with driving while intoxicated (DWI) (or driving under the influence (DUI)) is whether the arrest is a single aberrant incident or is indicative of a continuing pattern of criminal behavior on the part of the arrestee. This research is designed to examine whether people arrested for DWI have a significant history of prior criminal arrests. The hypothesis is that an arrest for DWI is not simply a single episode of criminal behavior, but rather is indicative of a continuing pattern of criminal activity. The examination of the data centers on arrests for

---

*   An earlier version of this chapter was presented at the Annual Meeting of the Academy of Criminal Justice Sciences, April, 1988.

crimes against persons, with the focus being on the relationship between alcohol use and aggressive criminal acts.

The presence of a criminal history record, particularly arrests, for the majority of individuals arrested for DWI was first reported by Waller (1967). Since that time other investigators (Pollack, 1969; Yoder & Moore, 1975; Zelhart, Schurr & Brown, 1975) have confirmed Waller's findings. Most recently Argeriou, McCarty and Blacker (1985) have reaffirmed these earlier findings and helped to establish the prior criminal arrest as a stable descriptor of individuals arrested for DWI.

As pointed out by Argeriou et al. (1985), there is an early an repeated identification of the relationship between criminal behavior and DWI arrests; however, the specific nature of the relationship has not been deeply explored. One of the problems with earlier studies was a lack of definition of what constitutes criminal behavior. Additionally, there is little information concerning the types and frequencies of the criminal offenses. According to Argeriou et al. (1985) this lack of definition of what constitutes criminal activity may account for the variation in the incidence of criminal behavior that has been reported in previous studies -- i.e., Waller (1967) 84 percent, Pollack (1969) 72 percent, Yoder and Moore (1973) 60 percent, Zelhart et al. (1975) 100 percent and Argeriou et al. (1985) 76.5 percent. In addition to the problem as presented by Argeriou, that of definition, the point in the criminal justice system at which the data is collected may result in different findings.

A relationship has been established between alcohol consumption and violent or aggressive crimes. For example, Wolfgang (1958) found that alcohol was present in either the victim, the offender, or both in 64 percent of the cases involving a homicide in Philadelphia, for the years 1948-1952. REsults similar to Wolfgang's have been found in other studies of homicides and other violent crimes, which indicates that those persons labeled problem drinkers have a disproportionate number of criminal arrests (Goodwin, Crane & Guze, 1971; Guze, Tuason, Gatfield, Stewart & Picken, 1982; Lindelius & Salum, 1973). Voss and Hepburn (1968) found that alcohol was consumed prior to the offense in 53 percent of the homicide cases they studies, and Amir (1967) reports that 34 percent of the rape cases he analyzed showed the offender has consumed alcohol prior to the offenses. Other studies involving rape found that even higher percentages, between 72 and 77 percent, of the reported incidents of rape were preceded by the consumption of alcohol (Johnson, Gibson & Linden, 1978; Rada, 1975). Additionally, 58 to 64 percent of reported assaultive behavior has been found to be preceded by alcohol consumption (Meyer, Magedanz, Kieselhorst & Chapman, 1978; Mayfield, 1976). This phenomenon is by no means restricted to the United States. Pernanen's (1979) research on a general population of adults from a community in Canada found that, in 52 percent of reported violent incidents, at least one of the parties involved had been drinking. Roslund and Larson (1979) report that 68 percent of the offenders they studied in Sweden were found to have been "drunk" when committing their crime.

A relationship has also been found between alcohol consumption and property crimes. Self-report studies of inmates reveal that alcohol had been consumed prior to, or was being consumed at the time of, the crime for which they were currently incarcerated (Roizen & Schneberk, 1977; Pittman & Gordon, 1958). Roizen & Schneberk (1978) report that for selected property offenses they found alcohol involvement in 39 percent of the robbery cases; 47 percent of the burglaries; 38 percent of the larcenies; 46 percent of the vehicle thefts; 38 percent of the forgeries; and 67 percent of the arsons.

Not only is there evidence of a relationship between alcohol and crime, but alcohol has been linked to aggressive behavior as well as to shifts in mood and emotions (Nathan & Lisman, 1976). Psychotic and violent behavior increases as the blood alcohol content (BAC) rises (Carpenter & Armenti, 1972: Nathan, Titler, Lownstein, Solomon & Rossi, 1970; Feldman, 1977). Further support for the tie between aggressive behavior and alcohol is shown by interviews with inmates. Peterson and Braiker (1980) found that 24 percent of the California inmates whom they interviewed reported they "got drunk and hurt someone" in the three years prior to their current incarceration.

As a matter of public policy and treatment, it is important that an investigation of patterns of aberrant behavior during the life history of an individual be considered in the evaluation of the individuals' DWI arrest and conviction. Our contention is that the offense of DWI is not just an isolated incident but a part of a continuing pattern of criminal behavior, and that the same pattern tends toward crimes of aggression or more appropriately, toward crimes against persons. This is consistent with many theories of criminality, such as control theory (Hirschi, 1969; Reiss, 1951; Nye, 1958), deviance and social reaction theories (Akers, 1973; Chambliss & Seidman, 1971), and theories dealing with criminality as a learned behavior (Sutherland, 1947; Wolfgang & Ferracuti, 1981); in each of these, it is contended that the whole individual, including his prior criminal history, and/or his environment, must be taken into consideration when evaluating a criminal act. This means that the individual cannot be properly assessed on just one crime, such as DWI, but that the assessment must be made on the total history of the individual. The point to be made is that DWI cannot be studied, nor can rehabilitative efforts be made, as long as drunk driving is though of as an isolated incident in the life of the individual.

According to Argeriou et al. (1985), most criminal justice systems and treatment programs treat the DWI as if he or she were a part of a homogeneous group. Donovan and Marlatt (1982) suggest that failure to identify the presence of subtypes, such as persons with a history of criminal activity, in the DWI population (Steer, Fine & Scoles, 1979; Sutker, Brantley & Allain, 1980) may be the reason for the high rate of unsuccessful DWI intervention programs.

Zelhart et al. (1975) suggests that the primary behavioral data, such as driving and criminal history records, should be developed and employed in identifying and subtyping persons charged with DWI because the currently-used personality tests are too gross to discriminate between the low- and high-risk drivers with any accuracy.

The present research compares the number and types of arrests in the criminal histories of a sample of persons arrested for DWI (DWI sample) and a sample of licensed (license sample) drivers in Louisiana.

In this study arrests were used, as opposed to convictions or even arraignments. The rationale for using arrest data rather than conviction data is that, historically, case dispositions (convictions or findings of not guilty) are not recorded as thoroughly as are arrests. In a recent nationwide survey of attorneys it was learned that criminal history records failed to show disposition information 42.9 percent of the time (Doernberg & Zeigler, 1980). A review of the Illinois Criminal Justice Information Authority revealed that of the 1.24 million arrest events reviewed, nearly 59 percent lacked any type of disposition information (1983 Illinois Annual Audit Report). The reporting and use of arrest incidents, while by no means complete, does not present as acute a problem as does disposition reporting.

> The OTA Report found that 18 percent of local arrests for 1982 were not reported to state central repositories. Two recent audits of arrest reporting in Michigan and Missouri also indicate that underreporting of arrests is a problem. Both studies indicate that somewhere between 20 and 30 percent of arrests are not reported to central repositories. The extent that arrests are not reported by local agencies can be attributable to a failure to fingerprint for minor arrest (Data Quality of Criminal History Records, 1985).

METHODS

Sample

The populations of interest are, first, males over the age of 17 who were arrested for DWI in Louisiana in 1985 and, secondly, all male drivers over the age of 17, licensed in the State as of 1985. A total of 723 adult males were selected for each sample to complete the comparison.

Procedure

The sampling frame for the DWI sample is the listing of all individuals who were tested by a police officer at one of the DWI testing stations in Louisiana during the year 1985. The actual listing comes from log sheets maintained at each DWI testing station and archived at the Louisiana State Police Headquarters. The information collected from the log sheets includes the offender's race, sex, age, time of test, date of test, whether or not an accident was involved, the breath alcohol reading or refusal to be tested, geographic area of arrest, and the DWI charge or alternate and/or additional traffic charges. The additional information that was necessary for this examination was gathered from two other archival sources: *traffic records* and *criminal history records*. A driver's license and criminal history record search was made on each person who was selected in the sample from the station log sheets.

No comprehensive printable list of all drivers in Louisiana is maintained by the state, therefore it was necessary to randomly generate a list of driver's-license-length numbers for the selection of the licensed sample and then to enter the number into the state computer. Only those individuals who met the criteria (males over the age of 17) were kept for the study.

The first step in gathering the historical information on individuals selected for both samples was a computerized check on traffic records, which was made from the Louisiana Department of Public Safety files. The driver's license number was used to gather information on the driving record. This number was not used to gather information on the driving record. This number was not used as an identification number for reasons of confidentiality. Only those traffic charges for which a conviction was received are recorded on the driving record. For the purposes of this study only those traffic violations which occurred prior to the date of the DWI test for the DWI sample, or prior to 1985 for the license sample, were recorded, regardless of the date of the convictions.

After the driver's license record was received it was then possible to check for the criminal history on each individual. These data were used to augment the information from the traffic records. This was necessary, first, because the traffic record does not include criminal history information, and, secondly, because traffic convictions are removed from the driver's record after three years, for moving violations; DWIs, reckless and careless operation of a motor vehicle, and accidents are removed after five years.

Table 10.1
Demographic Comparisons Between the Two Samples by Age, Race, and Geographic Area (Troop Area)

	DWI Sample n = 723*	License Sample n = 723
Age X(SD)	32.8** (12.7)	34.4*** (12.8)****
Race %		
White	69.9	69.9
Black	30.3	30.6
Other	0.9	0.4
Geographic Area n(%)		
Troop A	102 (14.1)	95 (13.1)
Troop B	90 (12.4)	97 (13.4)
Troop C	78 (10.8)	76 (10.5)
Troop D	47 (6.5)	55 (7.6)
Troop E	78 (10.8)	65 (9.0)
Troop F	39 (5.4)	46 (6.4)
Troop G	85 (11.8)	89 (12.3)
Troop H	31 (4.3)	37 (5.1)
Troop I	67 (9.3)	59 (8.2)
Troop K	43 (5.9)	37 (5.1)
Troop L	63 (8.7)	67 (9.3)
Total	723 (100.0)	723 (100.)

* Missing Cases = 18

** CI = 31.540 to 34.228

*** CI = 33.120 to 35.800

**** Approximately 1.3 years of difference can be detected as signficant between the two groups.

The person's date of birth, race, sex and driver's license were used to gather information on the criminal history records. Only persons who were licensed in Louisiana were included, since permission to use criminal history data from other states had not been granted at the time of the data collection. The above information was taken from the station log sheets and verified by the driving record information to ensure that the records used were those of the correct person. As with the driving record, only those arrests that occurred prior to the test date of the individual were recorded. The information of interest on the criminal history records was both the number and types of arrests and convictions. As mentioned previously, the arrest information was used in this study because more complete information is not available.

RESULTS

Complete data was available for 708 individuals in the DWI sample and 723 of the license sample. As shown in Table 10.1 there was no significant difference between the samples in race or geographic area. The comparison in the geographic area of arrest and residence for the two samples was important because of the diversity of cultures throughout the state. The geographic areas were defined by the boundaries of the 11 State Police Troops. There was a significant, but most likely nonmeaningful, difference between the two samples in age. The mean age of the DWI sample was slightly younger than that of the license sample (Table 10.1).

The first variable of interest was whether or not there was a history of criminal arrest, other than a traffic charge or another DWI. The information concerning arrest for a previous DWI or traffic charge is included in the study, but not in the criminal history arrest category. For the criminal arrests, the data for the six years prior to 1985 were examined. The listing was comprised of crimes against a person, which includes homicide, robbery, assault (sexual and other assaults), battery; crimes against property includes theft (fraud and forgery), burglary; drug offenses include possession and sale of controlled drugs; public order crimes, drunk and disorderly conduct, weapons carrying, vice and gambling; and other crimes (family abuse or neglect and other crimes); traffic charges which includes DWI, as well as major and minor traffic offenses.

Table 10.2
Number of Prior Arrests for the DWI Sample and the License Sample

	DWI Sample (n = 723)		License Sample (n = 723)	
Arrests				
Prior	63.4%	(447)	10.8%	(78)
No Prior	36.6%	(258)	89.2%	(645)
DWI				
Prior	46.2%	(327)	5.8%	(42)
No Prior	53.8%	(381)	94.2%	(681)

Number of Times Arrested %(n)
  (for those with a prior arrest)

	DWI	License
One	18.7% (131)	3.5% (25)
Two	15.6% (109)	2.4% (17)
Three	9.9% (69)	0.7% (5)
Four	2.9% (20)	0.6% (4)
Five	2.4% (17)	0.7% (5)
Six	2.9% (20)	0.1% (1)
Seven	0.3% (2)	0.1% (1)
Eight or more	7.0% (49)	1.0% (7)

Data Analysis

As mentioned previously, the major concern of this study is the comparison of the prior criminal history records of the DWI sample to a random sample of male drivers in Louisiana. A prior criminal history in either sample was considered to be any arrest for a violation of the Louisiana Criminal Code, except prior DWIs or traffic offenses which were counted separately. As has been hypothesized, significantly more individuals in the DWI sample in comparison to the licensed drivers sample had a prior arrest (X^2 = 425.05, df = 1, p < .005) (See Table 10.2).

The data revealed that 63.4 percent (n=705) of those arrested for DWI were found to have a prior criminal history, other than another DWI or a traffic offense; in the license sample only 10.8 percent (n=723) had a prior criminal history record. Within the license sample there are 42 individuals with a prior DWI offense. If the number of individuals with a prior DWI were to be removed from the license sample, the percentage would drop to 7.4 percent (n=723).

If the two groups are compared on the number of times they were arrested prior to 1985, there is again a statistically significant difference between the two groups (X^2 = 404.73, 8 df, p < .005). The actual breakdown shows that 282 of the individuals (39.9%) in the DWI group have no prior criminal history record and of the driver's license group, 648 individuals (90.0%) had no prior arrests. There were 131 individuals (18.7%) in the DWI sample who had one arrest, as compared to only 25 individuals (3.5%) in the license sample. The most significant finding in this breakdown is that of the DWI sample, 49 individuals (7.0%) had eight or more arrests, as opposed to 7 individuals (1.0%) of the license sample. (The full breakdown of the two samples by number of arrests can be found in Table 10.2).

The next analysis of the data concerns the comparison of the last three crimes for which a member of either sample was arrested. When the actual crime type is analyzed, we find that the largest spread between the two groups for the last three crimes listed in the criminal history sheet occurs in what would be considered the violent crime category, i.e., robbery, battery, assault and homicide. The license group is slightly more similar to the DWI group in non-violent crimes than in violent crimes, i.e., theft, burglary and disorderly conduct. The ration between the two samples for battery is approximately 19 arrests, in the DWI sample for each arrest in the license sample. In comparison, the ration of arrests for theft drops to 4 arrests in the DWI sample for each arrest in the license sample. There were a total of 27 homicide arrests made in the DWI sample and none made in the license sample. The largest number of crimes committed in any category for the DWI group is battery. The same analysis of arrests for the license group shows that burglary and theft are the most commonly committed crimes for the prior three arrests. This comparison becomes very important when the overall use of alcohol is considered in connection with aggressive or assaultive behavior.

Another interesting result of the data analysis is that 327 individuals (46.2%, n=723) in the criminal history group had been convicted of DWI in the 6 years prior to 1985. In the license sample 42 individuals (5.8%, n=723) had a prior DWI conviction. The data show that prior DWI convictions differ significantly between the two samples (X^2 = 304.74, 1 df, p < .005). This is a strong indicator of continuing alcohol use in the DWI group (Table 10.3).

Table 10.3
Sample Comparisons for the Last Three Arrests by Crime Type*

	DWI Sample	License Sample	Ratio
Robbery(%)	36 (82%)	8 (18%)	4.5:1
Burglary	127 (81%)	30 (19%)	4.2:1
Assault	66 (93%)	5 (7%)	13.2:1
Battery	292 (95%)	16 (5%)	19:1
Disorderly	75 (85%)	13 (15%)	5.6:1
Theft	127 (80%)	31 (20%)	4:1
Homicide	27 (100%)	0	
Other	134 (88%)	19 (12%)	7.3:1
Drug Offenses	67 (84%)	13 (16%)	5.1:1
Total	951	136	

*   A single individual may account for as many as 3 criminal arrests in this analysis, additionally, there are no time contraints placed on the data collection.

The last comparison to be examined is the total number of criminal arrests committed by the two groups in the last six years prior to 1985. The need for this analysis in addition to comparing the last three arrests comes as a result of the number of individuals in both samples that have several arrests in a short period of time. In looking at only the last three arrests, much information about the individuals and the number of crimes for which they were arrested may give an incorrect picture of the data. This analysis is done on two-year intervals and includes all the major categories, but does not include prior traffic offenses nor prior DWIs.

Table 10.4
Sample Comparisons of Total Number of Arrests for Last Six Years*

		DWI Sample	License Sample	Ratio	(p <)
Robbery	n	58	8	7.3:1	0.01
	mean	19.33	2.66		
	std.	1.47	1.08		
Burglary	n	156	30	5.2:1	0.05
	mean	52	10		
	std.	13.91	3.24		
Assault	n	132	8	15:1	0.025
	mean	44	2.66		
	std.	6.04	.041		
Battery	n	376	16	23.5:1	0.005
	mean	125.3	5.3		
	std.	6.79	1.08		
Disorderly	n	109	15	7.3:1	0.025
	mean	36.33	5.3		
	std.	4.71	0.71		
Theft	n	161	31	5.2:1	0.01
	mean	53.6	10.33		
	std.	2.16	5.31		
Homicide	n	23	0		
	mean	7.6			
	std.	1.63			
Other	n	197	19	10.1:1	0.005
	mean	65.66	6.3		
	std.	5.89	2.94		
Drug Offenses	n	95	13	7.3:1	0.005
	mean	31.66	4.3		
	std.	2.48	.41		
Total		1307	140	9.3:1	

*   The comparison is made on two-year segments over the six-year period.

During the six-year period there were 1,447 arrests recorded; of this number, the DWI sample accounted for 1,307 of the total arrests and the license sample accounted fro 140 of the total. The breakdown of the categories by crime type shows that for the six-year period the difference between the two samples in the number of non-violent crimes is smaller than the difference between the samples in the violent crimes category. The license sample had no arrests for homicide compared to 23 homicide arrests for the DWI sample. The arrest ratio for assault was 15:1 and for battery the ration was 23.5:1. When the non-violent crimes are compared we find that the ration of burglaries and thefts were both 5.25:1. The data show that the DWI sample differs significantly from the license sample for all crime categories (See Table 10.4).

Discussion

The data presented here describe individuals arrested for DWI in Louisiana and compares them to a sample of licensed Louisiana drivers. Although the data may not be representative of all people who drink and drive (i.e., those not arrested and those arrested but not licensed in Louisiana) or of all people who drive in Louisiana (i.e., those who drive but failed to obtain a license), most males arrested for DWI have prior experience with the criminal justice system and most licensed drivers do not have the same prior experience. Almost two-thirds (63.4%) of the DWI sample had at least one prior arrest as compared to 10.8 percent for the license sample. Argeriou et al. (1985) found that 51.2 percent (n=1406) of his sample had a prior arraignment for criminal activity. This research supports Argeriou et al. (1985) in the gross number of crimes committed by the persons charged with DWI, and goes one step further in its comparison with a control group.

Support is found for the argument of the need for a system of classifying DWI offenders into subgroups according to prior criminality, prior DWI offenses and prior types of crime committed. This is apparent when one makes a comparison of the ration of violent versus non-violent crimes between the two groups. Those DWI offenders who have been arrested for a prior crime are more likely to have committed a violent crime than a non-violent crime. During the six-year period the license sample shows arrests for 32 violent crimes (robbery, assault, battery and homicide) and 76 non-violent crimes (burglary, disorderly and theft). The trend for the DWI sample is the reverse, with more arrests for violent crimes (589) versus arrests for non-violent crimes (426).

SUMMARY

All the evidence presented here indicates that there is a connection between criminal behavior and the offense of driving while intoxicated. The review of the literature established a link between criminal activity and alcohol consumption. This very same alcohol consumption is the link between driving while intoxicated and criminal activity. As can be seen from the data analysis presented here, there is a strong connection between an arrest for DWI and a prior criminal history. This same connection does not exist in the regular licensed male population, and if those convicted of a DWI offense were removed from the licensed sample, the difference in prior criminal activity between the two groups becomes even larger. All indication are that the statement made by Joye, "DWI is the crime most commonly committed by a noncriminal" (Joye, 1983) is false. The present research suggests that an individual with a DWI arrest is more likely than an individual in the general licensed population to have had a prior arrest on another charge, and that the arrest is more likely to have come as a result of a violent crime against another person. This provides support for Argeriou's argument, for the necessity of subtyping of DWIs before an evaluation as to treatment or sentence is made by any public agency can be supported. To know the "whole picture" of an individual DWI offender, a system of subtyping is necessary before treatment or rehabilitation can be expected to have an effect. This is especially true of those individuals who have in addition to prior criminal activity, a prior DWI arrest or conviction.

REFERENCES

Akers, R.L. (1973). *Deviant Behavior: A Social Learning Approach*. Belmont, CA: Wadsworth.

Amir, M. (1967). "Alcohol and Forcible Rape." *British Journal of the Addictions*, 62, 219-232.

Argeriou, M., D. McCarty & E. Blacker (1985). "Criminality Among Individuals Arraigned for Drinking and Driving in Massachusetts." *Journal of Studies on Alcohol*, 46(6), 483-485.

Carpenter, J.S. & N.P. Armenti (1972). "Some Effects of Ethanol on Human Sexual and Aggressive Behavior." In B. Kissin & H. Begleiter (eds.) *The Biology of Alcoholism*, Vol. 2. New York: Plenum Press.

Chambliss, W. & R. Seidman (1971). *Law, Order, and Power*. Reading, MA: Addison-Wesley.

Collins, J. (1981). "Alcohol Careers and Criminal Careers." In J. Collins (ed.) *Drinking and Crime: Perspectives on the Relationships between Alcohol Consumption and Criminal Behavior*. New York: The Guilford Press.

Doernberg, D.L. & D.H. Zeigler (1980). "Due Process vs. Data Processing: An Analysis of Computerized Criminal History Information Systems." *New York University Law Review*, 55.

Donovan, D.M. & G.A. Marlatt (1982). "Personality Subtypes Among Driving-While-Intoxicated Offenders: Relationship to Drinking Behavior and Driver Risk." *Journal of Consulting and Clinical Psychology*, 50, 241-249.

Feldman, M.P. (1977). *Criminal Behavior: A Psychological Analysis*. London: Wiley.

Goodwin, D.W., B. Crane & S.B. Guze (1971). "Felons Who Drink: An 8-Year Followup." *Quarterly Journal of Studies on Alcohol*, 32, 136-147.

Guze, S.B., V.B. Tuason, P.D. Gatfield, M.A. Stewart & B. Picken (1962). "Psychiatric Illness and Crime with Particular Reference to Alcoholism: A Study of 223 Criminals." *Journal of Nervous and Mental Disease*, 134(6), 512.

Hirschi, T. (1984). "A Brief Commentary on Akers' 'Delinquent Behavior, Drugs, and Alcohol: What is the Relationship?'" *Today's Delinquent*, 3, 49-52.

Hirschi, T. (1969). *Causes of Delinquency*. Berkeley, CA: University of California Press.

Hirschi, T. & M. Gottfredson (1983). "The Distinction between Crime and Criminality." In T. Hartnagel & R. Silverman (eds.) *Critique and Explanation: Essays in Honor of Gwynn Nettler*. New Brunswick, NJ: Transaction.

Johnson, S.D., L. Gibson, & R. Linden (1978). "Alcohol and Rape in Winnipeg, 1966-1975." *Journal of Studies on Alcohol*, 39(11), 1877-1894.

Joye, R.I. (1986). "Drunk Driving: Recommendations for Safer Highways." In D. Foley (ed.) *Stop DWI: Successful Community Responses to Drunk Driving*. Lexington, MA: Lexington Books.

Lindelius, R. & I. Salum (1973). "Alcoholism and Criminality." *Acta Psychiatrica Scandinavica*, 49, 306-314.

Marcos, A.C., S.J. Bahr & R.E. Johnson (1986). "Test of a Bonding/Association Theory of Adolescent Drug Use." *Social Forces*, 65, 11.

Mayfield, D. (1976). "Alcoholism, Alcohol Intoxication and Assaultive Behavior." *Diseases of the Nervous System*, 37, 228-291.

Meyer, C.K., T. Magedanz, D.C. Kieselhorst & S.G. Chapman (1978). *A Social-Psychological Analysis of Police Assailants*. Norman, OK: Bureau of Government Research, University of Oklahoma.

Nathan, P.E. & S.A. Lisman (1976). "Behavior and Motivational Patterns." In R.E. Tarter & A.A. Sugarman (eds.) *Alcoholism: Interdisciplinary Approaches to an Enduring Problem*. Reading, MA: Addison-Wesley.

Nathan, P.E., N.A. Titler, L.H. Lowenstein, P. Solomon & A.M. Rossi (1970). "Behavioral Analysis of Chronic Alcoholism." *Archives of General Psychiatry*, 22, 419-430.

Nye, I. (1958). *Family Relationships and Delinquent Behavior*. New York: John Wiley.

Osgood, D.W., L.D. Johnston, P.M. O'Malley & J.G. Bachman (1988). "The Generality of Deviance." *American Sociological Review*, 53(1), 81-93.

Pernanen, K. (1979a). "Experiences of Violence and their Association with Alcohol Use in the General Population of the Community." Paper presented at the annual meeting of the American Society of Criminology, Philadelphia, 1979.

Pernanen, K. (1979b). *Alcohol and Aggressive Behaviour: A Community Study with a Cross-Cultural Perspective* (Addiction Research Foundation Substudy No. 1050). Toronto: The Foundation.

Peterson, M.A. & H. Braiker (1978). *Doing Crime: A Survey of California Prison Inmates* (draft with S.M. Polich). Santa Monica, CA: The RAND Corporation.

Pittman, D.J. & G.W. Gordon (1958). "Criminal Careers of the Chronic Police Case Inebriate." *Journal of Studies on Alcohol*, 19, 225-268.

Pollack, S. (1969). *The Drinking Driver and Traffic Safety Project*, Vols. 1 & 2. Springfield, VA: National Technical Information Service.

Rada, R.T. (1975). "Alcoholism and Forcible Rape." *American Journal of Psychiatry*, 132, 444-446.

Reiss, A.J. (1951). "Delinquency as the Failure of Personal and Social Controls." *American Sociological Review*, 16, 196-207.

Roizen, J. & D. Schneberk (1977a). "Alcohol in Crime." In M. Aarens, T. Cameron, J. Roizen, R. Room, D. Schneberk & D. Wingard (eds.) *Alcohol, Casualties and Crime*. Berkeley, CA: Social Research Group.

Roizen, J. & D. Schneberk (1977b). "Alcohol and Crime." Special report to the National Institute on Alcohol Abuse and Alcoholism, March, 1977.

Roslund, B. & C.A. Larson, (1979). "Crimes of Violence and Alcohol Abuse in Sweden." *International Journal of the Addictions*, 14(8), 1103-1115.

Steer, R.A., E.W. Fine, & P.E. Scoles (1979). "Classification of Men Arrested for Driving While Intoxicated and Treatment Implications: A Cluster-Analytic Study." *Journal of Studies on Alcohol*, 40, 222-229.

Sutker, P.B., P.J. Brantely & A.N. Allain (1980). "MMPI Response Patterns and Alcohol Consumption in DUI Offenders." *Journal of Consulting and Clinical Psychology*, 48, 350-355.

Sutherland, E.H. (1947). *Criminology*, 4th Ed. Philadelphia: Lippincott.

Voss, H.L. & J.R. Hepburn (1968). "Patterns in Criminal Homicide in Chicago." *Journal of Criminal Law, Criminology and Police Science*, 59(4), 499-508.

Waller, J.A. (1967). "Identification of Problem Drinking among Drunken Drivers." *Journal of the American Medical Association*, 200, 114-120.

Wolfgang, M.E. (1958). *Patterns in Criminal Homicide*. Philadelphia: University of Pennsylvania.

Wolfgang, M.E. & F. Ferracuti (1981). *The Subculture of Violence*. Beverly Hills, CA: Sage.

Yoder, R.D. & R.A. Moore (1973). "Characteristics of Convicted Drunk Drivers." *Quarterly Journal of Studies on Alcohol*, 34, 927-936.

Zelhart, P.F., B.C. Schurr & P.A. Brown (1975). "The Drinking Driver: Identification of High-Risk Alcoholics." In S. Israelstam & S. Lambert (eds.) *Alcohol, Drugs, and Traffic Safety*. Proceedings of the Sixth International Conference on Alcohol, Drugs, and Traffic Safety. Toronto, 8-13 September 1974. Toronto: Addiction Research Foundation, 1975, 181-198.

Section III

SPECIAL ISSUES

In addition to broad concerns regarding the relationships among drugs, crime, and the criminal justice system, the study of drugs and the criminal justice system also raises a number of special issues. These issues place new demands on the system or raise fundamental questions about our understanding of the problem. In the first chapter of this section, "The Accuracy of Self-Reported Drug Use: An Evaluation and Analysis of New Data," Thomas Mieczkowski addresses the fundamental problem of measuring the nature and extent of the drug problem. the use of self-report is one of the most widely used techniques for assessing drug prevalence, and yet the accuracy of such data is poorly understood. Mieczkowski compares self-reported drug use with the results of urine tests and concludes that self-reports are generally accurate. Beyond this general observation are some interesting, specific findings. In particular, the accuracy is relatively constant regardless of the extent of drug use, but does vary by the type of drug used. Cocaine users are more likely to deny use but test positive in a urine sample, while the opposite is true for marijuana users. In general, this study raises interesting questions regarding the use of self-report studies to assess drug use.

In the next chapter, James Inciardi traces the development of the AIDS problem in the United States and the implication of AIDS for criminal justice. While first associated with homosexuality, AIDS is more commonly being transmitted by IV drug users who share their equipment. As AIDS patients are increasingly drawn from the ranks of drug users, their impact on the criminal justice system also increases. Facing lawsuits from offenders with AIDS, offenders who do not wish to be exposed to AIDS, and criminal justice personnel who must handle both groups, police departments and prisons are finding it necessary to develop policies regarding AIDS. Aside from the personal problems involved, the handling of offenders with AIDS may become extremely expensive for the system if it is required to provide extensive medical treatment for those with AIDS-related illnesses. The criminal justice system may find itself the treatment center of last resort.

In the war on drugs, drug testing of employees and offenders is a weapon likely to have an impact on the average citizen. The question of drug testing raises a host of moral, political, and legal questions. While all citizens should be concerned about the role of drug testing in society, the issue has already been raised in the criminal justice setting, and court rulings in that setting are likely to establish the ground rules for testing in general. The chapter by Sorensen and del Carmen focuses on "Legal Issues in Drug Testing Offenders and Criminal Justice Employees." The authors discuss the types of tests which are currently available and the shortcomings of each. They then turn to the issue of testing offenders, noting that the legal restrictions on drug testing are greater for pre-trial arrestees than for convicted offenders. The authors note the constitutional issues raised in testing criminal justice employees and recommend policies for criminal justice agencies. It is clear that the problems raised by drug testing are not simply technical questions of accuracy, but include more fundamental questions about the relationship between a government and its citizens.

The problem of treatment for drug offenders is a particularly difficult one for the criminal justice system. Resources for treatment are in short supply and there is the question of the role of punitive institutions, such as jails and prisons, in providing therapeutic treatment. An alternative which minimizes these conflicting roles is the use of institutionally-allowed inmate self-help groups. In the final chapter, Mark Hamm describes one such group in the Baltimore City Jail. His account not only provides insights into how such treatment groups might facilitate recovery, but also reminds the reader of the problems involved in providing treatment in an essentially coercive environment. In such a setting, self-help groups also provide inmates with a power base which has interesting implications for the therapeutic environment. There is a constant struggle between the best interests of the group and the best interests of individual leaders who stand to benefit from the group. A study of this type of program is particularly important because it is likely that such self-help groups will flourish in the current political and economic environment in which jails and prisons operate.

11

The Accuracy of
Self-Reported Drug Use:
An Evaluation and Analysis of New Data[*]

Thomas Mieczkowski
University of South Florida

INTRODUCTION

Criminologists have vigorously discussed self-report methods and have come to a general consensus that they are valuable (O'Brien, 1985; Hardt & Peterson-Hardt, 1977). How they are obtained, and what meaning may be attached to them, however, is often controversial. Ever since Sir William Osler characterized opiate addicts as "inveterate liars" whose recitations were "totally unreliable," drug use self-reports have been especially suspect. Evaluating the accuracy of this type of data continues to be of interest. Self-report data on drug use has become particularly timely as Americans have become more concerned about illicit drug consumption, its dimensions and consequences. The ability to check self-report data against a highly accurate laboratory test is an appealing technique for validating data gathered by inter-

---

[*] I wish to acknowledge the assistance of the National Institute of Justice and its Director, James K. Stewart, for the grant funding which made this research possible. I would also like to acknowledge the help of John Spevacek, Office of Criminal Justice Research, for his help and assistance. This report reflects the point of view of the author and does not necessarily represent the position or views of the National Institute of Justice.

viewing drug users and dealers. Few would argue that these self-reports on drug-related and criminal activity should be accepted uncritically. But in what way should they be evaluated? This chapter will review the literature that has been developed in exploring this question. It will also present some new data for analysis. The new data is self-reported drug use by arrestees in Detroit, Michigan. I believe this chapter extends the scope of current evaluations of drug use self-reports. The present work compares responses to urinalysis results for both drug *type* and use *level*.

The ability to test the urine for the presence of drugs, while asking in an interview about recent drug use, is a powerful validation technique uniquely available to this type of research. In this context *validity* is a simple measure of the agreement or concordance between the respondent's reports and the urinalysis result. If the two agree, the response is valid. The percent of cases where self-report and laboratory results agree is the index of concordance. Such percentage distributions can be tested for significance and for correlational strength.

Historically, interest has been restricted to identifying drug users who deny their use. Although drug users who admit use and then test negative are also non-concordant, they have been of little interest. Such persons are generally assumed to be "clean" drug users. This consideration reflects the reality that there is a readily understandable motive for denial of actual drug use. For example, of the 24 studies reviewed in this article, 15 derived samples from populations which would be penalized if their drug use status was affirmed to authorities (they were either in treatment or on probation or parole). Most of the time, in the research settings considered here, there is no comparable equivalent motive to report non-existent drug use. In any event, findings appear to be the same if the sample is derived from a treatment or corrections population. Findings even appear to be unaffected when the respondent is *not* guaranteed anonymity (Leutgert & Armstrong, 1973).

While the practical logic of this comparative analytic approach is self-evident, the existing terminology is confused. Authors have used many different terms to describe concordance. "Validity" or "external criterion validity" have been the most popular terms. Some have used "reliability" as the appropriate referent. Some have argued that it can be either or both. Still others have created new terms such as "veridicality" (Bonito, Nurco & Shaffer, 1976). The limits of this measure are *perfect validity* (the report and urine result always agree) or *perfect invalidity* (the response never agrees with the urine test result). Generally, researchers have expressed the degree of validity as a percentage, the number of concordant responses divided by the total number of responses (11 of the 24 studies reviewed here, for example). Up until the 1980s no study ever reported less than 70 percent validity, and many reported validation percentages into the 90s. They unanimously reported concordance as "good" or "very good". It was not until Wish (1986) published his material that these findings were challenged. Of all the studies reviewed here, through 1988, 16 support validity as "good" while 7 are skeptical or in opposition to that conclusion. Virtually all the skeptical or contradictory re- . ports have appeared since 1986. Recent evaluations of drug use self-reporting have primarily reported percentage measures (concordant responses divided by all responses). Over the years there has not been great change in this approach. A recent study (Magura et al., 1988) has used a nominal concordance measure, Cohen's Kappa, which Magura argues to be superior to Chi-square and related measures (e.g., Phi). However, the conclusions they reached support what most studies have reported, that validity is quite good.

A 2x2 table which contains the response values (in rows) and urinalysis values (in columns) is an excellent way to display such data. The crosstab (urine results vs. report) can be evaluated by a significance test such as Chi-square. Some studies have estimated association by correlational measures (e.g., r, C, gamma). Such measures have suggested moderate strengths of association (Ben-Yehuda, 1980). Non-parametric techniques have been used and appropriately so. Population parameters for drug users are unknown and conceptually difficult to specify (Zinberg, 1984). Some researchers have used parametric tests assuming the sample and the population parameters equal (Bale, 1979: Bonito, Nurco & Shaffer, 1976; Maddux & Desmond, 1975; Page et al., 1977). Of the 24 studies listed in this bibliography, 19 relied on urinalysis or another external validator (e.g., second opinion, official record, earlier self-report, etc.). Percentage agreement was used in 11 cases as the reported index. In 5 of these cases Chi-square was used to test for significance, which was affirmed in every case. Three used Pearson's r, and for the balance a smattering of other parametric and non-parametric evaluations were used.

Review of the Literature

Table 11.1 is a summary presentation of validation research in this area ranging over the last 20 years. It reviews the validation technique, the size and nature of the population from which the sample was drawn, the inquiry procedure, the findings, and their associated quantitative measures. *External validation*, *urinalysis*, and *sampling populations in treatment programs* are the three most typical features of these studies. Most studies confirm the validity of self-reported drug use. More than two studies affirm the truthfulness of self-reports for every one which questions or denies it. Fifteen studies used urinalysis while nine used other validity criteria.

Table 11.1
Studies Evaluating the Validity of Responses to Drug Use

Author	Date	Validation Criteria	Number (N)	Sample	Method	General Conclusion	% of Validity	Statistical Measure
Clark & Tifft	1966	polygraph	45	students	Anonymous Questionnaires	high validity	92.5	percent agreement
Ball	1967	urine hospital records arrest records	59	former Rx patients	interview comparisons	good validity	70-90	percent agreement
Parry, Mitchell, Balter & Cisin	1970	prescription records	735	citizen volunteers	interview comparisons	good validity	74	t test
Stephens	1972	external evaluation	236	Rx patients	interview questionnaire	good validity	90-95	percent agreement
Whitehead & Smart	1972	not applicable	n/a	students	Test-Retest Dummy Question	good validity	n/a	n/a
Laugert & Armstrong	1973	internal questionnaire	514	students	questionnaire interview	not tested	validity not dependent on anonymity	Chi square
Petzel, Johnson & McKillip	1973	internal questionnaire	628	students	survey questionnaire	validity adequate	approx. 4 (+) on bogus question	Z scores
Cox & Longwell	1974	urinalysis	110	Methadone Rx patients	interviews	high validity	86	Chi square
Maddux & Desmond	1975	independent official records	248	Rx patients	interviews	validity good	71	r
Bonito, Nurco & Shaffer	1976	independent official records	349	known substance abusers	interviews	validity good	80-90	r
Amsel, Mandell, Matthias, Mason & Hocharman	1976	intraquestions test-retest urinalysis	1,500	Rx patients	interviews	validity good	74	percent agreement
Page, Davies, Ladner, Alfassa & Tennis	1977	urinalysis	896	arrestees	interviews	validity good	90+	Chi square multivariate analysis
Bale	1979	urinalysis	55	Rx patients	mailed questionnaire	validity good	76	r

Table 11.1
Studies Evaluating the Validity of Responses to Drug Use *(continued)*

Author	Date	Validation Criteria	Number (N)	Sample	Method	General Conclusion	% of Validity	Statistical Measure
Ben-Yehuda	1980	urinalysis	47	Methadone Rx patients	questionnaire	validity good	65	Chi square C gamma
Bachman & O'Malley	1981	internal analysis & comparison	16,654	students	survey questionnaire	validity questioned	generally low	Mean Ratio Expectancy
Bale, Van Stone, Engelsing, Zarcone & Kuldau	1981	urinalysis	272	ex-patients	interview	validity good	78	Chi square
Wish, Johnson, Strug Anderson & Miller	1983	urinalysis	631	"street criminals"	interview	validity good	80	percent agreement
Wish, Johnson, Strug, Chedekel & Lipton	1983	urinalysis	32	"street criminals"	interview	validity good	70-80	percent agreement
Wish	1986	urinalysis	4,847	PCP arrestees	interview	generally not valid	less than one-third valid	percent agreement
Carver	1986	urinalysis	6,738	arrestees	interview	generally not valid	48	percent agreement
Wish, Cuadrado & Martorana	1986	urinalysis	106	probationers	interview	not valid	underreported "grossly"	percent agreement
Wish, Brady & Cuadrado	1986	urinalysis	6,633	arrestees	interview	generally not valid	less than 56	percent agreement
Wish	1987	urinalysis	701	arrestees	interview	generally not valid	below 46 for cocaine	percent agreement
Magura, Goldsmith, Casriel, Goldstein & Spunt	1988	urinalysis	248	Methadone Rx patients	interview	"relatively inaccurate"	75	Kappa

Before the 1980s, urine-based investigations were infrequent. A very early example is Ball's 1967 work in Puerto Rico which could be called the "seminal piece" in this area. Using urinalysis and official records from both hospital and health authorities, Ball found that from 70 to 90 percent of a sample of 59 opiate users responded accurately to questions on drug use. He also argued that a substantial portion of the non-concordance was the result of mistakes, rather than intentional prevarication or evasion (Ball, 1967). Most of Ball's contemporaries were using non-urine based techniques, but came to similar conclusions. Clark and Tifft (1966) used polygraph results to validate questions on criminality, including drug involvement. They concluded that response validity exceeded 90 percent. Their work, however, elicited a scathing attack from Lois DeFleur (1967) on their use of the concept of validity. Defleur felt the method measured reliability, not validity. Three years after Ball, Parry, Balter, and Cisin (1970) questioned volunteer residents of a moderate-sized midwestern city about legal psychotropic drug use and validated the responses against prescription lists. This study was distinct in that it used a control group. The "control" was another group who were questioned on their use of non-psychotropic prescribed drugs. They rated validity as generally "good", showing an overall concordance rate of 74 percent. The percentage validity of the psychotropic experimental group was higher than the non-psychotropic control group. In a similar study Stephens (1972) used concordance measures between external evaluation by counselors compared to responses in interviews with patients at a drug treatment center. He concluded that 90 to 95 percent levels of validity characterized his sample.

Whitehead and Smart (1972), evaluating Canadian work in this area, concluded that both external and internal criteria studies in Canada established that validity of the drug self-report was "good." In the early 1970s, measuring validity by looking at internal consistency of response was also done. Leutgert and Armstrong (1973) and Petzel, Johnson, and McKillip (1973) evaluated the internal consistency of responses in order to estimate validity of student answers to questions on drug use. Leutgert and Armstrong found that validity was good, and interestingly that it did *not* differ among groups interviewed under anonymous and non-anonymous situations. Petzel et al. (1973) used a "fictional item" technique. They included a non-existent drug in their questionnaire. Roughly 4 percent of the respondents answered positively to questions regarding use of this fictional substance. They interpreted this figure as suggesting low levels of intentional misreporting.

A good example of a non-urine based validation was done two years later by Maddux and Desmond (1975) who used official records as criteria. They interviewed 248 drug treatment patients, and correlated selected responses to independent official police and health records. They rated validity at 71 percent for their sample. A year later, Bonito et al. (1976) interviewed 349 "known substance abusers" identified through police records, and compared their drug use responses to hospital and police data. They found "high validity" generally, rating overall performance of the sample as 80 to 90 percent valid. Only one non-urine based evaluation has challenged the prevalent findings, that drug self-reports have "good" levels of validity. Bachman and O'Malley (1981) analyzed data on drug use compiled for 16,654 high school seniors. Using an innovative approach, they tested responses for internal consistency by generating "expected" rates of use and compared the consistency of expectation rates within different time frames. Based on this analysis, they argued for skepticism about self-report use, arguing that their data showed both questionable validity and suggested underreporting of drug use. Because of the technique they were not able to attached a concordance value to the validity rate.

After Ball, Cox and Longwell (1974) reported the use of urinalysis as a validation technique. They asked methadone patients about their drug use and compared these responses to urinalysis results. They rated validity on questions of drug use as "high" (86%). Shortly after this Amsel, Mandell, Matthias, Mason, and Hocharman (1976) carried out a large-scale study to estimate validity of responses to drug use. Employing a sample of 1,500 they used five independent criteria, including urinalysis, to measure both internal and external validity of responses. Their sample was drawn from a treatment program population. Consistent with earlier work, they found validity to be generally high, rating the accuracy of response overall at around 74 percent.

The first study to use urinalysis, but not rely on treatment populations for a sample, was the work of Page, Davies, Ladner, Alfassa, and Tennis (1977). They interviewed arrestees within a jail shortly after their incarceration and also solicited a voluntary, anonymous urine sample from the participants. They had a substantial N of 896 cases, and rated the validity of response to the drug questions at "greater than 90 percent." Bale (1979) tested drug treatment patients by urinalysis and found that their response validity was "good." He rated it overall at 76 percent. This was true even though the questionnaire had been mailed to the respondents and a "surprise" follow-up including urinalysis was done to validate the questionnaire. They compared the written mailer responses with interview responses and urine results. Bale's study was particularly interesting because it reflected testing done under more candid conditions than earlier work. Ben-Yehuda (1980) randomly selected 47 patients from a methadone treatment program and interviewed them on their drug use, comparing their responses to urine tests for those substances. He rated the overall validity at around 65 percent, a relatively low figure compared with earlier studies. Bale, Van Stone,

Engelsing, Zarcone, and Kuldau (1981) interviewed 271 ex-patients of a drug treatment program and reported a concordance of 78 percent between question responses on drug use and urinalysis results.

Wish, Johnson, Strug, Anderson, and Miller (1983) were the first to urine test "street criminals" by directly interviewing them outside the context of criminal justice or treatment agencies. Interviewing and obtaining urine specimens from 631 "street people," they reported concordance at 80 percent. Wish, Johnson, Strug, Chedekel, and Lipton (1983a) interviewed a sample of 32 volunteer street criminals and used a new (at the time) and more sensitive urine screening technology (enzyme multiplied immune testing or EMIT). They reported validity rates for cocaine use to be consistent with earlier studies, between 70 to 80 percent. Also notable in this work was a caution regarding the reliability of earlier testing technology, which they called into serious question. Specifically, EMIT to TLC (thin-layer chromatography) comparisons suggested that TLC dependent studies were likely to report significant false negatives, resulting in substantial hidden underreporting. EMIT, administered under ideal conditions, will be 98 percent accurate. The 2 percent error is biased towards false negatives (Marshall, 1988; Field, 1987; Wish et al., 1983a). Generally, unless rather exceptional conditions are prevalent, cocaine and heroin can be identified with reliability up to 48 hours after use. Marijuana can be readily identified up to one week after use in sporadic users, and up to fours weeks after the last use of chronic, heavy users (Schwartz & Hawks, 1985).

In 1986, Wish et al. published a series of reports which challenged the level of validity reported in earlier concordance studies. Wish (1986) reported the self-reports of PCP users compared to urine results screened by EMIT showed substantial underreporting. Using a large N (4,847) of arrestees, Wish demonstrated that more than two-thirds of the sample had not accurately answered questions on PCP use. Furthermore, Wish's work suggested that earlier studies and their consequent validity rates (which were largely concerned with heroin use) might need to be revised when considering other substances.

Data compiled during the mid-1980s seemed to confirm this view. With rising cocaine use, and relative diminution of heroin use, validity measured by concordance rates were not sustaining the high numbers of the 1960s and 1970s. Carver (1986) reported that in pretrial drug screening of arrestees in Washington D.C., 52 percent of the self-reports on cocaine use were not concordant. Wish, Cuadrado, and Martorana (1986) found that, in a sample of 106 probationers, self-reported drug use was "grossly underreported." Depending on the substance in question, underreporting appeared to entail a range of use 2 to 10 times higher than report. Likewise, Wish, Brady, and Cuadrado (1986), reporting on 6,633 arrestees in New York, found that nearly one half (44%) were not concordant on drug use or their urinalysis results. Wish (1987), in examining cocaine use in New York, found that the concordance between response and urine result was less than 46 percent.

This recent series of reports is significant in raising questions regarding the "well-established" validity of drug use self-reports (Toborg & Kirby, 1984). There are two reasons which may explain why this recent work fails to sustain the older literature.

(1) New technology in chemical screening shifts the validity figures into the low range. It detects drug-positive urine specimens that would be reported as drug-negative with the older technology (thin-layer chromatography).

(2) Traditionally, heroin users have dominated the validation studies. With the diminution of heroin and the rise of cocaine, the level of validity may vary. Concordance indices may be sensitive to the type of substance reported, so that specification of drug type is critical. As the prevalence of drug types shift, validity figures will fluctuate.

This chapter will use self-reports and EMIT-analyzed urine specimens from 454 voluntary participant/arrestees to examine the following:

(a) What percent concordance index does this sample show when comparing self-reports on 3 illegal drugs (heroin, cocaine, marijuana) to EMIT-based urinalysis?

(b) Do these concordance levels have statistical significance?

(c) Do significant relationships in (b) have strong, weak, or moderate correlational measures?

(d) How do these relationships vary or rank by drug type and level of use?

The Methodology

This data is derived from a continuing research effort, the Drug Use Forecast (DUF), sponsored by the National Institute of Justice. In brief, four times annually a research team conducts interviews with recent arrestees within the Detroit Police Department central pre-arraignment detention facility. The interviews cover a broad range of topics, including both criminal and non-criminal behavior and an intensive drug use history. Each inter-viewee is asked to provide a urine sample for drug analysis. The data from the interview is correlated with the urinalysis result. An independent laboratory conducts the urinalysis using EMIT technology. The procedure is anony-

mous and confidential. The interviewees are volunteers who are not com-
pensated for their participation. Cooperation is very good, with more than 95
percent of all arrestees agreeing to the interview procedure, and more than
90 percent providing urine specimens. The information in this chapter is
based on 454 interviews, 364 males and 90 females. Using EMIT technology
we only expect about 10 cases to have urine specimens incorrectly reported as
false negatives. The interviewer asks, in sequence, if the respondent has ever
tried a substance, used a substance in the last 30 days, or used a substance
within the last 24 to 48 hours. In this chapter, the reply to the 24- to 48-hour
time span is used as the self-report. This is because for two of the three substances (cocaine and opiates) EMIT loses reliability with urines obtained
more than 48 hours after taking the substance. Their reported drug use over
the last 48 hours will be compared to the EMIT urine screen results on those
same substances. The test sensitivity, 300 nanograms/liter for cocaine and
heroin and 100 nanograms/liter for marijuana, reflect widely accepted standards currently used in drug screening (Marshall, 1988).

For any category of drug, the concordance between the self-reported use
and the results of a urinalysis for that substance can be expressed as a 2x2
table. Six 2x2 tables are presented in Tables 11.3 through 11.8. There is a
zero-order and first-order table for each category of drug (heroin, cocaine,
marijuana). The horizontal axis represents a "+" (yes) or "-" (no) response
on use of the substance within the last 48 hours. The vertical axis is the
EMIT urine result for that substance, either "(+)" or "(-)." Two tables are
reported for each substance, a zero-order table and a first-order table. The
first-order table reports only those respondents who had *one or more* urine-
positives *besides* the substance on which they were reporting. For each table
a Chi-square value, a phi coefficient, and a gamma value is reported.

In interpreting the cell meanings of these 2x2 tables, the following
conditions are used, as shown in Table 11.2.

Table 11.2
Interpretation of Concordance Conditions

Respondent	Denies Use	Admits Use
Lab (-) Urinalysis	1. Concordant Abstainer	2. Non-Concordant (-) User
Lab (+)	3. Non-Concordant (+) User	4. Concordant User

The 2x2 tables are interpreted as follows. Those subjects who are "double negatives" (Cell 1) are concordant abstainers. Interpretation of the concordance in this category is unambiguous. Likewise, for Cell 4, who are concordant users. In each case the laboratory results confirm their self-reported status. Cell 2, an admitted user who is urine-negative is problematic is the sense of departing from the direct concordance of cells 1 and 4. However, the assumption used here is to interpret such a combination as valid. This assumption is based on the argument that, first, such a status is quite conceivable. The user may be currently "clean," therefore their urine is negative. Second, drug use is generally stigmatized, overtly illegal, and since the data are gathered in a jail, it seems very unlikely that compelling or convincing motives to misreport deliberately (claiming to be a drug user when one is not) would be typically attractive to the respondents. Cell 3, is also non-concordant, as is Cell 2. But here there is no ambiguity. A denial of drug use with a corresponding urine-positive can only be interpreted as either a misreport or as a false-positive of the EMIT screen. EMIT screening, as noted, is quite accurate. It errs "conservatively;" if it does misreport it is likely to report a urine-positive as urine-negative. Thus it is reasonable to assume that the positives usually indicate the presence of the tested-for substance rather than a false reagent reaction. The values of the diagonal summed data (Cell 2 + Cell 3) will be used as the number of non-concordant responses. The data will show that the values in Cell 2 generally are small.

The Data

The results are described for three substances: heroin, cocaine, and marijuana. There is a pair of 2x2 tables presented for each of these three substances (hence, six data tables). The first table in each case will be the comparison of urine results with the self-reports on that substance within 48 hours of the interview. The second table will be the same variable comparison (oral report vs. urine result). However, this table will contain only those in the sample who are positive *on at least one other tested substance* besides the substance on which they are asked to report. Thus, in Cell 3 (cases of urine-positive denials) each person would be positive for at least two drugs. When we consider marijuana, this procedure will be slightly modified. Marijuana has a very long appearance time in the urine when it can be detected by EMIT (varying from 14 to 45 days). Therefore the marijuana tables are a self-report on use in the *last 30 days*, rather than the last 48 hours.

The tables will examine, then, not only concordance rates by discrete substance, but will also compare those whose use is more "intense." "Intense" users here means users who consume two or more substances simultaneously. "Intense" is also meant relative to the general sample population. The objective is to determine:

(1) the levels of concordance compared to "expected" values within the tables ("expected" meaning a marginal-dependent occurrence rate based on the Chi-square procedure),

(2) if the indices of concordance (expressed as a percentage of all responses) change from substance to substance, and

(3) if the indices of concordance change for those who use two or more substances simultaneously.

Table 11.3
Heroin Use, Total Sample

```
                      OP        Urine positive for opiates
                  By HER24HR    Used heroin in last 24-48 hrs

HER24HRD>   Count  ¦                 ¦
            Exp val¦  Deny  ¦ Admit  ¦ Row
OP          -------¦----------------¦ Total
               1   ¦   383  ¦    4   ¦   387
    NEG            ¦ (359.7)¦ (27.3) ¦  85.2%
          URINE    ¦--------¦--------¦
               2   ¦    39  ¦   28   ¦    67
    POS            ¦ (62.3) ¦ (4.7)  ¦  14.8%
                   \----------------/
            Column      422      32      454
            Total      93.0%    7.0%   100.0%


Chi-Square    D.F.  Significance      Min E.F.     Cells with E.F.< 5
----------    ----  ------------      --------     ------------------
138.65411      1      .0000             4.722      1 of    4 ( 25.0%)
144.80823      1      .0000      ( Before Yates Correction )

Statistic     Value
---------     -----
Phi          .56477
Gamma        .97132
```

Heroin

Tables 11.3 and 11.4 contain the self-reports and urine results for heroin users. Table 11.3, Cells 2 and 3 (the upper right and lower left), contain the non-concordant responses. Of all responses in Table 11.3, 9.47 percent were in contradiction to the verbal report. Less than 10 percent of the non-concordant responses were in Cell 2, the category we earlier identified as "clean users." The EMIT-confirmed non-concordant Cell 3 (denies use but has a positive urine) represents 39 of the 43 non-concordant responses. Thus, of the non-concordant responses, more than 90 percent consisted of respondents who denied using the substance which was identified in their urine. Table 11.3, which represents the entire sample of 454, shows that of 422 respondents who denied heroin use, about 9.2 percent tested heroin-positive. The lower figures (in parentheses in each cell) are the Chi-square expected values. For Cell 3 this figure is 62.3 percent. The actual count in Cell 3 achieves only about 62.6 percent of this value. Because the actual data count is lower than the expected value, the interpretation here is to characterize the data as "shifted towards concordance." That is to say, the responses are more concordant than they ought to be if random chance alone were involved. Furthermore, Chi-square shows a statistical significance to four places (.0000). The two measures of the correlational strength, phi (.56) and gamma (.97), show a moderate to strong relationship between the variables.

Table 11.4 shows the same variables, reported heroin use versus EMIT urine screen. This table, however, includes only respondents who tested positively for another drug as well. Thus, those who tested positively for heroin were also positive for either marijuana, cocaine, barbiturates, Valium, Darvon, methaqualone, amphetamine, phencylidene, or methadone. Those respondents negative for heroin were positive for one or more of these other drugs. We regard this second set of respondents as "more intensive," representing a higher level of substance use.

There are 133 respondents out of the 454 who appear in Table 11.4. We note that 12 have non-concordant responses (only 1 in Cell 2, and 11 in Cell 3). Thus 9.0 percent of the 133 are non-concordant, a percentage value almost equal to the value in Table 11.3. Within this group, 120 denied any heroin use in the previous 48 hours, and 11 tested positive, a value of 9.1 percent, also virtually the same as in Table 11.3. This table also shows a "shift towards concordance," with the actual values in Cell 3 achieving 52.8 percent of the expected value. Correlational strength measures, indicated by phi and gamma, show a slight increase. Phi increases from .56 to .65 and gamma from .97 to .98. In Table 11.3, 12.5 percent who admitted use tested negatively, while in Table 11.4, 8.3 percent did so.

Table 11.4
Heroin Use, One or More Additional Drugs

```
                        OP          Urine positive for opiates
                    By HER24HR      Used heroin in last 24-48 hrs

HER24HRD>    Count    ¦                    ¦ Row
             Exp Val  ¦  Deny  ¦  Admit   ¦Total
OP           -------- ¦------------------- ¦
                  1   ¦  109   ¦    1      ¦  110
    NEG           ¦  (99.2) ¦  (10.8) ¦  82.7%
                       ¦------------------- ¦
          URINE   2   ¦   11   ¦   12      ¦   23
    POS           ¦  (20.8) ¦  (2.2)  ¦  17.3%
                      \-------------------/
                  Column   120      13      133
                  Total   90.2%    9.8%   100.0%


Chi-Square    D.F.  Significance        Min E.F.      Cells with E.F.< 5
----------    ----  ------------        --------      -------------------
  51.02344      1     .0000              2.248        1 of    4 ( 25.0%)
  56.68739      1     .0000          ( Before Yates Correction )

Statistic     Value
---------     -----
Phi           .65286
Gamma         .98332
```

Generally, for heroin use, there is a higher than expected level of concordance, and very little to indicate that the second group "specified" by additional drug use is less concordant than the general sample. It also supports this interpretation of cell meanings, since few respondents appear to admit drug use which is not confirmed by urinalysis.

Cocaine

The same analytical approach is employed for cocaine. Several changes need to be highlighted, however, before examining the cocaine data. The DUF questionnaire asks about cocaine use in a variety of different ways. In Detroit the DUF team has uncovered several methods of consuming cocaine (see Mieczkowski, 1988). This report specifically asks about snorting, freebasing, smoking, and using crack cocaine. For the purposes of this analysis, all the various cocaine use methods have been collapsed into one variable, so that responses to cocaine use include all varieties of consumption techniques. This is appropriate because EMIT urine tests cannot distinguish between a particular method of use.

Table 11.5 reflects the concordance between urine test results and self-reported cocaine use for the 454 cases constituting the whole sample. There are 154 non-concordant responses (5 in Cell 2 and 149 in Cell 3) comprising 33.9 percent of the sample. This figure is between three and four times as high as the comparable figure for heroin. Almost 97 percent of the cases are in Cell 3, a pattern very much like the pattern found for heroin. Of the 354 respondents who denied cocaine use, 149 tested cocaine positive. This represents 42 percent of the negative self-reports. The comparable figure for heroin use is 9.2 percent. Thus the rate of denial coupled with positive urine exceeds the heroin rate by between 4 and 5 times. The comparability of actual values to expected values (measured as a percentage) narrows more for cocaine than heroin (cocaine-75.1%, heroin-62.6%). But even though this difference is distinctly smaller for cocaine, it (like heroin) shows a "shift towards concordance." The data distribution of actual-to-expected cell frequencies cannot be attributed to random chance. Chi-square values for Table 11.5 are significant to four places (.0000). Relational strength as measured by phi and gamma shows moderate to strong correlation (phi=.44, gamma=.93).

Table 11.6 shows the cocaine use and self-report relationship when restricted to those who test positive for at least one other substance. Of the 98 cases which meet this criteria, 35 are non-concordant (2 in Cell 2, 33 in Cell 3). Thus 94.3 percent of the cases of non-concordance are denial of cocaine use with an associated positive urine. This finding is consistent with the heroin data. Table 11.6 has a non-concordance index of 35.7 percent, slightly higher than Table 11.5 at 33.9 percent. Of the 70 respondents who denied cocaine use, 33 tested positive (47.1%), around 5 percent higher than Table 11.5. The actual values in Cell 3 of Table 11.6 attain 78.4 percent of the expected values, quite comparable to the values in Table 11.5. These are also (like Table 11.5) "shifted towards concordance." The Chi-square value for

Table 11.6 shows the distribution is significant (.0001) and has a phi value of .42 and gamma of .87, both slightly weaker than the values in Table 11.5.

Like the heroin data, the sample self-reports for cocaine are more accurate than chance expectation. The level of inaccurate denials is, however, considerably higher than that for heroin. This finding supports an interpretation of less credibility attached to cocaine use self-reports than heroin use self-reports. The number of cases falling into Cell 2 is small. Thus, this data also appears to support the supposition that few cocaine users appear to falsely report consumption. Decidedly more prevalent is the consumer who denies use.

Table 11.5
Cocaine Use, Total Sample

```
                         COC      Urine positive for cocaine
                    By CAINE24    Cocaine Use in the Last 48 Hours

CAINE24D>  Count  ¦                    ¦ Row
                  ¦ Deny  ¦ Admit      ¦ Total
COC        -------¦--------------------¦
                1 ¦  205  ¦      5      ¦  210
   NEG            ¦(163.7)¦(46.3)       ¦  46.3
                  ¦--------------------¦
        URINE   2 ¦  149  ¦     95      ¦  244
   POS            ¦(190.3)¦ (43.7)      ¦  53.7
                  \--------------------/
            Column    354        100       454
            Total    78.0       22.0     100.0


Chi-Square    D.F.  Significance    Min E.F.     Cells with E.F.< 5
----------    ----  ------------    --------     ------------------
 85.68953       1     .0000          46.256            None
 87.80496       1     .0000        ( Before Yates Correction )

Statistic          Value
---------          -----
Phi                .43978
Gamma              .92631
```

Table 11.6
Cocaine Use, One or More Additional Drugs

```
                        COC        Urine positive for cocaine
                   By CAINE24      Cocaine Use in the Last 48 Hours

CAINE24D>    Count  |                    |  Row
             Exp Val |  Deny  |  Admit  |  Total
COC          -------- -------------------
                 1  |   37   |    2    |   39
     NEG         |  (27.9) | (11.1)  |  39.8
                 |--------------------
          URINE  2  |   33   |   26    |   59
     POS         |  (42.1) | (16.9)  |  60.2
                 \--------------------/
              Column     70        28      98
              Total     71.4      28.6   100.0


   Chi-Square   D.F.  Significance      Min E.F.     Cells with E.F.< 5
   ----------   ----  ------------      --------     ------------------
   15.58907      1      .0001           11.143             None
   17.44494      1      .0000        ( Before Yates Correction )

   Statistic           Value
   ---------           -----
   Phi                .42191
   Gamma              .87160
```

Marijuana

The evaluation of marijuana requires a modification to one aspect of the comparison. In order to make the evaluation reflect the physiological realities of EMIT testing, the time frame must be adjusted. Both cocaine and heroin, under the conditions of the EMIT screen employed here, will be undetectable in the urine after about 48 hours. Marijuana, because of its affinity for lipids, is excreted rather slowly from the body and can appear in the urine for rather extended time periods. The exact time frame depends on several factors such as potency of the marijuana, amount ingested, if the user is a chronic consumer, and the like. A narrow prior time range (e.g., restricted to 48 hours) would artificially inflate the number of urine-positive denials. Thus the time frame used in these crosstabulations is 30 days.

Table 11.7
Marijuana Use, Total Sample

```
                        MJ          Urine positive for marjuana
                    By MJ30         MJ. IN LAST 30 DAYS

    MJ30D>    Count  !              ! Row
              Exp Val !  Deny ! Admit ! Total
MJ          --------!------------------!
               1  !   240  !   66   !   306
    NEG           !(182.0) !(124.0) ! 67.4%
                  !------------------!
         URINE  2  !    30  !  118   !   148
    POS           !  (88.0) !  (60.0) ! 32.6%
                  \------------------/
              Column    270     184      454
              Total    59.5%   40.5%   100.0%
```

```
Chi-Square   D.F.  Significance     Min E.F.      Cells with E.F.< 5
----------   ---   ------------     --------      ------------------
137.59564     1     .0000           59.982           None
139.99827     1     .0000         ( Before Yates Correction )

Statistic              Value
---------              -----
Phi                    .55531
Gamma                  .86931
```

The data Tables 11.7 and 11.8, which show the results on marijuana, are interesting. Of the 454 responses 96 (21.1%) are non-concordant. This figure is, in itself, reasonable. It falls about halfway between the value for heroin (9%) and cocaine (42%). But the cell distribution of these non-concordant responses represents a definite departure from the response pattern for either heroin or cocaine. For both cocaine and heroin, the percentage of responses in Cell 2 (the urine-negative and response positive) are a very small proportion of the non-concordant answers, while for marijuana this same cell represents a large majority of the replies. Of the 96 non-concordant responses on marijuana use, 66, or 68.7 percent, of them fall into this category. Thirty responses (31.3%) are contained in Cell 3 (the urine-positive denial). This represents a literal reversal of the findings for the other two substances. Of the 270 respondents who denied marijuana use, 30 tested positive (around 11%). This is comparable to the rate for heroin (9.2%) but dramatically less than the rate for cocaine (42%). The distribution of values in Table 11.7 is significant for Chi square (.0006), and the correlational strength is moderate, with the value of phi equal to .56 and the value of gamma at .87.

Table 11.8
Marijuana Use, One or More Additional Drugs

```
                      MJ         Urine positive for marjuana
                   By MJ30       MJ. IN LAST 30 DAYS

    MJ30D>     Count  :               :          : Row
               Exp Val :  Deny : Admit :  Total
MJ             ------- :-----------------:
                  1    :   39  :   24   :    63
    NEG               : (29.5) : (33.5) :  56.8%
                      :-----------------:
         URINE    2    :   13  :   35   :    48
    POS               : (22.5) : (25.5) :  43.2%
                      \-----------------/
               Column     52      59       111
               Total    46.8%   53.2%   100.0%


  Chi-Square   D.F.  Significance    Min E.F.    Cells with E.F.< 5
  ----------   ----  ------------    --------    ------------------
   11.90451     1       .0006         22.486            None
   13.26608     1       .0003      ( Before Yates Correction )

  Statistic    Value
  ---------    -----
  Phi          .34571
  Gamma        .62791
```

A similar pattern is observed in Table 11.8, the first-order table for marijuana. There were 111 respondents who were drug-positive for another substance. Thirty-seven of these cases were non-concordant (33%) for marijuana use. Of these 37 cases, however, 24 are in Cell 2, and 13 in Cell 3. In cases were marijuana use was denied in the last 30 days, 25 percent were urine-positive. This figure falls, as noted, approximately halfway between the figure for heroin and the figure for cocaine. It also is almost three times the rate as the zero-order marijuana data in Table 11.7. The correlational measures for Table 11.8 are somewhat weaker than the zero-order table. The phi value is .35, while the gamma value is .63.

Responses on marijuana use represent an interesting change compared with the first two substances. This may reflect some apparently distinctive attributes of marijuana use and self-report performance. The overall ratio of marijuana concordant to non-concordant responses is similar to heroin. In that regard, they support the conventional findings of "good validity." However, the internal distribution of the rates within non-concordant cells is strikingly different. There are almost no heroin users who admit heroin use and then test negatively in the urine, while there are a substantial number of marijuana users who do. The rate of urine-positives for those who deny marijuana use falls around midway between heroin use (low) and cocaine use (relatively high).

There are several ways that this distinction can be interpreted. Many people who admit marijuana use test urine-negative compared with both cocaine and heroin use. This may be a result of the test itself. Are these respondents "false negatives?" It may be that since the time span involves a 30-day period, these Cell 2 cases largely represent casual users who simply do not sustain detectable cannabinoid concentrations in the urine. This finding may also suggest that, compared to heroin and cocaine, there is a larger population of sporadic or casual marijuana users. It may be that respondents are more apt to admit marijuana use, since it is less stigmatized than "hard" drugs such as cocaine and heroin. Hence they may lack the same degree of motivation for denial. Employing a longer time frame for marijuana may also increase the likelihood of recall error. Of course, each of these aspects may operate simultaneously, so that the strong departure seen in the data represents some additive effect of all these factors.

CONCLUSIONS

The objective of this chapter was to examine whether self-reported drug use, when compared to urinalysis, would confirm or deny the validity of the sample's responses. The data examined support the following conclusions:

(1) There is more concordance in every category of drug and at each level of use within each drug category than can be attributed to random chance. All users of drugs appear to report their use with reasonably high degrees of accuracy. Generally, then, our findings confirm what most earlier studies have found.

(2) Substance type appears to be related to the probability of a non-concordant or invalid response. Cocaine users have a quite distinctly higher rate of non-valid denial when compared to users of the other tested substances. Thus, cocaine users appear within this sample as the most likely to report a non-concordant response. This likelihood is around 4 to 5 times as great compared to marijuana or heroin use.

(3) While substance type appears to be related to degree of validity, intensity of use (as measured here) does not demonstrate any such relationship. The movement from zero-order to first-order tables within each substance category does not show any notable lowering of concordance rates.

(4) Marijuana appears to have a distinctive distribution pattern within the non-concordant categories (Cell 2 and Cell 3). It shows an inverted distribution of responses compared with both heroin and cocaine. While heroin and cocaine support our interpretation of the substantive meaning of Cell 2 and Cell 3, marijuana fails to do so. In fact, it demonstrates a contrary state.

It appears that while the traditional findings of criminologists are confirmed in this study there is also support for a more critical evaluation of the validity issue, especially in regard to marijuana use self-reports. Generally, the self-reported data of drug users is a reasonably reliable source of information. Nothing here supports a position like Osler's contention of drug users as "chronic and inveterate liars." But specification of this large heterogeneous population by type reveals that there may be less candor among certain categories of users, perhaps based on the mode of drug psychoactivity. As Wish (1986) suggested in his findings on PCP users, it cannot be assumed that validation or honesty rates established in an era generally focused on sedatives, soporifics, and analgesics are applicable at present. The 1980s have been the age of the stimulant. Linking truthfulness to drug type and user type represents two ways to accurately evaluate self-report data on these populations.

DISCUSSION

This chapter treats validity as an operational concept. It is, for the purposes of this paper, "simple" concordance between two measurable states. In the most narrow technical sense, this is unambiguous. While subject to some level of measurement error, both the recording of responses and EMIT-based urinalysis are rather reliable devices or processes well-established in criminological drug use research. The issues of interpretation of the data, on the other hand, are problematic rather than simple.

Non-Concordance

Let us assume, momentarily, that there are no measurement errors in the self-reports or the urinalysis values. If every person answered perfectly honestly, and no respondent made a recall error, and every respondent knew the correct identity of the substances (and their contaminants) which they had ingested, then we would find a zero value in cells 2 and 3. That is, there would be no non-concordant cases. If every person was dishonest, the opposite status would prevail, with all cases distributed in the opposite diagonal. The tables show that we do not find such a condition, and it would defy common sense to expect it. To the extent the tables depart from this theoretical diagonal loading pattern, we note that they exhibit the property of non-concordance. But what does "non-concordance" mean? Of course, in a straightforward sense, it means, for our purposes, "non-validity" of response. But in exactly what way is this response invalid?

If the non-concordant state of the table is due to deliberate misrepresentation, it would be reasonable to call it deceit or lying. If the non-concordant values result from unintentional misrepresentations they are "errors." An interesting extension of this work would be to conduct a search for patterns of error and to differentiate them from intentional deceit. Recall error is often identified as a major source of unintentionally false self-reports. Rates of recall error may perhaps be estimated by using some known neutral comparator, and tables may be adjusted to accommodate such "non-intentional error." Thus tables may be tested for validity "controlling for" recall error.

It is also interesting to consider whether or not the psychotropic effects of the drugs themselves affect recall accuracy, and whether various drugs differ in this regard by identifiable and consistent values. Can such values can be determined and then tested independently across multiple time frames? An evaluation along this line, for example, could possibly be done with existing DUF data. It would be interesting to test out the conjecture that a subject, who is urine-positive for multiple drugs, and who misrepresents their use on one drug, would more likely misrepresent their use on another, or perhaps on some independent non-drug survey item. If such a pattern were identified, one could search for the specific combinations (if any) under which maximal misrepresentation occurs. Consider, as well, that it may also be possible that consumption methods may affect the process of accurate recall, independently or in combination with the psychotropic drug effects themselves. For example, a ritualized and repeated consuming process may enhance the likelihood of better recall than furtive, private, or sporadic use patterns. Stimulants may be more memory-negative than soporifics, and substances may be consumed in different fashion by different users, or differently at different times by the same user. Economic circumstances may drastically affect the degree to which a user plays close or scant attention to the incidence of use or the quantities of substance used. These and other factors all not only can affect the recall process, but also may act interactively upon it as well. Considering that all these factors can act simultaneously, it may be possible to model their relationships and weigh their relative contribution to accurate self-reports.

The Specificity of Drugs

One very interesting finding of this research is the relatively high rate of misrepresentation of cocaine use. Why is this so? It is interesting to consider whether the concepts discussed above could account for this result. Does cocaine lead to biochemical impairment of short-term memory? Does the use of cocaine increase the likelihood of a relatively severe sanction (e.g., compared to marijuana)? Does the fear resultant from such a sanction act as a conscious motivation to misreport? Is this further enhanced by the increased feelings of paranoia often associated with high-use levels of stimulants? It is interesting, in this regard, to note that heroin-use reports (heroin being a drug as severely sanctioned in the law as cocaine but a soporific) have a relatively low rate of non-concordance in these findings. Is it the relatively simple (compared to heroin) use procedure and the lack of a dramatic focal event (like injection) which accounts for less accurate cocaine-use recall? In a large enough data base, would there be non-concordance rate differentials between cocaine snorters, smokers, and injectors?

Examining the findings for marijuana also stimulates some interesting questions which deserve further empirical examination. Why are the rates of Cell 2 (urine-negative, report-positive) so high, literally reversed relative to heroin or cocaine? Perhaps the sheer volume of marijuana use, enhanced by the relatively mild consequences of use, make for conditions which promote accurate self-reports which are not confirmed using current rates of 100 nanograms/liter as a cut-off for EMIT. If one were to lower the concentration value required to define a positive response, perhaps this pattern would abate. That is, the data do not indicate non-users who choose to "lie" and report use when there is no use. Rather, users who consume very casually may not be sustaining high enough urine concentrates of the testable metabolites to register positive results. This hypothesis could be checked within existing DUF procedures by splitting the samples into two, and testing one component at very high sensitivity rates (e.g., 5 nanograms/liter). Or again, the action of marijuana may inhibit accurate recall, so that users fail to adequately report the timing of their use. They "confess" to marijuana which is more temporally distal, and thus show in the tables as "non-concordant abstainers." This feature may be even further aggravated by using a 30-day time interval, which undoubtedly will raise recall error rates compared to a 48-hour interval.

Policy Implications

Of course, it is quite fair to ask in a policy sense, What does "drug presence" mean? After all, what EMIT measures is mainly metabolic by-products or urinary remnants of the drugs. This tells us that these drugs have passed through the persons metabolism. But it does not reveal any other information regarding the drug and its broader meanings and impacts. Do drugs uniformly affect behavior? Do the qualities and quantities of drug-induced behavior apply relatively uniformly to people or not? And if the metabolite appears in the urine, how can that be interpreted in regards to behavior? Marijuana is especially interesting in this regard. Marijuana sustains a lengthy presence in the urine for days, weeks, and even months after it is last ingested. It may not have any effect on behavior, but it is still detectable in the urine. If this is the case, then how do we link observable behavior to drug use? It is somewhat fashionable to treat drug intoxication as leading to disordered behavior, but the opposite might also be true. In effect, we are delivered at the doorstep of the correlation/causation conundrum.

This leads to other policy implications, with interesting speculative possibilities. In a population broadly screened for drugs, and sanctioned in some fashion for the presence of such drugs, what can happen? Marijuana use among such a population is easy to detect. Is it possible, as a consequence, that broad drug screening will encourage people to use "fast" metabolic drugs, like cocaine and the opiates? Or will any such sanctions simply shift people into legitimate psychotropics, such as alcohol, or prescriptive psychotropics like Valium? Furthermore, is it possible that we will witness the emergence of the marketing of "testing neutralizers" designed to foil current drug-testing technology? Will a technological tete-a-tete break out between testers and "anti-testers?" If this seems far-fetched, consider the competitive battles between copy-protection-oriented software companies and the anti-copy-protection industry in personal computer software. Such a development in the-drug testing industry should be given serious thought. Could such "test-fooling" products be outlawed? Like legal problems with so-called "narcotics paraphernalia," could testing neutralizers be adequately legally defined to avoid constitutional infringements on commerce?

In any event, sanctioning such users represents problems of a whole different sort. To what extent are industries prepared to punish workers who would test positive in a "performance vacuum?" That is, a worker who is caught through random screening but has a virtually ideal work record, represents a dilemma. If workers are to be dismissed for positive drug tests, are there sufficient numbers of appropriate "drug-free" workers available to compensate in the labor pool if massive actions take place? If employees who are drug-positive are dismissed, to what are they dismissed? If companies must provide "rehabilitation" services, are they in effect subsidizing drug use? Will companies be allowed to ignore drug intoxication if they want? It may prove cost-effective for many companies to do just that. What about companies which will be forced to "certify" drug-free employees by contractual obligation? Suppose they test employees by contractual requirement (e.g., suppose they received a federal grant which required it) and the employer dismisses drug-positive employees. If those employees file suit for wrongful discharge (e.g., a botched test) will the requiring agency indemnify the contractor?

The drug-testing technology we currently possess represents a vast improvement over the technology of just a decade ago. It may be tempting, in the face of highly accurate and relatively cheap drug screens, to turn to this technology as a type of "silver bullet" for monitoring and controlling drug use. Linked with a punitive mentality, it can be a powerful force to bring to the workplace and public commercial life. In the clamor for a "quick fix" to drug abuse problems, and couched behind the widely held belief that drugs are the root cause of a vast amount of our current criminality, we may be making a mistake. We may be unleashing a technology which lacks a well thought-out social application, and which may hold some surprising consequences if implemented without careful thought.

REFERENCES

Amsel, Z., W. Mandell, L. Matthias, C. Mason & I. Hocherman (1976). "Reliability and Validity of Self-Reported Illegal Activities and Drug Use Collected from Narcotics Addicts." *International Journal of The Addictions*, 11:325-336.

Bachman, J. & P. O'Malley (1981). "When Four Months Equal a Year: Inconsistencies in Student Reports of Drug Use." *Public Opinion Quarterly*, 45:536-548.

Bale, R. (1979). "The Validity and Reliability of Self-Reported Data from Heroin Addicts: Mailed Questionnaires Compared with Face-to-Face Interviews." *International Journal of the Addictions*, 14(7):993-1000.

Bale, R., W. Van Stone, T. Engelsing, V. Zarcone & J. Kuldau (1981). "The Validity of Self-Reported Heroin Use." *International Journal of the Addictions*, 16(8):1387-1398.

Ball, J. (1967). "Research Notes: The Reliability and Validity of Interview Data Obtained from 59 Narcotic Drug Addicts." *American Journal of Sociology*, 72:650-654.

Ben-Yehuda, N. (1980). "Are Addict's Self-Reports to Be Trusted?" *International Journal of the Addictions*, 15(8):1265-1270.

Boone, D.J. (1987). "Reliability of Urine Drug Testing." *Journal of the American Medical Association*, 258(18): 2587-88.

Bonito, A., D. Nurco & J. Shaffer (1976) "The Veridicality of Addict's Self-Reports in Social Research." *International Journal of the Addictions*, 11(5):719-724.

Carver, J.A. (1986). "Drugs and Crime: Controlling Use and Reducing Risk through Testing." National Institute of Justice Report, SNI 199, Washington, DC.

Clark, J. & L. Tifft (1966). "Polygraph and Interview Validation of Self-Reported Deviant Behavior." *American Sociological Review*, 31:516-527.

Cox, T. & B. Longwell (1974). "Reliability of Interview Data Concerning Current Heroin Use from Heroin Addicts on Methadone." *International Journal of the Addictions*, 9:161-165.

DeFleur, L. (1967). "On Polygraph and Interview Validation." *American Sociological Review*, 32, 114-115.

Field, L. (1987). "Reliability of Urine Drug Testing." *Journal of the American Medical Association*, 258(18):2587-2588.

Hardt, R. & S. Peterson-Hardt (1977). "On Determining the Quality of the Delinquency Self-Report Method." *Journal of Research in Crime and Delinquency*, 14 (July):247-261.

Leutgert, M.J. & A.H. Armstrong (1973). "Methodological Issues in Drug Usage Surveys: Anonymity, Recency, and Frequency." *International Journal of the Addictions*, 8(4):683-689.

Maddux, J. & D. Desmond (1975). "Reliability and Validity of Information from Chronic Heroin Users." *Journal of Psychiatric Research*, 12:87-95.

Magura, S., D. Goldsmith, C. Casriel, P. Goldstein & D. Lipton (1988). "The Validity of Methadone Client's Self-Reported Drug Use." *International Journal of the Addictions*, forthcoming vol. 22.

Marshall, E. (1988). "Testing Urine for Drugs." *Science*, 241:150-152.

Mieczkowski, T. (1988). "The Damage Done: Cocaine Methods in Detroit." *International Journal of Comparative and Applied Criminal Justice*, 12(2):261-267.

O'Brien, R.M. (1985). *Crime and Victimization Data*. Beverly Hills: Sage.

Page, W.F., J.E. Davies, R.A. Ladner, J. Alfassa & H. Tennis (1977). "Urinalysis Screened vs. Verbally Reported Drug Use: The Identification of Discrepant Groups." *International Journal of the Addictions*, 12(4):439-450.

Parry, H., M. Balter & I. Cisin (1970). "Primary Levels of Under-Reporting Psychotropic Drug Use." *Public Opinion Quarterly*, 34:582-592.

Petzel, T., J. Johnson & J. McKillip (1973). "Response Bias in Drug Surveys." *Journal of Consulting and Clinical Psychology*, 40:437-439.

Schwartz, R.H. & R.L. Hawks (1985). "Laboratory Detection of Marijuana Use." *Journal of the American Medical Association*, 254(6) 788-792.

Stephens, R. (1972). "The Truthfulness of Addict Respondents in Research Projects." *International Journal of the Addictions*, 7(3):549-558.

Toborg, M. & M. Kirby (1984). "Drug Use and Pre-trial Crime in the District of Columbia." National Institute of Justice Monograph, U.S. Department of Justice, Washington, DC.

Wish, E., B. Johnson, D. Strug, K. Anderson & T. Miller (1983). "Concordance Between Self-Reports of Drug Use and Urinalysis Test Results from Active Unapprehended Criminals." Narcotics and Drug Research, Inc., New York.

Wish, E., B. Johnson, D. Strug, M. Chedekel & D. Lipton (1983a). "Are Urine Tests Good Indicators of the Validity of Self-Reports of Drug Use? It Depends on the Test." Narcotics and Drug Research, Inc., New York.

Wish, E., E. Brady & M. Cuadrado (1986). "Urine Testing of Arrestees: Findings from Manhattan." Narcotic and Drug Research, Inc., New York.

Wish, E., M. Cuadrado & J. Martorana (1986). "Estimates of Drug Use in Intensive Supervision Probationers: Results from a Pilot Study." *Federal Probation*.

Wish, E. (1986). "PCP and Crime: Just Another Illicit Drug?" In D.H. Clouet (ed.) *Phencyclidine: An Update, National Institute on Drug Abuse Monograph #63* Washington, DC.

_____(1987). "Drug Use in Arrestees in Manhattan: The Dramatic Increase in Cocaine from 1984 to 1986." Narcotic and Drug Research, Inc., New York.

_____(1987a) "Drug Use Forecasting: New York 1984 to 1986." National Institute of Justice Research Report, Washington, DC.

Whitehead, P. and R. Smart (1972). "Validity and Reliability of Self-Reported Drug Use." *Canadian Journal of Criminology and Corrections*, 14:83-89.

Zinberg, N. (1984). *Drugs, Set, and Setting.* New Haven: Yale University Press.

12

AIDS and Drug Use:
Implications for Criminal Justice Policy

James A. Inciardi
University of Delaware

Acquired Immune Deficiency Syndrome (AIDS) has been called many things. In 1986 the United States Surgeon General referred to the disease as the most serious health issue since the bubonic plague of the 14th century (Koop, 1986). Or similarly, in 1988 the Secretary of Health and Human Services called AIDS America's "Number One" public health problem (Bowen, 1988). By contrast, however, both God and "Nature" have also been brought into discussions of the disease. To some, AIDS is "nature's revenge" for the "crime" of homosexuality -- God's retribution for the perversions committed by "junkies and queers and whores" (See Black, 1986). And to many more, AIDS has become like syphilis, leprosy, and plague -- the contemporary metaphor for corruption, decay, and consummate evil.

The linking of AIDS with homosexual practice and intravenous drug use makes it easily susceptible to these metaphorical interpretations, as are other diseases that are transmitted through taboo behaviors or those with unknown etiologies (See Sontag, 1988). But these stigmatic misconceptions should not distract from the seriousness of the disease. AIDS confronts society in general, and the criminal justice system in particular, with a variety of concerns about such things as risk factors, disease vectors, susceptibility, contagion, and spread.

Within the context of these remarks, what follows is a brief history of AIDS; a summary of its pathology, epidemiology, and transmission patterns; and an analysis of its policy implications for both drug abuse control and criminal justice processing.

THE EMERGENCE OF AIDS

Acquired Immune Deficiency Syndrome was first described as a new and distinct clinical entity during the late Spring and early Summer of 1981 (Centers for Disease Control, 1981a, 1981b; Gottlieb et al., 1981; Masur et al., 1981). First, clinical investigators in Los Angeles reported five cases to the Centers for Disease Control (CDC) of Pneumocystis carinii pneumonia (PCP) among homosexual men. None of these patients had an underlying disease that might have been associated with the PCP, or a history of treatment for a compromised immune system. All, however, had other clinical manifestations and laboratory evidence of immunosuppression. Second, and within a month, 26 cases of Kaposi's sarcoma (KS) were reported among homosexual men in New York and California.

What was so unusual was that prior to these reports, the appearance of both PCP and KS in populations of previously healthy young men was unprecedented. PCP is an infection caused by the parasite P. carinii, previously seen almost exclusively in cancer and transplant patients receiving immunosuppressive drugs. KS, a cancer or tumor of the blood vessel walls and typically appearing as blue-violet to brownish skin blotches, had been quite rare in the United States -- occurring primarily in elderly men, usually of Mediterranean origin. Like PCP, furthermore, KS had also been reported among organ transplant recipients and others receiving immunosuppressive therapy. This quickly led to the hypothesis that the increased occurrences of the two disorders in homosexual men were due to some underlying immune system dysfunction. This hypothesis was further supported by the incidence among homosexuals of "opportunistic infections" -- infections caused by microorganisms that rarely generate disease in persons with normal immune defense mechanisms (Institute of Medicine, 1986a:195). It is for this reason that the occurrence of KS, PCP, and/or other opportunistic infections in a person with unexplained immune dysfunction became known as the "acquired immune deficiency syndrome," or more simply, AIDS.[1]

With the recognition that the vast majority of the early cases of this new clinical syndrome involved homosexual men, it seemed logical that the causes might be related to the lifestyle unique to that population. The sexual revolution of the 1960s and 1970s was accompanied not only by greater carnal permissiveness among both heterosexuals and gays, but also a more positive social acceptance of homosexuality. The emergence of commercial bathhouses and other outlets for sexual contacts among gays further increased promiscuity, with self-selected segments of the male gay population viewing promiscuity as a facet of "gay liberation." In fact, among the early patients diagnosed with AIDS, their sexual recreation typically occurred within the anonymity of the bathhouses with similarly promiscuous men. Some had had as many as 20,000 sexual contacts and more than 1,100 sex partners (Shilts, 1987:132).

Because of this, it is not surprising that such factors as frequent exposure to sperm, rectal exposure to sperm, and/or the body's exposure to amyl nitrate and butyl nitrate (better known as "poppers," and used to enhance sexual pleasure and performance), were themselves considered potential causes of AIDS. Yet while it was apparent that AIDS was a new disease, most of the gay lifestyle factors were not particularly new, having changed only in a relative sense. As such, it was difficult to immediately single out specific behaviors that might be related to the emerging epidemic.

Within a brief period of time, the notion that AIDS was some form of "gay plague" was quickly extinguished. The disease was suddenly being reported in other populations, such as intravenous drug users, blood transfusion patients, and hemophiliacs (Centers for Disease Control, 1982ab; Davis et al., 1983; Siegal & Siegal, 1983:86-95). And what these reports suggested to the scientific community was that an infectious etiology for AIDS had to be considered.

TRACKING THE EPIDEMIC

Almost immediately after the first cases of AIDS were reported in 1981, researchers at the Centers for Disease Control began tracking the disease backward in time to discover its origins. They ultimately determined that the first cases of AIDS in the United States probably occurred in 1977.[2] By early 1982, AIDS had been reported in 15 states, the District of Columbia, and two foreign countries, but the total remained extremely low -- 158 men and 1 woman. Although more than 90 percent of the men were either homosexual or bisexual, interviews with all of the patients failed to provide any definite clues about the origin of the disease.

Although it was suspected that AIDS might be transmitted through sexual relations among homosexually active men, the first strong evidence for the theory did not emerge until the completion of a case control study in June 1982 by epidemiologists at the Centers for Disease Control (Auerbach et al., 1984). In that investigation, data were obtained on the sexual partners of 13 of the first 19 cases of AIDS among homosexual men in the Los Angeles area. Within five years before the onset of their symptoms, nine had had sexual contact with people who later developed Kaposi's sarcoma or P. carinii pneumonia.

The nine were also linked to another interconnected series of 40 AIDS cases in 10 different cities by one individual who had developed a number of the manifestations of AIDS and was later diagnosed with Kaposi's sarcoma. Overall, the investigation of these 40 cases indicated that 20 percent of the initial AIDS cases in the United States were linked through sexual contact -- a statistical clustering that was extremely unlikely to have occurred by chance.

Yet even in the face of this evidence, there were those who doubted that AIDS was caused by some transmissible agent. However, when AIDS cases began to emerge in other populations -- among individuals who had been injected with blood or blood products, but had no other expected risk factors -- the transmission vectors for the disease became somewhat clearer. Such cases were confirmed first among people with hemophilia, followed by blood transfusion recipients and intravenous drug users who shared hypodermic needles. Then, when there were documented cases of AIDS among the heterosexual partners of male IV drug users, it became increasingly evident that AIDS was a sexually transmitted disease, and that "sexual preference" was not necessarily the only risk factor.[3]

In 1983 and 1984, scientists at the Institute Pasteur in Paris and the National Institutes of Health in the United States identified and isolated the cause of AIDS -- human immunodeficiency virus, more commonly known as HIV. More specifically, HIV is a "retrovirus," a type of infectious agent that had previously been identified as causing many animal diseases. The designation of "retrovirus" derives from the backward, or "retro-" flow of genetic information from RNA to DNA, which reverses the normal flow of genetic messages.[4] Subsequent studies demonstrated that HIV is transmitted when virus particles or infected cells gain direct access to the bloodstream. This can occur through all forms of sexual intercourse, the sharing of contaminated needles, blood, and blood products, and the passing of the virus from infected mothers to their unborn or newborn children.[5] And within this context, HIV, a continuum of conditions associated with immune dysfunction, and AIDS is best described as a severe manifestation of infection with HIV (Institute of Medicine, 1986b:353).

Subsequent to the discovery of HIV, an early priority was to fully verify its association with the diseases in question.[6] Using a variety of different laboratory tests, researchers in virology and molecular biology searched for antibodies against HIV in the blood of AIDS patients. Ultimately, they found that almost 100 percent of AIDS patients had HIV antibodies (Institute of Medicine, 1986a:20). The presence of specific antibodies in the blood indicates that a previous infection registered on the body's immune system. The antibody molecules that remain in the bloodstream act as scouts, so to speak; if the virus appears again, the scouts recognize it immediately and attempt to prevent it from getting a foothold.

This research led, in 1985, to the widespread availability of a commercial test for antibodies to HIV. The basic test is an enzyme-linked immunosorbent assay (ELISA). More commonly known as ELISA or EIA, it is not a test for AIDS, nor does it even detect the presence of the virus itself.[7] What the test does indicate is whether HIV has been noticed by an individual's immune system.[8]

As to where AIDS and HIV actually originated, the matter remains unsettled. However, there is considerable agreement that the source may have been Central Africa. The AIDS problem in Africa first became evident in 1982 when physicians in Belgium began seeing patients from Zaire and Burundi.[9] They had signs and symptoms virtually identical to what was being called AIDS in the United States. Further investigation led to a number of different theories. The first was that HIV existed for decades, nestled in remote regions of Africa and limited to small, relatively isolated populations (Institute of Medicine, 1989:107). The social mores of those populations may not have been conducive to the rapid spread of the disease, and the few cases that did develop could likely have escaped detection against the backdrop of multiple life-threatening infections that are common to the region. There were a number of factors that eventually changed this pattern. African cities grew dramatically after World War II, principally the result of many African countries gaining their independence. As in other parts of the world, the urbanization of Africa was accompanied by social changes and family disruptions, combined with the anonymity of urban life -- all of which increased the likelihood of behaviors that contributed to the spread of sexually transmitted diseases (multiple sex partners and prostitution). In time, the prevalence of HIV increased sufficiently to make AIDS visible as a new clinical entity in Africa, and elsewhere.[10]

An alternative theory suggests that the natural home of the AIDS virus is in an animal. The African green monkey has been singled out as a prime suspect, with the hypothesis that somehow, the virus mutated and jumped species, entering the human population when monkeys bit hunters who were attempting to capture them for food.[11]

Several investigations have also suggested that AIDS and HIV may have made their way to North America from Africa, via Haiti. More specifically, from the early 1960s through the mid-1970s, there was considerable migration from Zaire to Haiti, and many of these immigrants are believed to have settled in the United States (DeVita, Hellman & Rosenberg, 1985:304). In addition, at least one commentator has argued that African green monkeys were imported to Haiti from Zaire and kept as pets in male houses of prostitution (Altman, 1987:72). And finally, there is the point of view that Haiti was a popular vacation spot for gay Americans, who brought the disease home with them and infected the mainland population (Altman, 1987:72). Yet whatever the source or sources, by 1983 it was clear that AIDS was an epidemic disease with a 100 percent mortality rate.

THE EPIDEMIOLOGY OF AIDS AND HIV

From analyses of AIDS reports combined with data from HIV testing, it appears that there are at least three distinct patterns of AIDS across the globe (Mann et al., 1989).

Pattern-I seems to be typical of industrialized nations with relatively large numbers of AIDS cases, such as the United States, Canada and Mexico, many Western European countries, Australia and New Zealand, Brazil, and a few regions of South Africa (which are not industrialized). In pattern-I nations HIV probably began to spread extensively during the late 1970s. Most cases occur among homosexual and bisexual males, and urban intravenous drug users. Heterosexual transmission of the virus, although increasing, is responsible for only a small proportion of cases. There was transmission of HIV through some transfusions of blood and blood products in pattern-I countries between the late 1970s and 1985. However, that route of transmission has been practically eliminated in some countries and drastically reduced in others by convincing members of high risk groups not to donate blood and by the testing of potential blood donors for the presence of HIV antibodies. Unsterile needles, aside from those used by IV drug users, are not a significant factor in the transmission of HIV in pattern-I nations. Finally, relatively few women are infected in these countries, and as a result, perinatal transmission (from mother to infant) is also low. The current male-to-female ratio ranges from 10:1 to 15:1. This is rapidly changing, however, as is the incidence of perinatal transmission, due to the growing spread of the virus within populations of IV drug users and their sex partners.

Pattern-II can be observed in Haiti, a few other parts of the Caribbean, and several countries in central, eastern, and southern Africa. As in the pattern-I nations, pattern-II areas saw the initial spread of the virus during the late 1970s. Unique to this pattern, however, the male-to-female ratio is almost 1:1, with most cases occurring among heterosexuals. Transmission through homosexual activity or IV drug use is either absent or at a low level, whereas perinatal transmission is common.

Pattern-III prevails in sections of Eastern Europe, North Africa, the Middle East, Asia, and the majority of the Pacific. In these areas, HIV was likely introduced during the early and mid-1980s. Only small numbers of cases have been observed, and primarily in people who have traveled to pattern-I or pattern-II countries and had sexual contacts during their visits. Indigenous homosexual, heterosexual, and IV-drug transmission patterns have been documented only recently. Finally, some cases have been caused by imported blood products that were contaminated by HIV.[12]

In terms of the national dimensions of AIDS, as of August 31, 1989, there were a total of 105,990 diagnosed cases of AIDS in the United States that were reported to the Centers for Disease Control (1989:8). The majority of these were concentrated in the states of New York, California, Florida, New Jersey, and Texas, which collectively accounted for some two-thirds of all cases.

Table 12.1 provides an interesting portrait of the distribution of AIDS cases in the United States. Homosexual and bisexual men account for 61 percent of the cases in the adult/adolescent age category, followed by female and heterosexual male IV drug users (21%), and then homosexual/bisexual male IV drug users. Collectively, homosexual and bisexual men and IV drug users account for more than two-thirds of the known cases of AIDS in the United States. Importantly, however, although IV drug users (including those who are also homosexual and bisexual men) rank a distant second as a major risk group for AIDS, their numbers are proportionately increasing, expanding from 28 percent of all new cases in 1988 to 29 percent a year later. Furthermore, this represents an increase from 24 percent in late 1987 (CDC, 1987a).

The next exposure category in the adult/adolescent age cohort includes those infected through heterosexual contacts, and accounts for some 5 percent of all diagnosed cases. The number of individuals in this group is relatively small -- 4,807 since June of 1981. However, as suggested by Table 12.1, this group appears to be growing rapidly in that two-thirds of all cases were diagnosed during the last two years and 36 percent during the past 12 months. Persons who have had sex with an IV drug user or with an individual born in a pattern-II country account for the overwhelming majority.

Of interest in Table 12.1 is the distribution of pediatric cases -- persons under 13 years of age. Not surprisingly, there are few -- 1,780 since June, 1981, representing only 1.7 percent of all reported cases in the United States. However, the overwhelming majority (80%) are the result of perinatal transmission. Of all pediatric cases, moreover, some 82 percent were diagnosed at age 4 or less. And most importantly for this analysis, almost three-fourths (71%) of these perinatal cases were the result of the mother's IV drug use or her sexual contacts with an IV drug user.

THE AIDS/DRUGS CONNECTION

In 1987, the United States Public Health Service estimated that there were some 900,000 regular (at least weekly) IV drug users across the nation, 25 percent of whom were already infected with HIV (CDC, 1987b). At the same time, the CDC was reporting that IV drug users, as already noted, were the second highest risk group for AIDS, representing 24 percent of all reported cases in the United States. By early 1988, IV drug users had come to represent 26 percent of known AIDS cases in the U.S. (CDC, 1988), and by late-1989 that proportion was up to 29 percent (CDC, 1989).

Table 12.1
AIDS Cases by Age Group, Exposure Category, and Sex, Reported September 1987 through August 1988 and September 1988 through August 1989; and Cumulative Totals, by Age Group and Exposure Category, through August 1989, United States

Adult/adolescent exposure category	Males Sept. 1987-Aug. 1988 No. (%)	Males Sept. 1988-Aug. 1989 No. (%)	Females Sept. 1987-Aug. 1988 No. (%)	Females Sept. 1988-Aug. 1989 No. (%)	Totals Sept. 1987-Aug. 1988 No. (%)	Totals Sept. 1988-Aug. 1989 No. (%)	Cumulative total No. (%)
Male homosexual/bisexual contact	17,439 (65)	18,803 (64)	—	—	17,439 (58)	18,803 (57)	63,497 (61)
Intravenous (IV) drug use (female and heterosexual male)	5,241 (19)	5,843 (20)	1,617 (54)	1,775 (51)	6,858 (23)	7,618 (23)	21,370 (21)
Male homosexual/bisexual contact and IV drug use	2,082 (8)	2,079 (7)	— (0)	— (0)	2,082 (7)	2,079 (6)	7,379 (7)
Hemophilia/coagulation disorder	296 (1)	308 (1)	5 (0)	9 (0)	301 (1)	317 (1)	996 (1)
Heterosexual contact:	547 (2)	698 (2)	854 (29)	1,044 (30)	1,401 (5)	1,742 (5)	4,807 (5)
Sex with IV drug user	*189*	*351*	*553*	*659*	*742*	*1,010*	*2,402*
Sex with bisexual male	*—*	*—*	*94*	*76*	*94*	*76*	*300*
Sex with person with hemophilia	*1*	*3*	*12*	*11*	*13*	*14*	*41*
Born in Pattern-II country	*282*	*229*	*91*	*126*	*373*	*355*	*1,477*
Sex with person born in Pattern-II country	*19*	*16*	*4*	*10*	*23*	*26*	*74*
Sex with transfusion recipient with HIV infection	*4*	*10*	*16*	*22*	*20*	*32*	*70*
Sex with person with HIV infection, risk not specified	*52*	*89*	*84*	*140*	*136*	*229*	*443*
Receipt of transfusion of blood, blood components, or tissue	552 (2)	451 (2)	330 (11)	318 (9)	882 (3)	769 (2)	2,566 (2)
Other/undetermined	768 (3)	1,429 (5)	174 (6)	311 (9)	942 (3)	1,740 (5)	3,595 (3)
Adult/adolescent subtotal	26,925 (100)	29,611 (100)	2,980 (100)	3,457 (100)	29,905 (100)	33,068 (100)	104,210 (100)

Table 12.1 *continued*

Pediatric (<13 years old) exposure category

	29 (10)	34 (10)	—	1 (0)	29 (5)	35 (6)	102 (6)
Hemophilia/coagulation disorder	29 (10)	34 (10)	—	1 (0)	29 (5)	35 (6)	102 (6)
Mother with/at risk for AIDS/ HIV infection:	221 (74)	262 (76)	211 (85)	251 (90)	432 (79)	513 (82)	1,422 (80)
IV drug use	112	132	109	106	221	238	728
Sex with IV drug user	46	58	39	54	85	112	288
Sex with bisexual male	3	5	8	3	11	8	30
Sex with person with hemophilia	3	—	2	1	5	1	7
Born in Pattern-II country	22	25	15	27	37	52	155
Sex with person born in Pattern-II country	1	2	—	2	1	4	6
Sex with transfusion recipient with HIV infection	—	3	1	6	1	9	10
Sex with person with HIV infection, risk not specified	10	12	6	13	16	25	56
Receipt of transfusion of blood, blood components, or tissue	3	3	10	8	13	11	32
Has HIV infection, risk not specified	21	22	21	31	42	53	110
Receipt of transfusion of blood, blood components, or tissue	43 (14)	34 (10)	29 (12)	15 (5)	72 (13)	49 (8)	200 (11)
Undetermined	7 (2)	14 (4)	7 (3)	11 (4)	14 (3)	25 (4)	56 (3)
Pediatric subtotal	300 (100)	344 (100)	247 (100)	278 (100)	547 (100)	622 (100)	1,780 (100)
Total	27,225	29,955	3,227	3,735	30,452	33,690	105,990

SOURCE: Centers for Disease Control, *HIV/AIDS Surveillance Report*, September 1989, p.8.

Table 12.2
AIDS Cases by Age Group, Exposure Category, and Race/Ethnicity, Reported through August 1989, United States

Adult/adolescent exposure category	White, not Hispanic No. (%)	Black, not Hispanic No. (%)	Hispanic No. (%)	Asian/Pacific Islander No. (%)	American Indian/ Alaskan Native No. (%)	Total No. (%)
Male homosexual/bisexual contact	45,916 (77)	10,310 (37)	6,606 (42)	471 (75)	69 (50)	63,497 (61)
Intravenous (IV) drug use (female and heterosexual male)	4,322 (7)	10,710 (39)	6,234 (40)	24 (4)	24 (18)	21,370 (21)
Male homosexual/bisexual contact and IV drug use	4,389 (7)	1,899 (7)	1,050 (7)	11 (2)	21 (15)	7,379 (7)
Hemophilia/coagulation disorder	833 (1)	64 (0)	75 (0)	14 (2)	6 (4)	996 (1)
Heterosexual contact:	963 (2)	3,041 (11)	767 (5)	21 (3)	8 (6)	4,807 (5)
Sex with IV drug user	*538*	*1,222*	*629*	*8*	*3*	*2,402*
Sex with bisexual male	*158*	*97*	*39*	*4*	*1*	*300*
Sex with person with hemophilia	*36*	*3*	*1*	*1*	*—*	*41*
Born in Pattern-II country	*3*	*1,457*	*10*	*4*	*—*	*1,477*
Sex with person born in Pattern-II country	*21*	*49*	*4*	*—*	*—*	*74*
Sex with transfusion recipient with AIDS/HIV infection	*54*	*8*	*6*	*1*	*—*	*70*
Sex with person with HIV infection, risk not specified	*153*	*205*	*78*	*3*	*4*	*443*
Receipt of transfusion of blood, blood components, or tissue	1,878 (3)	395 (1)	233 (1)	52 (8)	3 (2)	2,566 (2)
Other/undetermined	1,334 (2)	1,385 (5)	798 (5)	36 (6)	6 (4)	3,595 (3)
Adult/adolescent subtotal	59,635(100)	27,804 (100)	15,763(100)	629(100)	137(100)	104,210(100)

Table 12.2 *continued*

Pediatric (<13 years old) exposure category

Exposure category						
Hemophilia/coagulation disorder	73 (18)	12 (1)	14 (3)	3 (33)	—	102 (6)
Mother with/at risk for AIDS/HIV infection:	209 (52)	849 (90)	353 (84)	3 (33)	4(100)	1,422 (80)
IV drug use	*100*	*428*	*196*	*1*	*2*	*728*
Sex with IV drug user	*43*	*140*	*104*	*—*	*—*	*288*
Sex with bisexual male	*11*	*15*	*4*	*—*	*—*	*30*
Sex with person with hemophilia	*5*	*1*	*1*	*—*	*—*	*7*
Born in Pattern-II country	*2*	*152*	*1*	*—*	*—*	*155*
Sex with person born in Pattern-II country	*—*	*5*	*—*	*—*	*—*	*6*
Sex with transfusion recipient with HIV infection	*5*	*3*	*2*	*—*	*—*	*10*
Sex with person with HIV infection, risk not specified	*9*	*25*	*19*	*1*	*1*	*56*
Receipt of transfusion of blood, blood components, or tissue	*10*	*12*	*10*	*—*	*—*	*32*
Has HIV infection, risk not specified	*24*	*68*	*16*	*1*	*1*	*110*
Receipt of transfusion of blood, blood components, or tissue	111 (27)	46 (5)	40 (19)	3 (33)	—	200 (11)
Undetermined	12 (3)	32 (3)	12 (3)	—	—	56 (3)
Pediatric subtotal	405(100)	939 (100)	419(100)	9(100)	4(100)	1,780(100)
Total	**60,040**	**28,743**	**16,182**	**638**	**141**	**105,990**

SOURCE: Centers for Disease Control, *HIV/AIDS Surveillance Report*, September 1989, p.8.

The ready transmission of HIV among IV drug users is the result of needle-sharing practices, combined with the presence of cofactors. Cofactors include any behavioral practices or microbiological agents that facilitate the transmission of HIV. "Booting" is one such cofactor, since the practice increases the amount of residual blood left in drug paraphernalia. Booting involves the aspiration of venous blood back into a syringe for the purpose of mixing the drug with blood, while the needle remains inserted in the vein. The mixed blood/drug solution is then injected back into the vein. Most IV drug users believe that this "pre-mixing" enhances a drug's effects. Since IV users often share needles and syringes, particularly if they are administering the drugs in "shooting galleries" -- places where users gather to take drugs -- booting increases the probability that traces of HIV from an infected user will remain in a syringe to be passed on to the next user. And finally, genital sores and infections from other viruses have also been found to be cofactors (Quinn et al., 1988), and because of their lifestyles, IV drug users are rather well-known as a population that hosts a wide spectrum of microorganisms (Young, 1973; Pace et al., 1974; Geelhoed, 1984; Des Jarlais et al., 1987).

Among some sociodemographic groups, IV drug use is the primary risk factor for AIDS. In one study of consecutive admissions of economically disadvantaged AIDS patients to three hospitals in New York, for example, almost two-thirds were heterosexual IV drug users and an additional 5 percent were homosexual IV drug users (Maayan, Wormer & Hewlett, 1985). Furthermore, and as is apparent in Table 12.2, both blacks and Hispanics are overrepresented in the number of known AIDS cases in the United States -- a phenomenon directly related to minority group representation within the IV drug population. Whereas blacks constitute only 12 percent of the U.S. population, for example, they account for 27 percent of the reported AIDS cases. Similarly, whereas Hispanics constitute only 8 percent of the U.S. population, they account for some 18 percent of the reported AIDS case. Finally, and as already noted, the majority of all perinatal/pediatric AIDS children in the United States are offspring of IV drug-using women.

Intravenous drug users, in addition to being the second-highest risk group for HIV and AIDS, also represent a population that appears difficult to impact with routine AIDS prevention messages. The potential for HIV transmission from infected needles and "unsafe" sex is likely known to most drug users. Yet most are accustomed to risking death (through overdose or the violence-prone nature of the illegal-drug marketplace) and disease (hepatitis and other infections) on a daily basis, and these generally fail to eliminate their drug-taking behaviors. Thus, for an IV drug user who risks disease and death on a daily basis, warnings that needle sharing or unsafe sex may facilitate an infection that could cause death perhaps five or more years down the road have little meaning.

It would appear that at least some IV drug users are willing to adjust a few behaviors related to the transmission of HIV, such as purchasing new needles, sterilizing used needles, and reducing the sharing of needles with others (Des Jarlais, Friedman & Hopkins, 1985; Selwyn et al., 1987; Seligman et al., 1987). However, the minimal research in this area has tended to be inconclusive, particularly since many of those who adjusted their behaviors nevertheless continued to share needles with friends, relatives, and others who appear healthy.

Shifting to a related aspect of the AIDS/drugs connection, there is an extensive body of literature offering a strong empirical basis for the notion that prostitution is a major means of economic support for IV drug-using women (James, 1976; Rosenbaum, 1981). Moreover, it is well established that there is a high incidence of prostitution among women IV drug users (Goldstein, 1979; Inciardi, 1986). As such, the IV drug-using prostitute is not only at high risk for contracting HIV, but for transmitting the infection as well (Newmeyer, 1987; Chaisson et al., 1987; Castro et al., 1988).

AIDS, DRUG USE, AND THE CRIMINAL JUSTICE SYSTEM

Although IV drug users have been recognized as a unique risk group for HIV and AIDS, outside of New York City (which has both the greatest number of AIDS cases and the highest concentration of IV drug users of any locale in the United States) they have not attracted the media attention as the other AIDS "at-risk" groups. Both homosexuals and hemophiliacs are members of organized groups and constituencies that can direct attention to their health problems. Such is not the case with drug users. Or as medical researcher Harold M. Ginzburg (1984) stated not too long ago:

Drug abusers in general, and intravenous drug users in particular, have no organized advocacy. On the contrary, these groups have been identified as reservoirs of medical problems (such as serum hepatitis) and social ills. Drug abusers are traditionally associated with self-destructive activities; high rates of unemployment and criminality among abusers are frequently reported. Despite these apparent similarities, drug abusers are an extremely heterogeneous group. They display no common type of social, economic, or political behavior that distinguishes them from the general population.

Figure 12.1

Any Drug, Excluding Marijuana:
Use by Female and Male Arrestees*

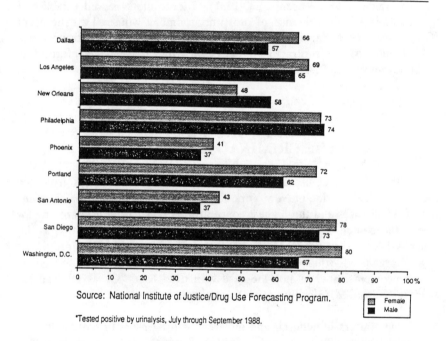

Source: National Institute of Justice/Drug Use Forecasting Program.

*Tested positive by urinalysis, July through September 1988.

Although drug abusers attempt to remain anonymous, they are typically identified in one of two circumstances: *as they seek treatment,* and *when they are arrested.* And since the number of drug treatment slots in the United States, combined with the fact that most drug users do not actively seek treatment, the criminal justice system, more than any other institutional sector, has the most concentrated contact with the largest number of users. In fact, there are data which suggest that at least in urban areas where both drug use and crime rates are high, drug users represent the major criminal justice clientele. As indicated in Figure 12.1, for example, during the third quarter of 1988, in seven of nine major cities where samples of arrestees were tested for the presence of drugs in their urine, the majority of arrestees were found to be positive for drugs. Other data from the National Institute of Justice's Drug Use Forecasting (DUF) program (1989) found that in all of the cities where testing was done, significant proportions of arrestees were not only using drugs, but injecting them as well. What all of this suggests is that the criminal justice system in the United States is faced with managing a growing population of HIV-infected as well as AIDS-diagnosed clients.

Since arrest is the entry point to the criminal justice, police officers in areas where drug use rates are high have the potential for dealing with HIV-infected suspects. This has led to considerable apprehension among many police officers, with some refusing to have any physical contact at all with homosexuals or drug users. Or as one Pennsylvania State Trooper put it early in 1989:

> What makes you think I can't be infected by a cough, a sneeze, or a sweaty palm. Yeah, I know what the training literature says -- there are no known cases of people getting it that way. But look what it says -- no known cases. Look at it from my point of view. I don't want to be the first known case of a cop getting AIDS because of some fag or junkie.[13]

Since most AIDS and HIV-related concerns within the ranks of policing relate to contacts with individuals known or suspected to be infected with HIV and with potentially contaminated blood, the National Institute of Justice has directed the following recommendations to all police agencies in the United States (Hammett, 1987: 35-36):

1.   Provide education and training on AIDS for law enforcement officers and other department staff.

2.   Issue specific AIDS policies and procedures, or revise existing communicable disease policies to address AIDS issues.

3. Educate officers on the low risk of HIV infection associated with assaults, human bites, and other disruptive behavior by subjects, but recommend reasonable precautions.

4. Ensure careful supervision of lockup areas to prevent incidents in which HIV infection may be transmitted among prisoners.

5. Counsel caution and use of gloves in searches and evidence handling, but educate on the low risk of infection.

6. Use masks or airways for CPR, but educate on the low risk of infection.

7. Follow infection control procedures for first aid.

8. Ensure that no staff touch bodies of deceased individuals unless authorized or necessary.

9. Provide clear education on the fact that HIV infection is not transmitted by any form of casual contact.

10. Coordinate educational efforts with public health departments, hospitals, emergency medical services, fire departments, community-based AIDS action groups and gay/lesbian organizations.

Shifting to the field of corrections, because of the ways that the HIV infection is transmitted, AIDS has become a special problem in contemporary jail and prison settings. Although health care personnel are uncertain over how quickly AIDS can be transmitted in correctional environments -- whether through drug use or sexual activity -- they believe that the incubation period might extend to as long as ten years. This would suggest that the full extent of the HIV and AIDS problem will not be known for many years to come. And there are other variables. As of October 1987, for example, there were some 2,000 correctional inmates in the United States diagnosed as having AIDS (Hammett, 1988) -- a rather small proportion of the total number of inmates in federal, state, and local prisons and jails. No doubt in the ensuing years this number has increased substantially. But even more importantly, this figure does not include those infected with HIV who have not as yet shown symptoms of the disease. And the number of inmates in this latter category may indeed be considerable. Studies indicate that in some locales as many as 70 percent of all IV heroin and cocaine users are already infected with HIV, and many of these eventually end up in detention and correctional settings. In this regard, the National Institute of Justice has made the following recommendations (Hammett, 1988: 92-93):

1. Quality medical care should be provided to all inmates infected with HIV.

2. Emphasis should be placed on proactive identification and monitoring of inmates at high risk of HIV infection and AIDS.

3. Comprehensive psychosocial services and pre-release planning are also essential for inmates with asymptomatic HIV infections and AIDS.

4. Costs of care for inmates with AIDS are very high, but may be reduced by eliminating unnecessary hospitalizations.

5. Most correctional systems still segregate or hospitalize inmates with AIDS, but there has been a noticeable trend away from blanket segregation of those with HIV. Systems should consider case-by-case housing and programming decisions based on the inmate's medical situation, need for protection, and likelihood of engaging in behaviors that may place others at risk.

6. Correctional systems should establish "universal precautions" for blood and body fluids. This is, unprotected contact with the blood or body fluids of everyone should be avoided.

7. Reasonable and consistent precautionary procedures should be established to help staff safely deal with a variety of situations, including altercations, blood spills, searches, CPR, and biting incidents.

8. Corrections systems should not adopt precautionary measures beyond those recommended by CDC for clinical staff.

9. Several correctional systems currently make condoms available to inmates in institutions, emphasizing that this is not to condone prohibited behavior but only to recognize that it occurs and to provide for reasonable risk reduction.

POSTSCRIPT

Throughout the 1990s the problems of AIDS and HIV will not only endure, but will escalate within populations of drug users, and hence, arrestees and inmates. This will place even greater pressures on all components of the criminal justice system than those that already exist. These pressures will not only involve the management problems associated with the handling of persons with communicable diseases, but significant health care costs as well. And beyond these, there are other difficulties with which the criminal justice system is already being confronted. Litigation is being brought by AIDS-infected inmates and arrestees alleging deprivations of basic constitutional rights involving violations of the Eighth Amendment ban against "cruel and unusual punishment," and the Fourteenth Amendment's "equal protection" and "due process" clauses (Moriarity, 1987). Litigation alleging inadequate medical treatment for inmates with AIDS is also emerging as the focus of lawsuits, as has the communicability of AIDS and HIV and the adherence to standards applied generally to communicable diseases. No doubt, too, that as more inmates are diagnosed with HIV and AIDS during the 1990s, correctional administrators and state and federal correctional agencies will be targeted with allegations of failing to protect inmates from contracting AIDS.

NOTES

[1]   By early 1982 the disease was known by a variety of names and acronyms. The most popular of these was GRID, for Gay-Related Immune Deficiency. But staff members at the Centers for Disease Control despised the GRID acronym and refused to use it, particularly since they were well aware that the disease was not restricted to homosexuals. When someone finally suggested the sexually neutral yet snappy acronym "AIDS" during the middle of 1982, it immediately replaced all others (Shilts, 1987:171).

[2]   There is some evidence of the existence of AIDS in the "pre-AIDS era" in the United States (Garry et al., 1988; Biggar, Nasca & Burnett, 1988); Africa (Sher, Reid, & Falcke, 1987); Canada (Rogan et al., 1987; Huminer, Rosenfeld & Pitlik, 1987); and in Norway (Froland et al., 1988). Most observers agree, however, that the evidence presented in these cases remains preliminary. See also, Huminer and Pitlik (1988).

3   For a discussion of the early history of AIDS, see Fettner (1987), Institute of Medicine (1986a).

4   DNA is the carrier of genetic information for all organisms, except the RNA viruses. See Institute of Medicine (1986a: 62-63).

5   Reprints of the early epidemiological and clinical studies of AIDS and HIV have been collected in Cole and Lundberg (1986) and Relman (1987).

6   HIV manifests itself in a variety of conditions, which has complicated efforts to define AIDS. The Centers for Disease Control formulated an initial definition of AIDS in 1982 that relied on the presence of certain opportunistic infections and malignancies (Centers for Disease Control, 1982b). "Opportunistic infections" in this original case definition included pneumonia, meningitis, and encephalitis caused by nine different viruses, bacteria, fungi, and protozoa; esophagitis (inflammation of the esophagus) caused by candidiasis, cytomegalovirus, or herpes simplex; progressive brain disease with multiple lesions; chronic inflammation of the intestine caused by certain protozoan parasites (lasting more than four weeks); and unusually persistent herpes simplex infections of the mouth or rectum (lasting more than five weeks).

7   The current standard for antibody testing for HIV requires both the ELISA test, which is a sensitive screening test, and a confirmatory Western Blot analysis. Without repeating the ELISA itself and the confirmatory Western Blot, the likelihood of false-positives rises considerably, particularly in large-scale screenings of low-risk populations.

8   For a long time, AIDS researchers believed that people exposed to HIV developed antibodies within six months of infection. In June, 1989, however, researchers from the UCLA Medical Center reported that one-fourth of a group of 133 homosexual men who engaged in high-risk sexual behavior were infected, but the long periods did not produce HIV antibodies, thus causing some uncertainties about the test.

9   Prior to gaining their independence in the early 1960s, Zaire and Burundi were part of the Belgian Congo, and those citizens with financial means still travel to Belgium for their major medical care.

10   The apparent cases of AIDS in the "pre-AIDS era" cited earlier in Note "4" suggest that HIV may have entered several communities before the

current epidemic.   In each case, however, the virus failed to gain a foothold in a large, sexually-active or needle-sharing population. When each lone carrier died, the chain of infection was broken.

[11]   See Essex and Kanki (1989); New York Times, November 21, 1985:A1; Institute of Medicine (1986a:72).

[12]   As of January 31, 1989, a total of 139,886 diagnosed cases of AIDS had been reported to the World Health Organization. Of these, 60.4 percent of the cases were in the United States, and 83.4 percent could be found in only ten countries, ranked as follows: United States, France, Uganda, Brazil, Tanzania, Italy, Federal Republic of Germany, Kenya, Malawi, and Spain. See Current AIDS Literature, 2 (March, 1989):110-111.

[13]   Personal communication, February 7, 1989.

[14]   The two most complete collections of studies on IV drug use and AIDS are Galea, Lewis, and Baker (1988), and Battjes and Pickens (1988).

REFERENCES

Altman, D. (1987). *AIDS in the Mind of America: The Social, Political, and Psychological Impact of a New Epidemic*. Garden City, NY: Doubleday.

Auerbach, D.M., W.W. Darrow, H.W. Jaffe & J.W. Curran (1984). "Cluster of Cases of Acquired Immune Deficiency Syndrome: Patients Linked by Sexual Contact." *American Journal of Medicine*, 76 (March):487-492.

Battjes, R.J. & R.W. Pickens (eds.) (1988). *Needle Sharing Among Intravenous Drug Abusers: National and International Perspectives*. Rockville, MD: National Institute on Drug Abuse.

Biggar, R.J., P.C. Nasca & W.S. Burnett (1988).   "AIDS-Related Kaposi's Sarcoma in New York City in 1977." *New England Journal of Medicine*, 318 (January 28):252.

Black, D. (1986). *The Plague Years: A Chronicle of AIDS, the Epidemic of Our Times*. New York: Simon & Schuster.

Bowen, O.R. (1988). "In Pursuit of the Number One Public Health Problem." *Public Health Reports*, 103 (May-June):211-212.

Castro, K.G., S. Lieb, H.W. Jaffe, J.P. Narkunas, C. Calisher, T. Bush & J.J. Witte (1988). "Transmission of HIV in Belle Glade, Florida: Lessons for Other Communities in the United States." *Science*, 239 (January 8):193-197.

Centers for Disease Control (1981a). "Pneumocystis Pneumonia-Los Angeles." *Morbidity and Mortality Weekly Report*, 30 (June 5):250-252.

_____ (1981b). "Kaposi's Sarcoma and Pneumocystis Pneumonia Among Homosexual Men -- New York City and California." *Morbidity and Mortality Weekly Report*, 30 (July 3):305-308.

_____ (1982a). "Epidemiologic Aspects of the Current Outbreak of Kaposi's Sarcoma and Opportunistic Infections." *New England Journal of Medicine*, 306 (January 28):248-252.

_____ (1982b). *Morbidity and Mortality Weekly Report*, 31 (September 24):507-514.

_____ (1987a). *AIDS Weekly Surveillance Report*, October 17.

_____ (1987b). "Human Immunodeficiency Virus Infection in the United States: A Review of Current Knowledge." *Morbidity and Mortality Weekly Report*, 36 Supplement (December 18).

_____ (1988). *AIDS Weekly Surveillance Report*, February 22.

_____ (1989). *HIV/AIDS Surveillance Report*, September 1989.

Chaisson, R.E., A.R. Moss, R. Onishi, D. Osmond & J.R. Carlson (1987). "Human Immunodeficiency Virus Infection in Heterosexual Intravenous Drug Users in San Francisco." *American Journal of Public Health*, 77 (February):169-172.

Cole, H.M. & G.D. Lundberg (1986). *AIDS: From the Beginning*. Chicago: American Medical Association.

Davis, K.C., C.R. Horsburgh, U. Hasiba, A.L. Schocket & C.H. Kirkpatrick (1983). "Acquired Immunodeficiency Syndrome in a Patient with Hemophilia." *Annals of Internal Medicine*, 98 (3):284-286.

Des Jarlais, D.C., S.R. Friedman & W. Hopkins (1985). "Risk Reduction for the Acquired Immunodeficiency Syndrome Among Intravenous Drug Abusers." *Annals of Internal Medicine*, 103 (November):755-759.

_____ E. Wish, S.R. Friedman, R. Stoneburner, S.R. Yancovitz, D. Mildvan, W. El-Sadr, E. Brady & M. Cuadrado (1987). "Intravenous Drug Use and the Heterosexual Transmission of the Human Immunodefiency Virus: Current Trends in New York City." *New York State Journal of Medicine*, 87 (May):283-286.

Devita, V.T., S. Hellman & S.A. Rosenberg (1985). *AIDS: Etiology, Diagnosis, Treatment, and Prevention*. Philadelphia: J.B. Lippincott.

Essex, M. & P.J. Kanki (1989). "The Origins of the AIDS Virus." In J. Piel (ed.) *The Science of AIDS*, 27-37. New York: W.H. Freeman and Co.

Fettner, A.G. (1987). "The Discovery of AIDS: Perspectives from a Medical Journalist." In G.P. Wormser, R.E. Stahl & E.J. Bottone (eds.) *AIDS and Other Manifestations of HIV Infection*, 2-17. Park Ridge, NJ: Noyes Publications.

Froland, S.S., P. Jenum, C.F. Lindboe, K.W. Wefring, P.J. Linnestad & T. Bohmer (1988). "HIV-1 Infection in Norwegian Family Before 1970." *Lancet*, (June 11):1344-1345.

Galea, R.P., B.F. Lewis & L.A. Baker (eds.) (1988). *AIDS and IV Drug Abusers: Current Perspectives*. Owings Mills, MD: National Health Publishing Co.

Garry, R.F., M.H. Witte, A. Gottlieb, M. Elvin-Lewis, M.S. Gottlieb, C.L. Witte, S.S. Alexander, W.R. Cole & W.L. Drake (1988). "Documentation of an AIDS Virus Infection in the United States in 1968." *Journal of the American Medical Association*, 260 (October 14):2085-2087.

Geelhoed, G.W. (1984). "The Addict's Angioaccess: Complications of Exotic Vascular Injection Sites." *New York State Journal of Medicine*, 84 (December):585-586.

Ginzburg, H.M. (1984). "Acquired Immune Deficiency Syndrome (AIDS) and Drug Abuse." *Public Health Reports*, 99:206-212.

Goldstein, P.J. (1981). *Prostitution and Drugs*. Lexington, MA: Lexington Books.

Gottlieb, M.S., R. Schroff, H.M. Schanker, J.D. Weisman, P.T. Fan, R.A.Wolf & A. Saxon (1981). "Pneumocystis Carinii Pneumonia and Mucosal Candidiasis in Previously Healthy Homosexual Men: Evidence of a New Acquired Cellular Immunodeficiency." *New England Journal of Medicine*, 305 (December 10):1425-1431.

Hammett, T.M. (1987). *AIDS and the Law Enforcement Officer: Concerns and Policy Responses*. Washington, DC: National Institute of Justice.

_____ (1988). *AIDS in Correctional Facilities: Issues and Options*, Third Edition. Washington, DC: National Institute of Justice.

Huminer, D. & S.D. Pitlik (1988). "Further Evidence for the Existence of AIDS in the Pre-AIDS Era." *Reviews of Infectious Diseases*, 10 (September-October):1061.

Huminer, D., J.B. Rosenfield & S.D. Pitlik (1987). "AIDS in the Pre-AIDS Era." *Reviews of Infectious Diseases*, 9:1102-1108.

Inciardi, J.A. (1986). *The War on Drugs: Heroin, Cocaine, Crime, and Public Policy*. Palo Alto, CA: Mayfield Publishing Co.

Institute of Medicine, National Academy of Sciences (1986a). *Mobilizing Against AIDS: The Unfinished Story of a Virus*. Cambridge: Harvard University Press.

_____ (1986b). *Confronting AIDS: Directions for Public Health, Health Care, and Research*. Washington, DC: National Academy Press.

_____ (1989). *Mobilizing Against AIDS*. Cambridge: Harvard University Press.

James, J. (1976). "Prostitution and Addiction." *Addictive Diseases: An International Journal*, 2:601-618.

Koop, C.E. (1986). Surgeon General's Report on Acquired Immune Deficiency Syndrome. Washington, DC: Department of Health and Human Services.

Maayan, S., G.P. Wormer & D. Hewlett (1985). "Acquired Immunodeficiency Syndrome (AIDS) in an Economically Disadvantaged Population." *Archives of Internal Medicine*, 45, 1607-1612.

Mann, J.M., J. Chin, P. Piot & T. Quinn (1989). "The International Epidemiology of AIDS." In J. Piel (ed.) *The Science of AIDS*, 51-61. New York: W.H. Freeman and Co.

Marmor, M., D.C. Des Jarlais, H. Cohen, S.R. Friedman, S.T. Beatrice, N. Dubin, W. El-Sadr, D. Mildvan, S. Yancovitz, U. Mathur & R. Holtzman (1987). "Risk Factors for Infection with Human Immunodeficiency Virus Among Intravenous Drug Users in New York City." *AIDS*, 1 (May):1607-1612.

Masur, H., M.A. Michelis, J.B. Greene, I. Onorato, R.A. Vande Stouwe, R.T. Holzman, G. Wormser, L. Brettmen, M. Lange, H.W. Murray & S. Cunningham-Rundles (1981). "An Outbreak of Community-Acquired Pneumocystis Carinii Pneumonia: Initial Manifestation of Cellular Immune Dysfunction." *New England Journal of Medicine*, 305 (December 10):1431-1438.

Moriarity, L.J. (1987). "AIDS in Correctional Institutions: The Legal Aspects." *Criminal Law Bulletin*, 23 (November-December):533-459.

National Institute of Justice (1989). Drug Use Forecasting (DUF), Third Quarter, 1988.

Newmeyer, J.A. (1987). "Role of the IV Drug User and the Secondary Spread of AIDS." *Street Pharmacologist*, 11 (November):1-2.

Pace, B.W., W. Doscher & I.B. Margolis (1984). "The Femoral Triangle: The Potential Death Trap for the Drug User." *New York State Journal of Medicine*, 84 (December):596-598.

Quinn, T.C., D. Glasser, R. Cannon, D.I. Matuszak, R.W. Dunning, R.L. Kline, C. Campbell, E. Israel, A Fauci & E.W. Hook (1988). "Human Immunodeficiency Virus Infection Among Patients Attending Clinics for

Sexually Transmitted Diseases." *New England Journal of Medicine*, 318 (January 28):197-203.

Relman, A.S. (1987). *AIDS: Epidemiological and Clinical Studies*. Waltham, MA: Massachusetts Medical Society.

Rogan, E., L.D. Jewell, B.W. Meilke, D. Kunimoto, A. Voth & D.L. Tyrrell (1987). "A Case of Acquired Immune Deficiency Syndrome Before 1980." *Canadian Medical Association Journal*, 137 (October 1):637-638.

Rosenbaum, M. (1981). *Women on Heroin*. Brunswick, NJ: Rutgers University Press.

Sher, M.B., B. Reid & H. Falcke (1987). "Seroepidemiology of Human Immunodeficiency Virus in Africa from 1970 to 1974." *New England Journal of Medicine*, 317 (August 13):450-451.

Shilts, R. (1987). *And the Band Played On: Politics, People, and the AIDS Epidemic*. New York: St. Martin's Press.

Siegal, F.P. & M. Siegal (1983). *AIDS: The Medical Mystery*. New York: Grove Press.

Seligman, P.J., R.J. Campbell, G.P. Keeler & T.J. Halpin (1987). *Human Immunodeficiency Virus Seropositivity in Intravenous Drug Users in Ohio*. Columbus: AIDS Activity Unit, Ohio Department of Health.

Selwyn, P.A., C. Feiner, C.P. Cox, C. Lipshutz & R.L. Cohen (1987). "Knowledge About AIDS and High-Risk Behavior Among Intravenous Drug Users in New York City." *AIDS*, 1:247-254.

Sontag, S. (1988). *AIDS and Its Metaphors*. New York: Farrar, Straus and Giroux.

Young, A.W. (1973). "Skin Complications of Heroin Addiction: Bullous Impetigo." *New York State Journal of Medicine*, 73 (June 15):1681-1684.

13

Legal Issues in Drug Testing Offenders and Criminal Justice Employees[*]

Jonathan R. Sorensen
Sam Houston State University

Rolando V. del Carmen
Sam Houston State University

INTRODUCTION

Drug testing has become common in the last few years in both the private and public sectors. This may be attributed to two factors:

(1) a growing awareness that drug abuse is a serious and widespread social problem; and
(2) advances in technology that allow tests to be done quickly, inexpensively, and accurately (Collins, 1986).

In the criminal justice system, a third factor has encouraged the use of drug testing -- the drug-crime link discovered in recent years (Inciardi, 1980).

[*] An earlier and limited version of this chapter appeared as an article titled, "Legal Issues in Drug Testing Probationers and Parolees," *Federal Probation*, December, 1988, pp. 19-27. Portions of this article also appear in a pamphlet titled, "Legal Issues in Drug Testing Probation and Parole Clients and Employees," published by the National Institute of Corrections, January, 1989.

The RAND Corporation's Survey of Jail and Prison Inmates, and subsequent writings on the career criminal and selective incapacitation, have received the most widespread publicity (Chaiken & Chaiken, 1982; Greenwood, 1982). These studies support the long-held assumption that career criminals are heavily involved in drug use. A disadvantage of urinalysis is that the procedure does not show *when* the drug was used. Whether the person was under the influence of drugs while working, or whether the person used drugs at some other time, cannot be determined through urinalysis.

Urinalysis has been popular primarily because it is the form of testing that manufacturing firms have developed and made available commercially. One author has identified the six major types of testing methods (Zeese, 1988:2-7). These tests are: *immunoassay tests, thin-layer chromatography (TLC), color* or *spot tests, gas chromatography (GC), high performance liquid chromatography (HPLC)*, and *mass spectrometry tests (MS)*. None of these tests in and of themselves are sufficient proof of drug use, but instead should be used in a screening/confirmation test format. Though some of the tests are used for both purposes, the first three are normally utilized as screening tests and the last three as confirmatory tests.

Screening Tests

Of the three forms of screening tests, immunoassay tests are the most widely used. Immunoassay tests measure the presence or absence of drugs when antibodies added to the urine form complexes with the drugs or their metabolites, which act as antigens. There are three types of immunoassay tests: *radio immunoassay tests (RIA), Flourescein polarization immunoassay tests (FPIA)*, and *enzyme immunoassay tests*.

The most widely used RIA is the Abuscreen, produced by Roche Diagnostic Systems of Belleville, New Jersey, and used by the armed forces. RIA measures the free or bound radioactivity after urine and radioactively-labeled drugs are mixed with antibodies. The measurement indicates the presence of drugs because both sets of drugs, those in the urine and those radioactively labeled, compete for binding sites on the antibody, and hence can be measured by the amount of radioactivity present after an incubation period.

The FPIA test has been used in drug testing by Abbott Laboratories in its Toxicology/Abused Drug Assays. This method employs fluorescent tracers that compete with drugs in the urine to bind with antibodies. The presence of drugs is measured by the polarization of light that occurs when the tracer is unable to locate binding sites.

Of the two popular forms of enzyme immunoassay tests, one -- EZ-Screen -- tests only for the presence of cannabis. It is a very simple test utilizing a card that turns color when drops of urine are added. This test is produced by the Environmental Diagnostics of Burlington, N.C., and costs about $7. The test most commonly used in the criminal justice system is one that measures the enzyme activity of the complexes (enzyme multiplied immunoassay technique -- EMIT) (Wish, 1988).

In EMIT, enzyme-labeled drugs are injected into the urine along with antibodies. Presence of drugs is measured by the binding of enzymes, which compete with the drugs in the urine for binding sites. If drugs are present, the antibodies bind with them. The reaction is recorded by a photometer (*Higgs v. Wilson*, 1985). The test merely notes the presence of various drugs and does not directly measure the amount of drugs present in the urine.

Created by the Syva Company of Palo Alto, CA, the EMIT test is easy to administer and is inexpensive. A small laboratory can be set up within the agency to test the urine samples at a cost of $3,500 (*Higgs v. Wilson*, 1985), or the samples may be sent to a larger laboratory to be tested at a cost of $5 per test (Wish, 1988). The inexpensiveness of these tests leads most criminal justice agencies to use them, either singly or in two separate tests, as screening and confirmatory tests, although experts and the makers of EMIT suggest confirmation of EMIT tests through other means.

The final two forms of drug-screening tests are the thin-layer chromatography (TLC), and the color or spot tests. TLC is a procedure whereby different molecular structures are separated and can then be identified on the basis of the distance the substance travels through a membrane in comparison to a solvent, *the Rfvalue*. The Rfvalue, color, and appearance after various applications, make the identification of many types of drugs possible; however, the accuracy of the technique depends, to a large extent, on the ability of the technician. It is a subjective method that should never be used without confirmation.

The color or spot tests use a strip of paper that turns color (after drops of urine are added) if drugs are present. These tests do not indicate which type of drug is present and there are substantial problems with cross reactions, making these forms of tests virtually useless.

Confirmation Tests

A form of confirmation test that is an outgrowth of TLC is gas chromatography (GC). GC is similar to TLC in that it functions by separating components from the mixture. GC separates the substances while they are in gaseous form swept through a column, and the measurement consists of how far up the column the components travel. However, GC should not be relied upon in a qualitative analysis to identify the substances, since many substances may travel the same distance.

High performance liquid chromatography (HPLC) is an outgrowth of GC, but measures the distances which separated liquids, instead of gases as in GC, flow. Its disadvantages are similar to those of GC.

The final form of confirmation test and the only acceptable method, according to a number of experts, is Mass Spectrometry (MS). It is used in conjunction with GC, in which GC separates the mixture into components so that MS can identify them. GC/MS operates by separating and fragmenting substances and then recording the responses of this fragmentation. The recording of peaks upon which the substances lose their ionization charge identifies them. Though the method has up to a 99 percent accuracy rate, a skilled technician must be used in identifying the peaks, or erroneous conclusions can be much more common. The elaborate procedures used in GC/MS cost $70 to $100 per test (Wish, 1988).

TESTING OFFENDERS

There are three main classes of offenders subjected to drug tests: *arrestees/pre-trial releasees*, *inmates*, and *probationers/parolees*. Though each group of offenders has a unique legal status, many of the issues involved in drug testing are shared by these groups. Other issues are unique to the various groups of offenders. A discussion of constitutional issues involved in drug testing offenders is next, followed by a discussion of other legal issues involved in testing.

Constitutional Issues

For the purposes of this chapter, within each category of constitutional rights, those that are common or unique to the three main classes of offenders are discussed in the following order: arrestees and pre-trial releasees, inmates, and probationers and parolees. Challenges to the collection and analysis of urine have involved five basic constitutional rights: the right against *unreasonable search and seizure*, the right to *due process*, the right to *confrontation and cross-examination*, the right to *equal protection*, and the right against *self-incrimination*.

The Right Against Unreasonable Search and Seizure

The Fourth Amendment protects persons from unreasonable searches and seizures. Searches can be made with a warrant based on probable cause or without a warrant in a number of instances. Persons have certain expectations of privacy and, as long as these expectations are reasonable, they can only be violated when the governmental interest in searching outweighs the individual's expectation of privacy. A body search is the most intrusive violation of personal privacy and as such requires the greatest protection against governmental intrusion.

The first issue in drug cases is whether the collection of urine is indeed a search and seizure, hence enjoying Fourth Amendment protection. Cases involving offenders have generally assumed that the collection of urine is a search and seizure. An example is *Macias v. State* (1983), in which the Texas Court of Appeals ruled that it had no doubt that the taking of urine from a probationer was a search. The court relied on *Schmerber v. California* (1966) and Texas cases allowing the taking of blood samples in concluding that the taking of urine was constitutional. The court in *Macias* wrote:

> The taking of a urine sample is analogous to the taking of a blood sample. Each involves an extraction from a human body. It has been held that the taking of blood constitutes a search and seizure under federal and state constitutional law. (1983:151-152)

Once it is determined that urinalysis constitutes a search and seizure, and is protected by the Fourth Amendment, the next question becomes: absent probable cause and a search warrant, is the search reasonable? In order to determine whether a search of this type is reasonable, the type of offender being examined must be considered separately. There is a need to look separately at arrestees and pre-trial releasees, detainees and inmates, and probationers and parolees.

Pre-trial Drug Testing

This type of testing has greatly expanded in recent years as a result of pilot projects funded by the National Institute of Justice in Washington, D.C. and New York City. In order to be considered reasonable, the governmental interest in the search must outweigh the intrusion into individual privacy. In the Washington, D.C. program, urination is observed by a staff member to avoid the possibility of tampering, a very intrusive procedure (Carver, 1986). The governmental interest in obtaining this information derives from the correlation between drug use and crime and is grounded on the protection of society. Proponents of pre-trial testing claim that the issue of intrusiveness is weak because arrestees voluntarily agreed to the searches and have therefore relinquished their Fourth Amendment rights (Carver, 1986). Opponents counter that the argument is suspect because offenders know that failure to submit to urine testing will likely result in confinement. The voluntariness of the waiver becomes an issue.

While case law is scarce, one circuit court opinion has pointed to the legal issues involved in drug testing prior to trial (*Berry v. District of Columbia*, 1987). In *Berry*, challenges that the District of Columbia's drug-testing program violated Fourth, Fifth, and Eighth Amendment rights were summarily dismissed by the District Court as being "far-fetched" and not presenting issues of "constitutional dimension."

On appeal, the Circuit Court was asked to consider whether the District's drug testing of all arrested persons -- pre-arraignment testing, and pretrial releasees -- was unconstitutional. The Circuit Court did not express an opinion on the issue of pre-arraignment testing, as no evidence was presented that the appellant had been tested prior to arraignment; the court also lacked a factual record necessary to determine the constitutionality of drug testing as a condition of pre-trial release. The court disagreed, however, with the District Court's finding that the challenge to the drug-testing program did not raise issues of constitutional dimension. The Circuit Court reversed and remanded the case for a full hearing on the constitutional issues involved. The Circuit Court did suggest that in order for the District to prove that its program does not infringe on constitutional rights, it must show the governmental interest in testing to be substantial, that there is in fact a positive correlation between pretrial drug use and criminality or failure to appear for scheduled court dates. Absent individualized suspicion, it must be shown, for the government's case to prevail, that the privacy interests implicated in the search are minimal, at least in comparison to the governmental interest in searching. Also, the search must be "reasonably related in scope to the circumstances which justified the interference in the first place," meaning it must be "no more degrading than is reasonably necessary."

Testing Jail and Prison Inmates

The reasonableness of a search of jail or prison inmates was discussed by the U.S. Supreme Court in *Bell v. Wolfish* (1979). The analysis involves "(b)alancing the significant and legitimate security interests of the institution against the privacy of the inmates..." In this case, the Court allowed body cavity searches to be conducted without probable cause or reasonable suspicion in jail because of the threat posed to institutional security by contraband. In *Hudson v. Palmer* (1984), the Court said that the Fourth Amendment right against unreasonable searches and seizures affords an inmate absolutely no protection for searches and seizures in his cell. Relying on these cases, a U.S. District Court upheld random urinalysis of prisoners in *Pella v. Adams* (1986). The U.S. Court of Appeals for the Eighth Circuit concluded that the narcotics problem that plagues prisons' security outweighs the prisoners' limited expectation of privacy in random urine collection and analysis (*Spence v. Farrier*, 1986). The court, however, emphasized the necessity of keeping the procedure totally random to prevent the harassment of specific inmates.

Testing Probationers and Parolees

In general, a search of a probationer or parolee "must be reasonable and based on the probation officer's reasonable belief that it is necessary to the performance of her duties," (*United States v. Duff*, 1987). Consistent with this standard, the court in *United States v. Duff* ruled that submitting to urinalysis was the least intrusive way of determining if *Duff* had refrained from drug use. The court in *Duff* did not decide the issue of whether drug testing was a search, but assumed it was a search based on prior decisions.

In *United States v. Williams* (1986), the U.S. Circuit Court of Appeals also refrained from deciding whether or not the taking of urine was a search. The court wrote:

> Assuming, without deciding, (citing 19 cases, but not all directly apply to the taking of urine) that the taking of a urine sample entails a search or seizure, we hold that the condition imposed here is reasonable and, accordingly, passes muster under the Fourth Amendment. (1986:1135)

The state appellate courts of Texas and Georgia have also upheld the taking of urine from probationers as not being a violation of the Fourth Amendment protection against unreasonable searches and seizures (*Clay v. State*, 1986; *Howard v. State*, 1983).

Drug testing, which necessarily involves the collection and analysis of urine, is a form of justified search and seizure under the Fourth Amendment. An unclear picture emerges in testing offenders who have yet to be convicted, case law being scarce. Testing inmates, probationers and parolees is a reasonable search, therefore neither probable cause nor reasonable suspicion is necessary to conduct drug tests. While random and mass testing of prisoners would most likely be constitutional because they hardly enjoy any rights under the Fourth Amendment, imposing drug testing as a condition of probation is best done on an individual basis, using as justification the fact that drug testing is reasonably related to the rehabilitation of the individual and/or the protection of society.

The Right to Due Process

A closely related claim by offenders concerns their right to due process of law protected by the Fifth and Fourteenth Amendments. These rights are often invoked when questioning procedures employed in testing; therefore, the challenge focuses on procedural rather than on substantive due process rights. These challenges involve test accuracy and chain of custody.

Test Accuracy

As mentioned earlier, EMIT tests are not very accurate when used alone. Experts recommend the use of another type of test to confirm initial positive findings. The costs of many of these confirmation procedures are prohibitive for criminal justice agencies; therefore, even when giving confirmatory tests, agencies often simply utilize a second EMIT (Wish, 1988). A major concern in drug testing is whether it meets acceptable scientific standards for use in court. The *Frye* doctrine in legal proceedings states that, before the results of scientific tests can be admissible as evidence in a trial, the procedures used must be sufficiently established to have gained general acceptance in the particular discipline to which the tests belong (*Frye v. United States*, 1923). The question, therefore, is whether drug tests have gained a sufficient level of acceptance in the scientific community, as determined by the courts, to be admissible as evidence in a legal proceeding.

It is axiomatic that complete accuracy is hardly attainable in a lot of scientific tests. In cases involving offenders, courts usually do not insist on the same quantum of evidence needed in trials. In a recent case, for example, the U.S. Supreme Court said that due process in prison disciplinary proceedings is not violated if "some evidence" on the record supports the decision (*Superintendent v. Hill*, 1985). In probation and parole cases, the standard of proof in revocation proceedings is not governed by the Constitution, but by state law or by court decisions. Most state courts adhere to a standard lower than probable cause, some courts validating revocations based on "slight evidence" (*Dickerson v. State*, 1975).

In cases where the proof of reliability of the testing procedure has not been established in the record, courts may not choose to accept test findings which are not confirmed by alternative methods or testing procedures. In a recent case challenging the reliability of EMIT tests in a prison disciplinary proceeding, the New York Supreme Court held that nothing in the record of the case established the reliability of the test, and that the test did not meet the requirements of the *Frye* doctrine (*Lahey v. Kelly*, 1986). Said the Court:

> The record before us is completely barren of scientific evidence which would establish the reliability of the test. Given this state of the record and the conflicting views on the matter, we cannot say the EMIT test results are generally accepted as reliable in the scientific community...The party offering the evidence bears the bur-

den of establishing its admissibility and, absent an adequate basis for the reliability of the test itself, mere evidence of the test is insufficient evidence to sustain a finding of misbehavior. (1986:188)

Prison Cases

Most federal courts deciding prison disciplinary cases have determined that EMIT testing is sufficiently reliable to meet the standard of "some evidence" required by the U.S. Supreme Court in *Superintendent v. Hill* (1985), citing studies that show the accuracy rate of EMIT tests to be about 95 percent when human error is not involved. The U.S. Court of Appeals for the Eighth Circuit, in *Spence v. Farrier* (1986), considered whether EMIT test results are admissible in disciplinary proceedings absent a showing that the test has been accepted by the scientific community. The court dismissed the claim as unmeritorious and stated that, "EMIT has been shown to be widely accepted."

Two recent federal district court cases help settle the issue of EMIT test reliability in prison disciplinary cases. In *Peranzo v. Coughlin* (1985) and *Higgs v. Wilson* (1985), the courts upheld the use of double EMIT tests in prison disciplinary hearings as affording adequate due process safeguards. Together with Spence v. Farrier, these cases appear to settle the confirmation issue (Collins, 1987:36). Double EMIT tests, rather than using TLC or GC/MS as confirmatory tests, are sufficient in prison disciplinary cases to meet the standard of "some evidence."

Probation and Parole Cases

In one of the earliest drug testing cases involving probationers, the court ruled that the EMIT could not be admitted in revocation proceedings (*Isaacks v. State*, 1983). The court stated that the test had not attained scientific acceptance and that the government witness did not understand the theory behind the test's performance. The court added that until the machine had been properly tested for reliability and accuracy, the results could not be admitted as evidence.

Despite the ruling in *Isaacks*, most state cases hold that EMIT results are admissible in revocation proceedings. In *Smith v. State* (1983), the court ruled that the trial court had not erred in allowing the EMIT test into evidence because of the expert testimony in the case attesting to its operation and accuracy. Since the trial court did not exceed its authority in deciding to admit, the admission of the test results into evidence was affirmed. In a second case, *Szili v. Carlson* (1985), a Florida court held that the evidence of probation violation using the EMIT test was admissible even if the test is only

80 percent accurate (Collins, 1986:70). In a third probation revocation case, the appellate court held that even though the EMIT test is not entirely accurate, it could be accepted as "reliable and probative evidence," (*State v. Johnson*, 1987). In this case, the defendant's pharmacological expert testified that the EMIT test had a 5 to 10 percent margin rate of error. The court held that a double EMIT test used as a screening and confirmatory test, though not conclusive, could be used if there is no showing by the defendant of unreasonable abuse of discretion by the probation officer.

It is evident from the above cases that EMIT results have been admissible in disciplinary and revocation proceedings despite the admitted lack of complete accuracy. The issue of whether a confirmation test is required has not been addressed decisively by the courts. In at least one case involving prisoners, and another case involving probationers, courts have upheld the use of single unconfirmed EMIT tests as being acceptable for disciplinary action and revocation (*In re Johnston*, 1987; *Smith v. State*, 1983). Most courts that have considered the reliability of unconfirmed tests have held that a positive result alone is insufficient to prove drug use (Zeese, 1988:8-7).

Recent developments in drug testing may soon render this issue less controversial, if not academic. A new study, conducted in January 1989, of 31 laboratories following the guidelines set by the American Association of Clinical Chemistry, has shown an accuracy rate of 97 percent in testing urine samples for narcotics. In the words of one expert, "After today, inaccuracies should not be used as an argument against drug testing." (*Houston Chronicle*, January 11, 1989, p. 4A.)

Chain of Custody

This challenge asserts that test results are invalid because of faulty custodial procedures in the handling of samples. In a case challenging the custodial procedures employed in a correctional institution in which the plaintiff claimed that someone had tampered with the sample, the court ruled against the plaintiff, even though no written record existed, because all of who had had access to the sample testified at trial that the sample had not been out of their sight from collection to analysis (*Wykoff v. Resig*, 1986). The court, however, did suggest that court time could be saved if better chain of custody procedures were followed. The court suggested:

> The Indiana DOC should seal urine samples in the presence of the inmate donor, keep a written record on the location and transportation of the urine samples at all times, and while the samples are still in the possession of the DOC, it should store the urine samples in locked refrigerators with very limited access. Further-

more, the minimum due process requirements defined in *Wolff v. McDonnell* requires that inmates receive a duplicate copy of the EMIT test results from the laboratory which conducted the test. (1986:1514)

In a probation case, a state court overturned a revocation because the physical evidence was no longer available (*People v. Moore*, 1983). In this case, the County preserved positive samples for 90 days, or longer if a request was made in a particular sample. The government failed, however, to show that such requests were routinely made and honored. The court ruled that the government must employ "rigorous and systematic" procedures to preserve the evidence, and that the government had failed to meet this standard. In the absence of a request by the defendant to retain the samples, the court ruled that it is the affirmative duty of the state to preserve the evidence.

The question of whether a sample has been properly maintained and is not mixed up with another's sample or tampered with in any way was addressed in *Stahl v. Commonwealth* (1987). In this parole revocation case, the appellant questioned the reliability of the laboratory tests because of the custodial procedures employed. An officer labeled the samples and placed them in a refrigerator they were mailed to the laboratory. The court ruled this procedure to be proper.

The Right to Confrontation and Cross-Examination

The Fifth Amendment right to confrontation and cross-examination protects persons from the hazards of hearsay evidence. Defendants should be convicted only when they have had a chance to confront and question their accusers. Prison disciplinary proceedings and probation revocation, however, are not trials, and consequently, these offenders are not entitled to the full panoply of constitutional rights guaranteed to presumably innocent defendants.

Prison Cases

In prison disciplinary proceedings, an inmate's right to call witnesses and present evidence is limited to situations when "permitting them to do so will not be unduly hazardous to institutional safety and correctional goals." (*Wolff v. McDonnell*, 1974) A recent case challenged the use of EMIT in disciplinary hearings as creating an irrebuttable presumption of guilt (*Spence v. Farrier*, 1986). The court ruled that such is not the case because inmates may challenge the accuracy of test results or rebut proof of urinalysis, but under

Wolff they have no right to independent confirmation tests or to present expert testimony. Most importantly, disciplinary hearings are meant to be expeditious, and as such, inmates have no right to confrontation and cross-examination. Prisoners and detainees have diminished constitutional rights and whatever rights they have left may be curtailed if, in general, there is a rational relationship between legitimate prison objectives and a policy of curtailment. Although inmates do have a limited right to cross-examination and confrontation in prison disciplinary cases, such rights can be as easily overcome by demonstrable considerations of institutional security and offender rehabilitation.

Probation and Parole Cases

Standing alone, test results deprive probationers and parolees of the right to confrontation and cross-examination. It is hearsay if the person who comes up with the results cannot be in court for cross-examination. The admissibility of hearsay evidence in revocation proceedings has been stated by a Pennsylvania court in *Jefferson v. Commonwealth* (1986). The court wrote:

> It has long been settled that hearsay evidence is properly admissible
> in parole revocation proceedings subject to a finding of good cause
> to deny the parolee his due process right to confront and cross examine adverse witnesses. (1986:497)

In this case, the court ruled that the laboratory reports were reliable and, hence constituted an exception to the hearsay rule for purposes of revocation.

Subsequent cases have been decided in accord with *Jefferson*. One case upheld the admission of laboratory reports based on the business record exception to the hearsay rule which provides that official records kept by a prison or organization in the regular course of business are admissible in court despite their being hearsay. The court noted that if the reports contained indicia of reliability and regularity (such as letterhead and signature), they could be admitted as evidence (*Damron v. Commonwealth*, 1987). If the laboratory report is verified by independent means such as a confession, it is also admissible (*McQueen v. State*, 1987). However the trial court may not automatically accept laboratory reports absent a showing of good cause for a witness not being present for cross-examination (*Powell v. Commonwealth*, 1986; *Whitmore v. Commonwealth*, 1986).

Federal appellate courts have also upheld the use of laboratory reports in probation revocation procedures. In one case, a laboratory report was accompanied by a letter from the laboratory president and was characterized by the court as both "trustworthy and reliable" (*United States v. Penn*, 1984).

The reliability of the report was upheld by the court in *Penn* because such reports were regularly issued to doctors and hospitals who acted in accord with the findings. Additional reasons listed by the court for not reversing the appellant's probation revocation were: (1) there was corroborating evidence that the probationer had been using drugs, and (2) good cause asserted by the government for not allowing confrontation and cross-examination outweighed the appellant's right to confront and cross-examine the testers. In order to allow confrontation and cross-examination in this case, it would have been necessary to obtain the presence and testimony of 20 to 30 persons who performed the tests.

In *United States v. Bell* (1986), the court, though remanding the case for other reasons, upheld the *Penn* decision of the Eleventh Circuit Court of Appeals. Citing the balancing process between the rights of the probationer and the grounds asserted by the government in the *United States v. Penn*, the Eighth Circuit held that the laboratory reports were admissible. The court reasoned that the reports themselves "bore substantial indicia of reliability" and that the probationer presented no evidence to contradict his drug usage.

The above cases strongly indicate that the use of drug test results does not violate offender's right to confrontation and cross-examination even though the evidence may be hearsay. Inmates' right to confrontation and cross-examination is not violated if written drug test results are admitted into evidence. In probation and parole hearings, drug tests are admissible under the various exceptions to the hearsay rule. Such exceptions come under the category of business records, reliability, and trustworthiness.

The Right to Equal Protection

The Fourteenth Amendment right to equal protection basically means that people cannot be treated differently unless there is sufficient legal justification for the differential treatment. While originally used mainly to proscribe racial discrimination, the equal protection clause has been used by courts to apply to various types of discriminatory treatment outside racial context. Together with the Civil Rights Act of 1964, the equal protection clause has established protected categories of individuals who cannot be treated differently unless legal justification exists.

In the context of drug testing, inmates, probationers, and parolees might claim that those subjected to drug tests are treated differently from offenders who do not have to undergo such testing and that, therefore, their constitutional right to equal protection is violated. Or, it might be alleged that isolating drug users as the group to be tested, while not probing into other offender tendencies or handicaps, such as AIDS or VD carriers, is a form of impermissible discrimination.

The constitutional right to equal protection has not been invoked often in drug-testing cases, perhaps because it is generally recognized that the challenge is weak and stands little chance of being upheld. Equal protection has been used with great success by offenders in cases where money makes a difference in whether a person goes to prison. In *Bearden v. Georgia* (1983), for example, the court held that a judge cannot properly revoke a defendant's probation for failure to pay a fine and make restitution -- in the absence of evidence finding that the probationer was somehow responsible for the failure, or that alternative forms of punishment were not adequate to meet the state's interest in punishment and deterrence. In that case, the only reason probation would have been revoked was that the probationer was too poor to pay the fine and restitution imposed by the court. Such is not the case in drug testing. No monetary issue is involved in drug tests (unless the agency makes the offender pay for the test), and the differential treatment is not based on money, but on drug use. An inmate, probationer, or parolee is treated differently from the rest of the offender population because he or she is using drugs. This is not an impermissible categorization and should be allowable as long as there is a rational relationship between the measure taken and the objective sought to be accomplished. Drug testing (the measure taken) does not probe into and may prevent drug use (the objective sought to be accomplished), hence a rational relationship is easy to establish. While the equal protection clause sometimes demands the establishment of a compelling state interest or legitimate state need before a right can be violated, such is not the case in drug testing because neither a fundamental nor a highly protected right is violated.

The Right Against Self-Incrimination

The Fifth Amendment protects against self-incrimination. In probation, this right has been used in cases where an offender is required to answer a counselor's question, submit to a search by a probation counselor, or provide a juror or prosecutor with information. Whether or not the right against self-incrimination can be invoked generally depends upon the type of proceedings wherein the evidence is to be used. If the evidence is to be used in a criminal trial, the claim to exclude is upheld (del Carmen & Vaughn, 1986).

There is no denying that to require an offender to submit to drug testing is self-incriminatory, but this type of self-incrimination is not what the constitution prohibits. What is prohibited is not physical self-incrimination, but testimonial self-incrimination. Thus an accused can be compelled to appear in a line-up, give fingerprints, or furnish handwriting exemplars because these are forms of physical self-incrimination. Drug testing is a form of physical self-incrimination and, therefore, falls outside the purview of constitutional protection. While the results obtained may indicate drug use and, therefore, incriminate the user, the test itself does not require an offender to verbally admit or confess guilt, the type of self-incrimination prohibited by the Constitution.

Summary and Suggestions

Criminal justice agencies may require clients to submit their urine for drug testing without violating the constitutional rights of inmates and supervisees. As the above discussion indicates, no constitutional challenge to drug-testing offenders has prevailed. This is because convicted offenders enjoy diminished constitutional rights, and whatever constitutional rights remain are balanced against the rehabilitation of the individual and/or the protection of society. Random testing of offenders has been upheld by the courts and such programs may be implemented for incarcerated offenders and those supervised under probation or parole.

To reduce the likelihood of legal challenges, agencies should take precautions when testing for drugs. Based on decided cases, jurisdictions and agencies may want to consider the following suggestions when implementing a drug-testing program for offenders:

(1) Ascertain whether or not a confirmation test is required by courts in your jurisdiction -- some courts require confirmation of positive results; others do not. In case of doubt, and if the issue is unresolved in your jurisdiction, it is advisable to play it safe and confirm test results. Generally, a second EMIT test is acceptable.

(2) In using a new form of drug testing, one without a proven track record, it becomes necessary to either confirm the results by alternative methods or to systematically test the accuracy of the procedure by including known clean and spiked samples.

(3) Ensure that drug test operators are trained and properly qualified, regardless of whether the testing is done in-house or by an outside public or private laboratory.

(4) Employ rigorous chain of custody procedures, such as sealing the samples in tamper resistant bottles, immediately labeling and having the offenders sign the seals, and making sure that

the transfer of samples is properly documented. In essence, the chain of custody rule ensures that the sample given by the individual is the substance tested and that the findings introduced and admitted into evidence were the result of testing the correct sample.

(5) In probation and parole, save the samples until the revocation date so it is available to the defendant if he or she wishes to have the test results verified by an independent laboratory.

(6) Have a clearly written policy on the use of drug testing and the resulting consequences of positive findings.

(7) Impose drug testing as a condition of probation or parole only in cases where such condition is "reasonably related to the rehabilitation of the individual." This does not necessarily mean a conviction for a drug-related offense, but rather that a defendant's status and criminal record could most likely be attributable to drug use. This covers a multitude of offenses (many, if not most, offenses can reasonably be attributed to or are caused by drug distribution or use), but also exclude others that cannot be linked to drugs.

TESTING CRIMINAL JUSTICE EMPLOYEES

Drug testing has become widespread in public and private employment in the United States. One source indicates that, in 1987 alone, employers required 4.5 million Americans to submit to urine tests as part of their job requirement. The same source states that the military has conducted over one million urine tests each year since 1981 and that former President Reagan's executive order in 1986 could add 1.1 million federal workers to the pool of tested Americans (Zeese, 1988:1-5).

In criminal justice agencies, testing has become increasingly routine. A recent survey of 33 large police departments found that 73 percent conducted drug-screening tests of applicants and virtually all had written policies and procedures for drug testing officers suspected of using illegal drugs (McEwen, Manili & Connors, 1986). In prisons, a recent survey showed that 19 of 48 responding state prisons and the Federal Bureau of Prisons drug test employees or applicants, four states plan to begin testing, and 13 are discussing such plans (Guynes & Coffey, 1988). The extent of testing other criminal justice employees has yet to be determined, but there appears to be a trend toward increased testing of all criminal justice employees.

Cases involving drug testing of employees raises essentially the same constitutional issues as those challenging offender testing. The difference is the scope of the constitutional right involved and the state's justification for curtailing that right. Two of the rights most often invoked by employees are discussed here: the right against unreasonable search and seizure and the right to due process. Other constitutional rights that may be infringed are the right to equal protection and the right against self-incrimination. Although sometimes invoked, these rights are not discussed in this article because they are less controversial and have been largely settled by lower court decisions in favor of constitutionality.

Constitutional Issues:
The Right Against Unreasonable Search and Seizure

Most lower courts that have addressed the question have ruled that such testing constitutes search and seizure and, as such, is protected by the Fourth and Fourteenth Amendments (Zeese, 1988:5-4). Some courts have analogized drug testing to the taking of blood. In *Capua v. City of Plainfield* (1986), the court said:

> The "taking" of urine has been likened to the involuntary taking of blood which the Supreme Court found to constitute a search and seizure within the Fourth Amendment. . . Though urine, unlike blood, is routinely discharged from the body so that no actual intrusion is required for its collection, it is normally discharged and disposed of under circumstances that merit protection from arbitrary interference. (1986:1513)

In two recent U.S. Supreme Court decisions on drug testing, the Court concluded that urinalysis comes under the Fourth Amendment (*National Treasury Employee's Union v. Von Raab*, 1989; *Skinner v. Railway Labor Executives' Association*, 1989). In both cases, the Court said that "where the Government requires its employees to produce urine samples to be analyzed for evidence of illegal drug use, the collection and subsequent chemical analysis of such samples are searches that must meet the reasonableness requirement of the Fourth Amendment."

In order for a search to be valid under the Fourth Amendment, it must be "reasonable." Court determination of the reasonableness of a search, absent a warrant or probable cause, "requires a judicious balancing of the intrusiveness of the search against its promotion of a legitimate governmental interest." In order to determine if the search is reasonable in urine testing cases, courts often focus on whether the individual has a reasonable expectation of privacy and, if such exists, whether the government's interest in obtaining the sample outweighs the individual's privacy right.

Right to Privacy

Although a separate and well-established constitutional right, the right to privacy is often discussed in the context of search and seizure cases. This is because in marginal search and seizure cases, the crucial question is often whether a person has a reasonable expectation of privacy that the state has an obligation to respect. A recent report (Manili, 1987) has identified the privacy rights that public employees legitimately expect. One privacy interest an employee has is to be free from exposure while urinating. In *Capua v. City of Plainfield* (1986), cited above, the court stated that the act of urinating is "traditionally private" and that "urine collection forces those tested to expose parts of their anatomy to the testing official in a manner akin to strip search exposure." The experience, according to the judge, is likely to be "very embarrassing and humiliating." Another judge has said that "one's anatomy is draped with constitutional protections" (Zeese, 1988:5-7).

A second privacy interest concerns the urine itself and whether the individual has a reasonable expectation of privacy in his or her discharged bodily fluid. In *Capua*, the court stated that the major reason a person has a privacy interest in his urine is that "urinalysis forces plaintiffs to divulge private, personal medical information unrelated to the government's professed interest in discovering illegal drug abuse." The search could discover such disorders as epilepsy or diabetes, and legally prescribed drugs the person may be taking for emotional or physical conditions. And, as stated by the lower court in *National Treasury Employee's Union v. Von Raab* (1987), "unlike one's hair or handwriting, one's urine is not routinely exposed to the public gaze."

Government's Interest

In a recent article, Jerry Higginbotham (1986), of the FBI, listed seven interests police departments have in testing their employees. These are: *public safety, public trust, potential for corruption, presentation of credible testimony, morale and safety in the workplace, loss of production,* and *civil liability.* Most of these interests can be extended to the field of corrections. The main governmental interest in testing correctional officers, however, stems from the necessity of preventing contraband from entering the prison, the assumption being that drug-using employees are more likely to smuggle drugs to inmates.

In most instances where public officials are involved, the courts have ruled that the governmental interest outweighs the individual's privacy interest, hence public officials may be tested. When and how the courts may test, however, is a different question. Courts often note the lessened expectations of privacy to which a public official is entitled and the enormity of the governmental interest involved in drug testing. Often the courts find that public employees are not entitled to the same privacy as the average citizen because of their sensitive positions. As the court stated in *Turner v. Fraternal Order of Police*:

> The police force is a para-military organization dealing hourly with the general public in delicate and often dangerous situations. So we recognize that, as is expected and accepted in the military, police officers may, in certain situations, enjoy less constitutional protection than the ordinary citizen. (1985:1008)

In the only Circuit Court decision regarding drug testing of prison employees, *McDonell v. Hunter*, the court noted that:

> While correctional officers retain certain expectations of privacy, it is clear that, based upon their place of employment, their subjective expectations of privacy are diminished while they are within the confines of the prison. (1987:1306)

In *McDonell*, the court restated the two main governmental interests in keeping correctional officers drug free: (1) so that they are fully capable of performing their duties, and (2) so that contraband is not smuggled into the institution. The court, however, did recognize the intrusiveness of a strip search or observation of urination, and suggested that "less intrusive measures can be taken to insure the validity of the specimen."

The two recent U.S. Supreme Court decisions found a strong governmental interest involved in drug testing. In *Skinner v. Railway Labor Executives' Association* (1989), the interest in testing employees stemmed from the risk of injury that could be caused by train crews impaired by drugs. Moreover, studies had shown drug and alcohol abuse to be major problems in the railway industry, and many prior train accidents were connected to employee alcohol and drug use. In *National Treasury Employee's Union v. Von Raab* (1989), the Court concluded that the government's interest in testing those involved in the interdiction of drugs results from the necessity of having persons of unimpeachable integrity and judgment in these positions, who would take the mission of drug interdiction seriously and not be susceptible to bribery from drug dealers. Public safety compels that customs employees who carry firearms also be drug free.

In both cases, the Court also noted the lessened right to privacy that employees may legitimately expect. The railroads and law enforcement agencies have always been highly regulated. In both, what may have been viewed as unreasonable intrusions of privacy in other contexts were seen as reasonable given the "operational realities" of these workplaces.

Level of Proof Needed to Search

Normally, the Fourth Amendment requires a warrant for the search to be carried out. The issuance of a warrant necessarily entails probable cause to believe that the evidence will be found. In drug testing public employees, it is not necessary to meet the requirement of probable cause to search, although some courts have required this standard (*Jones v. McKenzie*, 1986). Most courts allow drug testing on the lesser standard of "reasonable suspicion". While these terms are difficult to define with precision, reasonable suspicion requires a degree of certainty that is lower than probable cause or reasonable grounds, but higher than mere suspicion. In general, scholarly writings have endorsed the standard of reasonable suspicion as sufficient for drug testing (Lawlor, 1987; Westphal, 1987).

The "reasonable suspicion" standard applies to employees already on the job. This is because these employees enjoy property interests in that they have much to lose if the test is positive. Court decisions have said, however, that reasonable suspicion is not required in the following instances:

(1) Testing job applicants, trainees and probationary officers -- this is because in these cases, employees have no property interests as yet in the job;

(2) Routine physicals -- no search occurs because the urine sample has already been given as part of the procedure.

In these cases random and mandatory testing are acceptable. Both of the recent U.S. Supreme Court decisions on drug testing involved mandatory drug testing. In the *Railway Labor Executives' Association* case, employees were tested automatically after serious train accidents, and could be tested, at the discretion of management, after various safety violations. In the *National Treasury Employee's Union* case, persons applying for jobs where they would be directly involved in drug interdiction, carrying firearms, or privy to "classified" material were automatically tested. In both cases, after balancing governmental interest with employees' legitimate privacy expectations, the

Court concluded that mandatory testing in the absence of a warrant, probable cause, or individualized suspicion was acceptable. In the *National Treasury Employee's Union* case, while the Court noted the necessity of testing those privy to sensitive information, it remanded the issue of mandatory testing in these instances, because the relationship between certain positions and the type of sensitive information accessed was not clearly stated by the Custom's Service.

Most courts prior to these decisions concluded that individualized suspicion was necessary and that random testing was unconstitutional (Zeese, 1988:5-8). For example, in *Capua* the court held that individualized suspicion was necessary to conduct urinalysis. The court stated that "the reasonable suspicion standard requires individualized suspicion, specifically directed to the person who is targeted for the search." (1986:1517) In all police cases where random and mass testing of incumbents have been challenged, police officers have won.

Federal Drug-Testing Program

In September, 1986, former President Reagan announced a mandatory drug-testing program for federal employees. The program allows for the testing of federal employees. The program allows for the testing of federal employees in "sensitive" positions without individualized suspicion. An attempt by the Federal Bureau of Prisons to begin testing in accordance with this executive order was blocked by a U.S. District Court judge in California. The judge stated:

> The program would force law-abiding employees of the Bureau...to submit to urinalysis even though not suspected of any drug use nor of any wrongdoing, negligence or dereliction of duty...There are cases in which compulsory drug testing may be justified in the interest of public safety or security or the like. Not this one. (*Houston Chronicle*, July 30, 1988:17)

In a more recent development, a federal judge in Washington, D.C., on July 29, 1988, issued a permanent injunction against the testing program of the U.S. Department of Justice, under which that agency would test 1,800 employees in sensitive law enforcement positions. This program also comes under former President Reagan's September 1986 announcement of mandatory drug testing for federal employees. Agreeing that compulsory random testing constitutes unreasonable search and seizure, the judge ruled that such testing cannot be justified because the department does not consider drug use to be widespread in the agency. The federal government had justified the test based on a critical interest in the security of sensitive and classified law enforcement information and the integrity and the public image of the department (*Houston Chronicle*, July 30, 1988:17). This decision, currently on appeal, implies that the sensitive nature of the position is not enough to justify mandatory random testing. It must also be established that the agency considers drug use in that agency to be widespread. In *McDonell v. Hunter* (1987), the Eighth Circuit upheld the use of systematic random drug tests, adding that prisons are "unique places fraught with serious security dangers." The court added that the "strong government interest" involved prevailed over the employees' expectation of privacy in medium and maximum security prisons where such employees had regular direct contact with inmates. The court recognized three justifications for random employee testing:

(1) to ensure that employees are not working under the influence of drugs or alcohol,
(2) to ensure that officers are alert at all times, and
(3) officers who use drugs are more likely to smuggle drugs into the institution.

The Right to Due Process

Due process basically means fundamental fairness. It has two aspects: procedural due process and substantive due process. While these two terms are difficult to define, procedural due process generally means adherence to certain prescribed procedures to ensure that the process is fundamentally fair. Substantive due process, on the other hand, means that certain subjects are outside the ambit of government control, regardless of the procedure used (Peltason, 1982:199).

In employee testing, the concern is procedural due process, manifested in such issues as employee notification, chain of custody, test accuracy, and test confidentiality (Manili, 1987). Employee notification stresses the need for clear guidelines concerning how and when testing is to be done. Chain of custody goes into whether the specimen collected is in fact the specimen tested and whose results are later used in evidence. Test accuracy deals with false positives and false negatives and asks whether or not the results are scientifically reliable to a point where admission into evidence is fair to the individual. Test confidentiality is concerned not just with the improper disclosure of results, but also with whether the test reveals other information (such as medicine being taken) that is unrelated to government interest in drug testing.

All of the above issues require that the testing process be surrounded with safeguards against error and abuse. The concept is best illustrated in two court cases that reached opposite results because of the procedures used.

In *Capua v. City of Plainfield* (1986), the court disapproved of the practices of the agency and concluded that they violate due process. The court found the following procedures, among others, unacceptable:

(1) Not giving notice of intent to begin drug testing;

(2) Absence of a policy concerning the procedures and standards in the implementation of drug testing;

(3) Failure to protect confidentiality;

(4) Lack of verification procedures;

(5) Failure to give persons tested a copy of the laboratory report; and

(6) Immediate termination of those who tested positive and filing of criminal charges against them.

In contrast, the U.S. Supreme Court approved the testing program used in the case of *National Treasury Employee's Union v. Von Raab* (1989). Included in the U.S. Customs drug-testing program are the following key due process safeguards:

(1) Testing only for those persons voluntarily applying for sensitive positions;

(2) Giving five days notice prior to testing;

(3) Allowing the employee to withdraw his or her application at any time without any adverse inferences;

(4) Giving a form to employees at the time of the test on which he/she may list any medications taken;

(5) Employing strict chain of custody procedures including applying a tamper-proof seal to bottles, having employees initial labels affixed to seals and chain of custody forms, and maintaining both a tracking system and chain of custody records at the laboratory where samples are sent;

(6) Confirming positive EMIT results with a GC/MS test;

(7) Allowing employees to designate a laboratory to independently test the original sample in the event of positive results;

(8) Implementing a quality-assurance program that involves intermingling control samples with employee specimens to test the rate of false positives; and

(9) Using drug tests as an administrative tool only, and never bringing criminal charges.

The closer an agency's procedure is to the *Von Raab* model, the better its chances are of surviving a due process challenge.

The Two Recent Supreme Court Cases

Mention has been made above of the two cases decided on March 21, 1989 by the U.S. Supreme Court -- *Skinner v. Railway Labor Executives' Association* and *National Treasury Employee's Union v. Von Raab* (1989). Various aspects of the cases have been discussed, and both deserve an extended analysis because, despite peculiar facts, they constitute authoritative pronouncements from the Court in some facets of drug testing.

In *Skinner v. Railway Labor Executives' Association* (decided on a 7-2 vote), the Federal Railroad Administration promulgated regulations requiring railroads to see that blood and urine tests of covered employees are conducted following certain major train accidents, and also authorized, but did not require, railroads to administer breath or urine tests, or both, to covered employees who violate certain safety rules. Suit was brought in Federal District Court, which granted summary judgment for petitioners, concluding that the regulations did not violate the Fourth Amendment. The Court of Appeals reversed, saying that a requirement of particularized suspicion is essential to drug testing. On appeal, the Supreme Court held that the Fourth Amendment is applicable to drug and alcohol testing, but that in this case testing without warrant was justified because of the government's interest in regulating the conduct of railroad employees engaged in safety-sensitive tasks in order to ensure the safety of the traveling public and of the employees themselves. The government interest involved, said the Court, plainly justifies prohibiting such employees from using alcohol or drugs while on duty or on call for duty and the exercise of supervision to assure that the restrictions are in fact observed. The Court added that the interest involved presents "special needs" beyond normal law enforcement and therefore justifies departure from the usual warrant and probable cause requirements.

In the second case, *National Treasury Employee's Union v. Von Raab* (decided on a 5-4 vote), the U.S. Customs Service implemented a drug-screening program that required urinalysis tests of employees seeking transfer or promotion to positions having direct involvement in drug interdiction (the Service's primary mission), or requiring the incumbent to carry firearms or to handle "classified" material. The program was challenged by a federal employees' union and one of its officials, alleging a violation of the Fourth

Amendment. The Federal District Court upheld the petitioners' contention and enjoined the program. The Court of Appeals vacated the injunction, saying that the searches were reasonable because of their limited scope and the Service's strong interest in detecting drug use among employees in these positions. On appeal, the Supreme Court held that requiring employees to produce urine samples, the collection thereof, and the subsequent chemical analysis of such samples constitute searches that must meet the reasonable requirement of the Fourth Amendment. In this case, however, the Service's suspicionless drug-testing program was held reasonable because of the government's compelling interests in public safety and in safeguarding borders. Moreover employees seeking positions in the Service that required drug testing had diminished privacy interests. As for those seeking promotion or transfer to positions that involved handling of classified information, the Court remanded the issue to the court of appeals to determine whether the category of employees to be tested included only those likely to gain access to sensitive material.

The two cases were decided by the Court primarily under the Fourth Amendment issue of searches and seizures, the Court holding that both programs are reasonable and therefore do not violate constitutional rights. This means that the warrantless and suspicionless testing programs implemented by the agencies, given their circumstances, are valid. The cases did not address other issues raised in this article, particularly the issue of procedural due process often raised in the context of chain of custody and test accuracy. These concerns must therefore be considered unresolved by the Court. It must be noted that the two cases did not involve random mandatory testing. Both involved mandatory testing, but not at random. Whether or not random mandatory testing is constitutional has not been resolved by the Court; however, lower court decisions predominantly held that they are not. In the National Treasury Employees Union case, the Court said: "In sum, we believe the Government has demonstrated that its compelling interest in safeguarding our borders and the public safety outweigh the privacy expectations of employees who seek to be promoted to positions that directly involve the interdiction of illegal drugs or that require the incumbent to carry a firearm." In both cases, the Court gave great weight to the fact that compelling government interests were involved and that the government succeeded in establishing both.

Two issues raised by plaintiffs in the *National Treasury Employee's Union* case deserve special mention because they address issues likely to be raised in drug-testing cases. Petitioners contended that the drug-testing program implemented by the agency was unreasonable because it was not based on a belief that testing would reveal any drug use by the employees. The Court rejected this, saying that although the program was not motivated by any perceived drug problem among Service employees, it was nonetheless justified by extraordinary safety and national security hazards that are present if drug users are promoted to sensitive positions. Petitioners also maintained that the program did not justify intrusion on Fourth Amendment rights because illegal drug users could easily avoid detection by temporary abstinence or by secret adulteration of their urine specimens. The Court found this unpersuasive, saying that addicts may be unable to abstain even for a limited period or may be unaware of the "fade-away effect" of certain drugs. The fear of adulteration was rejected by the Court, saying that sufficient precautions were built into the program to ensure the integrity of the sample.

In sum, these two cases provide answers to some constitutional questions about drug testing, but leave other issues unanswered. The cases say that warrantless, suspicionless, and mandatory testing of public employees or of employees who come under the authority of the State are constitutional if a compelling government interest is involved and if the jobs are so sensitive as to warrant a diminution of employees' Fourth Amendment rights. The problem, however, is that these decisions were based on the nature of the government interest sought to be protected and the type of program implemented by the agency. These concerns vary from one agency to another and therefore will have to be addressed on a case-by-case basis. It is one thing to require drug tests; it is another to require probation officers, for example to do the same. The government interest involved and the sensitivity of the positions are not similar, but where the line can be drawn constitutionally is a difficult issue that the two cases did not address.

Summary and Suggestions

The safeguards used in employee testing and the instances in which police and correctional officers may be tested varies substantially from those of their clients. A study of existing literature and decided cases suggests ways whereby a drug-testing program can be so structured as to minimize vulnerability to a legal challenge. Considering the U.S. Supreme Court and lower court decisions, some measures agencies might consider to avoid litigation are as follows:

(1) Avoid random mandatory testing of personnel. Such tests are more vulnerable to court challenge, except for correctional officers working in maximum and medium security prisons.

(2) Avoid mandatory testing, even if it is not random (as in the *National Treasury Employee's Union* case where it was re-

quired for promotion or transfer) unless a compelling governmental interest is involved. Such interest is usually determined by the sensitive nature of the job in terms of possible bad effects on the public resulting from an officer's drug use.

(3) If possible, obtain a voluntary consent from the employee prior to drug testing.

(4) If the test is to be made without a warrant, have at least a "reasonable suspicion" before testing an employee. The only instances when individualized suspicion is not necessary are:

    (a) when the test is in conjunction with a routine annual physical examination, or

    (b) if the persons to be tested are job applicants or probationary officers.

(5) Have a written policy that states the procedure to be used in drug testing, and the resulting disciplinary action that will be taken in cases of positive results.

(6) Give employees a copy of the department's policy on drug testing.

(7) Maintain confidentiality of test results. Such results should be made available only to duly authorized persons. Do not go public with the information.

(8) Use drug tests only for administrative purposes, not for initiating criminal charges against the employee.

(9) Adopt a policy not to automatically terminate an employee when positive findings result; instead employees should be allowed to participate in a drug treatment program before final decision is made. This benefits employees who are willing to change and obviates lawsuits that usually come with termination.

CONCLUSION

Drug use has become alarmingly pervasive in American society. Recent studies have established a link between drug use and crime. Drug use deterrence and abstinence have, therefore, become priority goals in criminal justice. To achieve this, many criminal justice agencies, from arrest through parole, are drug testing clients.

This study concludes that there are no major legal barriers to drug testing prisoners, probationers or parolees. This is because convicted offenders have diminished constitutional rights, and whatever rights they have may be overcome by a strong governmental interest in institutional safety in prison, or rehabilitation of the offender and the protection of society in probation and parole cases. The legality or constitutionality of drug testing offenders therefore, should not pose much concern. Nonetheless, it is necessary that proper testing procedures be followed, the accuracy of the test be established, and the proper chain of custody procedures be employed if a possible successful legal challenge to drug testing is to be avoided or minimized.

Drug testing prison and police officers raises the same constitutional issues as those raised in testing offenders. Court decisions indicate that drug testing may be allowed under narrow and limited conditions. The courts will most likely disallow mandatory testing of police officers, and possibly prison officers, except if there is at least a reasonable suspicion that the employee uses drugs. Even then, proper safeguards must be employed before an agency can test and later take disciplinary action.

REFERENCES

Chaiken, J. & M. Chaiken (1982). *Varieties of Criminal Behavior: Summary and Policy Implications*. Santa Monica, CA: The RAND Corporation.

Carver, J. (1986). "Drugs and Crime: Controlling Use and Reducing Risk Through Testing." National Institute of Justice Reports, SNI 199. Washington, DC: U.S. Government Printing Office.

Collins, W. (1987). *Correctional Law*. Olympia, WA.

Collins, W. (1986). *Correctional Law*. Olympia, WA.

del Carmen, R. & J. Vaughn (June, 1986). "Legal Issues in the Use of Electronic Surveillance in Probation." *Federal Probation*, 50, 60-69.

Greenwood, P. (1982). *Selective Incapacitation*. Santa Monica, CA: The RAND Corporation.

Guynes, R. & O. Coffey (1988). "Employee Drug Testing Policies in Prison Systems." National Institute of Justice Research in Action. Washington, DC: U.S. Government Printing Office.

Higginbotham, J. (1986). "Urinalysis Drug Testing Programs." *Law Enforcement Bulletin*.

Inciardi, J. (1981). *The Drug-Crimes Connection*. Beverly Hills, CA: Sage.

Lawlor, J. (1987). "Drug Testing of Government Employees and the Fourth Amendment: The Need for a Reasonable Suspicion Standard." *Notre Dame Law Review*, 62, 1063-1082.

McEwen, J.T., B. Manili & E. Connors (1986). "Employee Drug Testing Policies in Police Departments." National Institute of Justice Research in Brief. Washington, DC: U.S. Government Printing Office.

Manili, B. (1987). "Police Drug Testing." National Institute of Justice. Washington, DC: U.S. Government Printing Office.

Peltason, J.W. (1982). *Understanding the Constitution*. New York: Holt, Rinehart and Winston.

Westphal, E.E. (1987). "Public-Sector Employee Drug Testing Programs: Has Big Brother Finally Arrived?" *John Marshall Law Review*, 20, 769-793.

Wish, E. (1988). "Drug Testing." *National Institute of Justice Bulletin*, NCJ 104556. Washington, DC: U.S. Government Printing Office.

Zeese, K. (1988). *Drug Testing: Legal Manual*. New York: Clark Boardman.

TABLE OF CASES

Bearden v. Georgia, 33 Cr.L. 3103 (1983).

Bell v. Wolfish, 441 U.S. 520 (1979).

Berry v. District of Columbia, 833 F.2d 1031 (D.C. Cir. 1987).

Capua v. City of Plainfield, 643 F.Supp. 1507 (D.N.J. 1986).

Clay v. State, 710 S.W.2d 119 (Tex. Ct. App. 1986).

Consolidated Rail Corporation v. Railway Labor Executives' Association, 845 F.2d 1187 (3d Cir. 1988).

Damron v. Commonwealth, 531 A.2d 592 (Pa. Commw. Ct. 1987).

Dickerson v. State, 136 Ga. App. 885 (1975).

Frye v. United States, 293 F.2d 1013 (D.C. Cir. 1923).

Higgs v. Wilson, 616 F.Supp. 226 (W.D. Ky. 1985).

Howard v. State, 308 S.E.2d 424 (Ga. App. 1983).

Hudson v. Palmer, 486 U.S. 517 (1984).

In re Johnston, 107 Wn. ___, No. 17745-1-I (Nov. 25, 1987).

Isaacks v. State, 646 S.W.2d 602 (Tex Ct. App. 1983).

Jefferson v. Commonwealth, 506 A.2d 495 (Pa. Commw. Ct. 1986).

Jones v. McKenzie, Vic. Act. No. 85-1624 (1986).

Lahey v. Kelly, 510 N.Y.S.2d 187, 125 A.D.2d 923 (1986).

McDonell v. Hunter, 809 F.2d 1302 (8th Cir. 1987).

McQueen v. State, 740 P.2d 744 (Okla. Ct. App. 1987).

Macias v. State, 649 S.W.2d 150 (Tex. Ct. App. 1983).

National Treasury Employee's Union v. Von Raab, 816 F.2d 170 (5th Cir. 1987).

Pella v. Adams, 638 F.Supp. 94 (D. Nev. 1986).

People v. Moore, 666 P.2d 419 (Cal. 1983).

Peranzo v. Coughlin, 608 F. Supp. 1504 (S.D.N.Y. 1985).

Powell v. Commonwealth, 513 A.2d 1139 (Pa. Commw. Ct. 1986).

Railway Labor Executives' Association v. Burnley, 839 F.2d 575 (9th Cir. 1988).

Schmerber v. California, 384 U.S. 757 (1966).

Smith v. State, 298 S.E.2d 482 (Ga. Ct. App. 1983).

Spence v. Farrier, 807 F.2d 753 (8th Cir. 1986).

Stahl v. Commonwealth, 525 A.2d 1272 (Pa. Commw. Ct. 1987).

State v. Johnson, 527 A.2d 250 (Conn. App. Ct. 1987).

Superintendent v. Hill, 472 U.S. 445 (1985).

Szili v. Carlson, No. TCA 84-7196 (N.D. Fla., 1985, unpublished).

Turner v. Fraternal Order of Police, 500 A.2d 1005 (D.C. App. 1985).

United States v. Bell, 785 F.2d 604 (8th Cir. 1986).

United States v. Duff, 831 F.2d 176 (9th Cir. 1987).

United States v. Penn, 721 F.2d 762 (11th Cir. 1984).

United States v. Williams, 787 F.2d 1182 (7th Cir. 1986).

Whitmore v. Commonwealth, 504 A.2d 401 (Pa. Commw. Ct. 1986).

Wolff v. McDonnell, 418 U.S. 566 (1974).

Wykoff v. Resig, 613 F. Supp. 1504 (D.C. Ind. 1986).

14

Addicts Helping Addicts to Help Themselves: The Baltimore City Jail Project*

Mark S. Hamm
Indiana State University

INTRODUCTION

Drugs in America. Hardly a day goes by without the media reporting to us the horrors of cocaine and "crack," "drive-by" shootings, teenage drug abuse, infant-born narcotic addiction, the latest terrorist activity of Latin American drug cartels, and the sinister spread of AIDS through needle-sharing. To be sure, current opinion polls refer to drugs as the nation's most pressing concern. Like the inveterate character in the Hollywood movie *Network*, the United States is, moreover, "Mad as hell and won't take it anymore!"

Accordingly, public officials have launched an unprecedented "war on drugs" which includes the death penalty for drug-related murder, life prison terms for people convicted of selling drugs to children, the use of illegally obtained evidence in drug trials, the increased use of drug testing in the

---

* This research is funded in part through a National Institute of Corrections Technical Assistance Grant (NIC T.A. 88-J1272). The ideas expressed in this chapter reflect the views of the author and do not necessarily reflect official NIC views or policies. The author wishes to thank Ralph Weisheit for his helpful comments on an earlier draft.

workplace, and the deployment of military personnel along America's southern borders (Inciardi, 1986; Shannon, 1988; Trebach, 1987). As a result, the American criminal justice system has begun to experience an enormous strain on its ability to effectively punish and treat drug abuse criminals.

Today over 580,000 inmates -- roughly equivalent to the population of San Francisco -- are confined to state and federal prisons, and nearly 60 percent of these prisoners had serious drug abuse problems before incarceration; many of whom were arrested for committing violent crimes and have extensive criminal records (Bureau of Justice Statistics, 1988a & 1988b). Few of these inmates, however, receive treatment for their drug problems while in prison, and there is little research on what constitutes effective rehabilitation for them (Wexler & Williams, 1986). In addition to the extraordinary bureaucratic problem of identifying and implementing the complex array of treatment strategies necessary for such a large number of offenders, there are two other reasons for the paucity of drug treatment programming in prison today.

First, drug abuse criminals elicit very little compassion from the public. Indeed, the President of the United States has recently called these offenders "a repudiation of everything America is" (Hamm, 1988a:104); whereas longitudinal research shows that the public is adopting increasingly more punitive attitudes toward the control of criminals in general (Flanagan & Caulfield, 1984; Rankin, 1979; Sheingold, 1984), and it is equally common for state-level politicians to justify punitive policies on the grounds that they fulfill the public's "will" (Cullen et al., 1985; Flanagan & McGarrell, 1986; Hamm, 1989).

Second (and somehow more importantly), drug abuse criminals generally distrust and often hate authority figures of any kind. That is, after years of subjecting themselves to numerous "treatment plans" and then leaving prison with great hope yet limited opportunity for a better future, many "career criminals" have grown weary of prison rehabilitation programs (Gendreau & Ross, 1987; Hamm & Schrink, 1989; Irwin, 1980). In turn, a new generation of youthful offenders has also come to avoid prison treatment programs through their association with these seasoned criminals (Sykes, 1986).

As an alternative to state-sanctioned rehabilitation, inmates -- becoming more and more concerned with their physical and emotional survival in today's overcrowded prison systems -- have therefore retreated to gangs (Jacobs, 1985; Martin & Ekland-Olson, 1987), religious fellowships (Lozoff & Braswell, 1989; Clear, 1989), and self-help groups (Abdul-Mu'Min, 1985; Irwin, 1980) in an attempt to relieve their "pains of imprisonment" (Johnson, 1987).

The Prisoner Self-help Movement
and the Drug Abuse Criminal

Prison inmates have demonstrated a strong and sustained interest in self-help organizations for over 20 years now (Burdman, 1974; Ellis, 1983; Irwin, 1980; Katz & Bender, 1976; MacNamara with Sagarin, 1971; Snarr & Wolford, 1985; Sagarin, 1969; Sands, 1964). This phenomenon is not hard to explain. In addition to inmates feeling abandoned by the state apparatus, the prisoner self-help movement has been closely linked to a broader social movement which has arisen from a general sense of alienation in society; the perceived failure of social institutions (such as schools, churches, and families) to provide nurturance and support for the truly needy. From the familiar Alcoholics Anonymous to the little-known Schizophrenics Anonymous and support groups for victims of AIDS, heart by-pass surgery, and domestic violence, the self-help movement currently reaches into many unexpected corners of our social world (see Liberman & Borman, 1979).

Today it is likely that there are hundreds of self-help groups operating in U.S. prisons (see Madura & Meese, 1988). Some of the most prominent are: the Seventh Step Program, Beyond the Wall, the Fortune Society, the Jaycees, Alcoholics Anonymous, Narcotics Anonymous, and the est program. These organizations share two common features. First, they all promise to relieve the "pains of imprisonment" by bringing together criminal offenders who wish to change their own lives and help other prisoners change their lives. Second, because they do not trust the state, these self-help groups are voluntary and there are no correctional staff involved to stimulate or guide group discussions and activities (Hamm, 1988b).

John Irwin, one of the nation's leading penologists, has found that more prison inmates belong to self-help groups than any other form of prisoner organization. This is so because "self-help programs remain an alternative to other, more political groups" (Irwin, 1980:93). Moreover, Irwin concludes that self-help groups offer "the first encouragement for a criminal to come out; convicts learn through the self-help process that they have nothing to hide or live down." Alas they can "unabashedly and proudly announce their past and open doors to a variety of conventional endeavors" (1980:94).

Like any other organization, however, there are also problems with prisoner self-help groups. Elsewhere I have shown that these problems emerge when prisoner self-help groups are viewed as threatening by administrators who are ambivalent about the whole notion of self-help in prison. Also, I have argued that successful prisoner self-help groups are non-threatening organizations which embrace a quasi-religious theology, and avoid activities that are foreign to the operations of corrections (Hamm, 1988b). Likewise, Wexler and Williams (1986) -- the only known researchers to examine the

effects of self-help on drug abuse criminals in specific -- discovered three im-
pediments to effective prisoner self-help treatment: *institutional resistance,*
severity of inmate problems, and *program inadequacies.*

We are therefore left with a simple set of propositions that can be used
to examine the value of self-help programming for drug abuse criminals in
American prisons today. On one hand, we would expect successful programs
to operate from a quasi-religious basis, be non-threatening to prison administrators, and engage in well-developed activities that are consistent with the
regular prison regime. On the other hand, we would expect unsuccessful
programs to be poorly developed and organized around principles antagonis-
tic to the prison administration, and run by prisoners who are thought to be
so criminally severe that they are beyond saving. This chapter so evaluates a
prisoner self-help program within a critical context, the Baltimore City Jail.

BACKGROUND

Anyone who has ever spent time in the Baltimore City Jail knows of its
dark and decrepit history. The facility is so old that the great poet Edgar
Allan Poe claimed to have served a week there for failing to repay a debt
back in 1831 (Quinn, 1941). Veteran guards speak of a later era when tor-
ture was commonly used to control inmate behavior. During the mid-1960s,
disciplinary procedures at the jail included the use of the "hard bed." Inmates
who were caught stealing or fighting were routinely taken to one of the jail
tunnels, where they were stripped of their clothing and placed belly-up on a
metal bedspring. Four sets of handcuffs were used to secure the inmate's
wrists and ankles to the frame of the bedspring, and then a rubber mat was
placed over the length of the inmate's body. The prisoner was left in this
condition for two or three days while they were routinely beaten and fed only
one substance -- cod liver oil.

At the end of the 1960s, guards and administrators witnessed the dawn
of a new era in the jail's history. From 1960 to 1968, the Baltimore Police arrested an average of about 500 narcotics violators per year. In 1969, however,
the police increased its number of narcotics arrests to 1,852, representing a
140 percent increase over 1968 figures. As a result, the jail became overcrowded for the first time in its history. Public officials concluded that increased arrests were caused by a spectacular growth in the number of Baltimore residents who had begun using heroin.

Research suggests that two primary factors led to this development.
First, heroin was generally associated with an emerging American ethos
known as "hip." Hip was the ionization of rebellion for white middle-class
youth of the 1960s; like many black Americans of the civil rights era, "hippies"

did not trust government either -- so they determined goodness for themselves through the expression of their own feelings. In essence, "hip" meant showing the utmost kindness to one's fellow sufferer in a world which was becoming progressively more flawed; and hippies sought their instant humanism with marijuana, psychedelics, amphetamines and heroin (Nicosia, 1984; Spitz, 1989). In this way, heroin became linked to the hippie subculture and its use expanded within the American population consistent with the increased use of other drugs (Hamm, 1986; Leech, 1972; Mitcheson, 1970; Ray, 1978; Trebach, 1982).

Second, the increase in arrests for heroin was also due to a dramatic rise in the number of police officers responsible for patrolling high crime rate areas of big cities which came as a result of the recommendations issued by the 1967 President's Commission on Law Enforcement and Administration of Justice (see Zalman, 1987). Over the next ten years, the number of police assigned to urban areas of the United States would double (Chambliss, 1988), thereby "widening the net" around narcotics users in the nation (Trebach, 1987).

Taken together, these developments begin to explain the major changes witnessed at the Baltimore City Jail over the course of the past two decades. Figure 14.1 reveals that arrests for narcotics violations in Baltimore rose from 772 in 1968 to 14,473 in 1987, representing an astonishing 1,878 percent increase. Yet increases in heroin use and police surveillance do not fully account for this trend. In 1984, the Baltimore Police Department embarked upon its most aggressive fight against narcotics in history. At the center of their attention was the new distillate of cocaine called "crack."

Crack is sold on the street in pea-sized pellets, usually two or three per vial, with an average dose of 125 milligrams costing around $20 (Hamm, 1987a; Lempinen, 1988). Among seasoned drug users, crack has become enormously popular for two reasons. First, it is intensively euphoric; when smoked, crack reaches the brain within ten seconds, and due to its pharmacological purity, produces euphoria sooner than other narcotic drugs (Haight-Ashbury Drug Detoxification Project, 1987; Taylor, Weisman & Gest, 1986). Second, crack requires no preparation; unlike heroin and powder cocaine, crack is ready to be smoked on purchase -- all one needs is a lighter and a pipe (Morganthau et al., 1986). Moreover, crack has become the cheapest and most accessible addictive commodity on the illicit drug market because today it is the drug of choice for many heroin addicts or users of injectable cocaine (Katchaturian, 1986; Press, 1986; Thomas, 1986). As such, the emergence of crack suggests the major reason for the dramatic increase in narcotic violations in Baltimore between 1985 and 1987, as displayed in Figure 14.1.

Figure 14.1
Arrests for Narcotic Violations, 1968-1987

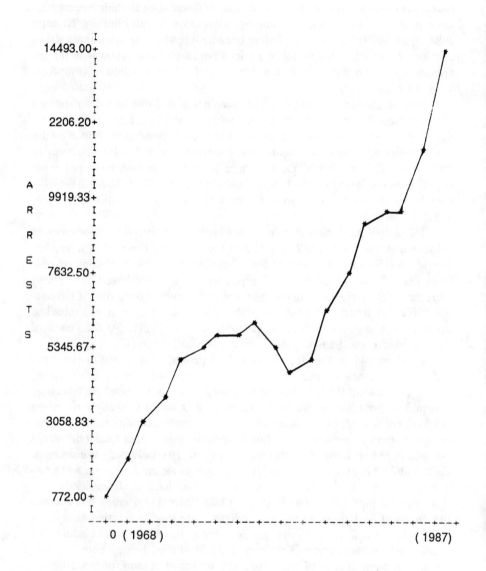

Hence the Baltimore City Jail has become seriously overcrowded. Currently the jail has a capacity of 1,900, yet approximately 3,000 prisoners are incarcerated there. About 80 percent of them are awaiting trial, and the other 20 percent are serving sentences. Eighty percent of the population are black and twenty percent are white. Approximately 70 juveniles are serving sentences. The jail is extremely dirty. Most prisoners spend their days watching television (often standing up because there is not enough room to sit down in the "day rooms"), roaming the cell blocks, or sleeping. Because of the crowding, filth, idleness, noise levels, and heat (most of the jail has no air-conditioning), veteran employees began calling the Baltimore City Jail a "powderkeg" during the brutal summer drought of 1988.

As might be expected, these conditions have severely impacted official resources for rehabilitation. The treatment staff of the jail consists of only two teachers, three psychologists, seven work crew supervisors, and one chaplain. Because there are no official programs for drug abusers, prisoners in the Baltimore City Jail have developed their own program of reformation. This program is sanctioned by the jail administration and is generally perceived by inmates, guards, teachers, and psychologists as being a model treatment regime. The purpose of this chapter, therefore, is to expose the operations, structure, and potential of this program. My observations are based on a two-day visit to the Baltimore City Jail, in the summer of 1988, where I interviewed a number of addicts, guards, treatment personnel, and administrators.[1]

THE CASH PROGRAM

In 1973, a group of heroin addicts in the Baltimore City Jail persuaded a cell-block captain that a self-help program was needed to deal specifically with the problem of narcotics addiction. The captain took this idea to the warden of the jail, and the warden subsequently approved the establishment of a prisoner self-help group known as Confined Addicts Seeking Help (CASH).

The CASH Philosophy

CASH was explicitly organized to appeal to the ever-increasing number of drug addicts incarcerated in the jail. The objective of the group is to assist addicts in their attempts to return to the mainstream of life. Membership is open to virtually any prisoner with a drug problem. Like other drug treatment programs such as Synanon and Narcotics Anonymous, CASH views the drug addict as being in social isolation. That is, addicts are seen by society as using drugs for reasons largely peculiar to their own deviant cohort. These reasons include the need for kicks or rebellion; or because of boredom or peer pressure to conform to counterculture norms (Adler, 1970; Moore, 1977). Because of this counterculture orientation, CASH looks upon drug addicts as an unusually antibureaucratic, disaffiliated group which cannot be reached by traditional social service delivery systems. Instead, the CASH model of treatment is based on a moral self-help approach designed to build an intense unity and esprit de corps among inmates who are addicted to drugs. This treatment paradigm is made explicit in the group's philosophical statements. All prisoners who join CASH are expected to memorize three different mottos. These mottos (which are transcribed verbatim from CASH literature) are presented below.

The Morning Motto

Up today, down tomorrow,
do your own thing, and every thing will follow.
Ain't nothing to it but to do it.
Regardless how you feel,
you'll find it in your heart, every thing for real.
For some of us the hill's a little steeper
so let's look after each other, we are our brother's keeper.
I may be in jail, but I am somebody.
I'll always care cause I am somebody.
Good Morning.

The CASH Philosophy

We are here, because there is no other refuge. Finally from ourselves a person can at last appear clearly to himself. Until a person confronts himself in the eyes and hearts of others, he is running. Until he suffers them to share his secrets, he has no safety from them. Afraid to be known, he can know neither himself nor another. He will be alone. Where else but in our common ground can we find such a mirror. Here together a person can at last appear clearly to himself, not as a giant of his dreams nor the dwarf of his fears, but as a man alive with a share and a purpose, in this ground we each that roots and grows. Not alone any more as in death but alive to ourselves and others.
Good Morning.

The Annex Philosophy

We, the deprived are here, held in bondage, awaiting one's fate, trying; hard to maintain a open mind, struggling to be educated and build our minds, bodies and understanding, towards the right things in life has to offer. Just because we are somebody.

JUST BECAUSE WE ARE SOMEBODY

To share knowledge, wisdom and understanding, guiding us along the road of right and wrong. Let us stand together

JUST BECAUSE WE ARE SOMEBODY

As a whole

JUST BECAUSE WE ARE SOMEBODY

Unite, forcefully, peacefully, and aware of the battle towards freedom, that we all need to stress. What it is

JUST BECAUSE WE ARE SOMEBODY

Our goal

JUST BECAUSE WE ARE SOMEBODY

Up-Town

JUST BECAUSE WE ARE SOMEBODY

Up-Town

JUST BECAUSE WE ARE SOMEBODY

Good morning men. Reach for the stars!

The Government and Law of CASH

CASH is a highly structured self-help group administered by well-intentioned and deeply concerned prisoners who are themselves recovering addicts. However, CASH is not a democratic organization. Rather, it is led by a "Dictator" who has risen to power within the prisoner subculture. As one Dictator is released from the Baltimore City Jail, he appoints his successor. (There are no women in the group.) The Dictator controls the CASH economy and its systems of law and government. He is given his choice of dormitory housing, and is also allowed to have a large refrigerator and permission to sell fruit, pie, soft drinks, and ice water. Consequently, the Dictator's living space is a storehouse of commodities, and a legal source of revenue and power. In order to help guide the activities of CASH, the Dictator has appointed three prisoners to fill crucial positions in his government. The first ranking officer of CASH is the "Floor Rep," who is responsible for recording all CASH points in two systems of government: the Merit Point System and the Rules and Penalty System. The "Judge" is second in command, and he is responsible for adjudicating organizational infractions. This cabinet is completed by the "Sergeant at Arms," who enforces all CASH law.

Table 14.1
CASH Merit Point System

MERIT SYSTEM

1. (10) points for the morning prayer: Moorish, Lord and Serenity.
2. (10) points for the morning motto.
3. (15) points for each seminar
4. (5) points for participation in seminars, classes, and groups (weekly total 20 pts.).
5. (5) points for beneficial information.
6. (5) points for current events (25 pts. total weekly).
7. (10) points bonus for outstanding resident during group and seminar sessions.
8. (15) points for AA and NA meetings.
9. (15) points for the CASH philosophy.
10. (5) points for doing extra detail work.

DEMERIT SYSTEM

1. (5) points for speaking out of turn in groups, seminars and morning meetings.
2. (10) points for leaving groups, seminars and morning meetings without permission.
3. (5) points for not participating in groups and seminars.
4. (10) points for sub-grouping.
5. (10) points for sleeping, nodding or otherwise being inattentive in groups.
6. (5) points for not being on time for groups.
7. (5) points for poor posture and attitude.
8. (10) points for receiving infraction.
9. (5) points for receiving a pull-up.
10. (10) points for horseplaying.

Any prisoner who joins CASH is required to sign a statement relinquishing all personal property and money to the Dictator. The prisoner is left with only the clothes he is presently wearing, and told to sign a second agreement to follow the CASH Merit Point System. CASH initiates must earn 2,000 points before they can get their property and money back. The CASH Merit Point System is displayed verbatim in Table 14.1. Most addicts who seek out the CASH Dictator are withdrawing from a serious narcotic addiction; therefore, they often participate in CASH while doing "cold turkey." Once 2,000 points are accumulated, the prisoner is given a graduation party by the Dictator, where he is rewarded his belongings and given a certificate of membership into CASH.

The Political Structure of CASH

The effectiveness of CASH can be measured in terms of the organization's ability to coerce prisoners into following the activities and regulations of the group. To the extent that CASH achieves order within its ranks, it will be perceived by officials as a stabilizing force in the old jail. Furthermore, if CASH can demonstrate its organizational stability, then perhaps CASH membership will be viewed positively in Pre-Sentence Investigation Reports prepared by the probation department, and ultimately by the courts.

The organizational stability of CASH rests upon an intricate system of rules and penalties. The Rules and Penalty Systems are displayed (verbatim) in Tables 14.2 and 14.3. Table 14.2 lists 34 rules of the organization and Table 14.3 lists 34 penalties to correspond with each rule if violated. For example, Rule 1 is "No Stealing" and Penalty 1 is "Reclassification, L-Section Lock-Up." Likewise, Rule 2, "No drugs or chemicals of any kind" corresponds with Penalty 2, "Reclassification, L-Section Lock-Up, possible street charge," and so forth. Notably, Table 14.2, Item 17, states that, "No one is exempt from rules and regulations."

Only the Dictator and the Floor Rep can bring charges against a CASH member. Each charge is documented on the CASH "Charge Sheet," and forwarded to the Judge. The Judge impanels a hearing which includes the defendant, the Chief of Security for the Baltimore City Jail, the CASH "Section Representative," and any witness to the infraction. After all arguments have been heard, the Judge records a disposition of the charge and his order is then carried out by guards and/or the CASH Sergeant of Arms.

Table 14.2
CASH Rule System

1. No stealing.
2. No drugs or chemicals of any kind.
3. No fighting or threats of violence.
4. No gambling.
5. No community materials to leave Annex.
6. Change only—NO BILLS.
7. No littering.
8. Everyone must go through the Chain of Command.
9. Residents must keep themselves and living quarters clean at all times.
10. No one can refuse a job assignment.
11. Everyone must be properly dressed at all times.
12. No skating—being in an area without permission.
13. No outsiders allowed in Community without permission.
14. No leaving group meetings or classes without permission.
15. Everyone has the right to call Special Meeting at any time.
16. You must sign Destination Sheet before leaving and returning to your floor.
17. No one is exempt from rules and regulations.
18. No one is to loiter in the hall areas.
19. No loud noises at any time.
20. No one is to be on the phones during Mass Movement.
21. No "horseplaying" at any time.
22. No one is to be in any bed area except his own, without permission.
23. No use of foul or abusive language.
24. No unnecessary "feedback."
25. No game playing, sleeping, nodding, etc. during program hours.
26. All directions from staff must be honored.
27. No weapons, or objects resembling weapons, allowed in Community.
28. No abuse/destruction of Annex property—telephone, bedding, school material.
29. No disrespect or dishonesty in deed or character at any time.
30. No hats, caps, shower shoes or slippers of any kind to be worn during program.
31. No going beyond designated areas when going to or coming from Dining Hall.
32. All passes must be honored on time.
33. Everyone must attend Meetings on time and be prepared.
34. Everyone must be in his own dorm after Mass Movement for the count.

Table 14.3
CASH Penalty System

1. Reclassification, L-Section Lock-Up.
2. Reclassification, L-Section Lock-Up, possible street charge.
3. Reclassification, L-Section Lock-Up.
4. Reclassification, and/or loss of commissary and visit.
5. One (1) week's loss of phone usage.
6. Officer may confiscate bills.
7. One (1) week's hard work contract and/or one (1) day's loss of phone usage.
8. One (1) day's hard work contract and/or one (1) day's loss of phone usage.
9. Two (2) days—Seminar.
10. Five-hundred (500) word essay.
11. One-thousand (1,000) word essay.
12. Four (4) days' hard work contract and/or two (2) days' loss of phone usage.
13. Five-hundred (500) word essay.
14. Five-hundred (500) word essay.
15. No penalty.
16. Five (5) days' hard work contract and one (1) day's loss of phone usage.
17. One (1) day's hard work contract.
18. Two (2) days' hard work contract.
19. One (1) day's loss of phone and/or Climb-the-Mountain.
20. Three (3) days' loss of phone.
21. Five-hundred (500) word essay.
22. One (1) seminar.
23. One (1) day's hard work contract and/or one (1) day's loss of phone usage.
24. One (1) hour Bus Stop.
25. One (1) hour Bus Stop or Climb-the-Mountain.
26. Three (3) days' hard work contract.
27. Reclassification, L-Section Lock-Up, possible street charge.
28. One-thousand (1,000) or more word essay.
29. Two (2) days' hard work contract and/or three (3) days' loss of phone usage.
30. Two (2) hours of Bus Stop or one (1) day's loss of phone usage.
31. Two (2) days' hard work contract and/or two (2) days' loss of phone usage.
32. Five-hundred (500) word essay.
33. Five-hundred (500) word essay.
34. Two (2) hours of Seminar.

CASH Program Activities

Upon waking each day at 6:00 a.m., CASH members gather together in the Baltimore City Jail and recite their own personal prayer. Next, they recite, in unison, the "Morning Motto," the "Annex Philosophy," and the "CASH Philosophy." Throughout the day, CASH members attend organizational activities which include seminars and classes in coping with narcotics addiction, stress management, high school equivalency preparation, and organizational development and management. In addition to these self-help offerings, CASH members are encouraged to take advantage of the limited educational, work, recreational, and chaplaincy services provided by the jail administration.

During the evenings, CASH members do homework and complete work assignments around the dormitory. As a result of these work details, CASH has been able to clean up their section of the jail, provide air-conditioning, and paint colorful CASH motifs around the cellblock. For example, the Dictator's living space (including his large refrigerator and warehouse of consumable goods) is bathed in a vibrant yellow. Combined with the Dictator's access to air-conditioning and personal television, his living condition is superior to all other living conditions in the jail. In fact, his living quarters stand in sharp contrast to those afforded the majority of offenders at the jail who are being double-bunked in cell spaces that barely meet minimum correctional standards.

DISCUSSION

Criminologist Donald Cressey made two useful observations about self-help groups for drug addicts. First, he wrote that "it is as ridiculous to try to 'cure' a man of drug addiction as it is to try to 'cure' him of sexual intercourse" (Volkman & Cressey, 1963:142). By this, Cressey meant that drug addiction is essentially a biological problem that can be handled most effectively with a medical solution. Therefore, counseling programs -- by themselves -- can only help a person stay away from drugs for a limited period of time. In this regard, self-help groups have a " 'success' rate higher than those institutions officially designated by society as places for the confinement and 'reform' of drug addicts" (1963:142). This is so, according to Cressey, because "the group relations method of rehabilitation (allows) newcomers (to be) truly integrated into the antidrug, anticrime" culture. This "group relations method" is based on the expressed willingness of an addict to submit one's self to a group that hates drug addiction, exalts sobriety and group cohesion, and provides ample opportunity to achieve status within the organization (Cressey, 1955). Simply put, Cressey's theory suggests that every time a drug addict is socially rewarded for denouncing someone else's addiction, the addict reinforces his or her own sobriety (Cressey, 1983).

Second, Cressey argued that self-help groups for drug addicts are "pretty much the product of one person" (1983:152). He goes on to suggest that these leaders are often "very authoritarian and mean." In the end, Cressey maintained that self-help group leaders become more concerned with publicity and politics, and less concerned with drug addiction.

To the extent that Cressey was right, he provided a challenge for contemporary self-help groups like CASH. If group leaders (e.g., the Dictator) allow their own self-interests to supersede the efforts they make to help addicts "stay clean," then they run the risk of tarnishing the organization's reputation. Once the reputation of a prisoner self-help group has been smeared in the eyes of the membership and staff of a correctional institution, the group begins to encroach on its own cohesion, undermining opportunities for what Cressey called "status ascriptions" (1963:135). In turn, the moral philosophy of the group begins to atrophy, until nothing is left of the self-help organization except obsolete stationery and meaningless creeds (Hamm, 1988b; McAnany & Tromanhauser, 1977).

Finally, in the spirit of his "group relations method," I am sure Cressey would call for the incorporation of democratic principles into contemporary addict self-help government. He would have seen such a display of democracy as providing the necessary checks and balances against abuses of power that obtain in any organization. On balance, Cressey would argue that addict self-help groups can retain their noble cause -- providing hope and human optimism even in the darkest corners of imprisonment -- on one condition: *Addict self-help groups must remain true to their cause.*

CONCLUSION

It is time the American criminal justice system and researchers began to recognize the inherent value of the prisoner self-help movement. Given the spectacular increase in recent incarceration rates caused by the war on drugs, this value may potentially be greater now than ever before. Although this chapter has discovered that the self-help group under analysis ran the risk of violating its fundamental purpose due to its internal political structure, this did not mean that the CASH project was unsuccessful. On the contrary, the program appeared to relieve many of the psychological and physical deprivations associated with the deplorable conditions of confinement at the Baltimore City Jail. Furthermore, the CASH program was found to offer a specific support system that met the needs of a particularly troublesome population of criminal offenders. In other words, the program seemed to provide immediate help for addicts in their struggle toward reformation. Consistent with previous research, this short-term success appears to be a function of CASH's quasi-religious orientation, its well-developed set of activities, and its ability to work in concert with administrators to improve the institutional regime. It is hard to imagine a reason for not allowing this sort of programming to flourish throughout our nation's embattled criminal justice system.

NOTES

1   I admit that two days' worth of observation is a very narrow time frame through which to draw conclusions about the Baltimore City Jail, let alone the workings of any of their inmate self-help programs. Because I had spent nearly 15 years as a prison guard, teacher, and administrator in the Arizona Department of Corrections, however, I was no stranger to professional standards of prison hygiene, staffing and management when I visited the jail. I was also no stranger to inmate subcultures; I had worked nearly a year as a teacher on death row at the Arizona State Prison in Florence, a year as the assistant warden of the Arizona State Prison in Tucson, a year as a guard in the maximum security unit of the Tucson prison, seven years as a teacher in prison classrooms throughout the state, and one year as assistant deputy director of the Arizona prison system.

I was invited to the Baltimore City Jail, by the National Institute of Corrections, to deliver a series of talks on a self-help program known as the Human Potential Seminar (see Hamm, 1987b). During my visit, I was in constant contact with jail officials; every discussion I had with other staff and individual inmates was conducted in full view of these administrators of the Baltimore City Jail. None of the information I received from staff and inmates was corrected, denied, or otherwise abridged by the attending jail administrators. That is, the administrators verified what I heard from staff and inmates to be true.

REFERENCES

Abdul-Mu'Min, E.M. (1985). "Prison Power and Survival." In Robert M. Carter, Daniel Glaser & Leslie T. Wilkins (eds.) *Correctional Institutions*. New York: Harper & Row.

Adler, N. (1970). "Kicks, Drugs, and Politics." *Psychoanalytic Review*, 57:432-441.

Burdman, M. (1974). "Ethnic Self-Help Groups in Prison and on Parole." *Crime and Delinquency*, 20:107-118.

Bureau of Justice Statistics (1988a). *Prisoners in 1987*. Washington, DC: U.S. Government Printing Office.

_____ (1988b). *BJS Data Report*. Washington, DC: U.S. Government Printing Office.

Chambliss, W.J. (1988). *Exploring Criminology*. New York: Macmillan.

Clear, T. (1989). "Devout Prisoners." Paper presented at annual meeting of Academy of Criminal Justice Sciences.

Cressey, D.R. (1955). "Changing Criminals: The Application of the Theory of Differential Association." *American Journal of Sociology*, 26:116-120.

_____ (1983). "Interview with Donald R. Cressey." In J.H. Laub (ed.) *Criminology in the Making: An Oral History*. Boston: Northeastern University Press.

Cullen, F.T., T.S. Bynum, K. Montgomery, G. Garrett & J.R. Greene (1985). "Legislative Ideology and Criminal Justice Policy." In E. Fairchild and V. Webb (eds.) *The Politics of Crime and Criminal Justice*. Beverly Hills: Sage.

Ellis, G. (1983). *Inside Folsom Prison*. Burlington, VT: Accord Publications.

Flanagan, T.J. & S.L. Caulfield (1984). "Public Opinion and Prison Policy: A Review." *The Prison Journal*, 64:31-46.

Flanagan, T.J. & E.F. McGarrell (1986). *Attitudes of New York Legislators Toward Crime and Criminal Justice: A Report of the State Legislator Survey -- 1985*. Albany, NY: Hindelang Criminal Justice Research Center.

Gendreau, P. & R.R. Ross (1987). "The Revivification of Rehabilitation: Evidence From the 1980's." *Justice Quarterly*, 3:349-407.

Haight-Ashbury Drug Detoxification Project (1987). *Smokeable Cocaine*. San Francisco: CINEMED, Inc.

Hamm, M.S. (1986). "Heroin Addiction, Anomie, and Social Policy in the United States and Britain." Washington, DC: American Academy of Higher Education.

_____ (1987a). "Policing the Crack Problem." *Indiana Sheriff*, Summer: 8-9.

_____ (1987b). "The Human Potential Seminar: A Strategy for Teaching Socially Adaptive Behavior in a Correctional Classroom." *The Journal of Correctional Education*, 38:4-7.

_____ (1988a). "Drug Policy and Applied Research: A Study of Users, Abusers and Politicians." *Journal of Crime & Justice*, 11:103-121.

_____ (1988b). "Current Perspectives on the Prisoner Self-Help Movement." *Federal Probation*, 52:49-58.

_____ (1989) "Legislator Ideology and Capital Punishment: The Special Case for Indiana Juveniles." *Justice Quarterly*, 6:219-232.

Hamm, M.S. & J.L. Schrink (1989). "The Conditions of Effective Implementation: A Guide to Accomplishing Rehabilitative Objectives in Corrections." *Criminal Justice and Behavior*, 16:166-182.

Inciardi, J.A. (1986). *The War on Drugs*. Mountain View, CA: Mayfield Publishing Co.

Irwin, J. (1980). *Prisons in Turmoil*. Boston: Little, Brown and Co.

Jacobs, J.B. (1985). "Street Gangs Behind Bars." In R.M. Carter, Daniel Glaser & L.T. Wilkins (eds.) *Correctional Institutions*. New York: Harper & Row.

Johnson, R. (1987). *Hard Time*. Monterey, CA: Brooks/Cole.

Katz, A.K. & E.I. Bender (1976). *The Strength In Us*. New York: New Viewpoints.

Kachaturian, A. (1986). "The Enemy Within." *Time* (September 15).

Leech, K. (1972). *Keep the Faith Baby: A Close Up of London's Drop-Outs*. London: The Camelot Press, Ltd.

Lempinen, E.W. (1988). "$3,000 a Day Makes Life Bearable: San Francisco Crack Dealers Tell Their Story." *San Francisco Chronicle* (April 7).

Liberman, M.A. & L.D. Borman (1979). *Self-Help Groups for Coping with Crisis*. San Francisco: Jossey-Bass.

Lozoff, B. and M. Braswell (1989). *Inner Corrections: Finding Peace and Peace Making*. Cincinnati: Anderson Publishing Co.

MacNamara, D.E.J. with E. Sagarin (1971). *Perspectives on Corrections*. New York: Thomas Y. Crowell.

Madura, E.J. & A. Meese (1988). *The Self-Help Sourcebook*. Denville, NJ: St. Clares Riverside Foundation.

Martin, S.J. & S. Ekland-Olson (1987). *Texas Prisons: The Walls Came Tumbling Down*. Austin, TX: Texas Monthly Press, Inc.

McAnany, P.D. & E.E. Tromanhauser (1977). "Organizing the Convict: Self-help for Prisoners and Ex-Cons." *Crime and Delinquency*, 23:68-74.

Mitcheson, M. (1970). *ABC's of Drug Addiction*. Bristol (England): John Wright and Sons.

Morganthau, T., N. Finke Greenberg, A. Murr, M. Miller & G. Raine (1986). "Crack and Crime." *Newsweek* (June 16).

Moore, H.A. (1977). *Drug Users and Emergent Organizations*. Gainseville, FL: The University Presses of Florida.

Nicosia, G. (1984). *Memory Babe -- A Critical Biography of Jack Kerouac*. New York: Grove.

Press, A. (1986). "Reality Versus Rhetoric: The Drug Crisis." *Newsweek* (September 8).

Quinn, A.H. (1941). *Edgar Allan Poe: A Critical Biography*. New York: D. Appleton-Century Co.

Rankin, J. (1979). "Changing Attitudes Towards Capital Punishment." Social Forces, 58:194-211.

Ray, O.S. (1978). *Drugs, Society and Human Behavior.* St. Louis: C.V. Mosby.

Sagarin, E. (1969). *Odd Man In.* Chicago: Quadrangle Books.

Sands, B. (1964). *My Shadow Ran Fast.* Englewood Cliffs, NJ: Prentice-Hall.

Shannon, E. (1988). *Desperados.* New York: Viking.

Sheingold, S.A. (1984). *The Politics of Law and Order.* New York: Longman Press.

Snarr, R.W. & B.I. Wolford (1985). *Corrections.* Dubuque; IA: William C. Brown.

Spitz, B. (1989). *Dylan.* New York: McGraw Hill.

Sykes, G. (1986). "Treatment of Captives: Ethical Implications." Paper presented at the Conference on Reaffirming Rehabilitation.

Taylor, R.A., A.P. Weisman & T. Gest (1986). "America on Drugs." *U.S. News & World Report* (July 28).

Thomas, E. (1986). "Crack Down." *Time* (August 18).

Trebach, A.S. (1982). *The Heroin Solution.* New Haven, CT: Yale University Press.

_____ (1987). *The Great American Drug War.* New York: Macmillan.

Volkman, R. & D.R. Cressey (1963). "Differential Association and the Rehabilitation of Drug Addicts." *American Journal of Sociology*, 69:129-142.

Wexler, H.K. & R. Williams (1986). "The Stay 'N Out Therapeutic Community: Prison Treatment for Substance Abusers." *Journal of Psychoactive Drugs*, 18:221-229.

Zalman, M. (1987). "Sentencing in a Free Society: The Failure of the President's Crime Commission to Influence Sentencing Policy." *Justice Quarterly*, 4:545-570.

SUBJECT INDEX

AUTHOR INDEX

Falcke, H. 320
Farnsworth, D. 116
Farrell, R. 171
Farrington, D. 219
Federal Strategy 141
Feldman, M. 259
Felson, R. 174
Ferracuti, F. 171-172, 259
Fettner, A. 321n
Fiddle, S. 148
Field, L. 282
Fine, E. 260
Finestone, H. 147, 154
Fishman, M. 155
Fitzpatrick, J. 148
Flanagan, T. 80, 187, 362
Flewelling, R. 173
Flueck, J. 215
Friedman, S. 315
Froland, S. 320

Galea, R. 322n
Gandossy, R. 141, 145, 147, 151, 221
Garry, R. 320n
Gary, L. 172
Gatfield, P. 258
Gawin, F. 152, 155-156
Geelhoed, G. 314
Gendreau, P. 45, 362
Gibson, L. 258
Ginsberg, I. 223
Ginzburg, H. 315
Glassner, B. 217
Glick, H. 45-46
Godshaw, G. 13
Gold, M. 217
Goldkamp, J. 57, 67
Goldman, F. 223
Goldman, M. 241
Goldstein, H. 90, 96
Goldstein, P. 139, 149, 153-154, 159,
    174, 187, 216, 221-223, 242, 315
Gooberman, L. 119-120, 125
Goode, E. 217, 224
Goodman, R. 174
Goodwin, D. 258
Gordon, G. 258
Gottfredson, M. 220, 230

Gottfredson, S. 45
Gottlieb, M. 304
Gould, L. 140
Graham, M. 187
Grant, B. 155
Greenley, J. 223
Greenwood, P. 330
Grinspoon, L. 113, 119, 122, 126, 131
Griswold, D. 228
Gropper, B. 187, 215
Guest, T. 365
Guttmacher, M. 172
Guynes, R. 344
Guze, S. 258

Haberman, P. 174
Haight-Ashbury Drug Detoxification
    Project 365
Hall, A. 65, 69
Hall, J. 151
Hamid, A. 43
Hamm, M. 274, 362-363, 365, 375-
    376n
Hammett, T. 317-319
Hamoway, R. 117, 125-126
Hansen, K. 219
Hanson, B. 159, 194, 196
Hardt, R. 275
Harwood, H. 153, 221
Hasin, D. 155
Hawkins, D. 113, 123
Hawkins, J. 219, 228-229, 237
Hawks, R. 282
Heffernan, R. 174
Hellman, A. 121, 127
Hellman, S. 307
Hepburn, J. 258
Hewitt, J. 173
Hewlett, D. 314
Higginbotham, J. 346
Hill, G. 217
Hillsman, S. 66
Hindelang, M. 217-218, 227
Hirschi, T. 218, 220, 228, 230, 259
Hocherman, I. 281
Hopkins, W. 315
Hore, B. 79
Horwitz, A. 228

About the Authors

Steven Belenko is presently Senior Fellow at the New York City Criminal Justice Agency, Inc. where he previously served as Acting Executive Director of Research. Prior to joining CJA, Dr. Belenko was a senior evaluator with the New York City Mayor's Criminal Justice Coordinating Council, a research psychologist at Mathematical Policy Research, Inc. in Princeton, New Jersey, and a senior research associate with the Vera Institute of Justice. He received his bachelor's degree in mathematics and his doctoral degree in Experimental Psychology from Columbia University. His research interests include pretrial misconduct, drug-crime interactions, alternatives to incarceration and program evaluation.

Henry Brownstein is Principal Research Specialist and Special Assistant to the Executive Deputy Commissioner at the New York State Division of Criminal Justice Services. Before joining DCJS, he taught sociology at Russell Sage College in Albany. He received his Ph.D. from Temple University in 1977. In addition to his work in the area of drugs and homicide he has written about alternatives to incarceration, the application of research to policy development, and the role of qualitative methods in policy-oriented research.

David L. Carter is Associate Professor of Criminal Justice at Michigan State University. He holds a B.S. and an M.S. from Central Missouri State University and a Ph.D. from Sam Houston State University in Criminal Justice Administration. He is the author and co-author of three books, including *Police Deviance* (Anderson, 1986), and numerous journal articles on policing issues, and has served as a consultant to a wide range of federal, state and local agencies on police policy issues. His fourth book, *Police Systems and Practices*, was published in 1989. A former police officer in Kansas City, Missouri, his expertise is in the areas of police misconduct, law enforcement intelligence operations and community policing. Most recently, Professor Carter directed the Police Executive Research Forum's project on Police Higher Education.

Rolando V. del Carmen is currently Professor of Criminal Justice at the Criminal Justice Center, Sam Houston State University. His publications include several articles on law-related topics in criminal justice. He has authored a number of books, including *Potential Liabilities of Probation and Parole Officers, 2d Edition* (Anderson, 1986), and is a consultant to various state and national criminal justice agencies. He travels and lectures extensively, and he has been appointed by the Governor of the State of Texas to a six-year term on the Texas Commission on Jail Standards.

Paul Goldstein is Deputy Director for Criminal Justice Research at Narcotic and Drug Research, Inc. Previously, he worked for the New York State Office of Crime Control Planning and the New York State Division of Substance Abuse Services. He received his Ph.D. from Case Western Reserve University in 1978. He is the author of numerous articles and chapters, a book, *Prostitution and Drugs*, and is co-author of the book *Taking Care of Business: The Economics of Crime by Heroin Abusers*. His primary interest in recent years has been studying the relationship between drug use and trafficking and violence.

Larry A. Gould is currently employed at Louisiana State University in the Department of Criminal Justice as an instructor and in the Department of Experimental Statistics as the Project Director for the Evaluation of Shock Incarceration in Louisiana. Current research interests include a research project investigating the differences in the characteristics (SEC, demographics and prior criminal history) of those individuals arrested and convicted of DWI and those arrested and not convicted of DWI. Recent publications include "Shock Incarceration in Louisiana: Retribution or Rehabilitation?" in the *Journal of Offender Counseling, Services and Rehabilitation*.

Mark S. Hamm is an Associate Professor of Criminology at Indiana State University and a former corrections officer, teacher and administrator of the Arizona Department of Corrections. He is the recipient of the 1980 Employee of the Year Award of the Arizona prison system, and author of *Heroin Addiction, Anomie, and Social Policy in the United States and Britain* (American Academy of Higher Education, 1986) and *The Abandoned Ones: A History of the Oakdale/Atlanta Prison Riots* (under review). He is currently working on a sociological study of the Skinheads.

James A. Inciardi is Professor and Director of the Division of Criminal Justice at the University of Delaware. He received his Ph.D. in Sociology from New York University, and has more than 25 years of experience in the research and clinical aspects of drug abuse. Dr. Inciardi has done extensive consulting work both nationally and internationally, and has published more than 100 articles, chapters, and books in the areas of substance abuse, history, folklore, criminology, criminal justice, medicine, law, public policy, and AIDS.

Bruce D. Johnson received his Ph.D. in Sociology from Columbia University in 1971. He is currently employed at Narcotic and Drug Research, Inc., a non-profit addiction research institute in New York City. Since 1977, he has served as principal investigator of five major NIDA- and NIJA-funded research grants. Based on this research, he has authored and co-authored 6 books, 9 monographs, as well as numerous articles, book chapters, agency publications, grant proposals, and professional presentations. His latest two books are *Kids, Drugs, and Crime* (1988), and *Taking Care of Business: The Economics of Crime by Heroin Abusers* (1985), both published by Lexington Books. Dr. Johnson routinely attends and gives presentations at professional meetings of the American Society of Criminology and the American Sociological Association.

Mitchell A. Kaplan received his Ph.D. in Sociology from the City University of New York Graduate School and University Center in 1987. After receiving his doctorate, Dr. Kaplan was awarded a National Institute on Drug Abuse post-doctoral fellowship to do research on issues related to drug addiction. Dr. Kaplan is currently employed as a Research Associate with the American Foundation for AIDS Research in New York City. He is a member of the American Sociological Association, the New York State Sociological Association, the American Public Health Association, and the New York Academy of Sciences. His scholarly interests include the social epidemiology of intravenous drug abuse and AIDS, the relationship between drugs and crime, the sociology of mental illness, and the sociology of aging.

Peter Kraska is an Assistant Professor in the Department of Criminal Justice Studies at Kent State University. He recently completed a National Institute of Justice grant on the criminal justice system's processing of serious drug offenders.

Doris Layton MacKenzie is an Associate Professor of Criminal Justice at Louisiana State University, on leave to the National Institute of Justice as a Research Fellow. Current research interests include a study of shock incarceration and parole in Louisiana, as well as a national study of shock incarceration.

Duane C. McBride is a Professor in the Behavioral Sciences Department at Andrews University in Berrien Springs, Michigan, and Chairman of that university's Institute of Alcoholism and Drug Dependency Research Center. He received his Ph.D. in Sociology from the University of Kentucky. He has been involved in drug abuse research since 1972. His work has primarily focused on the relationship between crime and drugs, the epidemiology of drug use, and most recently on the epidemiology of HIV infection among IV users. He is the author of a variety of publications in these areas.

Thomas Mieczkowski has been researching aspects of drug use and distribution since 1974. He has written on drug distribution mechanisms in the Caribbean, street heroin selling in Detroit, and is currently researching crack cocaine use and distribution. Dr. Mieczkowski has taught at the University of Michigan, taught at and chaired the Criminal Justice Department at Wayne State University, and is currently on the faculty in the Department of Criminology at the University of South Florida.

Peter Reuter is a Senior Economist in the Washington office of the RAND Corporation. He was awarded his Ph.D. in Economics from Yale University and was Guest Scholar at the Brookings Institution before joining RAND in 1981. His initial research dealt with the organization of criminal activities, resulting in the publication of *Disorganized Crime: The Economics of the Visible Hand*, (MIT Press, 1983). Since 1983 he has worked primarily on drug policy issues and has published a number of papers and studies on drug enforcement. His recent RAND publications include *Sealing the Borders* (a study of the effects of increased interdiction), *Drug Problems* and *Drug Problems in the Washington Metropolitan Area*. His current research deals with the role of drug selling in the economic life of poverty populations and with the proper allocation of resources among drug programs.

James Schmeidler received his Ph.D. in Statistics from Columbia University. He has worked as a statistical consultant for the New York State Division of Substance Abuse Services Bureau of Research. He is currently employed as a Statistical Consultant in the Department of Psychiatry and Biomathematical Sciences at Mount Sinai School of Medicine in New York City.

Jonathan R. Sorensen is a doctoral fellow at the Criminal Justice Center, Sam Houston State University. His current research interests include drug testing and capital punishment. He has co-authored several articles on capital punishment with James Marquat, and is currently researching the history of capital punishment in Texas.

James Swartz is presently Director of Management Information Systems at the Illinois Treatment Alternatives for Street Crimes (TASC) program. He has a master's degree from Loyola University of Chicago in Behavioral Research and is completing his doctoral work in Clinical Psychology at Northwestern University. The subject of his dissertation is an empirical investigation of the factors relating cocaine use and violent criminal behavior. He is also currently working on the design and development of an information system for the Illinois TASC program that will yield research data for future studies on drug use and crime.

Ralph Weisheit received his Ph.D. in Sociology from Washington State University and is currently an Associate Professor at Illinois State University. His research interests include women in crime and drugs in American society. He co-authored *Women, Crime and Criminal Justice* (Anderson, 1988). His current research, funded by the National Institute of Justice, focuses on members of mainstream society who become involved in domestic marijuana cultivation for profit. This study focuses on marijuana production in rural areas and includes marijuana growers, local law enforcement officials, and local community members.

Helene Raskin White is an Associate Professor of Sociology at the Center of Alcohol Studies, Rutgers University. Her research focuses on the etiology of adolescent substance use and delinquency and the consequences of alcohol and drug use. Currently she is engaged in two longitudinal studies, one examining the development of drug-using behaviors from early adolescence to adulthood and the other examining the consequences of prolonged marijuana use in a sample of mid-adults.